Conflicting Stories

Conflicting Stories

*American Women Writers
at the Turn into
the Twentieth Century*

ELIZABETH AMMONS

New York   Oxford
OXFORD UNIVERSITY PRESS
1991

Oxford University Press

Oxford   New York   Toronto
Delhi   Bombay   Calcutta   Madras   Karachi
Petaling Jaya   Singapore   Hong King   Tokyo
Nairobi   Dar es Salaam   Cape Town
Melbourne   Auckland

and associated companies in
Berlin   Ibadan

Library of Congress Cataloging-in-Publication Data
Ammons, Elizabeth.
Conflicting stories : American women writers at the turn
into the twentieth century /
Elizabeth Ammons.
p. cm. Includes index.
ISBN 0-19-506030-X
1. American fiction—Women authors—History and criticism.
2. Women and literature—United States—History—20th century.
3. Women and literature—United States—History—19th century.
4. American fiction—20th century—History and criticism.
5. American fiction—19th century—History and criticism.
I. Title. PS374.W6A48 1991
813'.4099287—dc20 90-47290

2 4 6 8 9 7 5 3 1

Printed in the United States of America
on acid-free paper

For Mark and Mo

Preface

I argue in this book that long fiction by women in the United States from the early 1890s through the late 1920s forms a diverse yet unified body of work. My primary aim is to pull together the work of writers who were contemporaries but who are in the criticism almost always treated singly or at best as couples or small clusters. In doing that, certain issues immediately come up. Identifying the turn of the century as a remarkable period of artistic achievement for women poses the question: What happens to our academic construction of the American literary past when we unite women writers at the turn of the century rather than scatter or ignore them? The book joins the deepening critical discussion of the disjunction for many women writers between gender and high art, especially at the turn from the nineteenth into the twentieth century, and provokes a number of questions about the relationship between political and social history and the production of art by women. The inquiry as a whole asserts the central and imperative need of bringing together into one account the work of white women writers and women of color.

It might be useful to pause here over several of these ideas.

First, grouping turn-of-the-century women writers raises significant questions about the connection between the enabling power of political activism and the production of art. It is no accident, I will argue, that the second great wave of the women's movement in the United States and the second great burgeoning of women writers as a group occurred at the same time. Just as the large group of very popular women writers that prospered during the midnineteenth century were energized, whether they knew it or not, by the first widespread popular growth in the women's movement in America, which drew much of its energy, it is important to remember, from the push for abolition, so women writers at the beginning of the twentieth century flourished in large part—as they do as I write in the 1980s—because of an intensified and pervasive feminist political climate. Whether consciously acknowledged or not, this political climate had the effect of empowering women, including writers, and of transforming cultural expectations about how many women could be publishing writers, how many of them could be "great," and what they could write about. The enabling relationship between politics and art—the connection between social and political struggle and the emergence of a sophisticated body of literature, much of it consciously political, by a group of people historically assigned inferior status in the culture—is one of the major themes that conceptualizing turn-of-the-century women writers as a group suggests.

For one thing it raises the possibility that the converse proposition may also obtain: that women artists *as a group* do not thrive when feminist political activism is in decline or nonexistent. The conservative 1950s may be a case in point. In any case, the question inescapably arises whether women artists disavowing their identity as women during actively feminist eras (which means disavowing their identification with women, women's movements, and women's issues even as they are the beneficiaries of gender-specific political action) play a dangerous game in their own survival. It may be that the attempt to have it both ways on the part of certain women writers at the turn of the century—to ride the crest of the women's movement and yet not identify as a woman writer—fed into the period's decline in the reactionary 1920s. If so, the issue, which, not surprisingly, has resurfaced in the late twentieth century in the debate among women writers over whether to identify as women or not,[1] raises important questions about the forces at work in the survival over time of women writers in significant numbers in American literature.

A second large consequence of grouping turn-of-the-century women writers is the creation of new perspectives on what we believe is already firmly established. Thinking about the turn of the century in terms of women writers, a number of whom were producing what the culture considered the artistically and intellectually most accomplished fiction of the day, prompts new ways of understanding the whole era. It becomes obvious, for example, that certain turn-of-the-century women writers were imitated by Theodore Dreiser, Sherwood Anderson, and Sinclair Lewis and then violently reacted against by yet another generation of men in the 1920s—F. Scott Fitzgerald and Ernest Hemingway are the most famous—who found people like Wharton and Cather and Stein, far more than any literary "father" of Harold Bloom's imagination, the real giants against whom they needed to define themselves. Dreiser's centering his first two novels on heroines or the early Sinclair Lewis's repeated interest in women's issues, followed by Hemingway's frantic misogyny and Fitzgerald, Faulkner, and Alain Locke's calmer, though equally evident, fear of female dominance, all occurred not in a vacuum but against the backdrop of women writers' enormous achievements and popularity in the early twentieth century. Although examining the impact of women's work on the careers of men falls outside the scope of this book, perceiving new patterns of influence and reaction constitutes one important subject that thinking about the turn of the century as a distinct literary period in many ways dominated by women calls into focus.

One of my chief concerns in the following discussion is the need to understand the relationship between the literary past of women of color and that of white women. In the far-reaching project now underway of rewriting American literary history, a project that has grown in large part out of the need to recover and take seriously literature by people of color and by white women, it is crucial that race in combination with gender be recognized and analyzed. Criticism that purports to talk about "women writers" but actually has in mind white women writers obviously reproduces the errors of the scholarship it seeks to revise; it is no different than the traditional white male critics' use of "American" to mean only white men (and usually privileged ones at that).[2]

The point here is not simply political (though it is that). By defining women to mean women, by telling the story of women of color and white women together, the story itself grows denser. Points of intersection—friction, harmony, alienation, appropriation, subversion, oppression—are forced into view from various sides, and they in turn throw into relief similarity, difference, and, most important, the possibility for new vision. For example, not only do we get the views on race and racism of women of color, a fundamental reality that frequently comes up when women of color become a focus, but as soon as women of color and white women are part of one study, we are forced to think at the same time about the attitudes toward race and the racism of white women, a subject that does not automatically come up in criticism about them, but should. How the complicated subject of race contributes to the literary historical picture that emerges, and certainly racism permeated American society at the turn of the century, represents a primary theme in my book, as it must, in my view, in a culture that systemically entangles the issues of race, gender, class, and sexual orientation to keep fundamental change from occurring.

Finally, and very important to any accurate reconstruction of American literary history, is the way in which grouping women writers at the turn into the twentieth century contributes to the ongoing revision of the still-popular modern thesis that the nation's "best" and most characteristic literature is antirealistic. Great American fiction, so the twentieth-century critical commonplace has run, is a literature of escape, a literature psychological, symbolic, cut off from topical social and political issues—a fiction fundamentally antisocial and adolescent: Huck and Jim on the raft; Ishmael and Queequeg on the *Pequod*. As Nina Baym has argued, the thesis itself is tautological.[3] Moreover, it has worked because American women writers have systematically been dismissed, scattered, ignored. The classic discussion in Leslie Fiedler's *Love and Death in the American Novel* (1960), for example, has to leap from Twain to Faulkner to make the thesis work; even Wharton and Cather are ignored.[4] A major premise of this book, like several other contemporary studies, is that if women writers are considered seriously—and there is certainly no aesthetic reason for not doing so, even by the most traditional aesthetic standards we might wish to invoke—then there is little question that much American fiction is social, adult, topical. The cherished view of ourselves as a nation whose "best" and most authentic literature is antisocial and antirealistic has to be profoundly reconsidered—if, that is, evidence is allowed to bear on the argument.

Medford, Mass.   *E.A.*
May 1990

Acknowledgment

For various kinds of aid I want to thank Awiakta, Nina Baym, Dorothy Berkson, Alanna Kathleen Brown, Cordelia Candelaria, Henry Louis Gates, Jr., Susan Gubar, Ruth Hsiao, Annette Kolodny, Paul Lauter, Amy Ling, Deborah McDowell, Sharon O'Brien, Marion Osmun, Linda Wagner-Martin, and Sandra Zagarell. Also I am grateful to the members of the Feminist Reading Group in Boston and to my colleagues in the American Studies workshop in Women's Studies at Tufts in 1983: VèVè Clark, Zella Luria, Susan Ostrander, and Maryanne Wolf. For keeping life funny I have to thank the Druids, especially, and as always, Mark.

I could not have written this book without released time from teaching. I am deeply indebted to the National Endowment for the Humanities for a Summer Fellowship in 1979 and for a Senior Fellowship in 1981–82; to Tufts University for a Faculty Summer Fellowship in 1988; and to the American Association of University Women for an American Fellowship in 1988–89.

Contents

Conflicting Stories

Fearful as the awakening was, it was better than to have slept through life.

Iola Leroy, 1892

Perhaps it is better to wake up after all, than to remain a dupe to illusions all one's life.

The Awakening, 1899

1 Introduction

For much of the twentieth century the picture of America's literary past provided by mainstream scholarship has been remarkably simple. The story has run something like this: Following a long period of development during the country's colonial and then early nation-building periods, American literature came of age in the early nineteenth century with the work of Irving, Cooper, and Poe and then exploded into brilliant creativity at midcentury in the work of writers whom F. O. Matthiessen labeled in 1941 as members of the "American Renaissance"—Emerson, Thoreau, Hawthorne, Melville, and Whitman. Fictive literature after the Civil War then underwent a change from romanticism to realism, the accepted story has held, with the major practitioners being Howells and James, the second of whom, along with Twain, and in some people's view Emily Dickinson as well, became the major literary figure of the latter half of the nineteenth century. The nation's literature then descended into a valley at the turn of the century before erupting in a second brilliant outpouring of talent, akin to that of the American Renaissance, in the 1920s, which saw the emergence of Hemingway, Fitzgerald, and most important, Faulkner.

At its crudest this portrait, which only recognizes white writers, grants American literature before the Second World War two periods of major achievement: the decade or so at the middle of the nineteenth century and the decade of the 1920s (spilling over into the early thirties). It also defines the romance, narrative that turns away from realistic depiction of social and cultural issues, as the nation's best and most important form.[1] In this view the turn of century represents a slump. There were some interesting naturalists—Stephen Crane, Frank Norris, Theodore Dreiser—in whose work we can see the beginnings of the rebirth of talent that emerged in the modernist twenties. Otherwise the years from the early 1890s through the teens are unimportant.

Those unimportant years, I will argue, saw the artistic triumph or emergence and maturation of the seventeen women whose work forms the primary focus of this book: Frances Ellen Watkins Harper, Sarah Orne Jewett, Kate Chopin, Edith Wharton, Willa Cather, Alice Dunbar-Nelson, Ellen Glasgow, Charlotte Perkins Gilman, Pauline Hopkins, Sui Sin Far, Gertrude Stein, Mary Austin, Humishuma or Mourning Dove, Anzia Yezierska, Jessie Redmon Fauset, Edith Summers Kelley, and Nella Larsen.

Clearly, my view of the turn of the century differs from that commonly described in the criticism.

As even a cursory look reveals, there occurred at the turn into the twentieth century a stretch of about thirty-five years (at its narrowest a two-decade span) that saw the careers of a number of the nation's most talented and accomplished women writers intersect and overlap. In 1892 Frances Ellen Watkins Harper culminated her literary career with the publication of *Iola Leroy*, as did Sarah Orne Jewett in 1896 with *The Country of the Pointed Firs*. Sixteen years later Jewett's admirer and friend Willa Cather successfully launched her own full-time fiction-writing career with *Alexander's Bridge*. Within these two decades, between 1892 and 1912, Kate Chopin published her last and best novel, *The Awakening*; Pauline Elizabeth Hopkins wrote *Contending Forces* as well as three serialized novels; Mary Austin brought into print her masterpiece, *The Land of Little Rain*; Alice Dunbar-Nelson published *The Goodness of St. Rocque and Other Stories*; Ellen Glasgow and Edith Wharton brought out their first best-sellers, *The Deliverance* and *The House of Mirth*; Gertrude Stein wrote *Three Lives*; Humishuma began *Cogewea*; Sui Sin Far published *Mrs. Spring Fragrance*; and Jessie Redmon Fauset started writing for the *Crisis*. Even if the field is limited to a selection of authors, the quantity and quality of literary production by women in the United States at the turn into the twentieth century are extraordinary. Between 1892 and 1929 there appeared "The Yellow Wallpaper," *Iola Leroy*, *The Country of the Pointed Firs*, *The Goodness of St. Rocque*, *The Awakening*, *Contending Forces*, *The Land of Little Rain*, *The House of Mirth*, *Ethan Frome*, *Three Lives*, *O Pioneers!*, *A Woman of Genius*, *The Custom of the Country*, *Mrs. Spring Fragrance*, *Herland*, *The Song of the Lark*, *Summer*, *Virginia*, *My Ántonia*, *The Age of Innocence*, *A Lost Lady*, *There Is Confusion*, *Weeds*, *Barren Ground*, *Bread Givers*, *Plum Bun*, *Death Comes for the Archbishop*, *Cogewea*, *Quicksand*, and *Passing*.

Grouping this fiction brings into view a large and important body of work. It is a body of work held together at one and the same time by common features and, even more important, by heterogeneity and difference. Fundamental divisions stemming from age, race, class, religion, and region, which translate into major differences in education, money, privilege, and opportunity, exist among the writers I discuss. Often tension is the major point of connection. There is no one story, no one kind of fiction, produced by this group. Variety—turmoil even—constitutes one of the strongest underlying themes holding serious women writers together across the faultline separating the Victorian era from the modern period.

At the same time the writers I discuss definitely belong together. They are united by gender, historical context, and self-definition. Writing within a historically coherent chronological period, which coincided with the second important wave in the women's movement in the United States—the three decades preceding and the one following the passage of the Nineteenth Amendment—they reflect an emerging, shared, and often defiant confidence in the abilities and rights of women that historians associate with the "new" middle-class American woman of the period. As such, these writers present a picture of a group of women clearly breaking with the past; and the major break, I will maintain, consisted in their avowed ambition, with few exceptions, to be artists. As a group they differed significantly from their most successful predecessors in the United States: middle-class white women at the middle of the nineteenth century, who, as scholars such as Nina Baym, Mary Kelley, and Judith Fetterley explain, conceived of themselves as professional writers rather than as artists—by which I mean, in the modern high-culture sense of the term in the west, makers of new, challenging, and typically idiosyncratic forms. In contrast, serious women writers at the turn into the twentieth century were determined to invade the territory of high art traditionally posted in western culture as the exclusive property of privileged white men.

What this resulted in, I argue throughout the following discussion, was the creation of a body of fiction apparently disparate but in fact complexly unified by two large concerns. First, much of the fiction shows an interest in radical experimentation with narrative form itself—a widespread attempt to break out of and disrupt the range of existing, inherited long forms available at the turn of the century. (Think of *The Country of the Pointed Firs, Three Lives, The Goodness of St. Rocque, O Pioneers!, Weeds*.) Second and related, the fiction of these authors addresses a network of recurrent, complicated themes which, though constantly shifting and even at times conflicting, finally interlock in their shared focus on issues of power: the will to break silence by exposing the connection among institutionalized violence, the sexual exploitation of women, and female muteness; preoccupation with the figure of the woman artist; the need to find union and reunion with the world of one's mother, particularly as one journeyed farther and farther from that world into territory traditionally marked off as forbidden; the corrosion of racism, including and often especially the oppression of women of color by white women; and the difficulty of dealing with multiple discrimination—being an immigrant, being lesbian, being black or Eurasian or Indian.

As even a sketch of the period suggests, in their exploration and rebellion ambitious women writers at the turn of the century were in many ways simply typical. As the historian Eileen Kraditor has observed, for privileged American women by the turn of the century (and women able to read, write, and attempt to make even part of their living by writing, no matter how hard their lives, are at least in some sense privileged), "The issue of abstract equality had been settled, and the debate now concerned the *meaning* of equality."[2] The Progressive Era, spanning at its broadest from the early 1890s through the middle 1920s, was for many American women a time of struggle and change.[3] Books and journal articles proliferated on the woman question, which encompassed everything from dress reform to the vote. Women pursued college and advanced degrees at unprecedented rates, increasing their enrollment in the first two decades of the twentieth century in public colleges by 1,000 percent, in private colleges by 482 percent.[4] New occupations opened up—typewriting, stenography, department store clerking, trained nursing—into which ambitious young women were beckoned and, especially if they were white, welcomed.

Politically, the issue of suffrage, which dramatically accelerated following the amalgamation in 1890 of the American Woman Suffrage Association and the National Woman Suffrage Association into the National American Woman Suffrage Association, heated up existing, mainstream political debate about women and women's rights. Because of white women's racism, suffrage finally divided white women and women of color more than it united them.[5] Nevertheless, agitation for passage of the Nineteenth Amendment vividly brought the issue of women's rights to the attention of the entire country; and gaining the vote represented an important goal for middle-class women across the color line, even if their reasons for wanting the ballot differed and their records of cooperation with each other sharply contrasted.

Likewise, the explosion of women's clubs at the turn of the century was a visible manifestation of middle-class women's widespread determination to make their power felt in the public realm. They used the clubs in two fundamental ways: to foster self-education and to involve themselves in reform movements. The black clubs, for example, worked to abolish the convict lease system and to end lynchings, and all of the clubs sponsored social reform campaigns that ranged from the establishment of kindergartens to the passage of pure food laws to the installation of women matrons in women's prisons.[6] Banding together on the basis of gender, middle-class women both within and without the clubs identified with women less advantaged than they, establishing settlement houses, working-girls clubs, and a multitude of community relief organizations. Fraught as these projects were with class bias, especially among white women, they nevertheless show the more privileged women's strong identification *as* women—their assumption of gender, and among African American women, of race as well—as a basic unifying fact that could be translated into public power. (Similar identification by gender often did not exist, at least not in the same way, among many poor, working-class, and immigrant women.)

In short, as the new century took hold, many women fortunate enough to live above the poverty line used various means—women's clubs, settlement house work, temperance agitation, antilynching crusades, and the campaign for suffrage—to assert their right to direct, active participation in the public affairs of the country. Viewed from this very broad perspective, it can be said that the turn of the century was a time when unprecedented numbers of women identified concertedly as women and engaged in focused, mainstream public action to achieve sexual—and even more pressing for women of color, racial—equality in the United States. It was a time of large-scale, visible, fractious political movements among women. It contained many internal tensions, a lot of them falling out along class, race, and regional lines. Most important here, however, is the fact that there were women's movements of sufficient vigor and complexity to have those tensions and that those movements played a major role in empowering women in the United States, not least of all women artists, as the nation entered the modern period.

The two largest groups of women organizing themselves to act in concert socially and politically at the turn of the century were middle-class white women and black women.[7]

To understand the emergence of a new generation of ambitious, socially engaged, middle-class white women, the historian Carroll Smith-Rosenberg points to certain large shifts in American culture that surfaced following the Civil War. As increasing urbanization transformed the nation from a small-town and rural economy held together in large part by networks of personal relationships—employer and employee met on the street as neighbors or were members of the same church—into an impersonal urban economy run by bourgeois managers numerous enough to form a distinct class, women changed along with men. No longer circumscribed by the antebellum white middle-class ideal of femininity that historian Barbara Welter has labeled the ideal of "True Womanhood," an ideal stressing domesticity, moral and sexual purity, submissiveness to authority, and removal from public affairs,[8] a generation of white women developed in the 1860s and 1870s who confidently combined household management and civic involvement. Drawn out of their homes initially to do Civil War work, this early generation never really returned; and their daughters, born during the second half of the nineteenth century, carried the invasion into the public sphere even further. As Smith-Rosenberg puts it: "If the urban bourgeois matron of the 1860s and 1870s alarmed, her daughter frightened. The 1880s and 1890s saw the emergence of a novel social and political phenomenon—the New Woman."[9]

Borrowing the term from Henry James, and intending by it to evoke his image of female independence and rebellion, Smith-Rosenberg uses *New Woman* to describe a specific group of privileged white women. They were born between the late 1850s and 1900; they married later than former generations or not at all; they had few or no children if they did marry; they attended college and had highly developed career and professional goals. They eschewed domesticity, and "by the early twentieth century, many had won a place within the new professions or carved career niches for themselves within the governmental and other nondomestic institutions that proliferated in the late-nineteenth-century city. In short," Smith-Rosenberg concludes, "the New Women, rejecting conventional female roles and asserting their right to a career, to a public voice, to visible power, laid claim to the rights and privileges customarily accorded bourgeois men."[10]

A similar pattern existed for black women. As the historian Paula Giddings explains, by the 1900s African American women in general were marrying later; and one-half of all married educated black women at the turn of the century had no children.[11] Statistics on 108 of the first generation of black clubwomen—those surveyed were born between the late 1850s and 1885 and thus for the most part were in the same generation as Smith-Rosenberg's New Women—confirm their strong career orientation. About 67 percent were teachers, with the remaining occupations including "clerk, hairdresser, businesswoman, and there was one bank president."[12] Three-quarters of the women in this group were married, and close to the same number worked outside the home. Only one-fourth of them had children. Moreover, some of the best known, interestingly, delayed marrying. "Mary Church Terrell, for example, was twenty-eight when she tied the wedding knot; Margaret Murray Washington was thirty-one, and Ida Wells-Barnett, thirty-three. All three had had to resolve the conflicts between what they wanted for themselves as women and what middle-class society expected of them as women."[13]

These accomplished, ambitious black women at the turn of the century in many respects resembled their white counterparts. They attended college, they had highly developed career goals, they married later than their mothers had or did not marry at all, and they had few or no children. However, the historical context that produced them contained some profound differences. Middle-class black women at the turn of the century were not the daughters of restless matrons rebelling against a restrictive Victorian ideal of True Womanhood. Most were the daughters or granddaughters of slaves. They descended from women whom racist America had defined as the complete antithesis of the True Woman—the female not as pure moral paragon, but as animal: woman as laborer and breeder. Symbolically, this was the heritage of *all* African American women, spokeswomen like Frances Ellen Harper, herself born to free parents well before the Civil War, insisted. The middle-class black woman at the turn of the century was not busy casting off a constricting ideal of Victorian femininity. She had never been included in it in the first place. Indeed, acquiring at least some of the benefits of that elevated definition of womanhood—respect, freedom from constant menial labor, interpretation as a morally pure human being sexually—represented an essential part of her emancipation as a woman.

Therefore Josephine St. Pierre Ruffin declared at the first National Conference of Colored Women in 1895: "Too long have we been silent under unjust and unholy charges." She emphasized that racist allegations of sexual immorality, "audaciously and flippantly made, as they often are, are of so humiliating and delicate a nature" that they serve "to protect the accuser by driving the helpless accused into mortified silence. It is to break this silence," Ruffin believed, that black women had to unite on the eve of the twentieth century. They had to form "an army of organized women standing for purity and mental worth."[14] This assertion of the moral purity of black womanhood, at a time when many white women of much the same educational and sociological background were trying to throw off sexual restrictions, defined one of the fundamental differences between the black women's movement at the turn of the century and the white women's. As Paula Giddings says of the "cult of True Womanhood": "If the cult caused Black women to prove they were ladies, it forced White ladies to prove that they were women."[15]

Striking correspondence exists between the profile of the turn-of-the-century New Woman as described by historians such as Smith-Rosenberg and Giddings and the Progressive Era women writers that I discuss. Excepting Harper, Jewett, and Chopin, who were born in 1825, 1849, and 1851, the writers I am concerned with were all born between the late 1850s and the early nineties: Pauline Hopkins in 1859, Charlotte Perkins Gilman in 1860, Edith Wharton in 1862, Sui Sin Far in 1865, Mary Austin in 1868, Ellen Glasgow and Willa Cather in 1873, Gertrude Stein in 1874, Alice Dunbar-Nelson in 1875, Anzia Yezierska in 1880 (or 1881), Jessie Redmon Fauset in 1882, Edith Summers Kelley in 1884, Humishuma in 1888, and Nella Larsen in 1891. Seven of the seventeen graduated from college: Mary Austin from Blackburn College in 1888; Alice Dunbar-Nelson from Straight College in 1892 (she also attended Cornell, Columbia, and the University of Pennsylvania); Willa Cather from the University of Nebraska in 1895; Gertrude Stein from Radcliffe College in 1898; Anzia Yezierska from Teachers College, Columbia University, in 1904; Jessie Fauset from Cornell University in 1905 (B.A.) and the University of Pennsylvania in 1919 (M.A.); and Edith Summers Kelley from the University of Toronto in 1903. Four attended college for a while or graduated from secondary academies or professional training schools: Sarah Orne Jewett (Berwick Academy, 1865), Kate Chopin (Academy of the Sacred Heart, 1868), Charlotte Perkins Gilman (Rhode Island School of Design for a while), and Nella Larsen (Fisk University, University of Copenhagen, and the Lincoln Hospital Training School for Nurses from which she received a diploma in 1915).

One-third of these women did not marry: Jewett, Hopkins, Glasgow, Cather, Sui Sin Far, and Stein. Of these six, it is known that three—Jewett, Cather, and Stein—plus Alice Dunbar-Nelson at various times, chose relationships with women that either were at the time or would be today understood as lesbian. Of the eleven who did marry—Harper, Chopin, Gilman, Wharton, Austin, Dunbar-Nelson, Kelley, Fauset, Yezierska, Humishuma, and Larsen—eight divorced their husbands or separated from them. Four formed new unions: Gilman and Humishuma remarrying, Dunbar-Nelson remarrying twice, and Kelley taking a common-law husband. The other four, Wharton, Austin, Yezierska, and Larsen, did not remarry.

This means that only three of the seventeen married and stayed in the marriage. All of the rest either did not marry or ended the marriage they did make, only four of them entering new unions, one of them common-law.

Moreover, it is important to emphasize that two of those who remained married until widowed, Harper and Chopin, were among the oldest in the group—representatives, it might be said, of a different generation. (Certainly this was true of Harper.) In addition, both wrote and published when they were not wives: in Harper's case before and after her four-year marriage, in Chopin's after she became a widow. This leaves only Fauset as an example of a woman who combined a first marriage with being an author. But it should be pointed out that Fauset did not marry until she was close to fifty, and as may or may not be germane, she quit publishing novels soon after she married.

Equally if not more striking is the childlessness of this group. If Kate Chopin and Edith Summers Kelley are excluded (Chopin had six children, Kelley three), the remaining group of fifteen woman produced four children. Each of these was an only child (and each, coincidentally, a daughter). They were born to Frances Ellen Harper, Charlotte Perkins Gilman, Mary Austin, and Anzia Yezierska. The other eleven women—Jewett, Wharton, Glasgow, Hopkins, Cather, Fauset, Stein, Dunbar-Nelson, Sui Sin Far, Humishuma, and Larsen—did not have children. Although some such as Humishuma helped rear children within their extended families and therefore should not be thought of as having no children to care for, the fact remains that they themselves did not become mothers.

The image that emerges is of a group of women clearly breaking with the past. Educated, worldly, career-oriented, they did not feel bound to marry or, if they did marry, to stay in the relationship when it proved self-destructive, as it did for most of them. Nor did they feel beholden to bear and raise children as their life's work; motherhood for the majority of them represented a choice, and it was a choice generally rejected. For the most part, the women writers I discuss did not believe that it was either possible or desirable to combine the traditional middle-class role of wife and mother with the role of artist.

Neither, of course, did their predecessors in the United States at the middle of the nineteenth century. The difference is that the earlier generation of fiction writers, made up almost entirely of middle-class white women, solved the conflict by making the opposite choice. They decided against being artists. They stayed within women's realm producing writing—but not ''art''—while they simultaneously raised families and ministered to husbands. Or so the popular picture of the respectable white midcentury woman writer maintained, and whether it was true or not in every case (and surely it was not), the image reflected the prevalent white middle-class ideology of separate feminine and masculine spheres, the former private and domestic, the latter public and commercial. As even the title of Mary Kelley's study suggests, *Private Woman, Public Stage: Literary Domesticity in Nineteenth-Century America*, the earlier generation of fiction writers tried to conceive of authorship as an occupation compatible with the pervasive middle-class feminine ideal of domesticity. They therefore thought of themselves as writers, not artists. As Nina Baym explains in *Woman's Fiction: A Guide to Novels by and about Women in America, 1820–1870*: "They conceptualized authorship as a profession rather than a calling, as work and not art."[16]

In contrast, the options possible by the turn of the century reflected a new historical context. Middle-class white women (at least in theory) could elect to pursue lifelong meaningful work outside the home. Educated black women, traditionally able—indeed, often required—to work outside the home, seemed to have access to a sufficient number of publishing outlets to consider writing a possible life choice, as did women of Asian ancestry such as Sui Sin Far and her sister, Winnifred Eaton. Intellectually, definitions of female mind and creativity grounded in theories of difference and inferiority were being openly challenged and debated,[17] which meant that they no longer reflected immovable facts. Politically, the idea of sexual equality appeared to be gaining strength steadily, even as the idea of racial equality—complicating matters for women of color—was clearly moving backwards. The effects of these changes on literature were dramatic. While the tradition of the domestic writer continued (as it does to the present day), especially among popular writers, most of the authors I am talking about either consciously broke with that heritage or never identified with it, declaring in the ways they lived their lives, in the statements they made about themselves as writers, and in the work they produced, that they were determined to be artists. In the high western tradition of art that they inherited, and were determined to invade, their declaration meant they had to situate themselves as creators in such a way that they could not be overwhelmed by the traditional demands of marriage and motherhood. They intended to claim for themselves the territory of Art—powerful, difficult to negotiate—that in western culture had been defined and staked out by white privileged men as their own.

Paradoxically, this claim both liberated and confined women. On the one hand, they found themselves free from many of the limiting definitions that had constricted women aspiring to be artists in earlier periods—Margaret Fuller or Phillis Wheatley, for example, or before them Anne Bradstreet. On the other hand, turn-of-the-century women writers found themselves, often in deep, subtle ways, emotionally stranded between worlds. They floated between a past they wished to leave (sometimes ambivalently, sometimes defiantly) and a future that they had not yet gained. They were full members neither of their mothers' world, at the one extreme, nor of that of the privileged white male artist, at the other. Further, the ways of living and types of writing associated with "art" had by and large been shaped by men; they were not necessarily compatible with the kinds of lives and types of stories that women writers wished to express. Tension between the tradition they aspired to enter and the lives and fictions they sought to create as women was inevitable.[18]

For women of color, the issues were multiply complicated. Almost all editors and reviewers were white, as were most book-buying readers. Pleasing this power block while remaining rooted in one's community and true to one's own artistic vision, which differed from individual to individual (a fact usually ignored by critics, most of them white), represented the almost intolerably schizophrenic challenge faced by turn-of-the-century writers in general who were people of color. For women, the situation was compounded. For a writer of Asian ancestry such as Sui Sin Far, there was absolutely no history of women writers like herself in the United States, no forebears and almost no contemporary context. Likewise for Humishuma, usually cited as the first Native American woman to publish a novel—*Cogewea* was begun in 1912 and came out at the very end of the period I am discussing, in 1927—the invention of herself as a writer was a literal, not a symbolic, act.[19] Similarly, black women writers, even though they had predecessors, faced large problems. On top of racism, they had to deal with sexism within the African American literary community, which manifested itself there as elsewhere in a willingness to see women as promoters and facilitators of men's work rather than as the authors of their own creations (Hopkins, Dunbar-Nelson, and Fauset all expended tremendous energy in the support of other people's work). They also had to contend with the racist misogyny of white America, which could conceive of black women as mammies, whores, or maids, but not as self-defined artists.

For white women, there was also the problem of sexism within the publishing world, as Ellen Glasgow, for one, learned when she delivered her first book manuscript to a publisher only to discover that he was more interested in her body than in her writing.[20] Equally difficult was the psychological issue of breaking with the past. If many white women found themselves happy to be liberated from woman's ''sphere,'' they were also, in disturbing ways, cut off from it. Whereas most white women writing fiction deep in the nineteenth century identified as women and were proud to be thought of as ''women writers,'' their descendants at the turn of the century who were determined to be artists became in many cases—as the modern masculine model of artist in the west quite logically dictated, of course—isolates, rivals, threats to each other. The often-remarked distance that Edith Wharton established between herself and other creative women is just one obvious, if exaggerated, example of this alienation, although too many modern critics, preoccupied with psychoanalysis rather than historical analysis, have tended to read it totally as an individual, family-scripted phenomenon. In fact, it was part of the author's historically explicable professional determination not to be categorized and dismissed as a woman writer.

In sum, if for many turn-of-the-century women writers being successful meant being an artist and being an artist, historically, meant being a man (and a privileged, white, erudite one to boot), then ironically being a successful, serious woman writer often meant saying that one was *not* a woman writer or a woman writer of color—that gender or gender and race (even as one wrote almost obsessively about nothing else) did *not* operate as part of the definition of who one was. Then as now both the benefits and the cost of this denial were considerable.

Certainly there were women in the United States who struggled with these issues of gender and art or gender, art, and race long before the 1890s. One of the most obvious is Emily Dickinson. In addition, along with Bradstreet, Fuller, and Wheat-

ley, one might point to Elizabeth Stoddard, Constance Fenimore Woolson, Harriet
E. Wilson, or Elizabeth Stuart Phelps. Turn-of-the-century literary women intent
on being artists had notable precursors scattered throughout American history. Furthermore, in England and on the continent Jane Austen, George Eliot, the Brontës,
Madame de Staël, and George Sand had already distinguished themselves brilliantly
as artists—as many turn-of-the-century women writers, citing them as models, well
knew. What is significant about the group I am discussing is not that they were
unprecedented, but that before them no historically coherent *group* of women of
comparable artistic ambition and accomplishment aspired to succeed as artists working primarily in fiction in the United States. They were the pioneer generation.
Before them were scattered individuals struggling with the problems of reconciling
gender and art or gender, race, and art. At the turn of the century, however—as
books in the period about women artists attest[21]—there erupted a whole group of
women struggling with the issues.

Grouping women writers, segregating by gender, carries with it certain dangers.
    As early as 1891, in her groundbreaking literary historical essay "Woman in
Literature," Helen Gray Cone opens her genealogy of women writers in America
with a vigorous protest against treating women separately. "In criticism, a classi-
fication based upon sex is necessarily misleading and inexact," Cone announces
three sentences into her essay, and the reason she gives for her aversion is straight-
forward and historical: "In practice, the evil effects which have followed the separate consideration of woman's work in literature are sufficiently plain. . . . The
dearest foe of the woman artist in the past has been the suave and chivalrous critic,
who, judging all 'female writers' by a special standard, has easily bestowed the
unearned wreath."[22] Cone—just like the women writers about to burst into view as
she wrote—was committed to an ideal of sexual equality, not difference. She understood that to allow "woman writer" as a separate category, as is still true, invites
ghettoization. In 1891 it risked encouraging separate lower standards for women
that would work against their being accepted as artists, and it was precisely that
figure—the woman writer on an equal footing with men—that Cone, thoroughly a
woman of the turn of the century, wished to protect.
    Cone's concern remains important. She found "the notion of ordained, invari-
able, and discernible difference between the literary work of men and that of
women" ridiculous—and worrisome.[23] To concede any difference is to run the risk
of conceding essential difference, and the idea of essential difference is what centuries of patriarchal criticism have used to exclude women.
    Recent scholars have raised similar issues. Myra Jehlen argues that generaliza-
tions about women writers need constantly to be tested against writing by men,
since after all "women cannot write monologues; there must be two in the world
for one woman to exist, and one of them has to be a man." Jehlen calls on "women
critics [to] adopt a method of radical comparativism," a method of talking about
literature by men and by women together rather than separately.[24] Peggy Kamuf,
sharing Audre Lorde's belief that "you can't dismantle the master's house with the
master's tools,"[25] points to the ways in which treating women writers separately
simply replicates the pattern of opposition and polarity at the core of white western

patriarchal thought and reifies the premises of generalization, exclusivity, and absolutism governing the patriarchal construction of knowledge. Kamuf asks: "If feminist theory lets itself be guided by questions such as what is women's language, literature, style or experience, from where does it get its faith in the form of these questions to get at truth, if not from the same central store that supplies humanism with its faith in the universal truth of man?" Likewise: "If feminist theory can be content to propose cosmetic modifications on the face of humanism and its institutions, will it have done anything more than reproduce the structure of woman's exclusion in the same code which has been extended to include her?"[26]

These dangers of ghettoization, erroneous generalization, and complicity in the institutional structures and methods of thought that have helped achieve the marginalization of women, men of color, and poor people in the United States are real and serious. At the same time, *not* to talk about excluded groups of writers separately, at least at this point in history, seems to me equally if not more dangerous. It guarantees perpetuating the silence and ignorance that have rendered most of these writers invisible. In American literature, the high white male tradition is so overdeveloped in the scholarship that it will take many years' work until other voices—those of white women, African Americans, Native Americans, Hispanic Americans, Asian Americans, working-class people—even begin to have the kind of developed, diverse interpretive context that, as Judith Fetterley eloquently points out in her introduction to *Provisions: A Reader from Nineteenth-Century American Women,* supports texts by making them psychologically and culturally accessible to the academy and therefore taught, read, known, heard, thought about, counted.

Additionally, grouping American women writers at the turn of the century contains strong historical logic. As I have suggested, the Progressive Era represents an unusually distinct period in women's history in the United States, which is vividly mirrored in the biographies of many of the writers I am discussing. Moreover, their work, in its very diversity and variety as well as in its shared focus on contemporary issues and on the question of form, displays a common determination among a number of women writers to write into the national record their presence as artists.

If existing literary history, as I will suggest, often hints at this presence of women writers as major figures at the turn of the century, the fact remains that most of the criticism and literary history that has been written until now does not look at them as a unit. Standard surveys such as the *Literary History of the United States,* Warner Berthoff's *The Ferment of Realism,* or Jay Martin's *Harvests of Change* occasionally juxtapose white women fiction writers of the period (most often paired are Glasgow and Cather). But singly or in couples they are almost always described as local colorists and conservatives, writers not caught up by large social and artistic questions pressing on the culture; and their achievements tend to be minimized, especially in comparison with their white male contemporaries, Jack London, Stephen Crane, Frank Norris, and Theodore Dreiser.

The prestigious *Literary History* in the 1974 revised edition illustrates the point. In it absolutely no attention goes to women of color at the turn of the century. (Black male writers do not fare well either, but at least some—Chesnutt, Dunbar, Du Bois, Johnson, Cullen, and McKay—are named.) And white women receive only minimal treatment. One paragraph is awarded to Kate Chopin, in which *The Awakening* receives no mention, and even when more time is spent on one or another turn-of-the-century white woman writer, condescension is the usual tone. Of Willa Cather it is said, for example:

> Her art is not a big art. It does not respond to the troubled sense of American might and magnitude realized but undirected, and felt so strongly by such men as Sinclair Lewis in the same decades. It is national in significance, but not in scope. Her colleagues among the men "sweated sore" over that job, whereas her books rise free and are far more creative than critical. She is preservative, almost antiquarian, content with much space in little room—feminine in this, and in her passionate revelation of the values which conserve the life of the emotions.[27]

While men, we are told, were writing big important sweaty books, Willa Cather was writing little feminine things with wings—books, incidentally, about American women becoming model farmers and world famous artists. Her work is "antiquarian" and lacks national "scope."

The passage on Cather does not need comment. It is a perfect example of what Mary Ellmann in *Thinking About Women* twenty years ago called "phallic criticism," and American literary history, as it should be, is in the process of being rewritten.[28] What does deserve dwelling on, however, because it anticipates the literary historical picture now emerging, is the *History*'s sense that Cather does stand apart from male writers of her era, and stands apart because she is a woman writer. There is a clear sense that Cather is doing something different from the men. The problem lies in the book's inability to identify accurately what that difference is, and then to take it seriously.

This is true not only in the treatment of Cather, but also in the *History*'s rare attempts at statements about turn-of-the-century white women writers in general. When the volume implicitly connects Wharton, Cather, and Glasgow by discussing them next to each other, the reason for juxtaposing them finally amounts to the fact that they represent awkward leftovers between discussion of the 1890s and Dreiser, on the one hand, and discussion of the 1920s and the white male writers of that era, on the other. Typical is this effort to provide some sort of unifying statement:

> While Mrs. Wharton deplores the corrosions of security, Ellen Glasgow fears only that the nobler aristocratic values will die out of America with her dying Virginians. And passion, nobly interpreted, is Willa Cather's chief theme. Indeed, it is Ellen Glasgow and Willa Cather, the two finest craftsmen and artists in this movement toward a summary literature of the secure and confident nineteenth century, who best illustrate the woman's contribution to American fiction at the end of an era.[29]

There is a desire here to think of women writers in relation to each other and *as* women writers, but beyond that there is confusion.

In contrast, a second class of books, decade books such as Larzer Ziff's *The American 1890s* or Grant Knight's *The Critical Period in American Literature* followed by *The Strenuous Age in American Literature,* typically group white women writers. They do so no doubt because they wish to reflect accurately the mood of the period they study. The 1890s, 1900s, and 1910s were highly self-conscious about the subject of women and the core of feminist issues loosely dubbed "the woman question" at the time, a phrase popular of course well before the turn of the century. (Significantly, Frederick J. Hoffman's decade book, *The Twenties: American Writing in the Postwar Decade,* groups no women writers, black or white—a difference reflecting the mounting antifeminism both of the period studied, the decade following World War One, and of the period in which the study was published, the decade following World War Two.) The most glaring failure of all of these studies is that not one talks about women writers of color. The second largest problem, even with Ziff's book, which is in certain respects quite perceptive, is that the decade construct is too narrow for the subject of women writers at the turn of the century. For example, the bond between Cather and Jewett is strong and important, yet Cather cannot be discussed in detail in a book about the 1890s and Jewett cannot be discussed in detail in a book abut the 1910s. Likewise the historical link between Harper in the 1890s, Hopkins in the 1900s, and Fauset in the teens and twenties must be ruptured when the continuity of the period is artificially segmented. Thus, while the decade approach can be a good one for the subject of women writers in terms of obliging critics and scholars to work closely with historical facts, it is a bad one in imposing arbitrary boundaries on what was in women's literary and social history a unified thirty-five-year period.

Especially important are critical books explicitly about women writers, among them Louis Auchincloss's *Pioneers and Caretakers,* Patricia Meyer Spacks's *The Female Imagination,* Ellen Moers's *Literary Women,* Barbara Christian's *Black Women Novelists: The Development of a Tradition, 1892–1976,* Josephine Donovan's *New England Local Color Literature: A Women's Tradition* and *After the Fall: The Demeter-Persephone Myth in Wharton, Cather, and Glasgow,* Carole McAlpine Watson's *Prologue: The Novels of Black American Women, 1891–1965,* Hazel V. Carby's *Reconstructing Womanhood: The Emergence of the Afro-American Woman Novelist,* Sandra M. Gilbert and Susan Gubar's *No Man's Land 2: Sexchanges,* Gloria T. Hull's *Color, Sex, and Poetry: Three Women Writers of the Harlem Renaissance,* Amy Ling's *Between Worlds: Women Writers of Chinese Ancestry,* or Judith Fryer's *Felicitous Space: The Imaginative Structures of Edith Wharton and Willa Cather.*[30] Many of these are excellent books. However, the mission of each, for different reasons, dictates interest in only some of the turn-of-the-century women writers brought together in this volume. Moreover, only some of these studies consider historical context important, and none develops analysis about both women of color and white writers, though only Christian, Watson, Carby, Hull, Fryer, Ling, and Donovan acknowledge this in their titles.

If we ask why turn-of-the-century American women writers have not been grouped and looked at historically, even when much of the criticism has obviously wanted to and various couples and combinations have always been offered, the answer requires, I think, some historical perspective.

American literature as a respectable academic field was born during the same decades that the women fiction writers I discuss distinguished themselves. As Paul Lauter explains, the institutionalization of American literature at the university level took place at the turn of the century; and with that professionalization of the study of American literature in the 1910s and 1920s, the authority over what was worthy and "best" passed out of the hands of readers, who were chiefly women, into the hands of a new, expanding, highly ambitious "professional" professoriat, which was overwhelmingly white, male, and middle to upper-middle class. American literature as a field, in other words, and the profession of professor as it is now understood emerged at the same time in American history; and that time, which was when women writers of the Progressive Era wrote, was, as Lauter's study makes dramatically clear, a period of mounting white male anxiety in the academy about the feminization of literature.[31]

At the annual meeting of the Modern Language Association in 1909, for instance, the chairman of the Central Division, focusing his address on "Coeducation and Literature," worried aloud about whether the high numbers of women enrolled in literature courses "may not contribute to shape the opinion that literature is preeminently a study for girls, and tend to discourage some men. . . . This is not yet saying," he hastened to add, "that the preference of women turns away that of men. There are many factors to the problem. But," he admitted, "it looks that way."[32] How to bring literary study more in line with "the ideal of masculine culture," to quote further from this 1909 convention speaker, constituted the challenge facing modern language professors on the eve of the second decade of the twentieth century.[33]

From the beginning, then, turn-of-the-century women writers faced strong forces of resistance. The era that saw women gain the vote, earn unprecedented percentages of college degrees, enter the professions in unheard-of numbers, lower the birthrate, raise the divorce rate, and stop the sale of liquor was also, it is important to remember, the era of San Juan Hill, the Rough Riders, World War One, and a political party named, not carelessly, the Bull Moose Party. If enthusiasm about women's new freedom ran high, so among privileged white males did anxiety about traditional masculinity (and this was inextricably connected to the renewed vigor of feminism, of course), as fiction from Norris to Hemingway dramatizes in passionate detail. The historian James R. McGovern provides an excellent summary of this crisis in white masculine culture in the Progressive Era, explaining that it gave birth to an intense

> "virility impulse." This may be described as an exaggerated concern with manliness and its conventional concomitants—power and activity. Social Darwinism is usually called upon to explain the phenomenon without inquiring why, in personal terms, it was so attractive to its supporters. . . . [The period] was marked by "superpresidents" and robust statesmen like Beveridge and Lodge who advanced the "rough and ready" philosophy of Mahan. Fears for our manly vigor were openly expressed by T. R. and Brooks Adams [brother of Henry], Roosevelt dynamically coping with the problem through lectures to women's organizations and gymnastics. While national foreign policy was ambitious, firm, and even belligerent, contemporary novelists like Dreiser and London exalted the Nietzchean hero and others like David Graham Phillips and Winston Churchill took hope in the Great Man.[34]

Given this cultural context, what happened to turn-of-the-century women writers as a group is in one way simple. The dominant-culture ideal of "masculine culture," to return to the MLA chairman's phrase in 1909, won. As Lauter makes clear, African American women writers were not written into American literary history to begin with, as has also been the case with writers of Asian, Native American, and

Latin descent, and then in the 1920s American white women writers got written
out. Whereas a few black men and a number of white female authors had found
their way into critical and historical studies before the twenties, or even during the
twenties and the thirties in work by such leftovers from old-fashioned "genteel"
literary culture as Fred Lewis Pattee or Arthur Hobson Quinn, the national literary
canon fashioned by the first generation of academic professionals in the 1920s, and
therefore destined to shape the field for half a century, was resolutely white and
masculine. Thus even as writers such as Edith Wharton, Willa Cather, and Jessie
Redmon Fauset were crowning their careers and others such as Edith Summers
Kelley and Nella Larsen were launching theirs, powerful forces had been set in
motion in the academy to scatter, trivialize, and finally to bury them. Not until the
profession of professor in the United States opened up at least a little to people of
color and white women in the 1960s and seventies would the model drawn in the
reactionary twenties begin to receive widespread, revisionary scrutiny.

Significantly, more than two decades before the MLA's "ideal of masculine culture"
began systematically to write women out of American literary history (or into such
minor roles that the same result was achieved), Helen Gray Cone, in the still pre-
professionalized early 1890s, sketched in "Woman in Literature" a rich tradition
of women writers in the United States. Though predominantly white, her group
does include Phillis Wheatley, and her essay recognizes slavery and abolition as
important forces motivating white women's literary tradition in America.
    Looking back, Cone decided of American women writers: "It is in fiction that
they have wrought with the greatest vigor and freedom; and in that important class
of fiction which reflects faithfully the national life, broadly or in sectional phases."[35]
Writing at the end of the period, in 1930, Pattee heartily agreed. He stated of turn-
of-the-century women novelists—of which his principal examples were Gertrude
Atherton, Willa Cather, Edith Wharton, Ellen Glasgow, and Zona Gale: "The work
of these women marks the highest reach to which the novel of characterization and
manners has attained in America during our period [1890–1930]. Perhaps no literary
phenomenon in our history has been more noteworthy than this feminine assumption
of leadership." Pattee continued: "The creation of fiction in most of its areas has
proved to be an art adapted peculiarly for the powers of women." Indeed, spurred
by discrimination, "woman has surpassed her male competitiors in workmanship,
in artistry, in the quality of work toiled over and finished."[36]
    Cone, in the early 1890s, could only imagine the field admired by Pattee. In
1891 only Jewett, Harper, and Chopin had appeared on the scene, and none had
produced her most important work. Cone records the puzzlement of "the just and
genial Colonel Higginson [who] expresses disappointment that woman's advance in
literature has not been more marked since the establishment of the women's colleges," and she offers in explanation the theory, which would prove especially true
for black women, that "the deed, and not the word, engages the energy of the
college woman of to-day." Yet she prophesies, "as these institutions grow into the
life of our land, that life will be everywhere enriched; and the word must follow in
happy time." Then, letting her hopes and imagination soar, she concludes by en-
visioning a utopian future of artistic accomplishment and equality for women. She

predicts that "individual genius for literature is sure sooner or later to appear within the constantly widening circle of those fairly equipped for its exercise. It would be idle to expect that the cases in which native power and an adequate preparation go hand in hand, will be frequent; since they are infrequent among men. The desirable thing was," Cone insists, "that this rare development should be made a possibility among women. It is possible to-day," she declares, and then ends her essay with the prediction: "Some golden morrow will make it a reality."[37]

How very close that golden morrow was in 1891 Cone could only guess. She could not name the women she knew had to be out there. She only knew that they must be there, about to speak.

A word of caution in conclusion. I do not think that the historical distinctiveness of Progressive Era women writers and the importance of that period in American literary history should be construed into an argument that these are the first "great" women fiction writers in America, that what they did is more significant (because more prestigious) than what their nineteenth-century predecessors did, or that their achievement should be set up as some sort of measure. I do think that they were an important group of individuals, and that it is good that an unusually large number of their books have managed to gain and retain recognition, even by people not interested in women writers per se. However, in grouping them I have no wish to contribute to the construction of literary history as competition, with winners and losers and everyone else ranked in between. Precisely that paradigm of literary-history-as-horse-race, with one track and one kind of winner (in horses the fastest, in men the most "brilliant"), is the mechanism that has served to exclude all but a very few women and a very few men of color from the "canon."

Indeed, one of my major purposes in pulling together turn-of-the-century women writers is to counteract the elitism that has allowed "in" one or two of them— usually Wharton and Cather—thus divorcing them from other women writers, both of their generation and before them, and consigning those writers not plucked out to oblivion. My purpose in telling the story of turn-of-the-century women writers is to contribute to the unfolding, complex, but nonetheless connected story now being recovered of American women writers as a whole. That many of the writers I discuss successfully invaded and in significant instances transformed such masculine territory as the high-art novel is very important. It also raises complicated questions. Women who choose to attempt the Great Novel, it can be argued, may confine their creativity in ways escaped by those who do not, or do not much of the time. Experimental work by Jewett, Gilman, Hopkins, and Austin, for example, suggests the liberating effect that *not* being able to concentrate only or mainly on novels can have.[38] Had Dunbar-Nelson not tried to write novels, might she have produced more short fiction and, gifted as she was, molded more exciting alternative structures? (Was her diary a stab at that?) At the same time, what most of these writers accomplished with the narrative forms that they inherited, including the novel, leaves little room for pining over what they might have done. Innovative, inventive, and dazzlingly adept in their manipulation of the status quo, many of them took possession of high-art fiction, the novel included, as no other generation of American women writers before them had.

Finally, the grouping of turn-of-the-century women writers that follows is not definitive. There are many authors not discussed or only mentioned—Mary Wilkins Freeman, Onoto Watanna, Gertrude Atherton, Zona Gale, Zara Wright, Renee Vivien, Helen Hull, Gertrude Dorsey Browne, and the list could go on—that other people will argue belong in a study such as this. I agree. What I am offering is not exhaustive. I am not attempting to talk about everyone in the period, nor about every work by the authors I do include. Moreover, emphasis in my discussion is uneven. Not every author included receives the same amount of attention and detail. In particular, well-known writers such as Wharton and Stein have, relatively speaking, little space allotted to them. Rather than repeat in detail the conclusions of other studies (my own among them), I point the reader to those studies, merely summarizing their views here, and thus free space for discussion of writers about whom less has been written. What I am offering in this book, in other words, is intended to be suggestive, a beginning. As Peggy Kamuf, wisely cautionary about the implications of method, argues: What we need is a new criticism that "leaves its own undecidable margins of indeterminacy visible, readable on the surface of the newly-contoured landscape" and recognizes "its own inevitable inaccuracy and lack of finality."[39] Likewise Annette Kolodny, calling for scholars of American literature at this point in time to immerse themselves in unfamiliar texts and traditions, urges acceptance "at the outset that the writing of literary history is never a static or completed process. In stark contrast to the authoritative tone of earlier histories, a certain tentativeness should mark" the new historical work being done.[40]

This book is offered as part of this new historical project. It represents one way of thinking about American women writers at the turn into the twentieth century. And just as I do not claim that my inclusion of authors is definitive or exhaustive, so my structure is not the only one possible. It has internal logic, I hope, but finally my form is simply an invention, one way of organizing a perspective on the material. Other organizing principles and combinations of authors could be used, each creating its own structural argument about both the parts and the whole.

To provide a map here, the structure I create in the following chapters roughly reflects chronology, brings together figures and works that are sometimes complementary and sometimes clashing, and varies from chapter to chapter in terms of isolating or grouping authors. In general, Chapter 2 focuses on Frances Ellen Harper; 3 on Charlotte Perkins Gilman; 4 on Sarah Orne Jewett; 5 on Alice Dunbar-Nelson, Kate Chopin, and Pauline Hopkins; 6 on Gertrude Stein and Mary Austin; 7 on Sui Sin Far; 8 on Willa Cather, with discussion too of Humishuma and of the whole issue of women writers and art; 9 on Jessie Fauset and Edith Wharton, plus a small section on María Cristina Mena; 10 on Anzia Yezierska, Ellen Glasgow, and Edith Summers Kelley; and 11 on Nella Larsen, with a glance at Zora Neale Hurston. Although I discuss other works as well, I talk in detail about *Iola Leroy*, "The Yellow Wallpaper," *The Country of the Pointed Firs*, *The Goodness of St. Rocque*, *The Awakening*, *Contending Forces*, *Of One Blood*, *The Land of Little Rain*, *Tender Buttons*, *Mrs. Spring Fragrance*, *The Song of the Lark*, *Sapphira and the Slave Girl*, *Cogewea*, *The Touchstone*, *Summer*, "The Vine-Leaf," *There Is Confusion*, *Comedy: American Style*, *Bread Givers*, *Barren Ground*, *Weeds*, *The Eatonville Anthology*, *Quicksand*, and *Passing*.

2 | Breaking Silence: *Iola Leroy*

The one mute and voiceless note has been the sadly expectant Black Woman,
　　An infant crying in the night,
　　An infant crying for the light;
　　And with *no language—but a cry.*

ANNA JULIA COOPER[1]

Anna Julia Cooper wrote of black women's need to speak in 1892, just one year after Helen Gray Cone had looked in vain for the new work by women writers that she knew had to be emerging. As if in prophetic answer to both Cooper and Cone, Frances Ellen Watkins Harper's *Iola Leroy, or Shadows Uplifted* (1892) appeared.

Harper's novel embodies what would become one of the core issues of serious writing by women at the turn of the century—the will to break silence by exposing the connection among institutionalized violence, the sexual exploitation of women, and female muteness. Construed most broadly, the linkage that black women writers understood to exist among lynching, rape, and voicelessness illustrates in extreme form the central concern with violence, sexual control, and silencing that white women writers of the period perceived and wrote about as well, as works from "The Yellow Wallpaper" in 1892 to *Barren Ground* in 1925 illustrate. As the historian Bettina Aptheker explains: "The Black female experience, by the very nature of its extremity, illuminates the subjugation of all women."[2] That premise, understood far better by black women than by white throughout American history, applies to the literary as well as to the social record.

The quiet shattered by African American women writers in the 1890s—the language found, where according to Anna Julia Cooper there had before been only silence—was not of course absolute. By 1892 Frances Ellen Harper had a long, strong female literary tradition behind her in the United States. White women had been publishing throughout the country's history; indeed, they had dominated the nineteenth-century fiction market. Black women, while not well represented in the novel, had been publishing poetry in America since the middle of the eighteenth century[3] and producing autobiographies throughout the nineteenth. They were also, as folklore and popular-culture studies have long recognized, though the academy has been slow to appreciate this fact, extraordinarily rich in oral literary tradition. The silence that Cooper felt herself piercing—the silence against which Harper wrote and, in so doing, opened this story in the early 1890s—was not literal silence. Rather, what set turn-of-the-century women's fiction apart from what came before it was an almost militant, shared—as opposed to sporadic—public determination among many women writers to *name* the systems of violence, sexual control, and silencing that governed the lives of countless American women. African American women, experiencing the most extreme forms of this systematic denial of voice, yet at the same time emboldened by a history of autobiographical writing and story-telling that was alive with the issue of freedom, were particularly determined to be heard. In 1892, with Cooper's *A Voice From the South,* Harper's *Iola Leroy,* and Ida B. Wells's *Southern Horrors: Lynch Law in All Its Phases,* they spoke out forcefully.

Although for most of the twentieth century *Iola Leroy* has been cited as the first novel published by an African American woman, it is important to understand that, in fact, it was not. Preceding Harper's novel was Amelia Johnson's *Clarence and Corinne; or, God's Way* in 1890 and Emma Dunham Kelley's *Megda* in 1891.[4] In addition, as the recent reissue of Harriet E. Wilson's *Our Nig* (1859) has empha-sized, the date of the earliest novel by a black woman in the United States extends back at least to the middle of the nineteenth century.[5] Still, Harper's novel does represent a substantive first, if not a literal one, for it was the first novel by a black American woman to gain both immediate and lasting recognition. Unlike the long fictions by Wilson, Johnson, and Kelley, *Iola Leroy* made a significant mark in its own day, going into second and third editions, and it never fell into oblivion; it consistently shows up in literary histories of African American writing (even if only to be disparaged). Perhaps most important, as Barbara Christian indicates by opening her study *Black Women Novelists* with a discussion of Harper's book. *Iola Leroy* is the novel that many twentieth-century African American women novelists them-selves have looked to, until very recently, as the first to be published in the United States by a black American woman. Full-length, secular, and literarily ambitious, it publicly and permanently opened the tradition of fiction by black women in the United States in the twentieth century—from Pauline Hopkins's *Contending Forces* in 1900 forward.[6]

From the 1890s through the 1920s, African American women published fiction at an unprecedented rate.[7] After *Clarence and Corinne, Megda,* and *Iola Leroy,* came Amelia Johnson's *The Hazeley Family* in 1894 and *Martina Meriden, or What is the Motive* in 1901. Victoria Earle Matthews brought out *Aunt Lindy* in 1893; Emma D. Kelley-Hawkins issued *Four Girls at Cottage City* in 1898; and Alice Moore Dunbar-Nelson published two volumes of short stories, *Violets and Other Tales* in 1895 and *The Goodness of St. Rocque* in 1899. Within three years after the publication of *Contending Forces,* Pauline Hopkins serialized three novels in the *Colored American Magazine,* for which she worked as an editor. In 1918 *Hope's Highway* by Sarah Lee Brown Fleming appeared; in 1920 Zara Wright brought out both *Black and White Tangled Threads* and *Kenneth*; in 1921 Lillian E. Wood published *"Let My People Go,"* and Mary Etta Spencer came out with *The Resentment.* Jessie Redmon Fauset, whose fiction had been appearing in the *Crisis* since 1912, published *There Is Confusion* in 1924, followed by *Plum Bun* in 1929, *The Chinaberry Tree* in 1931, and *Comedy: American Style* in 1933. Nella Larsen brought out *Quicksand* in 1928 and then *Passing* in the next year.

Throughout the three and a half decades from *Iola Leroy* to *Plum Bun* and

Passing, short stories by African American women, as well as an abundance of verse and essays, appeared in magazines and periodicals. Particularly they showed up in publications directed primarily to black audiences. Founded in the 1830s, this periodical press had developed to a peak of vigor in the 1850s and early sixties when debate about slavery and flagrant racism intensified immediately before and during the Civil War. It then went into a dormant period as possibilities for black people seemed to improve during Reconstruction. When Reconstruction collapsed, however, so too did the optimism that black Americans in the South would find themselves fully and fairly incorporated into the nation's economic and political life. At that time, as literary historian Penelope L. Bullock explains, the publication of black-owned and edited journals and periodicals began to increase dramatically. Magazines and periodicals proliferated through the 1880s, nineties, and the first decade of the twentieth century, culminating in the 1910 founding of the *Crisis,* the official publication of the newly formed National Association for the Advancement of Colored People, which had been organized primarily to combat lynching.[8]

Women wrote for this press from the beginning. Indeed, the first short story published by an African American in the United States is thought to be "The Two Offers" by Frances Ellen Watkins (later Harper), which appeared in 1859 in the *Anglo-African Magazine,* a publication founded by Thomas Hamilton and committed to printing only the work of black writers. The two most important magazines at the turn of the century for African American fiction writers were the *Crisis,* for which Jessie Fauset served as the literary editor until the mid-1920s, and before it the *Colored American Magazine* (1900–1909) during the years it was published in Boston, rather than in New York, under the literary editorship of Pauline Hopkins (up to 1904). In addition to essays, news stories, poems, travel writing, book reviews, and drama by women, these two periodicals alone published fiction by more than two dozen women before 1920.[9]

This outpouring of stories and novels by American black women from the early 1890s to the late 1920s was remarkable—and understandable. It was no accident that the work of these writers coincided exactly with the tremendous political ferment unleashed and mobilized within the black community, and particularly within the black women's movement, at the turn of the century.

The historian Rayford W. Logan has called the forty-year period following the collapse of Reconstruction "the nadir" for black people in the United States.[10] Against a national backdrop of rising prosperity, increasing global might, and ballooning patriotic self-congratulation indulged in by many white Americans, institutionalized racism gained ground rapidly during the Progressive Era in the form of lynching, Jim Crow laws, the convict lease system, disenfranchisement, unemployment, and ubiquitous segregation of public facilities and services. In the national press, repeal of the Fourteenth Amendment, granting the vote to black men, was openly proposed in articles such as "Have American Negroes Too Much Freedom?," "Negro Suffrage a Failure: Shall We Abolish It?," "The Black Shadow in the South," "The Race Problem: Disenfranchisement As a Remedy," and "Shall the Fourteenth Amendment Be Enforced?"[11] In white fiction, the turn of the century hosted an ominous upsurge in racist works, elevating authors such as Thomas Dixon, Joel Chandler Harris, and Thomas Nelson Page to extreme popularity.[12] Indeed, it was Dixon's virulently bigoted novel *The Clansman*, a best-seller in 1905, that provided the basis ten years later for D. W. Griffith's aesthetically acclaimed racist film about the creation of the Ku Klux Klan, *Birth of a Nation*.

Black Americans responded by speaking out, organizing, and working relentlessly to strengthen and empower themselves economically, politically, socially, and psychologically; and in this race work, black women were crucial and prominent. Principally through the network of women's clubs that sprang up and produced brilliant leaders—Fannie Barrier Williams, Ida B. Wells-Barnett, Mary Church Terrell, Charlotte Hawkins Brown, Nannie Helen Burroughs, Mary McLeod Bethune—black women organized themselves to combat racism through collectivity.[13]

The paramount issue for black women at the turn of the century was race.[14] While they suffered because they were women, they suffered more and primarily because they were black: If one or the other of the two issues had to take priority, it had to be race. As Elsie Johnson McDougald, a social worker by training who worked as an assistant principal in a public school in Harlem, explained in her 1925 essay, "The Double Task: The Struggle of Negro Women for Sex and Race Emancipation," the "feminist efforts [of African American women] are directed chiefly toward the realization of the equality of the races, the sex struggle assuming a subordinate place."[15] More than fifty years earlier, Frances Ellen Harper characterized her own position in reference to the Fourteenth and Fifteenth Amendments by observing that "when it was a question of race she let the lesser question of sex go." She added, with obvious anger: "But the white women all go for sex, letting race occupy a minor position."[16]

Because white women did not experience both systems of discrimination—indeed, they were active perpetrators of racism in many cases—they often treated sex discrimination and racism as rival issues to be played off against each other, to the obvious disadvantage of the race question every time, as Harper's bitter remark emphasizes. In contrast, black women were the direct recipients of both systems of discrimination. They were feminists because they were women *and* because they were black; they balanced and integrated their allegiance to the two causes. They never, however, placed black liberation second.[17]

This preeminence of race as the issue for black women—the idea that although sex discrimination in general may be bad, it is finally the peculiar brand of sex discrimination experienced by black women *because they are black* that must be named and dealt with—appears repeatedly in turn-of-the-century fiction by black women. It shows up most clearly, from *Iola* through *Plum Bun* and *Passing,* in the ubiquitous theme of "passing," which dramatizes again and again the fact that, even if the heroine wants to "pass" for white, disowning her race as the basic issue is not an answer. It may seem to be. It may appear that a woman can pass, that she can choose not to be black, choose simply to be a female human being—which in a racist white society means white. But the choice does not truly exist. In story after story heroines are tempted, in fact or fantasy, to be people not marked by race, but almost always the resolution is clear. As Jessie Fauset's heroine learns in a brutal confluence of racial and sexual humiliation in the 1920 novella, *The Sleeper Wakes,* it is not her sex but her race that a white man, enraged and powerful, hurls at her: " 'Nigger,' he had called her as she fell, 'nigger, nigger,' and again, 'nigger.' "[18]

Even if a black woman should want or try to escape it, race, in racist America, constitutes the primary issue of her life.

Simultaneously, however, and here the complexity and even paradox of the situation become evident, for black women no clear division between racial and sexual discrimination exists. African American women experience sexual discrimination as women who are black, and racial discrimination as blacks who are women. The two systems of sexual and racial discrimination entwine and support each other. Separating them in a culture that does not do so is a luxury unavailable to women of color, who throughout American history have experienced both concurrently. But that experience also means that women of color share a distinct and unusually encompassing and penetrating social perspective, for they have been uniquely positioned to understand the root connectedness of both systems of oppression. As Paula Giddings explains: "Because both are motivated by similar economic, social, and psychological forces, it is only logical that those who sought to undermine Blacks were also the most virulent antifeminists. The means of oppression differed across race and sex lines, but the wellspring of that oppression was the same. Black women understood this dynamic," Giddings concludes. "White women, by and large, did not." Therefore "white feminists often acquiesced to racist ideology, undermining their own cause in doing so"[19]—and in the process, I would add, defining themselves as a major part of the black women's problem.

Iola Leroy, as I will explain, deals with a complicated set of issues of deep concern to all black feminists at the turn of the century: the dominant culture's definition of black women as all-sexual, the reality and complex mythology of rape in a racist society, and the seemingly ineradicable racism of white "sisters."

Susan B. Anthony's request that Frederick Douglass, women's ally since the days of abolition, not attend the National American Woman Suffrage Association conference in Atlanta in 1894 lest his presence alienate Southern white women— or the declaration of the NAWSA five years later, still under Anthony's leadership, that women's suffrage and the black question were divisible—only confirmed black women's charges against white feminism. It is not surprising that, early in the 1890s when Fannie Barrier Williams and Anna Julia Cooper were invited to speak to the Columbian Exposition by the all-white board of Lady Managers, who had not of course included any women of color in the planning of the famous Woman's Building at the exposition, they took the opportunity to raise the subject of racism. The white women had probably expected Williams and Cooper to be polite, noncontroversial speakers.[20] Instead, they brought up the most highly charged issue possible: the alleged sexual promiscuity of black women.

The topic was fundamental to black women's counterattack on rape-lynch mythology. Although the overwhelming majority of lynchings were not even linked to a rape charge, the crime automatically evoked by a lynching in the eyes of white America was the rape of a white woman by a black man.[21] Respected white publications such as *Harper's* ran stories about the "new crime," and many white liberals—Jane Addams, for example—though opposed to lynching, subscribed to the image of the black man as rapist.[22] At the heart of this racist mythology were two elements: the allegedly monstrous libido of black men, who, freed from restraint by the collapse of Reconstruction, supposedly lusted uncontrollably after white women; and the presumed sensuality and insatiable sexuality of black women, whose carnality supposedly drove black men on. As one racist analysis put it at the time, it was finally the "wantonness of the women of his own race" which drove the black man to rape.[23] Rape-lynch mythology, in other words, was built on the bodies of black women. As one historian explains: "The dialects of the lynch mentality required the dehumanization of Black men (as rapists), Black women (as prostitutes), and white women (as property whose honor was to be avenged by the men who possessed them)."[24] For black women at the turn of the century, defending themselves against the racist charge of sexual immorality did not represent some misguided bow to outmoded Victorian morality. It represented an essential part of their life-and-death struggle *as women* against lynching in the United States.

Therefore, when Anna Julia Cooper, addressing the white Lady Managers in 1893, one year after Frances Ellen Harper published *Iola Leroy*, eloquently asserted that the real issue was not the black woman's supposed susceptibility to "temptations," but instead, in the wake of three centuries of white rape of black women, "the painful, patient, and silent toil of mothers to gain title to the bodies of their daughters,"[25] she was articulating a central—and agonizing—political and spiritual truth for black women. The issue of rape for African American women was not the supposed victimization of white women by black men. It was the real, documented, centuries-long institution of white rape of black women.

Further, when on the same occasion Fannie Barrier Williams said that black women's "own mothers can't protect them, and White women will not,"[26] she was calling into focus the racism of white women that many black women knew had to be exposed if either racial or sexual equality was to be realized. In 1920 Charlotte Hawkins Brown, one of four black women invited to speak at an interracial conference in Memphis, Tennessee, bluntly told her audience of white women: "We have begun to feel that you are not, after all, interested in us and I am going still further. The negro women of the South lay everything that happens to the members of her race at the door of the Southern white woman. . . . We feel that so far as lynching is concerned that, if the white women would take hold of the situation, that lynching would be stopped." She added, in what was certainly not a nonsequitur: "I want to say to you, when you read in the paper where a colored man has insulted a white woman, just multiply that by one thousand and you have some idea of the number of colored women insulted by white men."[27] Ida B. Wells in 1892 went even further in a Memphis editorial, later reprinted in *Southern Horrors*, by suggesting the truly unnameable: the possibility that white women were sexually attracted to black men. "Nobody in this section of the country believes the old thread bare lie that Negro men rape white women," she charged. "If Southern white men are not careful, they will over-reach themselves and public sentiment will have a reaction: a conclusion will be reached which will be very damaging to the moral reputation of their women."[28]

For her words, Ida B. Wells was threatened with the very sexual violence that she and other black people risked their lives to name. The editors of the Memphis *Press Scimitar* called on white men in the city "to tie the wretch who utters these calumnies to a stake at the intersection of Main and Madison Sts., brand him [*sic*] in the forehead with a hot iron and perform upon him a surgical operation with a pair of tailor's shears.''[29] The only reason that Wells escaped lynching was because she had left town. According to reports, she had left in response to the longstanding invitation of the famous activist and author Frances Ellen Watkins Harper.[30]

The overt political message of *Iola Leroy* is not complicated. Set during the Civil War and Reconstruction, the novel reclaims antebellum, Civil War, and Reconstruction history from a black point of view. Needing to combat deep, widespread prejudice and ignorance, Harper addresses many issues. She writes of the bravery of black troops; the ardent desire for freedom among slaves; the resistance and subterfuge exercised by them; the closeness of family ties among blacks both before and after the Civil War; the intense level of intellectual debate on issues of race and racism within the black community and between blacks and whites during Reconstruction; the discrimination faced by African Americans during that period; and the impressive, often heroic, commitment of countless black Americans to community self-help and solidarity. Set against these issues are Iola Leroy's successful search for her mother and her decision not to marry a white man from the North and spend much of her life "passing." Although raised to believe she is white, and fair enough to pass, Harper's heroine proudly identifies with her black heritage. She declares when she is fired from a job because the white salesgirls refuse to work next to a "colored" girl: "The best blood in my veins is African blood, and I am not ashamed of it.''[31] When the novel closes, Iola has chosen to marry a man of color, a physician who plans to dedicate his life to serving fellow blacks in the South, and the two will spend their lives working side by side in the black community.

Surely the announced political agenda of *Iola Leroy*—the novel's pride in race and vigorous commitment to inquiry, confrontation, and activism—came out of Harper's life. Already a published author for forty years by the time *Iola Leroy* came out, she was the best-known black poet in America between Phillis Wheatley and Paul Laurence Dunbar. As an artist in the oral tradition, she was by all accounts a genius.[32] She had devoted her life to writing and lecturing about injustice and reform, and for her—and this lies at the heart of her aesthetic—action and art were totally inseparable. As Hazel V. Carby puts it, there is no reason to wonder why at the age of sixty-seven "Harper chose to write a novel as a 'lasting service to the race.' . . . The production of *Iola Leroy* was rooted in the authority of Harper's experience as abolitionist, lecturer, poet, teacher, feminist, and black woman.''[33]

Harper's ardent belief in the political mission of literature aligned her with African American literary tradition that, from the stories and songs of slaves, to the narratives of ex-slaves, to the novels of Harriet Wilson and William Wells Brown, to the poetry of Harper herself and Dunbar, consistently used literature for protest. Also her commitment to protest aligned her with a major white female American literary tradition dating back most strikingly to Harriet Beecher Stowe, whom Harper admired.[34] That tradition, in the words of Helen Gray Cone, was forged in the "struggle between the art-instinct and the desire for reform." As Cone saw it, in contrast to most white men before the middle of the nineteenth century, talented white women in the United States, torn between art and action, often chose action. They followed their "passion for conduct," their "enthusiasm for abstract justice," especially during the abolitionist period, rather than remove themselves to some lofty aerie of Art. Then *Uncle Tom's Cabin*, in Cone's opinion, brought the two impulses together: "At last the artist's instinct and the purpose of the reformer were fused."[35] With Stowe's novel, according to Cone, a powerful, strong model for politicized fiction by women entered the national literature.

The art of *Iola Leroy* (in spite of Harper's claims that she was not an artist, but rather just a teller of truths) reveals how exciting but also how overwhelming the challenge was that faced her. Even with several friendly traditions behind her, how could she make a novel capable of embracing the huge complex of issues, obvious and hidden—even taboo—that had to go into the telling of even the most middle-class or "respectable" black woman's story in late nineteenth-century America? Obviously, the tidy, tight, highly controlled high-culture novel of Anglo-European derivation, such as what Henry James or even William Dean Howells might put together, could not begin to hold even the simplest version of the story that Harper, focusing on an African American heroine, had to tell. Neither could the domestic novel, crafted by white women in the middle of the nineteenth century, nor the standard nineteenth-century African American novel, shaped by men, offer Harper an easy answer to the question of how to put her narrative together.

The depth of Harper's formal struggle is clear in *Iola Leroy*. She herself invokes the common metaphor of weaving to describe her method, saying at the end of the book: "From the threads of fact and fiction I have woven a story whose mission will not be in vain if it awaken in the hearts of our countrymen a stronger sense of justice and a more Christlike humanity in behalf of those whom the fortunes of war threw, homeless, ignorant and poor, upon the threshold of a new era" (*IL*, p. 282). Teetering herself on the threshold of a new era, Harper offers a novel that, in its formal self-fracturing, speaks to the inadequacy of any single inherited long narrative form—the slave narrative, the domestic novel, the nineteenth-century African American novel, the white antislavery novel, the tight high-culture Anglo-European art novel—to serve her purpose of writing a political novel about a black woman in the United States. In *Iola*, Harper, "weaving," draws on and intermixes a conglomeration of inherited forms—melodrama, journalism, adventure fiction, slave narrative, abolitionist fiction, the realistic novel, oral tradition, the romance—to reach toward a new form. That form is imperfectly realized in this pioneering novel but nonetheless fascinating, especially as a harbinger. Harper enjambs realism and myth—or what in nineteenth-century fiction we would call melodrama, that is, narrative that is not literally credible but instead expresses *in*credible spiritual and moral "truths"—to create a vehicle for her deepest story, the relationship for Iola among sexual violence, silencing, and black female yearning for mother-daughter reunion.

This struggle of Harper as an artist, like many of the writers in this book, was not simply intellectual. As Audre Lorde notes, we have more poetry than long fiction from past generations of African American women because there are "enormous differences in the material demands between poetry and prose. As we reclaim our literature, poetry has been the major voice of poor, working class, and Colored women. A room of one's own may be a necessity for writing prose, but so are reams of paper, a typewriter, and plenty of time."[36] For forty years, as she traveled and lectured, Harper was able to write poetry; but not until late in her life did she have enough economic security as well as sufficient freedom from her commitments as an activist to write a long narrative. She herself addresses this point in *Iola Leroy*. Her heroine, who would like to be a writer, abandons her ambition for the time being, explaining more than three decades before Virginia Woolf's famous statement on the subject: "One needs both leisure and money to make a successful book" (*IL*, p. 262).

One also needs courage. When Harper did have leisure and money to make a book, she inscribed on its second page:

TO MY DAUGHTER
MARY E. HARPER,
THIS BOOK IS LOVINGLY DEDICATED.

Gift as well as protest, *Iola Leroy*, like the person to whom it was dedicated, came out of Frances Ellen Harper's flesh. The novel tells the story of black America as Harper had come to know it after years of laboring for abolition and then, after the Civil War, traveling alone through the South, never free from the threat of lynching and rape that accompanied any black woman journeying alone through racist territory to speak out against injustice. Recall the mutilation narrowly escaped by Ida B. Wells, who dared to speak her mind about lynching.

What most enabled Harper to publish a novel in the 1890s, however, was the explosion in vitality of the black women's movement at the time. Without it, all the political, economic, and personal motivation in the world could not, in all likelihood, have made Harper's attempt at long fiction any more lasting than Harriet E. Wilson's had been in 1859. While the differences between the era in which Wilson published *Our Nig* and the one in which Harper brought out *Iola Leroy* are vast, certainly one of the most important changes for black women writers was the emergence by the turn of the century of a vigorous, self-defined, middle-class women's movement in the black community. That movement simultaneously reflected and fostered the sense of powerfulness, mission, and possibility necessary to the emergence of art not simply by scattered individuals—a book here, a painting there—but by women as a group. The last decade of the nineteenth century saw African American women exercise their right to create art in every medium, including those proscribed as elite—untouchable—by the dominant culture. They published novels, short stories, and drama. In sculpture Meta Vaux Warwick Fuller enjoyed international acclaim; as an opera singer Marie Selika traveled and sang in Europe. As Paula Giddings cautiously observes: "It may have been no coincidence that during the same years that Black women began demanding to be recognized as 'an integral part of the general womanhood of American civilization' (as Fannie Barrier Williams had insisted), they also began to express the full range of their artistic talents."[37] I would be less tentative. Historically, now as then, for women artists the sense of personal power and possibility that a climate of feminist self-definition creates is almost impossible to overestimate. When we ask why Frances Ellen Harper in 1892 was able to publish the novel commonly cited as the "first" full-length novel by a black woman in the United States, a book which came out the same year that Anna Julia Cooper brought out *A Voice From the South* and Ida B. Wells published *Southern*

Horrors, the answer surely must include some acknowledgment of what the political activism of the 1890s meant for black women.

Another way of making the point is to look no further than the name Harper chose for her heroine. Iola was the penname that Ida B. Wells used in her political journalism.[38] Symbolically as well as literally, the line connecting women's politics and women's art—or to phrase it directly, the political enabling of women's art in the 1890s—is in Harper's case powerful and clear.

As a novel about a black woman, *Iola Leroy* is revisionist and propagandistic. The book, as Deborah E. McDowell observes, sets out to revise negative stereotypes of the African American woman and to elevate her image, in large part, by drawing it in terms of positive Victorian ideals of feminine gentility, piety, domesticity, and purity. McDowell astutely argues that in one way this simply produces a new stereotype, an image no closer to reality for most black women at the turn of the century than the degrading stereotype it replaces.[39] At the same time, Harper's insistence on black female moral purity, read against rape-lynch mythology, responds defiantly to the long history of racist violence and sexual exploitation—epitomized in the systematic rape of black women during slavery—that comprised the nation's (not just black people's) inheritance.

References to lynching appear throughout *Iola Leroy.* Aunt Linda, once a slave and now the witness of white "lynching, burning, and murdering," states that "it's rarely orful how our folks hab been murdered sence de war," and adds, "but I don't think dese young folks is goin' ter take things as we's allers done." Uncle Daniel, also an ex-slave, responds with unconcealed approval for the younger generation: "We war cowed down from the beginnin' . . . but dese young folks ain't comin' up dat way." And Salters, another former slave, joins in: "My gran'son, looking me squar in de face, said: 'Ain't you got five fingers? Can't you pull a trigger as well as a white man?' I tell yer, Cap, dat jis' got to me, an' I made up my mind dat my boy should neber call me a coward" (*IL,* p. 171). Iola's mother, Marie, worries that if she leaves the South her brother, when trying to vote, will "be murdered, as many others have been" (*IL,* p. 202). Dr. Gresham, the white man who wants Iola to marry him, observes: "The problem of the nation . . . is not what men will do with the negro, but what will they do with the reckless, lawless white men who murder, lynch, and burn their fellow-citizens" (*IL,* p. 217). In the penultimate chapter Iola, told by the man she will marry that she "brood[s] too much over the condition of our people," states: "They never burn a man in the South that they do not kindle a fire around my soul" (*IL,* p. 269).

Set against this white violence is Harper's heroine. Through her, the novel reveals white men's sexual exploitation of black women, the courage and moral integrity of black women in the face of that oppression, and the respect of black men—the alleged animals of rape-lynch mythology—for black women. Given these realities, the charge of black male sexual rapacity, accounted for in the popular racist mythology by the supposed "wantonness" of black women, becomes grotesque. Sexual purity and mutual respect are as valued in the black community as in the white—indeed, more so—this book maintains. Iola declares of the "outrages heaped on" her as a slave that she was "tried, but not tempted . . . I was never tempted." She explicitly contrasts her own sexual integrity with the depravity and sexual brutality of white men: "I never fell into the clutches of an owner for whom I did not feel the utmost loathing and intensest horror. I have heard men talk glibly of the degradation of the negro, but there is a vast difference between abasement of condition and degradation of character. I was abased, but the men who trampled on me were the degraded ones" (*IL*, p. 115).

In *Iola Leroy* black men's sexual appetite is not at issue. White men's is. Harper's heroine is characterized as a moral paragon—linked to an elevated Victorian image of womanhood—to demonstrate the vicious untruth of the "wanton" theory underlying rape-lynch mythology. As anyone as politically shrewd and committed as Frances Ellen Harper knew, dismantling that theory was crucial: Without the black woman as whore on which to build the whole racist structure of alleged black sexual abandon, insatiability, and aggression, the myth collapses. Some reason other than the allegation of rampant black lust must be found to explain why black men, and some black women, were being mutilated and murdered in the United States.

In this political argument, Iola's switch from "white" to "black" is central. Brought up to believe herself white, Harper's heroine is sold into slavery when her planter father dies. The melodrama is thematically essential. *Iola Leroy*, although written by a woman who was never a slave, contends that the heritage of all African American women, no matter how "white" or middle class or educated, is slavery. (Pauline Hopkins's *Contending Forces*, published eight years later, would agree and also choose slavery as the starting point for the narrative.) According to Harper's novel, in racist America every black woman, regardless of who she is, is constantly vulnerable to definition as sexual property by white America. No matter how high she lifts herself up, she is always only a trip of the lever away from definition as legitimate rape target. That is the meaning of Iola's story. In slave times, the transformation was literal and legal. The very same woman who was pure and safe when "white"—Iola—is instantaneously defined as corrupt and available when "black." Plunged into slavery, Iola discovers that "any white man, no matter how coarse, cruel, or brutal, could buy or sell her for the basest purposes." She has "no power to protect herself from the highest insults that lawless brutality could inflict upon innocent and defenseless womanhood" (*IL*, p. 39). This radical redefinition of Iola's sexual identity from sacrosanct to corrupt occurs solely because the color of her skin changes. "I was sold from State to State as an article of merchandise," she declares, and "I had outrages heaped on me which might well crimson the cheek of honest womanhood with shame" (*IL*, p. 115). For white readers forced to confront this instantaneous redefinition of Iola from pure woman to sexual object, the meaning of race prejudice for black women, presumably, takes on new force.[40] The fact of being a black woman in racist America, Harper's book says in 1892, means living with the sexual legacy of slavery—which means living with the constant reality of being defined by white America as sexual prey.

Writing at a time when the United States, through lynching, Jim Crow laws, disenfranchisement, institutionalized segregation, and the convict lease system, was moving deeper and deeper into a return to the ethos of slavery, Harper insists on keeping before her readers the meaning of slavery for black women. Iola, recalling what it was like "to be hurled from a home of love and light into the dark abyss of slavery," tells a white character: "You cannot conceive what it [was like] . . . to be in the power of men whose presence would fill you with horror and loathing, and to know that there is no earthly power to protect you from the highest insults which brutal cowardice could shower upon you" (*IL*, p. 273). Although Iola's stated conclusion to this speech is optimistic— "I am so glad that no other woman of my race will suffer as I have done" (*IL*, p. 273)—the fact that Harper reiterates the theme of the sexual exploitation of black women under slavery throughout the book (this mention of it appears less than ten pages from the end) suggests how important she believes the subject of black women's sexual exploitation to be for a contemporary audience, and not simply as a history lesson. The root message of Iola's life is this: As long as she was white, she was safe. As soon as she became black, she became open sexual territory in the eyes of white America.

In short, the theme that commanded Harper's attention most urgently in *Iola Leroy* was the racist sexual mythology that assaulted black women in white America. The same ideology that denied sexuality to respectable white women of the middle and upper classes—the ideology that Kate Chopin would attack in *The Awakening*— defined black women as nothing but sexual. Good white women were asexual; all black women were all-sexual. Given these sharply contrasting sexual mythologies, *Iola Leroy* is perfectly—absolutely logically—conceived. Sexual liberation for turn-of-the-century African American women, a group defined for three hundred years by white America as animalistic, libidinous, and depraved—defined, in a word, as the antithesis of respectable womanhood, regardless of a given individual's character, occupation, family, or position in life—did not consist of the right to be more sexual. It consisted of the right to be *less* sexual, the right, even, to be *un*sexual.

Embedded deep within *Iola Leroy*'s overt political argument about black women's right to sexual self-definition is an even more subtle fable about their struggle for verbal self-definition.

Iola Leroy is a parable about surviving rape. It tells the story of a black woman who, bought and sold, assaulted and defiled by white men, restores herself to herself, and does so in two ways crucial not only to women's freedom, but also to women's fiction. She names the outrage against her—she puts into language the sexual crime committed against her. And she reunites with her mother; she recovers the bond of mother-daughter wholeness deliberately ripped apart by slavery, a system of racist sexual violence and silencing that in Harper's book, as I have suggested, did not end with emancipation.

The essential drama in *Iola Leroy* is the violent theft of Iola's safe, "pure" identity as a privileged "white" woman (an isolating, very limited identity, it turns out, compared with the mature Iola), her brutal redefinition by white men as sexual prey and property, and her successful reclamation not only of autonomy and sexual self-possession but, equally important and related, of speech. As the white daughter of Eugene Leroy, Iola is visible and has language: We can see and hear her. As the free black woman survivor of slavery, Iola likewise has physical presence and language (this Iola exists most obviously in the book, occupying a central place in the narrative). As the enslaved black woman, however, Iola has virtually no direct presence or speech in the text. Separated from her black mother—totally in the control of white men—this Iola, as the subject of her own story, almost entirely disappears. In part, the disappearance reflects Harper's Victorian reticence; she hints at but cannot show Iola's sexual victimization. But also this invisibility and silencing operate as a powerful metaphor. We can hear Iola only when she is free. We can see her—truly see her—only when she has speech and self-definition, both of which are possible only when she is connected with (or has the possibility of being connected with) her mother.

It is therefore significant that in the climactic scene of the novel, Iola, triumphantly self-possessed, delivers a speech on the "Education of Mothers." The act connects her to traditional feminine values. More important, it dramatically links female autonomy, fully articulated language (recall the unlanguaged cries of Anna Julia Cooper's Black Woman in the epigraph to this chapter), and mother-daughter bonding, as opposed to father-daughter bondage. Through her own words—using her own language—Iola restores herself intellectually and emotionally, and for us symbolically as well, to the black woman who first gave her language.

At the center of *Iola Leroy* is, then, this simple parable: A privileged "white" girl (Iola) is turned into a raped black woman (Iola) is turned into—chiefly through her own agency—a self-defined black woman able to name the sexual violence she has suffered, and assert her essential intactness, even untouchedness, regardless. Although the book is in many ways disguised and trapped in Victorian convention (Harper, it is important to remember, was born in 1825), it speaks clearly, even if in code. The book opens with black people speaking in code—talking about the Civil War by discussing fresh butter and eggs, hanging sheets out to dry in symbolic configurations, and wearing books in their hats. With this Harper tells us that we must look not simply at the literal language of people told to be silent. We must also look at their coded language, their disguised speech, if we truly want to hear what is being said.

Speaking in code, Harper's novel celebrates Iola Leroy. It reaches into black women's history to find in the bought, sold, raped, and reborn black woman an image for the 1890s, a coded message for the next century, of a people's determination to survive despite racist white America's continuing commitment to genocide. The healing reunion of Harper's heroine with her mother symbolically fractures the cycle of black women's betrayal and violent abuse at the hands of white men. Iola's mother trusted and married one white man (Eugene Leroy) only to have him, in the body of his double (Alfred Lorraine), sell her and her children into slavery. Although she could perpetuate this past, Iola refuses. She will not marry a white man. Reunited with her mother and brother, she chooses a man who, like herself, has chosen to be black (he is so fair that could "pass" if he wished). Iola decides in favor of her "brother" (literally and figuratively) and, above all, her mother.

In the system of oppression described in *Iola Leroy*, the role of white women matters.[41] Harper opens her novel with a portrait of the white woman not, as in Stowe for example, as black people's friend. She is their enemy. To be sure, Harper's Mrs. Johnson, the mistress of a large working plantation, is no Simon Legree or, more to the point, Marie St. Clare. Rather, she is just an ordinary, benevolent, racist white woman. As such, she is a powerful enforcer of black people's oppression. Literally she has authority because her husband is off at war. Figuratively, she appears as the first white authority figure in the book to introduce Harper's strong views on the active and instrumental racism of white women.

Significantly, the first glimpse of this nondescript white woman involves a crime against a black woman. Mrs. Johnson selects (steals) a black child to raise "as a favorite slave. She had fondled him as a pet animal, and even taught him to read," we are told; and "notwithstanding their relation as mistress and slave, they had strong personal likings for each other" (*IL*, p. 7). (Lest we give undue emphasis to this second statement, we learn in a few more pages that the white woman "had taught him to read on the same principle she would have taught a pet animal amusing tricks. She had never imagined the time would come when he would use the machinery she had put in his hands to help overthrow the institution to which she was so ardently attached" [*IL*, p. 16].) Naive, spoiled, and completely out of touch with the true feelings of the black people of whom she is supposedly so fond, Mrs. Johnson, a woman prone to fainting spells and headaches, is no less racist—or dangerous—for being mildly ludicrous.

Her white sisters appear throughout the novel. Before the war there is the cruel mistress who prevents a black woman from burying her dead infant, whips another woman for arriving in the fields late because her husband was sick, and turns a blind eye to her sons' frequent and repeated rape of black women (*IL*, pp. 27–28). There are also the white women who refuse to visit the Leroy plantation after Iola's father marries her mother, a former slave (*IL*, p. 76). After the war there are a number of candidates: the white women who run an asylum for fallen women but turn black women away; the white working girls who will not work side by side with Iola; the white Christian working girls' association that refuses a room to a black Christian working girl; and the white temperance women who set up segregated black associations for their sisters in struggle (*IL*, pp. 232, 206, 208, 234). Drawn with a light touch, the racism of white women, particularly as it is directed against black women, emerges as a significant supporting theme in *Iola Leroy*.

It is ironic and yet fitting, then, that the piece of fiction by a white woman in the 1890s that probably has the most in common with Harper's, although at first glance it might not seem the case, was written by Charlotte Perkins Gilman, a writer and thinker whose racism severely diminished and damaged her vision. Published the same year that *Iola Leroy* appeared, "The Yellow Wallpaper"—short where Harper's fiction is long, immediately horrifying and gripping where Harper's story is for the most part calm and intellectual—raises many of the same issues as *Iola Leroy*. Both deal with the need to break with an oppressive past and create a new future, the right of women to self-definition and speech, the call to meaningful work, and perhaps most important, the need for a new woman writer—though how to liberate her voice in a world controlled by men hostile to her interests remained unclear.

Writing Silence:
"The Yellow Wallpaper"

> At best, woman was counted little more than man's toy among the upper classes, and his beast of burden among the lower social elements. In some countries even denied a soul, in none was she supposed to have any particular mental power, nor any need for its development.
>
> JOSEPHINE SILONE-YATES[1]

Harper was thirty-five-years old when Charlotte Perkins was born. Their paths seem not to have crossed, and certainly their perspectives diverged. Harper, an avowed feminist, put race first. Gilman, an unreflecting racist, put gender first. She was exactly the type of white woman whom Harper, as far back as 1869 (when Gilman was nine years old), criticized because of her blindness to the paramount importance of the race issue.

Yet as authors, what Harper and Gilman shared across race and generation is powerful. They, perhaps more than any other two writers in my group, resolutely and constantly fused their political and their literary missions. Not claiming to be "artists"—though of course they were, and even had strong opinions about what art should do, their own included—they were immovably committed to the literary tradition that Helen Gray Cone identified in 1891 as women's "struggle between the art-instinct and the desire for reform, which is not likely to cease entirely until the coming of the Golden Year."[2] Related to Harriet Beecher Stowe by self-declared affinity on the one hand (Harper) and by blood on the other (Gilman), the two, along with Pauline Hopkins, actively carried into the new era a tenacious nineteenth-century belief in the overt political—even evangelical—function of literature.

At the same time, placing Gilman and Harper side by side immediately calls into focus difference. Although *Iola Leroy* and "The Yellow Wallpaper" both deal with middle-class issues, and specifically with women's claim to physical self-definition and self-possession, crucial historical and contextual differences obviously separate the two texts. For middle-class white women, the issues of violence, sexual exploitation, and silencing were played out against a backdrop not of rape-lynch mythology but of domestic ideology; and the contrast clearly appears in the two works. Iola's story takes place in the world; Gilman's heroine is confined to one room of one house. Iola rejects the claim to her body of white men as a group; Gilman's narrator rejects the claim of one white man, her husband, to her body.

Iola "speaks," despite the systematic effort to silence her (and all black people), by committing herself to a life of action and service in the world. Gilman's narrator "speaks," despite the effort to silence her, by writing her body on the walls of one room.

Gilman had to know that "The Yellow Wallpaper" would be shocking when it first came out. When she sent the story to William Dean Howells in the early 1890s in the hope of seeing it published in the *Atlantic Monthly*, she received in reply from the editor this terse rejection:

DEAR MADAM,
   Mr. Howells has handed me this story.
   I could not forgive myself if I made others as miserable as I have made myself!
      Sincerely yours,
      H. E. Scudder[3]

After the story appeared in the *New England Magazine* in 1892, a reader complained to the Boston *Transcript*: "It certainly seems open to serious question if such literature should be permitted in print." This letter, titled by the newspaper "Perilous Stuff," concludes with the question (already emphatically answered in the negative): "Should such stories be allowed to pass without severest censure?"[4] Although some readers responded favorably, praising the story for its realism, its remarkable "delicacy of . . . touch and the correctness of portrayal,"[5] the shocked reactions of Horace Scudder and of the reader signed simply "M.D." in the Boston *Transcript* suggest how powerful the silence was that Gilman was breaking. Neither charged Gilman with lying. Rather her story was too true, the information in it too depressing. It should remain buried, untold.

   "The Yellow Wallpaper" tells the story of a middle-class white woman's attempt to claim sexual and textual authority. Forcibly stripped of choice and voice, Gilman's narrator furiously affirms her right to self-determination—in the flesh, in the written word. She does so in the face of the fact that her right to write herself has been systematically denied her, the story maintains, by the violent process of feminization to which she, as a privileged white American woman, has been forced to submit.[6]

   To expose as sadistic this standard white middle-class process by which a grown woman, under the supervision of a "benevolent" male expert, was required to turn herself into a helpless, docile, overgrown infant—that is, a feminine adult—Gilman evoked as context for "The Yellow Wallpaper" the late Victorian rest cure. Having been a patient once herself, she believed that it was in many ways simply an exaggeration of the "normal" process of feminization operating in the culture anyway. The intent of the cure, like the Victorian ideal of femininity it sought to instill, was to render a woman simultaneously and paradoxically all-body and yet (supposedly) asexual, a process that entailed strict prohibition of intellectual activity, fixation on physical reproductivity, and enforcement of childlike submission to masculine authority. Originally devised to treat soldiers incapacitated by the trauma of battle (the terror and profound lethargy that resulted were termed, rather benignly, "fatigue"), the rest cure responded to middle-class white women's trauma of unsuccessful role adjustment, which the medical establishment labeled "hysteria," by instituting a rigid and highly symbolic therapeutic regimen of enforced idleness and induced, infantile dependence.

In a typical scenario, the hysterical patient was admitted to the care of a learned physician and his attendants and then confined. Whether her disease manifested itself in symptoms of depression or of heightened excitability—she might be apathetic, morose, uncontrollably tearful, hypersensitive, delusional, or any combination of these—the patient found herself forcibly relieved of all physical and mental responsibility. Denied freedom of movement and intellectual stimulus (books, friends, writing, or drawing) in the first stage of treatment, she was transformed into nothing but body, a mass of pure passive, ostensibly desexualized flesh without self-control. As one historian explains in a discussion of the regimen created by S. Weir Mitchell, the most famous of the late nineteenth-century American rest-cure specialists and the physician whose treatment nearly drove Charlotte Perkins Gilman insane, he "made it clear to his patients that he was in total control and that their feelings, questions, and concerns must be disregarded."[7] With the physician properly installed as the sole authority, therapy then consisted of isolation, inactivity, and excessive feeding. In Mitchell's words:

> At first, and in some cases for four to five weeks, I do not permit the patient to sit up or to sew or write or read, or to use the hands in any active way except to clean the teeth. . . . I arrange to have the bowels and water passed while lying down, and the patient is lifted onto a lounge for an hour in the morning and again at bedtime, and then lifted back again into the newly-made bed.[8]

To summarize Mitchell's treatment: "The nurse spoonfeeds the patient, gives her a sponge bath, administers vaginal douches and rectal enemas, and may read to her for brief periods."[9] These reading periods, after a couple of weeks, could be extended to several hours, presumably, as a kind of reward.

The symbolism of this treatment is dramatic. Fattened, purified, and ceremoniously carried about like a sacred object, the re-covering Victorian patient of Mitchell's rest cure blows up to resemble a woman steadily and unchangingly six-months pregnant, or a pudgy baby that cannot yet walk. The two are the same, of course, in falling outside the conventional Victorian definition of what is sexual, a pregnant woman officially considered extrasexual, a baby supposedly presexual. Endlessly with child and at the same time a child, the successfully refeminized woman is at first forced and then later learns cheerfully to place her whole being in the hands of another, who, not accidentally, is a physician: the new priest, the new male authority, of the new scientific era.

Violence defines the physician's power in Gilman's story. When "The Yellow Wallpaper" opens, the heroine has been taken back in time by her physician-husband, forcibly carried away from modern, urban America to "ancestral halls," a "colonial mansion," a "hereditary estate."[10] There, in a "haunted house" "long untenanted" (*YW*, p. 9) that perfectly symbolizes the repressive Victorian "separate sphere" to which she is being returned, the narrator is held prisoner in a room filled with images and symbols of coercion, torture, and death. Empty except for one piece of furniture, a bed, which is nailed to the floor and shows signs of having been gnawed by some previous inmate, the room has barred windows, a heavy gate at the top of the stairs, and rings in the walls. When the narrator asks to be released from this prison, she is told by her husband, in a joke worthy of Poe, that he would be happy to take her "down to the cellar, if I wished, and have it whitewashed into the bargain" (*YW*, p. 15).

The relationship between this violent setting and the sexual exploitation and silencing of a privileged—in this case, literally a "kept"—woman emerges directly in "The Yellow Wallpaper." Under the supervision of modern medicine, the narrator has been moved back in time to be forcibly resocialized into conventional white middle-class femininity, a highly sexualized set of behaviors according to Gilman (despite its surface infantilism), and muteness. Against her will she is to learn in this "colonial" space, simultaneously imaged as a torture-chamber and a nursery, how to be a docile middle-class wife and mother and how to suppress her desire to write, the two in many ways being the same. Indeed, as this story about writing, about taking possession of language, proceeds, we realize that the desired transformation of the narrator has already *been* written on the domestic environment designed to contain her. The symbols of restraint—the nailed-down bed, the gate, the bars, the rings in the walls—announce the repression and self-denial, the excruciating idleness and physical inactivity, expected of her. The repellent flowery paper, with its repeating disembodied head that "lolls like a broken neck and two bulbous eyes [that] stare at you upside down" (*YW*, p. 16), images the grotesque, idiotic cheerfulness endlessly required of her. The severe isolation and circumscription of the space (even the view is highly limited) declare the narrow slit of experience and vision permitted.

That this ugly, imprisoning environment is a bedroom emphasizes how sexualized Gilman believed the supposedly asexual Victorian ideal of femininity to be.[11] The aggressive sexual content of the classic rest cure, with its assault on almost every orifice of the passive adult female body, is obvious. To be sure, the narrator's torture-chamber is officially a nursery, a place where she is treated like a baby. Her erudite husband carries her to bed, reads to her, calls her "little girl," and smothers her in baby-talk, exclaiming, "Bless her little heart! . . . She shall be as sick as she pleases!" (*YW*, pp. 21, 23, 24). Cuddled and coddled, the narrator, in accord with the Victorian ideal of femininity into which she is being forcibly reinducted, is expected to be helpless and dependent. Still, all of this infantilization takes place, it is important to remember, in a room inhabited by an adult and one piece of furniture: a bed. Immovable, gnawed, only it has been left in the room. From the point of view of the physician, the male architect of the narrator's resocialization, the concept of the space in which she is confined is very simple. It is a jail; it allows an extremely limited view of the world; and it has at its center a bed. Site for a woman not only of birthing, dying, and sleeping but also, and probably most important for this story, of sexual intercourse and therefore a potent reminder in late nineteenth-century America of male sexual privilege and dominance, including violence, a bed, to the exclusion of all else, dominates the room in which the narrator has been confined and forbidden to write.

Yet she does write. Simultaneously denied her adult female body by the room (a "nursery") *and* defined as nothing *but* that body by the bed, the narrator, ostensibly shattered by the schizophrenic space/ideal, defiantly inscribes her body on and through the wall(paper). The political content of this act remains vivid almost a century later. As the late twentieth-century critic Helene Cixous argues: "Woman must write her self: must write about women and bring women to writing, from which they have been driven away as violently as from their bodies—for the same reasons, by the same law, with the same fatal goal. Woman must put herself into the text—as into the world and into history—by her own movement."[12] Writing as a subversive act, as a dangerous move because it threatens the system of control constructed to contain women, is the subject of "The Yellow Wallpaper." To be written is to be passive. To write is to be active, to take action, to be the actor—to own and create one's self. And the action taken by Gilman's bound and silenced narrator, quintessential image of Victorian femininity, is radical. Venting her rage on the very domestic space that confines her, she permanently violates the silence imposed upon her by, as a theorist such as Cixous might put it, writing her body: both on the room, which physically bears her defiant inscription, and on the printed page before us. In doing so the narrator accomplishes a fundamental change in her relationship to the violence in the story. She moves from the position of victim to that of agent.

Initially, the wallpaper attacks the narrator. The paper displays "lame uncertain curves . . . [which] suddenly commit suicide—plunge off at outrageous angles, destroy themselves in unheard of contradictions" (*YW*, p. 13). It thrusts at her "a recurrent spot where the pattern lolls like a broken neck and two bulbous eyes stare at you upside down" (*YW*, p. 16). It "strangles" (*YW*, p. 30). It shelters "a strange, provoking, formless sort of figure, that seems to skulk about" (*YW*, p. 18). It turns backsomersaults and "slaps you in the face, knocks you down, and tramples upon you" (*YW*, p. 25). By the end of the story, however, this exterior "surface" violence transforms into what it has been in part all along: the external manifestation of the narrator's internalized rage. The suicide, the dangling head, the suffocation and skulking and pummeling all reflect the narrator's feelings, the abuse she has absorbed and turned on herself. Now she releases those feelings outward. She gets "in" the paper, and its violence, formerly directed *at* her, becomes her articulated fury and agony. Paper as enemy gives way to paper as self as she and the strong woman "behind" the tortured wallcovering (the narrator's double, of course) work together to shake their bars. Liberating other women also trapped behind paper/violence, they rip and shred the hideous paper-for-decoration (fitting symbol of the creative limits of the domestic world to which the narrator has been consigned). They turn the room into, metaphorically, the liberated, torn text of a woman's body.

Inscribed on the flowery walls of the narrator's cell, then, is a parallel text to the one in our hands. The story anticipates Cixous' statement that "women must write through their bodies, they must invent the impregnable language that will wreck partitions, classes, and rhetorics, regulations and codes, they must submerge, cut through, get beyond the ultimate reserve-discourse, including the one that laughs at the very idea of pronouncing the word 'silence.' "[13] Gilman's narrator, like Harper's Iola, declares in her flesh one woman's triumph over the system of violence, sexual exploitation, and silencing instituted to control women. Supposed to be passive, she lashes out at her nursery/prison/boudoir. She bites the bed, rips the

rebellion = victory

walls, and threatens to kill anyone who touches "her" paper (*YW*, pp. 34, 33). On one level an image of defeat—the narrator has finally gone mad—this concluding picture also represents victory. Violent, wild, physical, the narrator is the complete antithesis of the inhibited "lady" that Victorian America so carefully nurtured as a symbol of male power.

Feminist

Read optimistically, "The Yellow Wallpaper" dramatizes the failure of the modern era's attempt to recycle Victorian ideology. The regime in the nursery does not work. All the right things are done: The narrator is secluded, sheltered from stress, waited upon by a faithful servant, flattered and pampered by a loving husband, and given plenty of rest, fresh air, and modest exercise. To no avail. The trip back in time fails. Women such as the narrator will go mad before they will submit to the lives of infantile dependence prescribed as ideal by Victorian America.

But the story is also very dark and hopeless. By the end the narrator has lost her mind. Moreover, the idea that women will band together in mutual support and accomplish as a group what cannot be won by any one individual remains just that, an idea. For the narrator, solidarity exists with the imaginary women in the paper. In real life, the other women in the story collude in the system's resocialization of the narrator. The principal executor of the system is another women, paid for the purpose by the man in charge, and if there is any thought that the narrator's mother and sister might support her rebellion, it is quickly abandoned. Their visit on the Fourth of July leaves the narrator's situation unchanged (*YW*, p. 18): In real life and real terms, there is no Independence Day for the isolated woman in Gilman's tale. Viewed from this vantage point, the system has worked. The heroine has become the cripple her class has worked hard to create. Literally crawling, she offers a horrible picture of what the bourgeois white nineteenth-century ideal of femininity often really meant: bondage, masochism, madness.

racist meaning

The ways in which class and race limit Gilman's argument in "The Yellow Wallpaper" are very important. As Susan S. Lanser explains in an excellent essay, white feminist claims that the story is universal ignore its ethnic, class, and, perhaps most important, racial context. Focusing on the color of the paper itself, Lanser thinks about yellow in its turn-of-the-century context and theorizes that the paper is repulsive for Gilman precisely because it is yellow, the color that racist white Americans at the time, including Gilman herself, associated with Asians, Jews, Italians, and Eastern European immigrants. Unconsciously encoded in the wallpaper, in other words, is Gilman's own racism, and with it the limits of this story's "universality." Just as the class context of "The Yellow Wallpaper" establishes narrative boundaries, so the story's horror of yellowness articulates its racial boundaries and hidden racism.[14]

purpose

There is no question that Gilman's specific political agenda had to do solely with white women like herself. In her autobiography she recalls telling William Dean Howells, when he asked for permission to reprint "The Yellow Wallpaper" in *Great Modern American Stories* (1920): "I was more than willing, but assured him that it was no more 'literature' than my other stuff, being definitely written 'with a purpose.' In my judgment it is a pretty poor thing to write, to talk, without a purpose." Her purpose, she explained, "was to reach Dr. S. Weir Mitchell and convince him of the error of his ways."[15]

Whether or not Gilman influenced Mitchell,[16] her story contains a clear response not only to his rest cure but also to the larger cultural argument out of which his philosophy developed: the widespread, mounting scientific insistence at the turn of the century on fundamental difference between the sexes—and between races as well, even though Gilman was not perturbed by that part of the reactionary argument; indeed, she openly subscribed to and used it in some of her writings.[17]

As the historian Rosalind Rosenberg points out, for certain privileged, well-educated American women, by the turn of the century "the very basis of women's understanding of themselves was changing." Increased opportunities for higher education plus decades of political activism had produced a generation of professional women able to challenge traditional Victorian dogma about sexual differences. "Once the seed of doubt was planted," Rosenberg explains,

> it germinated in all directions. From questioning the extent of biological differences, women proceeded to challenge the universally accepted belief that men's and women's social roles were rooted in biology. Before they were through, they had challenged every tenet of the Victorian faith in sexual polarity—from the doctrine that women are by nature emotional and passive, to the dogma that men are by nature rational and assertive.[18]

This assertion of equality in the work of turn-of-the-century white female social scientists, which is equally obvious in fiction by women of the period, black and white, developed against a backdrop of intensifying scientific argument about white middle-class women's biological destiny. As historians explain, the increasing emancipation of middle-class white women at the turn of the century and the mounting reactionary power of medical science in the period are connected. It is not accidental that the most advanced men of medicine (Freud, for example) focused more and more brilliantly on defining women as a class as inferior and biologically determined at the same time that a growing number of women were representing more and more of a threat to the traditional Victorian order of society.[19] As organized religion gradually lost its power to dictate and enforce belief, science took over. The new dogma-maker, it pronounced the sexes innately and radically different.

One year before Gilman wrote "The Yellow Wallpaper," an article in *Forum* put the mainstream scientific conclusion for a general audience this way:

> All that is distinctly human is man—the field, the ship, the mind, the workshop; all that is truly woman is merely reproductive—the home, the nursery, the schoolroom. There are women, to be sure, who inherit much of male faculty, and some of these prefer to follow male avocations; but in so doing they for the most part unsex themselves; they fail to perform satisfactorily their maternal functions.[20]

Resexing the narrator, a middle-class white woman who is a new mother who rebelliously wants to use her brain and who therefore is failing in the performance of her maternal destiny, represents the scientific challenge—which Gilman presents as insane, of course—in "The Yellow Wallpaper."

Popularized by the turn of the century, the scientific insistence on difference, which owed a great deal to Darwin and Spencer,[21] was initially and most influentially developed for the general medical and scientific community by the American physician Edward H. Clarke. Offering biological "evidence" for inequality, Clarke maintained in *Sex and Education* in 1874 that the male and female brains were basically different. "The organs whose normal growth and evolution lead up to the brain are not the same in men and women," he argued; "consequently their brains, though alike in microscopic structure, have infused in them different though excellent qualities."[22] Among the different excellencies of women's brains, being smaller and lighter, was the fact, in Clarke's view, that they were not as capable of intellectual exertion as men's. The physician agreed with Spencer that women who pushed themselves mentally risked enfeebling themselves physically[23]—precisely the argument, of course, used by the narrator's physician-husband in "The Yellow Wallpaper."

Reasoning such as Clarke's generated a vigorous scientific and then popular literature about women's alleged intellectual inferiority to men, which was in turn used as evidence in arguments about the biological imperative of motherhood. The argument maintained that nature designed the sex to be breeders not thinkers. S. Weir Mitchell, for example, declared:

> Worst of all, to my mind, most destructive in every way, is the American view of female education. . . . To-day the American women is, to speak plainly, physically unfit for her duties as woman, and is, perhaps, of all civilized females, the least qualified to undertake those weightier tasks which tax so heavily the nervous system of man. She is not fairly up to what Nature asks from her as wife and mother.

Then, letting the political cat completely out of the bag, he asks: "How will she sustain herself under the pressure of those yet more exacting duties which nowadays she is eager to share with man?"[24] Ostensibly the argument holds that bourgeois women cannot even meet the demands of maternity, so how could they ever handle the more difficult challenges to which they aspire in the masculine realm of public accomplishment and action? Covertly, however, Mitchell is issuing a warning. If middle-class women are not contained in a separate sphere of maternal and domestic obligation, what is to prevent them from invading man's world wholesale and permanently?

That the argument was racist and class-ridden as well as sexist, though, again, Gilman was concerned only with the latter, becomes overwhelmingly clear in the many alarms about "race suicide" raised at the turn of the century. When Theodore Roosevelt wrote from the White House in 1902 to the authors of *The Woman Who Toils: Being the Experiences of Two Ladies as Factory Girls* (1903) that the "woman who deliberately avoids marriage, and has a heart so cold as to know no passion and a brain so shallow and selfish as to dislike having children, is in effect a criminal against the race, and should be an object of contemptuous abhorrence by all healthy people,"[25] the President of the United States was not worrying about women of color or immigrant women forsaking motherhood for work. Turn-of-the-century intellectuals and scientists asserting the biological imperative of motherhood wanted to control a specific group of women. As "The Yellow Wallpaper" demonstrates, what obsessed and frightened them was the possibility that middle class, American-born white women might actually believe in their own right to self-determination.

Blind to the antifeminism of her own racism, Charlotte Perkins Gilman was inspired by exactly the same idea.

Finally, the anger that drives "The Yellow Wallpaper" was in many ways intensely personal. Most obviously, Gilman's experience with Mitchell's rest cure, which was the consequence of her depression as a wife and mother, provided the impetus for the story. As a new mother the heroine of "The Yellow Wallpaper" epitomizes, according to the most advanced elite masculine scientific theory of the day, woman at her most "natural"—meaning, according to the experts Clarke, Mitchell, and the narrator's husband, woman speechless. The power struggle in which Gilman's narrator finds herself—like Wharton's Charity Royall in *Summer* sixteen years later, or Larsen's Helga Crane in *Quicksand* almost forty years later, *or* Gilman herself before "The Yellow Wallpaper" was written—is one of resisting the shifting but seemingly inescapable patriarchal definition (self-fulfilling, of course, in male-dominant culture) of motherhood as prison, flesh as destiny, and voice as silence. That Gilman never got paid for "The Yellow Wallpaper" because her male agent kept the money it earned seems almost unbelievably fitting.[26]

Less obviously, "The Yellow Wallpaper" probably had deep roots in Gilman's childhood. In her autobiography, the account she gives of her growing up focuses on the misery of her mother, a woman who adored her husband and loved having babies, only to have her husband leave and her babies grow up. Deserted, Gilman's mother—in the daughter's telling—grew bitter and fiercely repressed, deciding not to show any affection for her daughter in order to toughen the child. Life, as Gilman's mother had come to know it, brought women terrible disappointment and denial. Only in the dead of night would she allow herself to hug her daughter.

As a story about her mother, the early portions of Gilman's autobiography construct a family drama in which sexual desire in a woman leads to babies and death. (According to Gilman, her mother was warned that one more pregnancy would kill her, at which point the father left the family.)[27] On the other hand, denial of sexual desire, the celibate life that Mary Fitch Perkins knew when her husband left, resulted in furious repression and frustration. Either way, female sexual desire, motherhood, and masculine power were bitterly entangled for Gilman's mother, who even after years of separation and rejection remained her husband's prisoner, calling for him on her deathbed.[28] Looked at from the child's point of view, and Charlotte Perkins Gilman clearly both admired and hated her father, Frederick Beecher Perkins's power over his wife was so strong that she had to stamp out all that was free and physical and warm in herself, and try to do the same to her daughter. In a sense the woman on her knees at the end of "The Yellow Wallpaper," the prisoner of a charming man and an ugly empty domestic life that she cannot escape, is Gilman's mother as the child experienced her while growing up—humiliated, angry, crushed.

Even more salient, the alienation of women from each other and from their own bodies that Gilman learned in her childhood is deeply written on "The Yellow Wallpaper." It shows a powerful male figure designing the emotional misery of his "little girl" (in the story the wife, in Gilman's childhood the daughter), which is then carried out for him by an unbending, mature woman (in the story Jenny, in

Gilman's life her mother). Indeed, the narrator's emotional torture probably reflects the pain that Gilman felt not only as an adult but also as a child. Certainly the secret nocturnal relief achieved in the story by the narrator's surreptitious writing and secret connection with the women creeping around behind the wallpaper echoes Gilman's desperate, secret strategies for escaping the emotional and physical amputation from her mother that she felt as a child during the daytime. Gilman describes how she waited in the dark to connect with her mother: "She would not let me caress her, and would not caress me, unless I was asleep. This I discovered at last, and then did my best to keep awake till she came to bed, even using pins to prevent dropping off, and sometimes succeeding. Then how carefully I pretended to be sound asleep, and how rapturously I enjoyed being gathered into her arms, held close and kissed."[29] Escaping only at night and in secret into the female arms that promised refuge from the emotional prison she knew during daylight hours, the plotting child clearly anticipates the fictitious grown woman's furtive nocturnal escapes into a female world of intimate bonds and wild physical abandon. The narrator waiting to get into the wallpaper's embrace and the child waiting to get into her mother's arms flee the same thing, a spiritually killing world created by a man who supposedly loves them—and run by a woman who acts as his enforcer. And they seek the same thing: a world where women rebel, unite, touch.

The importance of this echo is that it lays out in biographical terms what is also obvious in the story, the scope of Gilman's subject. The drama of patriarchal control in "The Yellow Wallpaper" is the same one that Charlotte Perkins Gilman felt as a child, saw in her mother's life, and then experienced again herself as a young wife and mother. The story is not limited to just one stage of her life as a woman, but applies potentially to all stages, from childhood to old age. It is not, moreover, simply a story about the desire for escape from male control. It is also a story about the desire to escape *to* a female world, a desire to unite with the mother, indeed with all women creeping and struggling in growing numbers, through the paper, behind the wall.

Above all, "The Yellow Wallpaper" is about using paper to connect women, a theme doubly insisted upon in Gilman's story—on the wall, on the page—and repeatedly voiced and demonstrated in the work of women writers at the turn of the century. The union and reunion pictured at the end of *Iola Leroy* and of "The Yellow Wallpaper"—homey and evangelical in the first instance, ghastly in the second—represent dreams of female connectedness and reconnectedness that recur throughout the period. The mother-loss that permeates both texts—Iola's literal search for and reunion with her mother, the narrator's rupture from her mother and subsequent bond with the women in the wall—foretells a major concern of women writers in America at the turn into the twentieth century as, collectively and individually, they faced the issue of leaving the old century.

Finding Form:
Narrative Geography and
The Country of the Pointed Firs

I am amused that so many of the reviews of this book begin with the statement:
"This book is hard to classify." Then why bother? Many more assert vehemently that it is not a novel. Myself, I prefer to call it a narrative.

WILLA CATHER[1]

Sarah Orne Jewett's *The Country of the Pointed Firs* is so matrifocal that
it is easy to forget that it takes its shape from a myth about a daughter living not in
one but in two worlds, one mother-defined, the other male-defined; and in fact it is
in the second of these worlds that Persephone, like Jewett's woman writer, spends
most of the year. Mysterious, dark, ruled by a sexually powerful male, it is a world
that Persephone gladly escapes each June to join her mother, Demeter, in a region
of light and renewal. Some versions of the myth stress masculine violence and
brutality as the cause of the daughter's separation from the mother. They show
Persephone raped and forcibly dragged off to the male-dominant world where she
spends the winter of each year. Others emphasize the erotic appeal of the world to
which she goes. Persephone falls in love with Pluto and comes within only a few
pomegranate seeds of total and permanent exile from Demeter before realizing how
profoundly she needs to stay connected to her mother. Whichever version Jewett
had in mind (and it is possible, of course, that she had both), she constructed her
fable of mother-daughter yearning and reunion in *The Country of the Pointed Firs*
on a well-known myth about the daughter's permanent separation from her mother's
world. The daughter might go back for a while, but she would never live there
again.

The yearning for mother in Harper's novel and Gilman's autobiography (and
symbolically in her story), the desire to find union and reunion with the world of
one's mother even as a woman—a heroine, a writer—journeys farther and farther
from that world, winds a common thread through texts by women at the turn of the
century. Iola's need to find her mother, Gilman's narrator's complicated bonding
with the generations of mute women in the wall, Edna Pontellier's willingness to
slip into the seductive sensuous world of Madame Ratignolle in Kate Chopin's *The
Awakening,* the young woman's faith in an ancient fortuneteller in Alice Dunbar-
Nelson's lead story in *The Goodness of St. Rocque*—all of these, like the writer-
narrator's love affair with Mrs. Todd in Jewett's *Country of the Pointed Firs,* reflect
a shared, felt need among many women writers at the turn into the twentieth century

to stay attached to nonrational, maternal creativity even as they claimed the traditionally masculine territory of daring, brilliant art as their own.

Owning both realms as an artist was Jewett's challenge. Like Harper, but unlike almost every other writer in my group, all of whom were younger, Jewett by the turn of the century had largely worked out the conflicts involved in being a person permanently relocated from an old world to a new one. As Josephine Donovan explains in an excellent analysis of Jewett's 1884 novel about female ambition, *A Country Doctor*, the story of Nan Prince, a character whose very name predicts the gender integration at which Jewett would finally arrive, recounts the struggle and conclusion reached by Jewett herself as she faced the question "of remaining within the women's world or of entering the mainstream of patriarchal production. Nan's decision to become a professional doctor and not a woman-herbalist," Donovan suggests, "parallels Jewett's determination to become a professional author and not just a scribbling woman."[2] For Jewett the decision no doubt included feelings of loss as well as of liberation; but as she shows in Nan, as in her father, Dr. Leslie (again an androgynous name), she believed that synthesis was possible.

Jewett in many ways modeled herself on her father, a country doctor, whom she believed perfectly fused "feminine" sympathy and intuition with "masculine" knowledge and training. In addition, she came out of a tradition of New England regionalist writing dominated by women and focused on the short story and sketch rather than on the novel, a genre in which most nineteenth-century American women writers, even when very successful, did not take themselves seriously as "artists." Because of these personal and literary influences, Jewett felt, as Sharon O'Brien argues in *Willa Cather: The Emerging Voice*, that it was possible to be a woman writer fully connected to both the world of one's mother and of one's father.[3] Like other writing women of the period, she immersed herself in and revered celebrated white male writers such as Flaubert and Tolstoi, as well as an occasional female counterpart such as George Sand, who everyone agreed was so exceptional that she belonged in elite male company anyway. But Jewett also found powerful lifelong models in nonelite women writers such as Harriet Beecher Stowe. She did not consider Stowe the artist she did Flaubert,[4] yet she did admire her and regard her as an important forerunner. That is, for Jewett, like Harper, the midnineteenth-century middle-class feminine ideal of special, elevated maternal values was still psychically real and positively available at the turn of the century.[5] By the time that *The Country of the Pointed Firs* came out in 1896, the same year, coincidentally, that Harriet Beecher Stowe died, Jewett had already resolved issues of antithesis and alienation that younger women writers would later struggle with.

The reconciliation that Jewett worked out, as expressed in *The Country of the Pointed Firs*, was not simple. Conceptually and, even more important, formally, the book offers a fusion of traditionally gender-dichotomized western ethics and aesthetics that is so subtle and complex as to appear quite simple. But that simplicity, much like the famous aesthetic of simplification that Jewett's friend and protégé Willa Cather articulated in "The Novel Démeublé" several decades later, is an illusion. For if it can be said that in *A Country Doctor* Jewett philosophically worked out the conflict she felt between, metaphorically, allegiance to the world of her mother and entrance into the world of men, in *The Country of the Pointed Firs* she approached the conflict formally. Whereas architecturally *A Country Doctor* is quite conventional, structurally *The Country of the Pointed Firs* is anything but. What Jewett achieves in it, with brilliant success, is *formal* realization of the complex integration of spheres/ethics/aesthetics at which she had, by the mid-1890s, arrived.

To be sure, *The Country of the Pointed Firs*, looked at one way, reads like a traditional novel. It presents a linear story of the writer-narrator's progress from ignorance to enlightenment, her change from an author obsessed with solitary, unproductive, schoolhouse writing into one able to enter fully into the corporate Bowden family reunion with its communal aesthetic. At the feast that climaxes and effectively concludes this narrative line, the narrator comes to understand that literature should be created to be devoured—turned into flesh and blood, into life itself—by the eaters/readers for whom it is written.

Coexistent with and embracing this storyline, however, is a very different structure, one that is not linear but vortical, centric, weblike. Focused not on the individual, the narrative's narrator, but grounded instead in the relationship between the narrator and Mrs. Todd, *The Country of the Pointed Firs* seen from this vantage point goes nowhere; it simply, as the opening chapter "The Return" announces, re-turns and re-turns, growing out from its center in concentric waves of relationality and community but essentially staying put, deepening, widening, shrinking, swelling, ebbing—but "going" nowhere. Seemingly random patterns of constantly shifting attachment and detachment, patterns that do not conform to traditional white western conventions of linear dramatic plotting from Aeschylus forward, shape and move *The Country of the Pointed Firs*.

But ironically, of course, my separation of these two patterns is exactly what Jewett, I will argue, did not do. She made them simultaneous: discrete and fused, coexistent and interdependent. Although we can pull them apart like transparencies and look at them individually, they can—indeed *should*, Jewett's book says—finally be held together in one whole.

At the same time that *The Country of the Pointed Firs* was serialized in the *Atlantic Monthly* during the spring of 1896 (it came out in book form the following November), there appeared in the *Forum* an essay called "Family Life in America" by Marie Thérèse de Solms Blanc, translated by her friend Sarah Orne Jewett. Comparing France and America, Blanc praises the position of the "single woman in the United States," calling it "infinitely superior to [that of] her European sisters," but then she expresses deep reservations about the new female freedom. She disapproves of women avoiding marriage because of their ambition *"to be somebody, to do something*, to distinguish themselves in a career, and to escape from the common ways." The independence and dignity available to the single woman in America appeal to Blanc, but the possibility for mass self-centeredness does not, and she worries about what may get lost. She does not want women to relinquish "a good share of that spirit of self-sacrifice which may be called nothing but foolishness, though it is a sacred foolishness of a most heroic kind." Nor does she want them to give up the separate ways of knowing and dealing with the world that they have developed: the idea "that experience is above all systems, that our instinct is a power not to be suppressed, while it ought to be directed, and that certain things felt quite naturally by them [women], are more precious than what may be acquired by learning."[6] This ambivalence about change must have been easy for Blanc's translator to understand. While the Frenchwoman's nostalgia for a feminine past, with its separate ideals and codes of behavior, is in one way simply reactionary, it also raises the key question of the period for Jewett as well. Is it possible for one to find freedom as a woman in the modern world without losing the best of what white middle-class women's culture in the nineteenth century encouraged and allowed women to be?

Blanc's essay is torn between a new ideal of personal fulfillment for women, one of intense individualism, and the old-fashioned attractions of a separate and supposedly morally superior feminine culture, epitomized most obviously in the bourgeois nineteenth-century reverence for motherhood. That such a separate culture, as "The Yellow Wallpaper" insists, often harmed women more than it helped (or that it may have existed more in mind than in fact for thousands of American women) is not an issue for Blanc. Her issue is that middle-class white women, in declaring individual freedom to be their right and their highest good, as privileged American men had long been doing (at least in theory), stood to lose their identity as part of a separate, corrective, or at the very least alternative, ethical culture, one supposedly committed to cooperation rather than competition, nurturing rather than aggression, healing rather than killing, the group rather than the individual.

Precisely such an idealized separate feminine sphere is where Jewett takes her woman writer in *The Country of the Pointed Firs*, her parable about connecting the two worlds of freedom and nurture that Blanc—who of course is merely representative—can only imagine as antithetical.

Recalling Persephone's journey home to Demeter, *The Country of the Pointed Firs* opens with its narrator's "Return" to Maine in late June to arrive at Dunnet Landing "when the busy herb-gathering season was just beginning."[7] The journey carries the writer to a predominantly female world that, far from being remote, seems the very "centre of civilization of which her affectionate dreams had told" (*CPF*, p. 2). In this dreamy place, she is welcomed by motherly, ample Almira Todd, an herbalist whose last name rhymes with *god* and whose first name brings to mind the Latin word *alma*, soul. (The name recalls her precursor, Mrs. Goodsoe—as one critic points out, "good soul"[8]—in Jewett's earlier tale, "The Courting of Sister Wisby.") Perhaps Almira's name is also intended to evoke the legendary upstate New York town Elmira, named to commemorate the bond between a daughter and her mother who called the little girl so often and loudly (not unlike Demeter, who also called long and loud) that the community in 1828 changed the name of its town from Newtowne to Elmira.[9] In any event, like Persephone's mother, Jewett's Almira Todd, a supernaturally attuned and yet ultra-earthbound "mother," will spend the summer resuscitating a lost world for her liberated "daughter" up from the city.

At first this estranged daughter balks. She has brought with her from the city several writing assignments, and she plans to recreate in the Maine woodland her city-self, an independent, industrious, modern woman in charge of her time and actions. But a different and more important job awaits her. Although the narrator has made a "shrewd business agreement" for the summer with Mrs. Todd, she soon finds herself not only prevented from conducting her own business (writing), but actually so immersed in Mrs. Todd's "business" that she has become *her* "business partner" (*CPF*, p. 6). So good at it that the herbalist declares her "very able in the business," the narrator desperately seeks a "change in our business relations" (*CPF*, p. 7). This woman writer did not come to Dunnet Landing to sit around all day dispensing herbs and talking with women. To escape, she flees to the vacant schoolhouse where she will, with pointed pencil and commanding desk, resume *her* proper business, writing. But she cannot escape. As Jewett's insistence on "business" indicates (she uses the word five times in four paragraphs), the narrator's job for the summer *is*, whether she recognizes it or not, to become the business partner of Mrs. Todd. Her work in the city is valuable (we would not have the book if she was not a writer), but it is not the work of this summer.

When she arrives, Jewett's writer has complete confidence that her kind of creativity—creativity grounded in private, individual labor and resulting in polished, published writing—can and should dictate her life in Dunnet Landing. Sitting alone at the teacher's desk in the schoolhouse, as if she were that "great authority," she violently fends off the onslaught of nature (bees) that threatens her concentration. She desperately tries to do her city work; she has little success; she cannot write. "For the first time I began to wish for a companion and for news from the outer world," she admits, and she says of this "disastrous change of feeling," that it makes her "remember that I did not really belong to Dunnet Landing. I sighed, and turned to the half-written page again" (*CPF*, pp. 18–19). The unfinished page is the narrator herself. Until she turns away from the outer world and toward the country of the pointed firs, until she quits trying to do her business and takes up instead the business of Mrs. Todd—which is in this book the business of women's culture, defined by Jewett as tending human relationships and using nature beneficently—she will remain incomplete, half-written.

At this point there appears—for excellent reason—a character named "Littlepage." He interrupts both the narrator and the narrative to serve as a living illustration of precisely the type of bookishly solitary, climax-oriented, city-focused literature—significantly coming from a man and totally about men—that the narrator, sequestering herself in the local dispensary of traditional knowledge and inherited forms, the schoolhouse, has too unquestioningly, perhaps like the schoolmistress she sits in for, accepted as the model. Littlepage tells a story of adventure, scientific quest, masculine competition, failure, and finally death. It is too long and frequently boring. In both of these respects—in its virile content and in its dominance of space—it serves as an exemplum of the kind of story—self-indulgent, learned, male-focused, aggression-based—that does not otherwise show up in *The Country of the Pointed Firs*, and that the narrator, like the narrative, must leave behind.

Mesmerized by Milton (who could be more authoritative in western tradition than Milton?), Captain Littlepage rehearses his last voyage out. He tells how he sailed on the *Minerva* (the motherless goddess makes a fitting symbol of wisdom in patriarchal mythology) and explains how the journey ended, not surprisingly, in shipwreck. Stranded in the frozen north, this sea captain met another lost mariner, a crippled man named Gaffett, who had "shipped on a voyage of discovery" (*CPF*, p. 35). Gaffett's scientific voyage led, in Jewett's grisly allegory of modern science's disconnection from emotional reality, to a kingdom of the walking dead. It was a "great town" located in an icy wasteland and inhabited by "fog-shaped men," "blowing gray figures that would pass along alone, or sometimes gathered in companies as if they were watching" (*CPF*, p. 37). Cold, speechless, disembodied, these wraiths "stood thick at the edge o' the water like the ridges o' grim war; no thought o' flight, none of retreat. Sometimes a standing fight, then soaring on main wing tormented all the air. And when they'd got the boat out o' reach o' danger, Gaffett said they looked back, and there was the town again, standing up just as they'd seen it first, comin' on the coast" (*CPF*, pp. 38–39). This narrative of masculine adventure, purgatory, and death appears immediately after the narrator has yearned for news from the "outer world." Ironically, in other words, she gets her wish. Littlepage's story gives her the outer world—cold, impersonal, populated by men only—that represents the opposite pole to the one at which the woman writer, Jewett's refugee from the city, should spend her growing season.

This ultramasculine, death-filled story-within-a-story symbolizes the narrative structures men inherit from each other (Littlepage has it from Gaffett à la Bunyan and Milton) as opposed to those women pass to each other (the various tales the narrator has from Mrs. Todd and her friends). As such, as its prominent placement early in the book suggests, it is quite important to the woman writer. "The story of the wreck of the Minerva, the human-shaped creatures of fog and cobweb, the great words of Milton with which he described their onslaught upon the crew, all this moving tale had such an air of truth," the narrator tells us, "that I could not argue with Captain Littlepage" (*CPF*, p. 12). If Jewett's writer-narrator began by finding Littlepage's narrative "a little dull" (*CPF*, p. 19), she ends by being so affected that she would not be surprised if Almira Todd, mumbling an incantation and placing her under a spell, "would now begin to look like the cobweb shapes of the arctic town" (*CPF*, p. 31). But of course she never would. What the narrator has to learn is that Almira Todd is not in Littlepage's story. When Almira assumes shapes, they will not be out of his bleak frozen tradition. They will be out of hot classical myth and passionate witchlore.[10]

Littlepage's story is crucial. It is to be confronted early on, appreciated, and then moved beyond. Told about the narrator's interesting afternoon with Littlepage in the schoolhouse, Almira Todd divines, "I expect he got tellin' you of some o' his great narratives," and she pronounces, "Some o' them tales hangs together toler'ble well." She then promptly takes the narrator in a completely different direction: to Green Island. It is, she explains, "where mother lives" (*CPF*, pp. 29–30).

The Littlepage chapters inject into *The Country of the Pointed Firs* the impressively learned, high literary tradition, by definition masculine, that the narrator moves away from for the summer. The world of which Littlepage speaks is real. It is to traditional masculine, and by adoption women's, psychohistory in the west what Dunnet Landing is to conventionally socialized middle-class western feminine consciousness. But seen through the eyes of the woman writer in the land of Demeter, Littlepage's masculine tale of conquest, science, Milton, cities, and mind-boggling knowledge (each sea captain is described as imperially read in some specialty such as farming, medicine, history, or poetry—making each ship a kind of floating isolate of disconnected encyclopedic material), is unessential—interesting but finally ancillary, distant, of minor importance. (Placing Milton in the category of minor may be the most radical thing that *The Country of the Pointed Firs* does.)[11] What is of primary importance in this story is that the narrator get out of the schoolhouse. Intent upon attacking her writing in solitude and with "great authority" at the beginning of the summer, Jewett's woman writer, following the metaphoric evocation of that little-page world by Captain Littlepage, continues to spend time in the little building of books, but she also spends more and more time with Mrs. Todd. She opens herself up to an alternative course of development as a writer, one of learning that art can be communal, physical, female. She turns into a different type of writer from the one who left the city and arrived at Almira Todd's house in June, with her pointy pencils and obsessive, solitary work habits.

At the celebration that ends the book, the Bowden family reunion, there is no written Miltonic language such as Captain Littlepage introduced. Rather, to conclude the rural feast provided by and for the large extended family to which Almira Todd belongs, the assembled company—the narrator included—eat language. On the cakes and pies laid out by the women, "dates and names were wrought in lines of pastry and frosting on the tops." The reunioners gobble this language up. Moreover, "there was even more elaborate reading matter on an excellent early-apple pie," the narrator explains, "which we began to share and eat, precept upon precept. Mrs. Todd helped me generously to the whole word *Bowden*, and consumed *Reunion* herself." Most spectacular is a "renowned essay in cookery" that is totally non-verbal—"a model of the old Bowden house made of durable gingerbread" (*CPF*, p. 108), which everyone greedily devours.

This, Jewett says, is "literature." Delicious, corporate, maternal. And here the narrator's growth ends. She participates, literally, in a feast of women's language that fortifies her as she prepares to depart the mother realm to reenter the outer world of men and print. Brilliantly, Jewett uses the most traditional narrative structure of *The Country of the Pointed Firs*—the writer's linear move away from Littlepage and the schoolhouse to the reunion, away from an individualistic to a group aesthetic (from words on paper that won't come, to words in the mouth that turn into body)— to chart her growth as a writer, for the summer at least, away from precisely those traditional masculine models, modelers, and modes of literature-making—those Miltonic quests—that the shape of this plot mirrors.

But if Jewett's linear plot is important, it is also very loose—clearly secondary in *Pointed Firs*, as linear plotting is in almost all of her best work. The more important formal dynamic of Jewett's classic narrative of mother-daughter reunion is anti-linear.

Jewett complained as a young woman that she did not know how to create conventional plot. She wrote to the *Atlantic Monthly* editor Horace E. Scudder in 1873, almost twenty years before Gilman would shock him with "The Yellow Wallpaper":

> But I don't believe I could write a long story as he [William Dean Howells] suggested, and you advise me in this last letter. In the first place, I have no dramatic talent. The story would have no plot. I should have to fill it out with descriptions of character

n moving forward, as opposed to sideways, up and down, backwards,
nsionally). The result is narrative structure that works on a ladder
tion and tension mount as we progress through the fiction to its climax,
nt, situated close to the end. (The word climax itself comes from the
ax, meaning ladder.)[15]

tt's line from the schoolhouse to the reunion evokes that form, the largest
The Country of the Pointed Firs does not. It reproduces instead a pattern
pment and experience based on retaining and maintaining relationships
ectedness, as opposed to achieving radical individuation, as the most im-
dult challenge and human need, a process traditionally associated with
ne'' values and perspectives in the west and embodied in Jewett's narrative
compassing structure that is webbed, networked.[16] Instead of being linear,
pe of this design is nuclear. The narrative constantly moves out from its base
ven point and back again, out to another point and back again, out again,
again, and so forth, like arteries on a spider web. Instead of building to an
metric height, it collects weight at the middle: The most highly charged ex-
nce of the book, the visit to Green Island, comes at the center of the narrative
the eighth through eleventh of twenty-one chapters), not toward the end. And
ead of being relationally exclusive, it is inclusive and accumulative: Relation-
ps do not vie with but complement each other. The narrator does not go through
series of people to reach some goal; she adds new friendships onto her life mul-
directionally.

Like a web, which consists of strands radiating from a common nucleus, *The
Country of the Pointed Firs* at its largest level begins with, constantly returns to,
and ends in the relationship between the narrator and Mrs. Todd. Symbolic of that
nuclear bond, which deepens and broadens but does not undergo fundamental or
unexpected change—it is steady, solid, unshakable—is Mrs. Todd's house at Dunnet Landing, place of shared habitation and point of repeated return and embarkation.
The events of the narrator's summer ray out from this central edifice/relationship in
disparate and seemingly random directions, but they always return (until the end
when the narrator heads out alone to the city). Jewett makes the image "circle of
friends" a literal, geographical reality in *The Country of the Pointed Firs*. She labels
the first chapter "The Return," and the emphasis this places on the writer-narrator's
coming back to Dunnet Landing after her winter's work in the city is crucial. The
whole concept of re-turn, of turning (a circular movement, of course) back to where
one has been—this circularity comprises the first "action" in the book—is structurally paradigmatic. The narrative continually turns back to where it has been,
enriched by its journey out, but not needing to alter or improve upon the nucleus:
the relationship between the narrator and Mrs. Todd. All that "happens" in this
large, encompassing plot is that the circle expands.

One might map *Huckleberry Finn* as a backwards capital L; the action moves
down the Mississippi and then heads West. A map of *The Sun Also Rises* might
look like a slightly slanted capital I, with a line starting in Paris and running down
into Spain. A map of Jewett's encompassing plot in *The Country of the Pointed Firs*
might look, in contrast, scattered and indecisive, with many lines raying out, some
straight, some crooked, some looped, from the Dunnet Landing heart of the book.

and meditations. It seems to me I can fu.
and the scenery, and the audience, but the

At this early point in her career (she was twei
to produce traditional dramatic structure.

> I could write you entertaining letters perhaps,
> was in most charming company, but I couldn't n
> very much bewildered when I try to make these
> what shall be done with such a girl? For I wish to
> very best I can. [12]

Although, as *The Country of the Pointed Firs* its
into a writer who could provide the traditional "play
never did excel at conventional plotting. Her attempt to c
novel in *The Tory Lover* (1901) is notably unsuccessful;
pleasant, are very ordinary. Probably because convention
tures requiring exposition, complication, climax, and resolu
tagonist-antagonist model—did not work well for her, she
The problem of how to sustain a long narrative without relyin
on stock dramatic architecture was not easy to solve. She cou
job with conventional form if her subject matter was fairly p
Country Doctor; but even this novel, interesting thematically,
exciting aesthetically. It remained for *The Country of the Point*
Jewett's problem of putting together a long piece of fiction that wo
exclusively, or even primarily, on conventional western dramatic struc
be unified and exciting. Reproducing two patterns—one of web, the
scent—that in the west, at least in modern times, are associated mo
"feminine" than with the "masculine" accomplished that end for her.

It can be argued that conventional, western, written narrative such
inherited reflects a mainstream, western, masculine pattern of growth and
ence. Systematically taught from an early age in a society such as the United
this pattern emphasizes separation and aggression—vigorous individuation—
than connection or interdependence as the fundamental issues of successful a
development and adjustment. It involves a process of moving away from a negat
point through a series of challenges and conflicts to a positive point. Narrative for
itself, as Joseph A. Boone argues in a discussion specifically focused on Henry James
and the marriage plot, is not gender-free. "Traditional theories of the structural
dynamics operative in prose fiction," Boone points out, largely reflect men's experience and assumptions. They "assume that narrative consists of a rhythmic se-
quencing of event and crisis culminating in a final relaxation of tension variously
experienced by the reader as a 'significant discharge,' a 'spending' of passion, a
'pleasurable expenditure.' "[14] Such climax-release theories probably describe quite
well the basic form of much traditional western dramatic narrative. That basic form
is linear (starts at one point and moves forward to another point); pinnacle-oriented
(moves by stages or steps, often clearly identifiable, to a climactic high point);
asymmetric (the high point usually occurs close to the end); and relationally exclusive rather than accumulative (relationships compete with and replace each other to

(This seeming disorder may explain how Willa Cather came to edit the structurally altered version of the book that was reissued in 1925, containing Dunnet Landing stories not included in Jewett's original 1896 composition.)[17] The central principle of Jewett's narrative, very much like the web of women's relational experience it reproduces, is aggregation. Experiences accumulate in many directions.

First, the narrator renews her bond with the land and moves in with Mrs. Todd ("The Return" and "Mrs. Todd" are Chapters 1 and 2). Then the narrator heads inland from their shared home to her meeting with Captain Littlepage and carries the experience back to Mrs. Todd. The next unit of narrative (Chapters 8 through 11) follows Almira Todd and the narrator out to Green Island, the home of Mrs. Todd's mother, Mrs. Blackett. Within this bigger trip out from land is a smaller one out from Mrs. Blackett's earthy home to a sacred grove, virtually a shrine, where the intimacy between the narrator and Mrs. Todd deepens. They both carry this experience back, first to Mrs. Blackett's home, then to their own on the mainland. For the fourth cluster of chapters (12 through 15), Almira's friend, Susan Fosdick, arrives as a houseguest at Dunnet Landing; the circle of two expands to three and then in spirit to four as they journey imaginatively out to and then back from the bleak world of Almira's hermetic relative, Joanna Todd. The penultimate narrative unit, which like the Green Island trip is four chapters long (and of symmetrical weight thematically as well), shows Mrs. Todd and the narrator journeying out once again from Dunnet Landing, this time inland, with Mrs. Blackett enlarging the circle, to attend the Bowden family reunion, a ritualistic celebration of what is colloquially known as an extended "family circle." The last person added to the narrator's summer is Elijah Tilley, a widower whose grief for his lost mate does not diminish with time. Following that chapter (the twentieth) is the narrator's leave-taking, appropriately titled in this book of journeying forth and carrying back, "The Backward View."

These separate narrative units do not lead inexorably one to the next. They could be scrambled—the Green Island chapters could be switched with the Bowden reunion section, for example, or the Elijah Tilley meeting with the Captain Littlepage one—and the book would not disintegrate. The composition of Jewett's narrative, like the composition of the women's days she chronicles, does not follow an inviolable order.[18] Our understanding of each event is not built on our knowledge of what preceded it; the narrative does not stair-step. Yet there is pattern. *The Country of the Pointed Firs* is not aimless. The large weblike structure Jewett creates has its own coherence, its own rhythm, its own emotional and intellectual logic.

Most obvious is the book's alternation of joyful and sorrowful episodes. We first meet robust Mrs. Todd, then sad Captain Littlepage, then lively Mrs. Blackett, then tragic Joanna, then delighted Bowden reunioners, then tearful Elijah Tilley. Certainly this pattern of affirmation and depression, of happiness and sadness constantly exchanging places, mirrors the reality of many people's, and especially women's, emotional lives. If relationships are the focus rather than the background of one's world, as has traditionally been the situation of women in patriarchal culture (as Nancy Chodorow succinctly states, "Women's work is 'emotion work' "[19]), one inevitable rhythm, since we are mortal and sentient, is constant oscillation between vitality and morbidity, happiness and sadness, life and death, addition and loss. The rocking structure of Jewett's narrative echoes, in other words, many women's domestic, affectional experience, which is defined less by the attainment of unique, individual goals than by process and repetition.

A second large pattern noticeable in *The Country of the Pointed Firs* is the way that the male figures (Captain Littlepage, William Blackett, Elijah Tilley) move in and out of the narrative singularly. Whereas women function in groups—the narrator, Mrs. Todd, and Mrs. Blackett visit on Green Island and later travel together to the reunion; the narrator, Mrs. Todd, and Susan Fosdick visit for days and talk at length about Joanna—the men in the book show up solitarily. Captain Littlepage wanders alone into the schoolhouse; William Blackett is so shy that at first he hides from the narrator when she visits Green Island (and he does not come along to the reunion even though his mother and sister wish he had); Elijah Tilley is not at all outgoing—he normally communicates only with three other people and "appeared to regard a stranger with scornful indifference" (*CPF*, p. 186). The widely spaced introduction of these men, each separate from the other and each surrounded by narrative in which women relate warmly and easily with one another, calls attention to the gap between the emotional world of women and the emotional world of men in this book. In part, as critics have pointed out, the small number and isolation of men in *The Country of the Pointed Firs* are realistic; the great seafaring days are gone and with them the men who made their living from ships. But Jewett's presentation of men individually and as outsiders is not merely economic. From the perspective of women's community, which is the perspective of this book, men are secondary characters. They are not *as a group* of major importance in women's deepest psychological reality. They appear and disappear as individuals, passing through women's emotional life intermittently and singly. Only occasionally is a man essential in certain women's relational lives, as William is in his mother's and sister's (but not, it should be noticed, in the narrator's, although she is very close to both women in his family). The affectional world of women, this book shows structurally as well as thematically, resides mainly in bonds with other women, a fact that accords with the historian Carroll Smith-Rosenberg's argument that female friendship was emotionally primary for women in white middle-class nineteenth-century America.[20] In *The Country of the Pointed Firs*, men are quite literally isolated, relatively unimportant presences.

Holding together these large designs of oscillation and the solitary appearance of men is Jewett's fundamental web pattern. Much as the radial lines of a spider's structure support various surface networks, web undergirds the book both mechanically and psychically. Mechanically, the repeated trips back to Dunnet Landing create cohesion by tying the separate strands of narrative to one unifying point, home. Psychically, the aggregative structure of Jewett's narrative reproduces women's relational reality as it had been developed and shaped historically in white middle-class America, which in the nineteenth century, as Smith-Rosenberg argues, was grounded in mother-daughter connection and continuity, not rupture.[21] Neither linear nor exclusive, that reality consists of a process of valuing relationships above other goals in life (it is not accidental that the narrator's work degenerates almost into oblivion over the summer) and of developing friendships in an interconnected pattern that has at its core a powerful myth of primal female love. That myth, I now wish to suggest, generates Jewett's most powerful structuring device.

If Willa Cather edited a mangled version of Jewett's book, with chapters added where none were wanted, she certainly did not mistake the book's controlling energy. Introducing the 1925 edition, she begins her concluding paragraph: "If I were asked to name three American books which have the possibility of a long, long life, I would say at once, 'The Scarlet Letter,' 'Huckleberry Finn,' and 'The Country of the Pointed Firs.' "[22] The grouping is not as eccentric as it may look. Although these three books differ in many ways, they share an essential similarity. At the emotional center of each stands not an individual but a relationship, a couple: Hester and Dimmesdale, Huck and Jim, the narrator and Mrs. Todd. Moreover, each is a love story, though unconventional. The standard man/woman/marriage love plot is replaced with a narrative about a passionate bond between two people whose relationship falls outside that narrow frame. (The same is true of the bond between the principals in Cather's own *Death Comes for the Archbishop*, which appeared more than thirty years after *The Country of the Pointed Firs*, and which prompted the remark about form quoted in the epigraph to this chapter.)

Jewett makes the dramatic center of *The Country of the Pointed Firs* the tenth of her twenty-one chapters. In "Where Pennyroyal Grew," the narrator and Mrs. Todd descend together into a silent, sacred, lush, female space in nature where past and present, self and other, myth and reality, merge. In journeying "down to the pennyroyal plot," a place Mrs. Todd explicitly calls "sainted," the two women leave behind "the plain every-day world" (*CPF*, pp. 78, 77) to come together in the presence of the sacred earth, the healing Mother herself. As Marjorie Pryse says in an excellent introduction to a recent edition of the book: "It is clear that Mrs. Todd, in her role as guide, herbalist, and priestess, is here helping her summer visitor to go directly to the source of all vision and inspiration."[23] That source is primal, archetypal female love.

Christine Downing in *The Goddess: Mythological Images of the Feminine* speaks poetically of the Great Mother, Gaia, grandmother and great-grandmother to Demeter, Hera, Hestia, Athene, and Artemis. She is

the mother of the beginning. . . . She is the mother who is there before time . . . a mother from whom we are not separated, as in time, in consciousness, we find ourselves to be separated from the mother of the present. She is a fantasy creature behind the personal mother, construed of memory and longing, who exists only in the imagination, in myth, archetypally—who is never identical with the personal mother.

Although this figure "is there from the beginning," Downing points out that "our discovery of her is always a return, a re-cognition."[24] Most often this re-turn, or re-cognition, occurs in nature. It comes about by journeying into the earth, giver of life and death, progenitor of us all, symbol of the Great Mother. For Downing the descent occurred at Delphi in the company of a beloved woman friend. As the two women sat together in a pine grove, she "never had such a sense of a deep communion with another human being. It seemed to me as though my soul entered her body as hers had entered mine." Years later, Downing learned that before the grove at Delphi had been dedicated to Apollo, it had been Gaia's. The communion she and her friend experienced was not appolonian but primal and female; it partook of the mysterious energy of the Great Mother.[25]

This descent into a sacred female space in nature, a grove, a cave, is retold, not invented, by Downing. In a letter to a woman friend in 1900, Jewett described her own feelings for Greece, with its "blinding light" over a sea "dazzling and rimmed by far-off islands and mountains to the south," and her intense attraction to myth and ritual—for example, "the Bacchic Dance"—as "too much for a plain heart to bear."[26] It is the journey Thea Kronborg takes in Cather's *The Song of the Lark* when she descends into the canyon of her spiritual forebears, Native American mothers and artists, and finds her creative strength reborn. Likewise it is the journey the narrator and Mrs. Todd take to the sacred plot of pennyroyal on Green Island at the center of Jewett's *Country of the Pointed Firs*. Mrs. Todd shows the narrator a treasured picture of her mother and then bares her feelings, taking the narrator into her most intimate confidence. In so doing Almira Todd evokes for the narrator the ancient, perhaps timeless, grief and courage of all women: "She might have been Antigone alone on the Theban plain. . . . An absolute, archaic grief possessed this countrywoman; she seemed like a renewal of some historic soul, with her sorrows and the remoteness of a daily life busied with rustic simplicities and the scents of primeval herbs" (*CPF*, p. 211).

Mrs. Todd's "favorite" herb is pennyroyal (*CPF*, p. 211). The special herb of women, specifically of the womb, pennyroyal is the most important symbol in *The Country of the Pointed Firs*. The herb is used in childbirth to promote the explusion of the placenta and thus to facilitate a successful birth. Or it can be used as an emmenagogue, an agent that induces or increases menstrual flow, and therefore it is useful for abortion.[27] Pennyroyal, in other words, is associated with both the beginning and the end of new human life, with a woman's power to create or kill. Womb-herb, it suggests archetypal maternal power itself: the central, awesome power of women, like the earth, to give or not to give life.

Home of "such pennyroyal as the rest of the world could not provide" (*CPF*, p. 76), the sacred female place to which Jewett's two women descend, receives them. The narrator says, "I felt that we were friends now since she had brought me to this place" (*CPF*, p. 77). Here the two women know each other fully. They enter into a communion with each other and with the earth that can only be expressed ritualistically: "There was a fine fragrance in the air as we gathered it [the penny-royal] sprig by sprig and stepped along, carefully, and Mrs. Todd pressed her aromatic nosegay between her hands and offered it to me again and again" (*CPF*, p. 76).

As the dramatic core of Jewett's narrative, the descent of these women into the lush, secret, and earthily female place where pennyroyal grows might be described as concentric, even vortical, rather than climactic. The emotional energy of the book collects in this chapter, from which, in every direction, like rings spreading out when a stone is dropped in a pool, emanates Jewett's drama of female love, which is noncombative and nonlinear. Just as Dunnet Landing, point of constant egress and return, holds the book together mechanically, and the similarly weblike pattern of building relationships out in circles gives the book psychic coherence, so this chapter—"Where Pennyroyal Grew"—in its reproduction of basic female mythic material, holds the book together dramatically and emotionally. At the center, rather than near the end, Jewett's love story grows most concentrated, and nothing on either side of this midpoint significantly diminishes, conflicts with, or changes that basic female drama.

The artistic geography of *The Country of the Pointed Firs*—a book, as its title signals, about geography—is complex. It replicates the contrasting yet coexistent and interlocking psychic and narrative patterns grounded in gender that the woman writer as artist—Jewett's narrator—must negotiate. One is linear, traditionally conceived of as masculine in white western culture, and leads to independence, freedom. The other is webbed, traditionally associated with women and femininity in Jewett's world, and has as its goal nurturance and relationality. For Jewett, both must be home to the woman artist. Their polarization reflects a false dichotomy. Yet because the polarity exists—it is "real" since the culture insists upon it—it must be dealt with; and the way for the woman writer to deal with it, Jewett's narrative argues, is to lay claim to both worlds. The writer-narrator must learn to live biculturally— in two ethics/aesthetics—and out of that duality to produce union, synthesis, a new and perforce complex wholeness. Bridging and integrating these polarized worlds— embracing Littlepage's story within the land of Demeter, and then taking the summer back to the city—is what the narrator's bond with Mrs. Todd, a figure both "masculine" (professional and independent) and "feminine" (nurturant and dependent), means. Likewise the co-mingling of narrative forms in *The Country of the Pointed Firs*—one linear, the other concentric or weblike—"says" that synthesis and integration are possible.

The contemporary psychologist Jessica Benjamin argues that regardless of gender the true human need, at least in our culture, is to be both independent and connected. Modern white middle-class western society, however, has systematically polarized these desires (which do differ and therefore lend themselves to dichotomization) and then assigned to them gender, associating the first with father, and hence manhood, maleness, and masculinity, and the second with mother, and therefore womanhood, femaleness, and femininity. One result is that "the principle of polarity [itself], of either/or, becomes a normal way of experiencing the world." A second result is that the norm or model for individuation (independence) is defined in male terms. "The image of human subjectivity is 'purified' of the other (female) pole of human experience. A subject is no longer one who recognizes others, who nurtures others, who identifies with others. *He* is above all defined by his opposition to a world of objects, nature, woman, all that is other."[28]

Dissatisfied with this traditional, oedipal scenario of human development, Benjamin theorizes a different route to independence, which is grounded in maintenance rather than severance of the mother-child bond. Individuation or autonomy results not simply from separation from mother, Benjamin argues, but also from connectedness to her: "Human beings require recognition to develop a sense of their own agency. Autonomous selfhood develops, and it is later confirmed briefly by the sense of being able to affect others with one's acts. Ultimately, such confirmation also allows us to develop an appreciation of the other's subjectivity, to recognize another person.'' Separation and dependence, in other words, connect: "Developing the awareness of self and the awareness of other are really parts of the same process. Paradoxically, the need for recognition means that we are dependent upon another person to acknowledge our independence. In our very attempt to establish independence from the other person, we are dependent on that person to confirm or recognize our independence.''[29]

Benjamin's portrait of development and personality puts together in one relationship—typically that of mother and child, since the mother spends the most time parenting in modern western culture—what the oedipal model (the dominant theoretical paradigm in modern, western, partriarchal culture) pulls apart into two separate and conflicting scripts: the desire for freedom and the desire for nurturing, the former customarily associated with the father, the latter with the mother. Benjamin offers a model of finding both in relatedness to the mother, rather than in divorce from her. It is a model that Jewett anticipated almost one hundred years earlier, formally as well as conceptually, in her structurally integrated myth about the woman writer's staying attached to the mother tongue as the route to *both* freedom and nurturing.

The Country of the Pointed Firs offers a positive view of the past. Unlike Gilman's writer-narrator, who is forcibly carried back in time to find in nineteenth-century domestic ideology a prison, Jewett's narrator, a single woman, *chooses* to go back. Since she is not part of a heterosexual couple and is therefore free to design her own life, she can move back and forth between the gender poles laid out by society, creating her own circuit of wholeness over the course of her life. She spends most of her time in the city, which represents the present, the world of modern "masculinized" opportunities for urban middle-class women. Yet she is able to remain attached to the past, to the country of the pointed firs, where she finds not only a supportive network of women but behind that a mysterious mother-realm of archetypal, primal power. Insistent, as Jessie Fauset would be more than thirty years later in *Plum Bun*, on the imperative need for the woman artist to stay connected to the world of her origins and ancestors while she moved deep into regions historically defined as the sole province of privileged white men, Sarah Orne Jewett found a way to link old and new worlds. She saw how to connect the nineteenth-century white middle-class ethos of mother-daughter continuity and bonding to a classical world of female struggle and triumph and then both of those to an archetypal myth of primal, omnipotent, female love. For Jewett the past was a source of strength.

The Limits of Freedom: The Fiction of Alice Dunbar-Nelson, Kate Chopin, and Pauline Hopkins

The need to make sense of clashing worlds pressed as hard on Alice Dunbar-Nelson, Kate Chopin, and Pauline Hopkins as it did on Jewett. For all of them issues of form, freedom, and connection to a strong enabling female past were critical. For all of them creating themselves as artists—not just writers—was a central issue.

It is true that strong differences set Dunbar-Nelson, Chopin, and Hopkins off from Jewett and from each other. All three, like Harper and Gilman but unlike Jewett, had to deal with reconciling heterosexual desire and artistic vocation (Dunbar-Nelson had to work out her relation to both heterosexual and lesbian desire). Moreover, each had difficult individual questions to negotiate. For Dunbar-Nelson writing about human experience without being forced to focus on race presented a fundamental problem. For Chopin imagining some meeting ground between traditional white middle-class femininity and rigorous, passionate commitment to art defined a basic (and irreconcilable) tension. For Hopkins telling the truth in a racist, sexually hypocritical society about the violent silencing of the black woman artist represented an underlying issue.

Beneath these crucial differences, however, there runs through the major work of each writer—Dunbar-Nelson's *The Goodness of St. Rocque and Other Stories*, Chopin's *The Awakening,* Hopkins's *Contending Forces* and *Of One Blood*—powerful formal as well as thematic expression of each author's fierce desire for freedom as an artist. Even too fierce, it might be argued. These books were their authors' last major published works of fiction, and not because they wished to quit writing. In fact, they tried to continue their fiction-writing careers, but defying what was expected of them, they found for complicated and different yet nevertheless very clear reasons that they were unable to continue writing or publishing (or both) much fiction, if any at all.

In Alice Dunbar-Nelson's case, defiance may at first be hard to grasp. What could be less belligerent than the deft little collection of stories and sketches that she titled, sweetly, *The Goodness of St. Rocque and Other Stories?*

The book was Dunbar-Nelson's second published volume. In 1895 she had brought out *Violets and Other Tales,* a collection of verse and fiction. Four years later *The Goodness of St. Rocque* appeared; it was the last book of original fiction that she would publish even though she lived until 1935. The firm of Dodd and Mead advertised it and Paul Laurence Dunbar's *Poems of Cabin and Field* as companion pieces, the idea being, presumably, to attract a wide audience with this unusual offering of two books by an African American husband and wife. What actually happened, Ora Williams suggests, was that the two volumes were played off against each other, and the one damaged more in racist America was *The Goodness of St. Rocque.*[1] However much Alice Dunbar's illustrious (and shortlived) marriage did hurt her as a writer, and however much, as I will consider, her own actions in the face of racist prescriptions undermined her art, the fact remains that, although she is quoted as late as 1928 as saying that her fiction best represented her, and she continued writing and trying to publish fiction all of her life,[2] she did not survive or thrive as a fiction writer.

A major part of the problem was the white literary establishment at the turn of the century. That establishment expected black writers to fit a stereotype, which meant that they were supposed to limit themselves to racial themes, provide plenty of stock plantation characters, and write in dialect. William Dean Howells's notorious advice to Paul Laurence Dunbar to stick to dialect verse reflected the established editorial world's attitudes. Howells fondly believed that African American literature was at its best when it displayed, as he put it, "those charming accents of the Negro's own version of our English." Such advice infuriated Alice Moore even before her marriage to Paul Laurence Dunbar in 1898.[3] As for herself, she adamantly refused to cater to race-fiction expectations, and *The Goodness of St. Rocque* showed it—and paid for it. Although the book was praised in some quarters for its beauty and subtlety (The *Nation,* for instance, gave it a good review),[4] it was scorned or dismissed in others. "We should not forget," one condescending white reviewer observed, "that the Negro is practically but thirty years old, so far as modern conditions are concerned, and that we must give him time."[5] Black writers, in other words, were bound to produce inferior writing: They were not able, thirty years out of slavery, to pull off successful, sophisticated narrative.

Dunbar-Nelson's rebellion against such racist preconceptions is completely understandable. In her determination to break free from limitations placed on her simply because she was black, she anticipated James Weldon Johnson's argument three decades later that the black writer (Johnson speaks particularly of poets) "is always on the defensive or the offensive. These conditions are suffocating to breadth and to real art."[6] Faced with demeaning, racist prescriptions about what black artists should and should not do, Johnson, like Dunbar-Nelson, conceived of "real art" as freedom from race prescriptions: production above and beyond the narrow, confining dictates of race-minded America. Intent on being an artist, Dunbar-Nelson was determined in her fiction not to be bound by race in any direct way, either linguistically or thematically.

The problem with this choice, as Henry Louis Gates, Jr., points out in an excellent discussion of black poets' relation to dialect writing in the United States, is that there is no such thing as expression beyond race. As Gates explains of Johnson: "While we can understand Johnson's anxiety and desire to see the black artist escape the confinements of protest—to escape, in effect, from 'the race problem'—there is in his argument a not-so-latent urge to the universal, which universal, in practice at least, tended to demand the sacrifice of all that was not somehow Judeo-Christian.'' To decide not to write out of black experience and language in order to transfer oneself from the category of race writer to the category of artist, and by extension to place literary work by black authors in general into the mainstream of high art—the great white western tradition—may look politically wise, but is in fact suicidal. As Gates emphasizes: ''No poet, ultimately, knows more than race. 'Mere race' was not to be risen above but to be plunged into.''[7] To do otherwise was to commit to a level of self-denial that, as Gloria T. Hull observes of Dunbar-Nelson, can only be destructive. Dunbar-Nelson's separation of her stories from her own personal experience as a black woman was, as Hull rightly notes, unfortunate. Hull concludes, with great persuasion, that we can only ''wonder what novel, play, or story she might have developed if she had held a non-ivory tower concept of creative literature and had not maintained so rigorously the separation between her real life and daily concerns, and her art.''[8]

Yet it may be that denial is not the whole story; a misguided attempt to write around race may only partially define Dunbar-Nelson as a fiction writer. It seems to me that at another level, a level other than language and overt subject matter, *The Goodness of St. Rocque* affirms and celebrates the very fact of difference so airily denied on the surface of the narrative. That ''level''—that site of resistance, which I will argue represents not negation but instead a kind of secret, playful, yet serious affirmation of difference—is formal.

It is important to emphasize that Dunbar-Nelson did not disavow being black. In several stories written after *The Goodness of St. Rocque*, ''The Stones of the Village'' being the most obvious and interesting, she either focused on race or made it an important element.[9] Moreover, in her journalism in the 1920s and in her social activism and public school teaching in the first two decades of the twentieth century, she publicly and proudly identified as African American. What she did reject was the *way* that race was handled in fiction and the idea that true art could or should be tied to any particular political issue or mission. The complete antithesis of Frances Ellen Harper, she argued throughout her life against placing ''art'' in the service of race politics. Her praise for Nella Larsen's novel *Passing*, published thirty years after the appearance of *The Goodness of St. Rocque*, captures her sentiments. She says of Larsen's book (as could certainly be said of hers), ''Slight the story, you feel as you read it, slight, if absorbing''; and then she draws from that observation the conclusion that ''the subtle artistry of the story lies in just this—its apparent innocuousness, with its universality of appeal.'' Explaining this ''universality,'' Dunbar-Nelson argues that *Passing* is not about race:

> The real situation is not that Clare ''passed.'' It is that she came back into the life of Irene and she loved Brian. She did not have to be a near-white woman to do this, nor did the others have to be colored. It is a situation that is so universal that race, color, country, time, place have nothing to do with it. Of course, the author was wise in hanging the situation onto a color complex: the public must have that now. But the book would have been just as intriguing, just as provocative, just as interesting if no mention had been made of color or race. Clare might have been any woman

hungry for childhood friends; Irene and her brown skinned friends any group out of
the class of the socially elite.[10]

This review reveals more about Dunbar-Nelson than it does about *Passing* (though
it reveals a lot about *Passing*, particularly in its suggestion that the book is not
only—or primarily—about color, an argument made recently by Deborah E.
McDowell as well).[11] Dunbar-Nelson's belief that art could and should achieve
"universality" did encourage her to produce a regrettable amount of fluff: genuinely
innocuous fiction. But her review of Larsen also identifies her own real gift as a
fiction writer: her deep love of subtlety and her conviction that literary art operates
best when it dissembles, when it *appears* to be slight, appears to be be innocuous,
appears to be about one thing but is really about another.

Why *The Goodness of St. Rocque* was Dunbar-Nelson's last published book of
fiction is an important question. After *St. Rocque* she continued to try to publish
fiction, and while she was successful in placing some short stories, most of her
efforts met rejection. As Hull explains, Dunbar-Nelson did begin work on at least
two collections of short fiction, one to be called *Women and Men* and the other a
grouping of, in her words, "tenement" stories, but was told by an editor that
volumes of short stories were "the most difficult thing in the market" and therefore
unpublishable. She proposed expanding her unpublished story about passing, "The
Stones of the Village," into a novel but was told by Bliss Perry at the *Atlantic
Monthly* that "the American public had a 'dislike' for treatment of 'the color line.' "
She tried novels but was unable to get them published. The result of all this rejection,
as Hull explains, was that Dunbar-Nelson largely abandoned her ambition to be a
publishing fiction writer, though she continued to want to be one and attempted
again toward the end of her life to find a publisher for a long novel she called *This
Lofty Oak* (ca. 1932–33)."[12] The narratives that she wished to write—collections
of short stories and sketches or, as her idea about "The Stones of the Village"
suggests, long fiction about the color line—were not wanted. What publishers
wanted, if they actually wanted anything from a black American woman, was something Dunbar-Nelson was not good at: novels. Two supposedly impartial market
considerations—one a bias against feminine fiction (collections of sketches and local
color stories), the other a conveniently invoked bias against black subjects—kept
Dunbar-Nelson from being able to develop as a fiction writer after the publication
of *St. Rocque*. She was forced away from the fruitful experimentation of *St. Rocque*
into the conventional and, for her, uncreative terrain of the novel.

Like Sarah Orne Jewett, Dunbar-Nelson had trouble with plot all of her life. As
Hull records, "Contemporary critics were on target when they noted that she was
good at description, but weak with plot." The author's 1900 effort at a novel, *The
Confessions of a Lazy Woman*, was rejected because it lacked "action, plot, and
climax." A second manuscript, titled *A Modern Undine* (ca. 1901–3), was said to
be in need of "more development—more incident—more character drawing of the
sort that makes the characters reveal themselves in speech & action." Similarly,
her third and most ambitious attempt at long fiction, *This Lofty Oak*, failed in large
part, Hull says, because it "raises expectations of plot and style that are not fulfilled."[13]

What I want to suggest is that it is precisely this difficulty with conventional, preferred narrative form, as in Jewett, that identifies the place where Alice Dunbar-Nelson, as a self-determined artist struggling to find her voice at the turn of the century both as an African American woman writer and *not* as an African American woman writer (paradoxical and impossible as those conflicting goals may be), turned resistance—difference—into successful alternative art. On the one hand, *The Goodness of St. Rocque* does deny difference by asserting itself, in effect, as an aracial book. On the other hand, it can be seen as representing an exciting, rebellious move toward a new kind of African American fiction at the turn of the century. Not unlike Du Bois' experimental *Souls of Black Folk* four years later, *The Goodness of St. Rocque* attempts to exploit and explore form itself as the vehicle for thinking about difference.

To point to form as an important issue in *The Goodness of St. Rocque* may at first seem strange. As a volume of short stories, the book can be read as no more than a random collection of pieces designed to be read individually and bearing no through line.

In another way, though, the volume invites contemplation as a whole. Reading through the fourteen stories and sketches is like entering a room hung with a series of watercolors and drawings, each with a different subject but all done in the same location and hung as part of one exhibit. Moving in and out of the French Quarter, the pieces offer a series of views of life in New Orleans; and the volume does have a strong unifying principle: multiplicity. Even more specifically, in addition to place (which shifts constantly throughout the volume within the general area of New Orleans), what holds the book together is the irresolution of difference. To use an image encouraged in the book itself, and to which I will return, the design of the volume reflects the most famous institution of the city: Carnival, a constantly changing collection of figures, emotions, traditions, rhythms, meanings, and moods all brought together in a kind of random, self-generating urban dance that refuses to resolve into one event, meaning, or even, most dear to western narrative, duality.

Indeed, the first story sets the pattern by dissolving polarity. Based on a classic dark-fair split, "The Goodness of Saint Rocque" opens with the young woman Manuela (her name, like Nan Prince's, evokes both genders) afraid that she is losing Theophilé, her fiancé, to frothy, blonde Claralie. Manuela therefore rushes nervously down St. Rocque Avenue to the dilapidated cottage of an ancient fortuneteller who works charms. Calling up many traditions, this clever old woman lives in a "little and old and weather-beaten" cottage situated in a weed-choked flower garden back from the street. As Manuela enters from the one "yellow-washed" step at the end of the crumbled red-brick path, she finds "a small sombre room within, with a bare yellow-washed floor and ragged curtains at the little window. In a corner was a diminutive altar draped with threadbare lace. The red glow of the taper lighted a cheap print of St. Joseph and a brazen crucifix." The female figure that Manuela needs to find then emerges from the shadows. She is "a little, wizened yellow woman, who, black-robed, turbaned, and stern, sat before an uncertain table whereon were greasy cards." With her wild garden, greasy cards, painted step, lace-draped altar, turbaned head, black robe, and shiny crucifix, this ancient female figure deliberately confuses archetypal pre-Christian, African, Creole, fairy-tale, and Catholic realms. She speaks in harsh, croaking tones and has no name. She is called simply "the Wizened One," or "the Mistress of the Cards."[14]

This seer knows what Manuela wants even before the girl can tell her. Shuffling the mysterious cards "in her long grimy talons," she discloses that Manuela's lover

> was true, but "dat light gal, yaas, she mek' nouvena in St. Rocque fo' hees love."
>
> "I give you one lil' charm, yaas," said the Wizened One. . . . "I give you one lil' charm fo' to ween him back, yaas. You wear h'it 'roun' you' wais', an' he come back. Den you mek prayer at St. Rocque an' burn can'le. Den you come back an' tell me, yaas. Cinquante sous, ma'amzelle. Merci. Good luck go wid you." (*GSR*, pp. 8–9)

At the nearby shrine of St. Rocque, Manuela lights her candle and fairly sails out into the sunshine. When later she sees Claralie at the shrine lighting her own candle, the young woman rushes back to the Wizened One. " 'H'it ees good,' said the dame, shaking her turbaned head. 'She ees 'fraid, she will work, mais you' charm, h'it weel beat her' " (*GSR*, p. 12).

And of course it does. Although Claralie "fluffed her dainty white skirts, and cast mischievous sparkles in the direction of Theophilé" at a party the following week, the young man chooses to present Manuela, "tall and calm and proud-looking, in a cool, pale yellow gown," to his mother (*GSR*, p. 14), and the issue is settled. The charm has worked, and Manuela and Theophilé will marry.

Dunbar-Nelson's opening story then ends with this series of if's:

> If you had asked Manuela, after the wedding was over, how it happened, she would have said nothing, but looked wise.
>
> If you had asked Claralie, she would have laughed and said she always preferred Leon.
>
> If you had asked Theophilé, he would have wondered that you thought he had ever meant more than to tease Manuela.
>
> If you had asked the Wizened One, she would have offered you a charm.
>
> But St. Rocque knows, for he is a good saint, and if you believe in him and are true and good, and make your nouvenas with a clean heart, he will grant your wish. (*GSR*, p. 16)

Dunbar-Nelson's ultra-simple last sentence, sounding like a mother's goodnight reassurance to a small child, or the conventional moral at the end of a folktale, does not wrap up the story. As Claralie's experience shows, novenas to St. Rocque without the Wizened One's charm do *not* work. A person needs both. Thus if the narrative shows that the Wizened One is responsible for Manuela's happiness, and the last line says that St. Rocque is, then it is clear that the whole issue of the assignment of responsibility (as the five different if's at story's end illustrate) is not what matters. What matters is that *both* the Wizened One and St. Rocque are responsible. That is, the two mysterious figures are, at some level, coordinate.

St. Roch was a fourteenth-century miracle worker and healer. He does not show up in high, learned, ecclesiastical sources but instead in legend and folk material. Born in Montpellier, he apparently belonged to no religious order, but spent his life as a peasant, wandering among the poor and the sick, whom he cured simply by making the sign of the cross over them. In one account he fell ill himself and was miraculously fed by a dog. He survived to return to Piacenza where he cured more people, and their cattle as well (a detail Dunbar-Nelson picks up and echoes in her last story); and shrines to the saint, such as the famous one in the cemetery on St. Roch Avenue in New Orleans, sprang up throughout the Christian world.[15]

Viewed conventionally, the two miracle workers in Dunbar-Nelson's story represent polar opposites. St. Rocque and the Mistress of the Cards stand for male/female, Old World/New World, "white"/"black," Christian/Vodoun. Yet these contrasts do not exist in opposition in *The Goodness of St. Rocque*. They reveal themselves instead to be coexistent and conjunctive. It is not that Dunbar-Nelson erases difference. The magic of the Wizened One, contained in the physical charm Manuela wears close to her body, and the miracle of St. Rocque, purchased with the lighting of a candle, are distinct; they derive from different traditions and systems of belief. Red and especially yellow (symbol of good luck in the folk tradition Dunbar-Nelson evokes[16]) are the colors associated with the Mistress of the Cards. Her yellow skin, yellow doorstep, and yellow floor repeat in the yellow dress that Manuela wears on the night that Theophilé decides to make her his wife. In contrast, white is the color worn by Claralie, who is protected only by St. Rocque, the Christian saint, the gates to whose shrine shine white in the sunlight (*GSR*, p. 9). "The Goodness of Saint Rocque," in short, insists on difference. But instead of perceiving it as a problem that demands resolution—a manifestation of opposites that somehow have to be reconciled or bridged, as in Jewett for example—here realities usually assumed to be polar opposites in need of mediation are shown to be part of a complex, multiple coexistence of possibilities that do not need resolution, but simply acceptance. (The two symbolic figures themselves cross over and partake of each other's worlds, the Wizened One with her shrine to St. Joseph and crucifix, St. Rocque with his peasant background and supernatural powers emanating from "superstitious" folk tradition. The lines, even in the originals, blur.) Who "saves" Manuela? The old woman? The dead saint? Both? Neither? Why worry/choose/struggle to arrange, order, decide? this story asks. Why buy into the whole framework of polarity itself, the basic construct of inherited white western thought? Why not, like the heterogeneous world pictured in Dunbar-Nelson's book, entertain the possibility that difference need not be hierarchical, opposites need not be in conflict, polarity need not be the basic principle?

The result, to speak structurally, is that *The Goodness of St. Rocque* is neither linear nor centric but simultaneous and random. Place does hold the book together. But place, in the case of the New Orleans that Dunbar-Nelson creates, is itself a conglomerate, an unstirred mixture of different streets, neighborhoods, and people held in suspension and therefore affecting and intermingling with each other, but nevertheless not dissolving, not fusing. The book does not force all of its parts into one sequential narrative. Instead, it presents pieces in a collage or abstract mosaic, the "argument" of which is simultaneity, multiplicity, and incompletion.

This refusal to make opposition and especially duality central—yet at the same time the insistence on difference—seems to me to bear on Dunbar-Nelson's treatment of race. Who in *The Goodness of St. Rocque* is Italian, French, German, Creole, Irish, poor, rich, young, old, blue-eyed, black-eyed, sick, well, happy, or sad, we can easily say. But who—the obsessive American question—is "black" and who is "white," we often cannot say, and are usually not invited to ask. Some of her characters are obviously black: the "niggers" who fight back against racist whites in "Mr. Baptiste." Others are obviously white: Tony in "Tony's Wife." But there exists a large area in between. In most of the stories the characters are Creole, a term which was (is) itself relative. White people at the time Dunbar-Nelson wrote typically insisted that "Creole" should apply only to whites. In an 1892 essay titled "Creole Women," Mary L. Shaffter declared: "Creoles are the descendants of French or Spanish, born in Louisiana. Incorrectly the term is applied to any one born and living in New Orleans or its vicinity."[17] Despite such efforts at purism, however, "Creole"—as Shaffter's protest indicates—popularly was used for any-one of mixed heritage in New Orleans. Clearly, this is what Dunbar-Nelson meant by the term. The people in her stories are characterized not by race (an arbitrary method of categorization anyway) but by admixed ethnic and cultural background. That mixture in New Orleans—and particularly in the network of streets and neigh-borhoods that Dunbar-Nelson focuses on, the densely populated and highly heter-ogeneous area fanning out from the Mississippi River between Canal Street and St. Roch Avenue—can include some or all of the following: French, Italian, Spanish, African, German, Native American, Anglo, Irish—and any number of combinations thereof.

Dunbar-Nelson's refusal to write obvious race fiction was, as suggested earlier, conscious. In a letter written to Paul Laurence Dunbar in the 1890s not long before they were married, the woman who would publish *The Goodness of St. Rocque* explained: "Somehow, when I start a story I always think of my folks as simple human beings not as types of a race or an idea—and I seem to be on more friendly terms with them."[18] Like other women writers of the period who were determined to assert their right to create "art" rather than social tracts—Kate Chopin, Willa Cather, Jessie Redmon Fauset, to name some—Alice Dunbar-Nelson even as a very young writer rebelled against using literature for bald social or political purposes. Over the course of her life, she wrote scores of articles on various aspects of the race issue. In her newspaper columns in the late 1920s, she produced numerous pieces on topics ranging from white rape of black women and the exploitation of black domestic workers to the omission of blacks in American textbooks.[19] In her fiction, however, she wanted complete freedom. Her letter to Dunbar states outright her "dislike of writers who 'wedge the Negro problem and social equality and long dissertations on the Negro in general into their stories.' " She considered that kind of writing, in the words of Ora Williams, "too much like a 'quinine pill in jelly.' "[20] Even more pointed, given the fact that she was writing to Dunbar, she openly protested against surrendering to the pressure to produce dialect-writing just because one was black:

> You ask my opinion about the Negro dialect in Literature? Well, frankly, I believe in everyone following his bent. If it be so that one has a special aptitude for dialect work why it is only right that dialect work should be a speciality. But if one should be like me—absolutely devoid of the ability to manage dialect, I don't see the necessity of cramming and forcing oneself into that plane because one is a Negro or a Southerner. Don't you think so?[21]

This ostensibly ingenuous, unpolitical position was, of course, highly political. To her era's prescriptive demands based on race, Dunbar-Nelson responded with emphatic disobedience. She would not specialize in Southern black dialect; she would not use fiction to educate bigoted whites about the history and problems of "the Negro." They could learn those things somewhere else. She would express her pride in race and self by acting on her right as a free human being to create art as she saw fit, not as she was told to. Anzia Yezierska records how Richard Wright, a very different writer, would later charge that racist America expected blacks to be nothing but menials: " 'Some folks think that's all we're fit for—*art* is only for white folks.' "[22] Art was not only for white folks in the view of Alice Dunbar-Nelson at the turn of the century any more than it was for Wright three decades later. Her highly resistant stance was that she as a black woman could make fiction according to the dictates of her own personal vision regardless of what the dominant society said that vision should or should not be.

This flagrant defiance of racist prescriptions was so politically radical in 1899 as to be virtually suicidal, as Dunbar-Nelson's evaporating career as a publishing fiction writer showed, and as I think she herself, at some level, recognized even in *The Goodness of St. Rocque*. As a work of art, the book is extremely self-assured. Although published when Dunbar-Nelson was only twenty-four, it is the adroit, confident work of an author secure in her right to be an artist not bound by racist prescriptions, an artist free to write about a wide variety of people and to adapt to her own ends certain oral patterns of African American literary tradition, as well as the sketch and regional tradition developed largely by white women throughout the nineteenth century. Underneath this calm, secure surface, however, stir terrible fears and doubts.

The only woman in *The Goodness of St. Rocque* who dares to think about being an artist is the young singer Annette in "The Fisherman of Pass Christian"; she is bitterly betrayed by a brilliant male artist who leads her on only to reject her for the famous, established soprano with whom he co-stars. Then, immediately following this story, we meet the most passionate artist in the book, the old man M'sieu Fortier in "M'sieu Fortier's Violin"; he is deprived first of his orchestral position by the opera's new owners, an American "syndicate, a company immense and dishonest" (*GSR*, p. 76), and next of his violin by the ensuing poverty that forces him to sell the instrument to a rich, spoiled, young white man who simply wants it as a toy. Although M'sieu Fortier gets his violin back, and the story ends "happily" in that respect, he does not have any public place in which to play it for pay. He must make his living by rolling tobacco leaves.

The only slightly buried pessimism of these two stories about making art—one about a talented young woman whom a brilliantly accomplished man betrays, the other about a poor old man whom rich people exploit and discard—is reinforced by the bitterness and fear expressed in Dunbar-Nelson's two important stories about women wishing or actually attempting to transgress gender boundaries, "Sister Josepha" and "A Carnival Jangle." In "Sister Josepha" a fifteen-year-old brown-skinned girl (*GSR*, p. 156), left an orphan at three, has the opportunity to leave the convent she hates if she will agree to be adopted. When this child meets her prospective parents, the woman suits her, "but the man! It was doubtless intuition of the quick, vivacious sort which belonged to her blood that served her. Untutored in worldly knowledge, she could not divine the meaning of the pronounced leers and admiration of her physical charms which gleamed in the man's face, but she knew it made her feel creepy, and stoutly refused to go" (*GSR*, p. 159). The threat of sexual violence and very probably of rape forces her back into the overprotected separate sphere, the all-female world she loathes and longs to escape. When she later thinks of running away, her ignorance of life in the heterosocial/sexual world, her lack of identity, and her beauty again keep her in. The journey from the convent's safe but suffocating female space into the dangerous world of white men, given the level of violence against women in that world, is too treacherous to make alone, and she will remain, forever presumably, imprisoned in the virginal walled world of women she hoped to leave behind.

"A Carnival Jangle" offers an even grimmer perspective on female freedom. During Mardi Gras a young woman cross-dresses as a handsome male troubadour at the insistence of a glamorous young man named Mephisto. Thus lured across the gender line—and it is, of course, very significant that the costume she assumes is that of a white male artist—the woman is murdered. Her mother gazes "wide-eyed and mute at a horrible something that lay across the bed. Outside the long sweet march music of many bands floated in as if in mockery, and the flash of rockets and Bengal lights illumined the dead, white face of the girl troubadour" (*GSR*, p. 134). The meaning of this story for a generation of women beckoned and tempted to leave their mothers and cross over into traditionally male territory, including and especially the white male territory of high Art, is deeply cautionary and depressing.

To a profound degree Dunbar-Nelson's own story as a publishing fiction writer reveals itself in this macabre murder story, which enacts a twist on the usual theme of passing. As an artist Dunbar-Nelson insisted on her right to cross both the color and the gender line; she believed in her right to exercise complete imaginative freedom. Beyond question, this dissociation from race fiction reflected a level of denial that undermined her strength as an artist. To write as if race or gender or class is not part of one's identity, as Hull and Gates explain, is to silence huge central parts of oneself. In her swing away from submission to the William Dean Howellses of the American publishing scene, Alice Dunbar-Nelson, not above elitist derogatory comments about "niggers" in her private correspondence,[23] cut herself off destructively from black subject matter. Yet, as Ora Williams asks, what is black subject matter? Who is to say what being a black writer means?[24] The issue is not at all simple. Alice Dunbar-Nelson believed that she as a black woman was capable of defining herself for herself. For her, that meant being free to range incognito and without restriction through the territories of class, race, and gender that she as an artist saw as contiguous, separate, overlapping, blurred, oppositional, indistinguishable, central, irrelevant—in short, whatever she wished.

The personal pain of this decision not to focus on race gets hinted at in two unpublished pieces that Dunbar-Nelson wrote early and late in her life: "The Stones of the Village," composed between 1900 and 1910, and "Brass Ankles Speaks," written sometime after 1928. A bitter short fiction about silencing, self-hatred, and madness, "The Stones of the Village," as Gloria T. Hull argues, clearly displaces onto a male protagonist the torment that Dunbar-Nelson herself felt as a very fair-skinned, middle-class black woman in racist America. Even more overt as auto-biography is the essay "Brass Ankles Speaks," well summarized by Hull as "an outspoken denunciation of darker-skinned Blacks told by a 'Brass Ankles,' that is a Black person 'white enough to pass for white, but with a darker family back-ground, a real love for the mother race, and no desire to be numbered among the white race.' " Understandably unwilling to publish this essay under her own name, Dunbar-Nelson could not find an editor who would publish it pseudonymously and therefore the piece, like "The Stones of the Village," never appeared during her lifetime. Her personal anguish and anger remained well hidden.[25]

If we add to this stress and repression Alice Dunbar-Nelson's need to hide her bisexuality, especially at a time when same-sex love relationships between women were undergoing radical redefinition in the dominant culture as pathological, the complexity of her personal situation becomes enormous.[26]

Yet the fact that Dunbar-Nelson found it necessary to hide many of her experiences and feelings from the public does not necessarily mean that she was as a writer effectively silenced. All her life she played with form—tried new genres, adopted new masks. Beginning with her first book in the mid-1890s, *Violets and Other Tales*, itself a potpourri of fiction, poetry, and prose, she wrote stories, sketches, poems, essays, novels, plays, newspaper columns, and personal journals. There is no form she did not try. One conclusion to draw is that she was restless and thwarted as a writer. Another is that she was various and unbounded: As with her sexual and racial identities, so in her artistic identity she did not feel the need to observe the dominant culture's obsessive insistence on rigid demarcation and fixed categories.[27]

Which brings me back to Carnival, the image that is central, I believe, to un-derstanding both the ethic and the aesthetic which animate *The Goodness of St. Rocque*.

Carnival presents a kaleidoscope of human emotions, experiences, stations in life, rituals, belief systems, and sexual and national identities—like *The Goodness of St. Rocque*. It does so under the guise of being harmless, sheer entertainment, nothing but surface—also like *The Goodness of St. Rocque*. However, it really represents in its content and form a fundamental challenge to the social order; it subverts and radically confuses the status quo in its independent creation of a dif-ferent arrangement of values, moral and aesthetic—which is also certainly true of *The Goodness of St. Rocque* (as well as the entire female sketch tradition out of which the book comes, it can be argued). Because it represents a sanctioned con-tainment of rebellion, an approved place for it to occur within the existing order, Carnival is in one way fundamentally conservative and self-defeating. Nonconform-ity, allowed to burst out a few hours of the year—a few books of an era—is tolerated in the short run but silenced in the long run, which was the fate, quite obviously, of *The Goodness of St. Rocque*. At the same time, however, Carnival's very fa-miliarity, the fact that it does operate from within, may be its most insurgent feature. As the theorist Mary Russo explains:

> The masks and voices of carnival resist, exaggerate, and destabilize the distinctions and boundaries that mark and maintain high culture and organized society. It is as if the carnivalesque body politic had ingested the entire corpus of high culture and, in

its bloated and irrepressible state, released it in fits and starts in all manner of recom-
bination, inversion, mockery, and degradation. The political implications of this
heterogeneity are obvious: it sets carnival apart from the merely oppositional and
reactive. . . . In its multivalent oppositional play, carnival refuses to surrender the
critical and cultural tools of the dominant class, and in this sense, carnival can be
seen as a site of insurgency, and not merely withdrawal.[28]

Like Carnival, from which it takes much of its inspiration in my opinion, form in
The Goodness of St. Rocque—the combination of a group of fictions bound together
not by an obvious political message but instead by place and by the principles of
exuberant variety and multiplicity—declares Dunbar-Nelson's "site of insurgency"
as a black American bisexual woman writer at the turn of the century. As much as
or more than content, the book's form asserts Dunbar-Nelson's determination to
break the rules and lay claim to all of American culture; her determination to write
from her position, supposedly "underneath," however she wished.

From one point of view, Alice Dunbar-Nelson could be said to have lost her bid
for freedom. She ebulliently describes Carnival as

a brilliant Tuesday in February, when the very air gives forth an ozone intensely
exhilarating, making one long to cut capers. The buildings are a blazing mass of
royal purple and golden yellow, national flags, bunting, and decorations that laugh
in the glint of the Midas sun. The streets are a crush of jesters and maskers, Jim
Crows and clowns, ballet girls and Mephistos, Indians and monkeys; or wild and
sudden flashes of music, of glittering pageants and comic ones, of befeathered and
belled horses, a dream of colour and melody and fantasy gone wild in an effervescent
bubble of beauty that shifts and changes and passes kaleidoscope-like before the
bewildered eye. (*GSR*, 127–28)

Caught up in this brilliant riot, a young woman dresses as a male artist and ends up
dead. No one but her mother even seems to notice. The relative silence of Alice
Dunbar-Nelson as a publishing fiction writer in the thirty-five years that followed
the publication of *The Goodness of St. Rocque* seems tragically foretold in "A
Carnival Jangle."

Also foretold, however, and it is very important to recognize this, were the
strength and endurance of the author. Although she would not publish any more
volumes of original fiction, she did persevere as a poet, journalist, essayist, and
diarist, and though she could not find a publisher for them, she did try her hand at
novels. If Dunbar-Nelson could imagine defeat and even murder in *The Goodness
of St. Rocque*, she could also envision tough survival. In what may be the volume's
finest piece, "The Praline Woman," a feisty old woman hawks pralines outside the
archbishop's chapel on Royal Street. Cunning, adaptable, thorny, she flatters and
pleases some customers, insults and cons others. She is tender-hearted, bigoted,
caustic, maudlin, sincere. No one emotion or theme—unless it is survival, but
survival on her own terms, it must be emphasized—can be applied to the sketch
any more than it can to the whole volume, or to Dunbar-Nelson's life and career.[29]
Like the Wizened One whose magic in cahoots with snowy St. Rocque opens the
volume, the Praline Woman, an obscure, ordinary, powerful old hag, reminds us
that there exists behind the present a long, tough, enduring female past. Probably
nowhere else in the period, except in Jewett's *Country of the Pointed Firs* and

perhaps Mary Austin's *The Land of Little Rain*, does the assertion of nonconformity and resistance surface with as much deceptive calm and self-assurance as in *The Goodness of St. Rocque*. Also, however, nowhere else in the period does the promise of a young writer's fiction-writing career get extinguished as prematurely. Certainly the two were related.

Twenty-four years older than Alice Dunbar-Nelson, Kate Chopin wrote in her diary five years before the publication of *The Awakening* (1899):

> If it were possible for my husband and my mother to come back to earth, I feel that I would unhesitatingly give up every thing that has come into my life since they left it and join my existence again with theirs. To do that, I would have to forget the past ten years of my growth—my real growth. But I would take back a little wisdom with me; it would be the spirit of perfect acquiescence.[30]

This declaration is remarkable for many reasons,[31] but perhaps most of all for the clear division it suggests in Chopin's mind between the state of being an artist (what she would give up) and the condition of being close to her mother and loved by a man (what she misses). The two were no more reconcilable in the author's life, this diary entry implies, than they would be in her famous novel. For Kate Chopin, as for Alice Dunbar-Nelson, the journey out of a separate protected female space into the sexually dangerous world of art carried with it fundamental threats.

From the first page of *The Awakening*, separate spheres—oppositional realms— define the book, which like "The Yellow Wallpaper" and *The Country of the Pointed Firs*, embodies the basic gender division of middle-class white America in a literal split between city and country. The book opens with bespectacled Leonce Pontellier occupying himself at Grand Isle, an island resort outside New Orleans, by restlessly working his way through the city newspaper, which he constantly has to read one day late because he is so far removed from his natural urban habitat. Indeed, the busy man's principal activity in this languid summer retreat consists of leaving it. Repeatedly he goes either to the all-male club to which he belongs, "Klein's," or to his job in the city's financial district, which we are told constitutes New Orleans' version of Wall Street, the perfect symbol of masculine economic enterprise and power. His wife, Edna (another of the many masculine-based hero- ines' names in the period), effortlessly communicates with this important man non- verbally, mutely holding out her hand in their first encounter so that he can deposit in it the expensive rings that are the legal and material symbols of the authority which binds her to him.

We might expect this initially voiceless woman to represent the other half of the drastically bifurcated world so solidly introduced by Leonce. Instead, however, that feminine sphere finds embodiment in Edna's friend, Madame Ratignolle, soft, pink and white, pregnant, delicious. The simple, extreme, gender dichotomy established by this polarity of Leonce Pontellier and Adele Ratignolle becomes the background for Edna's drama, her complicated negotiation of the city territory of art and sex— masculine terrain—in the heart of the book. Edna's is a journey away from both Leonce and Adele, and it is played out against combined race and class issues, the former in the author's control far less, in most ways, than the latter.

On the island, deep in the bosom of maternal territory (even the primary busi-
nessperson in the area, Madame Lebrun, is a woman), Edna luxuriates in the lush,
erotic aura of "delicious" Adele Ratignolle, "heroine of romance," "fair lady of
our dreams," "sensuous Madonna," "queen."[32] Attracted to her "physical charm"
in a bond called sympathy, which we are told should really be understood as "love"
(*A*, p. 15), Edna moves with Madame Ratignolle through a sensuous, fecund region
of brilliant flowers, ripe vegetables, and laden lemon and orange trees (*A*, p. 15)
down to the edge of the sea. The scene, like Jewett's in "Where Pennyroyal Grew,"
celebrates a female intimacy that is simultaneously maternal, filial, sororal, sensual,
and mystical; and Chopin is even more explicit than Jewett. Her two women sit on
the porch of the beach house, Edna with her "long, clean, and symmetrical" body,
Madame Ratignolle opulent in her "rich luxuriant beauty," while Edna fans their
overheated bodies (*A*, p. 16). The pregnant woman strokes Edna's hand, at first
unnerving her but then stimulating a very physical sequence of memories and associations. Touched by Adele, Edna thinks first of her sisters, then of the female
friends she had as a girl, and then, climactically, of the erotic infatuations she
developed in early adolescence, first for a cavalry officer and finally for a famous
tragedian who, like the opera singer in Dunbar-Nelson's "The Fisherman of Pass
Christian," has no place in his rarified realm for mere girls. Edna declares that she
would give her life but not her self for her children and then "put her head down
on Madame Ratignolle's shoulder. She was flushed and felt intoxicated with the
sound of her own voice and the unaccustomed taste of candor. It muddled her like
wine, or like a first breath of freedom" (*A*, p. 20). In this sensuous intimacy with
a gorgeous maternal goddess/lover—a mythic ideal that has endured well into late
twentieth-century fiction, as *The Color Purple*, for example, illustrates—female
speech and freedom are born. Out of the bond with the mother (Mother Earth,
mother lover, mother sister), language, as opposed to silence, becomes possible.
Then, however, as I will examine shortly, reality rips the fantasy. The pretty picture
is disrupted by the arrival of the white women's children and their bitter, nameless
black nursemaids.

The literal, central issue of *The Awakening* can be stated simply. Edna Pontellier
awakens to the realization that she is not a "mother-woman," an individual happy
to conform to the nineteenth century's middle- and upper-middle-class maternal
ideal that Virginia Woolf would later immortalize as the Angel in the House. Coming
to her senses literally as well as figuratively, Edna realizes that she has sexual and
creative desires, and the conflict between the two drives the story. In Edna's world
sex and art do not meet. To be an artist and to be an erotic woman are mutually
exclusive (Mademoiselle Reisz vs. Madame Ratignolle). Furthermore, neither is
available to Edna. She lacks the talent and discipline of Mademoiselle Reisz. As an
artist Edna will never be more than a dabbler, despite the fact that she sells her
drawings and sketches; and even if she were brilliantly gifted, she is not interested
in being celibate. On the other hand, freely expressing herself heterosexually is
equally impossible. Such expression requires a partner, and men in Edna's world
either cannot accept her as a free sexual agent (Robert) or do so because they read
her as a mistress (Arobin). In either case, Edna herself knows that sex as an outlet
for creativity and independence has no depth. "To-day it is Arobin," she admits to

herself; "tomorrow it will be some one else. It makes no difference to me' " (*A*, p. 113).

What she really wants, to be both sexual and an artist, is out of the question. She begins to learn how to leave the old world that holds her in its cage like the cursing bird that opens the narrative. Ritualistically she prepares for a new future. Asking no one's permission, she travels with Robert to the cottage of a woman on the very edge of the village, where she sleeps alone and long "in the very center of the high, white bed" smelling of laurel (*A*, p. 37). She awakens to cleanse herself in a basin of water provided by the country woman and then enacts a solitary communion: "Edna bit a piece from the brown loaf, tearing it with her strong, white teeth. She poured some of the wine into the glass and drank it down." Ready for the new age, she exclaims to Robert: "How many years have I slept? . . . The whole island seems changed. A new race of beings must have sprung up, leaving only you and me as past relics. How many ages ago did Madame Antoine and Tonie die? and when did our people from Grand Isle disappear from the earth?" (*A*, p. 38). Robert tells her that she has slept one hundred years (would that she had), but of course he is lying. No New Age awaits Edna. She can purify herself of the old, but cannot single-handedly will the new. She cannot even fully imagine it (as if any one person could); she can only yearn for it.

The Awakening dramatizes oppositions, theses and antitheses, for which no synthesis materializes, no dialectic is conceivable, because the oppositions exist within white western culture itself, over which Edna, especially as a woman, has no control. She can try to step outside of the system—try to find the "wild zone" dreamed of and longingly imagined by certain women from her day to the present,[33] but no such place exists. Especially for a heterosexual woman, the dream of freedom is illusory: within Edna's culture men (and women too) inevitably carry with them patriarchal assumptions and values. Within her society there is no free zone beyond the rules of patriarchy, no neutral space capable of permitting female self-realization uncontrolled by androcentric values.

There is the suggestion that Mademoiselle Reisz, in her lofty artist's garret, has transcended the rules. But if that is so, it is because she has genius and is willing to be celibate, neither of which is true of Edna. Moreover, the price Mademoiselle Reisz has paid for her independence and brilliant artistry is personal crippling. She sits at her piano generating breathtaking sound, "and the lines of her body settled into ungraceful curves and angles that gave it an appearance of deformity" (*A*, p. 64). Chopin's willingness to trade her life as an artist for the nurtured existence she knew as a beloved daughter and wife is not hard to understand. Truly to create art in *The Awakening* is to suffer great loneliness and pain; it is to cross over into a realm not defined by or for women, one that within Edna's culture demands self-deforming sacrifice and sexual self-denial. And there is no alternative. Outside of culture is death.

At the other extreme is Madame Ratignolle. Vitality, fertility, health. The cost of her life, however, is complete obedience to the rules and what appears to be endless subjection to the pain and danger of childbirth, which Chopin does not idealize despite her own happiness as a mother. Moreover, Madame Ratignolle's sexual life offers no real model to Edna. The straightjacket of a baby garment on which she works through the hot summer, in a book that ends in nudity, is a garment that allows nothing but the infant's eyes to be exposed. Clearly, erotically fulfilled as Madame Ratignolle might seem to be, her ideas about body and sexuality are as conventional as the rest of her life.

Given this extreme polarization of alternatives, neither of which answers Edna's needs and between which there appears nothing, Edna's awakening can only lead out of culture itself. Only in the sea, in the womb of life, in the arms of the Great Mother, can Edna experience the liberation—the "wild zone"—impossible even to conceive of within culture, where even the human imagination, unavoidably, is socially structured. On land the wild, primordial maternal power that Jewett and Dunbar-Nelson are able to embody in living women—Almira Todd, the Mistress of the Cards—is in Chopin's work disastrously split apart into the separate figures of Madame Ratignolle and Mademoiselle Reisz. Motherless, the would-be woman artist drowns. Edna's story is one of profound modernist angst, of great personal desperation and pain.

It is also one, it is important to recognize, of great privilege. Edna Pontellier is able to swim dreamily to her death for one very clear and highly political reason: Black women will raise her children.

The background of *The Awakening* is filled with nameless, faceless black women carefully categorized as black, mulatto, quadroon, and Griffe, distinctions which, significantly, do not even show up in Alice Dunbar-Nelson's book. Also, Mexican American and Mexican women play crucial subordinate roles in *The Awakening*. Taken together, all of these women of color make Edna Pontellier's "liberation" possible. As menials they free her from work, from cooking to childcare. As prostitutes they service/educate the men in her world. Chopin is both in and out of control of this political story.

Compared to a Thomas Nelson Page or Thomas Dixon, Kate Chopin had liberal, enlightened views on the subject of race.[34] One of the ways that she shows how despicable Victor Lebrun is, for example, is by providing glimpses of his racism—his contempt for black people in general, his verbal abuse of the black woman who insists on doing her job of opening the door when Edna knocks, his arrogant assumption of credit for the silver and gold cake which he orders two black women to create in his kitchen (A, p. 59, 25). It is also possible to argue that, as Edna awakens, black characters change from nameless parts of the scenery to individuals with names and voices. On Grand Isle the blacks who tend white women's children, carry messages, sweep porches, and crouch on the floor to work the treadle of Madame Lebrun's sewing machine (a child does this) so that Madame's health is not imperiled move through the narrative speechless and nameless. As the book progresses, however, individuals emerge: the "boy" Joe who works for the Pontelliers in the city, the "mulatresse" Catiche to whose tiny garden restaurant in the suburbs Edna repairs, the capable "Griffe" nurse who sees Madame Ratignolle through the birth of her baby. Yet as even these mentions betray, the individual people of color who do emerge from the background, as the book traces Edna's increasing distance from the rigid class- and gender-bound world of her marriage, are finally no more than types, human categories—unexamined representatives of the novel's repressed African American context. Minor white characters are not identified by the cups of Irish or French or German blood in them. In other words, even an argument that claims progression in the individualization of black characters has to face the fact that images of black people in *The Awakening,* a book about a woman trying to escape a limiting, caging assignment of gender that stunts her humanity and robs her of choices, are stereotypic and demeaning.

Deeper is the problem that the very liberation about which the book fantasizes is purchased on the backs of black women. If Edna's children did not have a hired "quadroon" to care for them night and day, it is extremely unlikely that she would swim off into the sunset at the end of *The Awakening* in a glorious burst of Emersonian free will. Edna's story is not universal, although most white feminist literary criticism has failed to acknowledge the fact. It is the story of a woman of one race and class who is able to dream of total personal freedom because an important piece of that highly individualistic ideal (itself the product of the very capitalism that Edna in some ways gropes to shed) has already been bought for her. Though she does not see it, her freedom comes at the expense of women of other races and a lower class, whose namelessness, facelessness, and voicelessness record a much more profound oppression in *The Awakening* than does the surface story of Edna Pontellier. The great examined story of *The Awakening* is its heroine's break for freedom. The great unexamined story, one far more disturbing than the fiction privileged in the text, is the narrative of sororal oppression across race and class.

Toni Morrison argues in her groundbreaking essay, "Unspeakable Things Unspoken: The Afro-American Presence in American Literature," that it is not the why but the how of racial erasure that constitutes the truly important question: "What intellectual feats had to be performed by the author or his critic to erase me from a society seething with my presence, and what effect has that performance had on the work?"[35] The answer to this question in *The Awakening* is in one way quite simple. The repression of black women's stories—and with them Edna's identity as oppressor as well as oppressed—plunges not just Edna but also Chopin into a killing silence from which neither returns. It is widely agreed that Kate Chopin did not write much after *The Awakening* because the hostile reviews of the novel devastated her. I am sure that is true. One might ask, however, after *The Awakening,* unless Chopin was willing to confront race, what was there to say? The book brilliantly spins the privileged white female fantasy of utter and complete personal freedom out to its end, which is oblivion—the sea, death. The fantasy itself deadends. (Willa Cather's irritation with the novel, which she criticized for its "over-idealization of love" and its shallowly "expecting an individual and self-limited passion to yield infinite variety, pleasure, and distraction," does not seem so cranky when viewed from this perspective.)[36] Cut off from the large, urgent, ubiquitous struggle for freedom of African Americans in Chopin's America, a struggle hinted at but repeatedly repressed in the text, the utterly individualistic and solipsistic white female fantasy of freedom that *The Awakening* indulges in can only end in silence—in death.

Yet I also want to ask: Did Chopin succeed in keeping black women out? Complicating *The Awakening*'s final silence is the vocal form of the book. The mother of six children, Chopin shaped her novel into thirty-nine parts, which is just one chapter short, any woman who has borne a child knows, of the "normal" forty-week human gestation period.

Structured as a pregnancy, *The Awakening* participates at a deep, formal level in a female expression of creation that not only crosses class, race, religious, and national lines, but also, in Chopin's and Edna's world, involves white women intimately with black women. Those black women are white women's servants. Yet looked at another way, they are white women's guides and mentors. The novel makes very clear that white maternity as Chopin knew it exists totally within the context of black female wisdom, expertise, and hands-on labor. A black woman sees Madame Ratignolle through her confinement and delivery. Other black women tend and rear Adele and Edna's children. The experience of white maternity in Chopin's world, in other words, cannot be separated from the presence of black women. It is shaped and controlled by them, even as they are in the employ of the white women. Similarly, as the novel also makes clear, childhood in Chopin's privileged white world, the time during which people form language and first learn how to tell stories, is in basic ways affected by black women. As I will explain later, both Ellen Glasgow and Willa Cather explicitly recognized that their art as storytellers came from the black women who were in their lives when they were little girls. To say, then, that *The Awakening* is based formally on the experiences of pregnancy and maternity, given how Chopin as a privileged Southern white women knew those experiences, is to introduce the idea that *The Awakening* formally derives from African American culture.

In "Unspeakable Things Unspoken" Morrison urges reexamination of nineteenth-century American literature for "the ways in which the presence of Afro-Americans has shaped the choices, the language, the structure—the meaning of so much American literature. A search, in other words, for the ghost in the machine."[37] I am suggesting that at the level of form *The Awakening*, so deliberately repressive of race on its surface, admits the "ghost in the machine," the influence of African American culture and art on Chopin.

Critics have noted that the composition and flow of *The Awakening* do not evoke conventional, white, western, masculine plot structure. Comparing *The Awakening* with *Sister Carrie*, Emily Toth points out that, whereas Dreiser's novel is "linear," adhering to "a masculine model of incremental public success," *The Awakening* is "lyrical, epiphanic, concerned with moments of consciousness rather than upward striving."[38] Peggy Skaggs notes that the "very structure" of Chopin's novel connects it to the "basic, natural rhythm of the human gestation cycle,"[39] a structure by definition female and, as the word *cycle* suggests, nonlinear. In short, we might argue that if the content of Chopin's story is insistently privileged and western, the *way* the story unfolds, its overall rhythm and shape, is not. Its rhythms of repetition, cycle, and multiple, irregularly sized units accumulating into a thirty-nine-part whole, which is marked by unusual lyricism or musicality (recall the emphasis on music in the book), suggest a narrative form rooted in maternal and African American aesthetics.

Thus Chopin's novel sends a complicated, even contradictory, message. Its surface is preoccupied with privileged white middle-class dreams of unlimited personal freedom—dreams that are grounded in oppression of women by women across race and class. Yet structurally *The Awakening* comes out of and evokes shared female and, to the extent that it can be said of any human possibility, potentially universal female experience: pregnancy. Even more important, in deriving formally from one white woman's experience of pregnancy, which we know black women profoundly shaped, the book is indelibly marked by black women's consciousness. At its deepest formal level *The Awakening* articulates a primary, shared, female, creative pattern fundamentally influenced in Chopin's world by African American women. In doing so, this novel about the hard labor sometimes ending in stillbirth— silence—of trying to give birth to one woman's independence, voice, sexuality, and art delivers a new and rebellious form. Like Jewett's *Country of the Pointed Firs* or Dunbar-Nelson's *Goodness of St. Rocque,* though in still yet a different way, *The Awakening* refuses to march, mount, explode, and relax. Its design—the complex fluidity and cyclicness that for thirty-nine sections, beginning and ending on the island, embrace the straight line of Edna's awakening—announces the novel's fierce commitment to determining its own shape as a work of art.

Chopin said of Guy de Maupassant, the writer she consciously admired more than any other, that he "had escaped from tradition and authority . . . had entered into himself and looked out upon life through his own being . . . and told us what he saw."[40] Certainly this is what *The Awakening,* grounding its largest artistic design in an inherently female rather than a male experience of creation and genesis, does. What Chopin probably did not see, but what we cannot help but see, is her debt not only to Maupassant but also, prior and far more important, to black women's art as midwives, nurses, and storytellers. As with Dunbar-Nelson, ironically it may be the form of Chopin's book that, finally, speaks most resistantly—most insurgently—to the world that could, and did, silence her as an artist.

Published one year after *The Goodness of St. Rocque* and *The Awakening,* Pauline Hopkins's *Contending Forces* (1900), following in the tradition of *Iola Leroy,* takes on the race issue; and if lynching and rape are the great buried subjects of *Iola Leroy,* they are blatant in *Contending Forces.* The preface of Hopkins's novel, published eight years after Harper's came out, states directly that the book is appearing in "days of mob violence, when lynch-law is raising its head like a venomous monster," and she maintains that the difference between black people's situation in the past and in the present "is so slight as to be scarcely worth mentioning. The atrocity of the acts committed one hundred years ago are duplicated today, when slavery is supposed no longer to exist." This book will present "both sides of the dark picture—lynching and concubinage,"[41] Hopkins announces, and it does.

While the lines connecting Dunbar-Nelson, Chopin, and Hopkins are chiefly theoretical, the link between Pauline Hopkins and Frances Ellen Harper is historical. It is possible that Dunbar-Nelson and Hopkins met. In the 1890s, before she married Paul Laurence Dunbar, Alice Moore spent time in West Medford, Massachusetts,[42] which is close to Cambridge, where Hopkins lived. Given the size of the black middle-class community in Boston at the time, it is conceivable that the two writers met, but whether they actually did and whether they knew each other's work are unknown. In contrast, the literary bond between Hopkins and Harper is clear. Hopkins opens the section on "Literary Workers" in her series "Famous Women of the Negro Race," which appeared in the *Colored American Magazine* in 1902, with a long, celebratory profile of Harper, of whom she says with obvious admiration: "By personal effort alone she has removed mountains of prejudice."[43] At the same time, though, inspired and strengthened as she was by Harper's example, Hopkins also differed considerably from the well-known author and activist. She was much younger. She was far more ambitious as an artist. She was, in print at least, much angrier.

Like Harper, Hopkins chose as her avowed mission as a writer to counteract racism by attacking prejudice and injustice and by creating positive images of black Americans and of black American middle-class life. Advancing the race effort was her stated goal. A biographical sketch published in the *Colored American Magazine* in 1901 (and no doubt written by Hopkins herself) states: "Her ambition is to become a writer of fiction, in which the wrongs of her race shall be handled as to enlist the sympathy of all classes of citizens, in this way reaching those who never read history or biography. 'Contending Forces' is her first published work." However, this biographical sketch also states with barely concealed bitterness: "Pauline Hopkins has struggled to the position which she now holds in the same fashion that *all* Northern colored women have to struggle—through hardships, disappointments, and with very little encouragement. What she has accomplished has been done by a grim determination to 'stick at it,' even though failure might await her at the end."[44] The anger here (tragically, Hopkins *would* find failure waiting for her "at the end," and it was a literary end only three years away from the appearance of this profile) strikingly sets Hopkins apart from Harper.

Even a glance at their fictional representations of women artists emphasizes this difference. When Iola Leroy finds it impossible to realize her dream of being a writer, she calmly gives it up to devote herself instead to improving people's lives through social service. In Harper the desire to make art is outweighed by an even greater desire (consciously at least) to serve the black community in whatever way one must. In Hopkins there is no such calm surrender of artistic ambition. Her female artist figures are brutally assaulted and silenced by white men. Sappho in *Contending Forces* and Dianthe in *Of One Blood* (1902–3) are raped, deceived, abused, and in the second book, finally murdered into silence. Sappho survives barely, like her namesake whose verse we have only in fragments. Dianthe, her name evoking the Greek goddess of the hunt and of powerful purity—or as it is put in the fiction, "the flower of Jove"[45]—perishes.

Passionate, gorgeous embodiments of female creativity and power, including sexual power, Hopkins's female artist figures suffer terrible silencing, against which they struggle but with little or no success; and the story of Pauline Hopkins herself, as with Dunbar-Nelson and Chopin, seems foretold in her fiction. After being forced out as literary editor of the *Colored American Magazine* in 1904, she showed up in print for another year or so in the *Voice of the Negro*, then later in the *New Era* in 1916, and then disappeared as an artist. She supported herself by working as a stenographer at MIT, and she died in Massachusetts in the Cambridge Relief Hospital in 1930. She was seventy-one and, as the result of an accidental fire in her home, had burns covering her entire body.[46]

Occupying the foreground of Hopkins's first published long fiction, *Contending Forces*, are lynching, the connection between lynching and white rape of black women, and the relationship between white rape of black women and silencing.

As Hazel V. Carby states in her long and excellent discussion of Hopkins in *Reconstructing Womanhood,* in "*Contending Forces*, Hopkins reconstructed an interdependent history of the colonized and their colonizers as a narrative of rightful inheritance in which lynching and rape were the central mechanisms of oppression.''[47] Certainly Hopkins's evocation of lynching in *Contending Forces* is direct and forceful. She provides excrutiating detail, as in her reproduction of this white ''newspaper account'':

> Jim Jones, a burly black Negro accused of the crime of rape against the person of a beautiful white woman, was taken from his home by a number of our leading citizens, and after being identified by his victim, was carried into the woods, where, before an immense concourse of people, he was bound to a tree, pieces of flesh were stripped from his body, his eyes were gouged out, his ears cut off, his nose split open, and his legs broken at the knees. After this the young woman stepped forward and poured oil upon the wretch, and the wood being piled about him, she applied the torch to light the fire which was to consume the black monster. Leaving some of the party to watch the funeral pile, a posse went into the city and brought to the scene of vengeance Sam Smith, Bill Sykes and Manuel Jackson, who were accused of hiding the guilty wretch from the justice of the populace. These three men were hanged to the nearest trees in full sight of the burning wretch, who made the day hideous with his cries of agony. We think the Negroes of this section have been taught a salutary lesson.— *Torchlight*. (*CF*, pp. 223–24)

Hopkins explicitly relates this horror to white rape of black women. At the height of the antilynching meeting that she places at the center of the novel, she has Will Smith state:

> We come now to the crime of rape, with which the Negro is accused. For the sake of argument, we will allow that in one case out of a hundred the Negro is guilty of the crime with which he is charged; in the other ninety-nine cases the white man gratifies his lust, either of passion or vengeance. None of us will ever forget the tales [of lynching and white rape of black women] told us tonight by Luke Sawyer; the wanton passions he revealed and which it has taken centuries of white civilization to develop, disclosing a dire hell to which the common crime of the untutored Negro is as white as alabaster. And it is from such men as these that the appeal comes for protection for women's virtue! . . .
> Lynching was instituted to crush the manhood of the enfranchised black. Rape is the crime which appeals most strongly to the heart of the home life. Merciful God! Irony of ironies! *The men who created the mulatto race, who recruit its ranks year after year by the very means which they invoked lynch law to suppress,* bewailing the sorrows of violated womanhood!
> No; it is not rape. If the Negro votes, he is shot; if he marries a white woman, he is shot; if he accumulates property, he is shot or lynched. . . (*CF*, pp. 269–71)

As in *Iola Leroy*, the issue in *Contending Forces* is not the supposed rape of white women by black men but the actual lynching of black men by white people and, even more central to Hopkins's story, the rape of black women by white men.

Hopkins encapsulates this whole history of rape in the story of Grace Montfort. As Carby brilliantly explains:

> In a graphic and tortured two-page scene, Hopkins represented the brutal rape of Grace in the displaced form of a whipping by two of the vigilantes. Her clothes were ripped from her body, and she was "whipped" alternately "by the two strong, savage men." Hopkins's metaphoric replacement of the "snaky, leather thong" for the phallus was a crude but effective device, and "the blood [which] stood in a pool about her feet" was the final evidence that the "outrage" that had been committed was rape.

Carby concludes that this "ravishing of 'grace' at the hand of Southern brutality established the link that Hopkins believed existed between the violent act of rape and its specific political use as a device of terrorism."[48]

Appearing historically in the figure of Grace, the rape victim in the present for Hopkins is Sappho Clark. Arriving at the Boston boardinghouse of Will Smith's mother seemingly out of nowhere, Sappho is a typist and stenographer (which, as noted, is how Hopkins frequently made her living), and she keeps to herself. She refuses to talk about her past, and though she has artistic talent, it shows up only in hints: the literary name she has assumed, the way she beautifies her room, her creation of a gorgeous son, her employment of writing (although completely drained of creativity) to make a living. Sappho's tragic story comes out at the antilynching meeting at the center of the book. There the description of the abduction, rape, and coercion into concubinage of a fourteen-year-old New Orleans girl named Mabelle Beaubean results in Sappho's having to be carried from the room in a faint because the story is her own. Raped by a white uncle and forced by him into a brothel where she was not found for three weeks, the child Mabelle, upon being rescued, entered a convent where she bore a son. When she left the convent, her name was Sappho Clark.

This fable of "Sappho" at the heart of *Contending Forces* says that the black woman writer in the United States—a figure in hiding, a figure able to express herself only in fragments and by indirection—has been brutally silenced by the systematic exercise of white sexual terrorism. She has been forced to deny her own creativity (her son), the brutal past that is her true story (the rape), and the sisterhood of black women who have selflessly mothered and rebirthed her (the women in the convent). *Yet*, Hopkins's story says, this woman has and will survive the violence against her. The fable, in other words, is not a simple story of victimization. Raped by her white uncle (conventional patriarchal symbol for the United States), the black child Mabelle ("my beauty") has turned herself, with the help of the black female community of the convent, into the woman Sappho, forebear of generations of women artists. Out of the violence and sexual outrage of the black woman's experience in America will come—*despite* the effort to silence her—great art. In short, Hopkins's career as a fiction writer opens with images both of anger and of hope.

Perhaps it was this hope—this cautiously arrived-at belief in the African American woman artist's survival—that freed Hopkins herself as an artist in the three serialized novels that she wrote for the *Colored American Magazine* after *Contending Forces*. The first two, *Hagar's Daughter* (1901–2) and *Winona* (1902), show her beginning to grow experimental. As was true of Chopin and Dunbar-Nelson, Hopkins crossed traditional boundaries both in her adoption of subject matter and, even more significantly, in her experimentation with form, manifesting itself in her case in intense and radical conflations of realistic and allegorical dramatic structures.

In many ways *Hagar's Daughter* does not differ strongly from *Contending Forces*. It mixes realism and melodrama to tie the modern black American woman's story to slavery and to the issues of veiled, lost, and violated identity that that institution automatically evokes. In contrast, *Winona* shows Hopkins trying less conventional material. Although still concerned with the effects of slavery on the present, this novel places the drama in a Native American context, making the heroine's mother a runaway slave and her father, "White Eagle," a white man who chose to leave Anglo-America to live as an Indian. Taken together, *Hagar's Daughter* and *Winona* suggest Hopkins's step-by-step movement in the direction of fantasy and allegory, both of which become foregrounded in her last serialized novel, *Of One Blood*.

Whereas the symbolic story of Sappho comprises one element in the large, social documentary that marked Hopkins's entrance into long fiction in 1900 with *Contending Forces*, by the time she brought out *Of One Blood* in the *Colored American Magazine* two years later, the symbolic story of the woman artist embraces the entire narrative. Described by Carole McAlpine Watson as "a strange and complicated fairy tale" with "a fantastical plot,"[49] *Of One Blood* is generically radical. Ordinary western concepts of realism and fantasy are deeply challenged.

The narrative opens on a bleak winter night in Boston. Staring out his window, Reuel Briggs, a brilliant young Harvard medical student who has hidden his African American identity, contemplates suicide for the hundredth time and then sees, materializing against the dead landscape, the face of a woman. The face takes on body when Reuel's privileged white friend Aubrey Livingston brings him to hear, for the first time in his life, the Fisk Jubilee singers. Onto the stage steps the woman whose face came to Reuel in his desolation: Dianthe Lusk. She is the soprano soloist (the same role Hopkins took when she appeared with her family in the 1880s as part of the Hopkins Colored Troubadours)[50] and her art is incomparable. "There fell a voice upon the listening ear, in celestial showers of silver that passed all conceptions, all comparisons, all dreams; a voice beyond belief—a great soprano of unimaginable beauty, soaring heavenward in mighty intervals" (*OB*, p. 453). She sings the spiritual "Go Down Moses," and "all the horror, the degradation from which a race had been delivered were in the pleading strains of the singer's voice" (*OB*, p. 454). So fair that she could, like Reuel, deny her race, Dianthe instead affirms and soars with it. She uses her "power of genius" (*OB*, p. 453) to fuse completely her commitment to her people with the production of unparalleled art. This black woman artist—breathtakingly gifted and brilliantly vocal—inspires Reuel's life, literally breathes new vitality into it, and in so doing launches Hopkins's allegory.

Dianthe appears first as an image in Reuel's window, then as the lead soprano of the Jubilee singers, then as an apparition in the woods on Hallow-Eve (a time when all spirits can walk the earth), and then as a corpse among a group of trainwreck victims that Reuel, far ahead of his time scientifically, resuscitates. Dianthe's appearances and disappearances, her ability to cross the line between natural and supernatural reality, which amounts to free movement in time and space that includes crossing the barrier of death, identifies her as extraordinary. Likewise the pattern of mutual revitalization between Reuel and Dianthe—first she brings him out of his living death of suicidal depression, then he brings her out of the physical death into which she has sunk—suggests the tremendous power that in Hopkins's view is contained in the black woman artist: her spirituality, erotic energy, and indestructibleness. The depth and vitality of this power magnify as, with the fable's unfolding, we see Dianthe's ancestresses: her mother Mira, a slave, who has the power to appear from the spirit world to influence human events; her grandmother Hannah, also a slave, who has lived to an incredible age and is "the most noted 'voodoo' doctor or witch in the country" (*OB*, p. 603); and before either of these women, the African queen Candace, monarch of the hidden city of Telassar, descended from the ancient, fabulous, Ethiopian kingdom of Meroe.

Hopkins invokes this rich legacy of female creative power to tell a horrible story: that of the black woman artist's rape and murder in the United States. The white man, Aubrey Livingston, supposedly Reuel's friend, steals, rapes, silences, and finally kills Dianthe. This happens because Aubrey, representing dominant-culture designs in the book—he is white, sexually rapacious, all-powerful, and evil—stands at the center of a hideously effective system. That system of human theft, blackmail, and sexual enforcement, including murder if need be, manipulates and renders powerless the white woman (Livingston drowns his white fiancé) and divides black men and black women, removing and thus disempowering the former (Livingston sends Reuel to Africa) and appropriating and controlling through rape the latter. Perhaps the most pernicious way in which this oppression works, however, is not through its blatant structure of lies, sexual assault, and murder, but through its insidious genocidal power of encouraging black people to deny and disown their racial identity, and therefore each other—the community, the group. Recall that the novel opens with Reuel's suicide wish. Aubrey Livingston is able to destroy Dianthe not only because of what he does, but also because of what Reuel, the black man, does not do. After Reuel brings Dianthe back to life, she has no memory: She does not know that she was a Jubilee singer or that she is black; and Reuel, passing himself, does not tell her. He lets her believe that they are both white and marries her. Because of this denial, because Reuel keeps Dianthe from knowing that she is black and therefore that he knows it too, Aubrey is able to blackmail her into leaving Reuel by threatening to tell him that she is African American. Although there is no question that blame for Dianthe's death falls on Livingston, the powerful white man who symbolizes the system that kills her, there is a level at which Reuel, the black man, tragically abets the white man's evil by his silence—as Reuel in the end recognizes. Hopkins's allegory about racism in the United States, in other words, is both as simple and as complex as the system it excoriates.

Deepening further the levels of meaning, at the end of *Of One Blood* Hopkins discloses that Dianthe, Reuel, and Aubrey are sister and brothers. The three had the same mother, Mira. Her mother, Hannah, secretly replaced her white master's dead son with her own grandson, the infant Aubrey—which means, of course, that Aubrey is not really white. The terrible fact that all three are "of one blood" reveals that Dianthe has married first one brother (Reuel) and then the other (Aubrey). With dramatic force, this double incest exposes the literal horror of slavery. It also lays bare the insanity and arbitrariness of the whole idea of "race."

Most important, however, is the figurative meaning of the incest in *Of One Blood*. Symbolically, it shows that the black woman is abused and killed by her white "brother" to keep her from union with her black "brother," whose reciprocal bond with her can, the jealous white brother knows, offer strength and the miracle of resurrection to black people in the racist United States (the mutual resuscitation we see between Dianthe and Reuel). To prevent such racial wholeness and healing, according to Hopkins's literally incredible but symbolically accurate plot, the white man will lie, steal, rape, commit incest, and kill.

This allegorical vision of the black woman artist in *Of One Blood* is frightening and bleak. Despite her intermittent appearances (at the window, with the Jubilee singers, on Hallow-Eve), the American black woman artist exists in Hopkins's fable in a state of living death, from which, even if she is resuscitated, she emerges memoryless. Without memory there can be no identity: Dianthe can only be who other people tell her she is; and in racist America, that will not include being an artist.

Of One Blood boldly locates the origins of western culture in Africa. There, separated from Dianthe, Reuel discovers who they as black people really are; he meets the living past of which both he and Dianthe have been robbed. The scientific expedition in which he participates is searching for lost records that will prove, in the words of the scholar leading it, the "primal existence of the Negro as the most ancient source of all that you value in modern life, even antedating Egypt" (*OB*, p. 520). Evidence appears in the form of the hidden city of Telassar, created by Africans descended from the inhabitants of the ancient kingdom of Meroe; the city is filled with gorgeous statuary, mosaics, gardens, fountains, wealth, and erudition. A white American member of the party exclaims: "You don't mean to tell me that all this was done by *niggers*?" The bookish British expedition leader replies: "Undoubtedly your Afro-American are a branch of the wonderful and mysterious Ethiopians who had a prehistoric existence of magnificence, the full record of which is lost in obscurity" (*OB*, p. 532).

The particular significance of this scientific find for the story of the black woman artist is embodied by Hopkins in the mysterious figure of Candace, the queen of Telassar, whose statue shows a majestic female figure on whose knees crouch two enormous silver serpents. A virgin monarch, Candace's human identity is passed down among women. In every generation a new girl is chosen to replace the aging queen and become "Candace," who waits for the appearance of her mate, Ergamenes, with whom she will restore the lost kingdom of Meroe to its former power and magnificence.

Meeting Candace, Reuel is stunned to realize that she is strangely like Dianthe (*OB*, p. 568). The association links Dianthe, the modern African American woman artist, to her powerful, gorgeous African foremother, the queen Candace, who though underground is still alive. It also reiterates Hopkins's play with form itself, her deliberate (con)fusion of the credible and the incredible. Very far removed from the social-documentary style of *Contending Forces, Of One Blood* mixes in unstable and therefore highly productive and unsettling combinations the ingredients of narrative realism, travelog, allegory, and dream prophecy. Unlike Harper's work, in which much the same mixing of forms suggests generic searching, Hopkins's fusion, confusion, and irresolution of genre—the strange complexity of *Of One Blood*'s "fantastical plot," to recall Watson's characterization—suggests brilliant, even if not totally realized, purpose. Hopkins is not entering herself in the American romance tradition. She does not, like Hawthorne, use the supernatural as symbol. Rather, like Toni Morrison after her, she asserts the supernatural as reality. She breaks boundaries—enters the secret, long lost kingdom of black power in Africa—not in a mind trip but in a *real* trip, as *Of One Blood*'s literal volatility of form expresses. She moves with complete logic and ease between material and supernatural reality, past and present. In Charlotte Perkins Gilman's work about a woman artist, spirits and the supernatural are products of mind—and of deranged mind at that (the wobbling heads in the wallpaper, the creeping female forms). In Hopkins's narrative, experience from the other side (of life/of the world) is not the product of mind, much less of insanity. It is part of what is here. To "say" this in fiction—to say the opposite of what a Poe or Gilman might imply in their contextualizing of the supernatural in madness, or what Hawthorne might suggest in using the supernatural as moral or psychological symbol—Hopkins *does* create, by "realistic" high-culture western standards, a most strange and fantastical narrative: elaborate, dense, utterly decentered in its instability as realism. Clearly her last published long fiction, *Of One Blood*, suggests her desire to break out of the inherited high western narrative tradition, her desire to craft new form by drawing on antidominant realities of multiconsciousness and pan-African wholeness.

As an allegory about art, Hopkins's elaborate, bitter story shows the black woman artist, whose roots go deep into African history, half-dead and then completely dead in the United States. Dianthe, Candace's spiritual double and daughter, should be strong like her African forebear: regal, powerful, constantly renewed by the society in which she lives, and ready to unite with the black man to redeem the past and create the future. In Hopkins's myth, however, this tremendous possibility for creativity, including union with her black brother, meets total destruction at the hands of the white man, whose policy it is to deceive, silence, exploit sexually, and finally kill the black woman if she attempts to free herself from him. Whatever guarded optimism Hopkins might have felt about the future of the African American woman artist at the time she wrote *Contending Forces* was gone by the time she wrote *Of One Blood*. Grounding the black woman artist's story in unrequited heterosexual desire, violent sexual violation by white America, and erasure of her empowering African heritage, Hopkins tells in her "fairy tale," her wildly unbelievable fiction (if looked at in conventional western realistic terms), the awful truth about the African American woman artist's reality at the beginning of the twentieth century. In *Of One Blood* the black American woman artist *has* a past. It is ancient, potent, brilliant—full of voice. What she does not have is ownership of that past, or a future.

The twentieth-century author Margaret Walker has said that people cannot write when they are hungry, sick, tired, or worried; that every writer needs a time and place in which to work; and that racism is hardest on black woman.[51] For Pauline Hopkins in the first decade of the twentieth century, these observations practically forecast the silence into which she would be forced. In 1904 she lost her job at the *Colored American Magazine*, which had provided the money, time, place, and outlet that made her fiction-writing possible. Apparently, she was forced out because certain of her literary practices, such as the portrayal of racially mixed marriages, were too radical for white readers and, even more instrumental, because her refusal to endorse Booker T. Washington's accommodationist policies drew the opposition of the powerful Tuskegeean, who addressed the problem by secretly buying the magazine out from under its prolific, uncooperative literary editor.[52] To publish another novel was not an option because the production of long fiction, then as now, was very expensive. Publishing *Contending Forces* had nearly bankrupted the Colored Co-operative Publishing Company, which, given its responsibility for bringing out the *Colored American Magazine*, could not undertake any more separate novel-publishing ventures.[53] Although Hopkins did form her own publishing firm after leaving the magazine—P. E. Hopkins & Company, located in Cambridge, Massachusetts—the venture seems to have had a short life, producing little or nothing after issuing Hopkins's 1905 pamphlet *A Primer of Facts Pertaining to the Early Greatness of the African Race and the Possibility of Restoration by its Descendants— with Epilogue*.

With *Of One Blood* Pauline Hopkins changed history. She pushed narrative form fully over into the mode of allegorical vision, prophecy, and dream projection that African American fiction, and particularly fiction by women—Toni Morrison, Rosa Guy, Gloria Naylor—would brilliantly mine later in the twentieth century. Without the *Colored American Magazine*, however, Pauline Hopkins, whose last major fiction in that magazine dramatized the violent silencing and death of the black American woman artist, disappeared as a productive artist.

6 | Form and Difference: Gertrude Stein and Mary Austin

> Somewhere in print I have said that women as a class are indifferent to form.
> Take it that I was then behaving in a characteristically feminine way, but do not
> forget that the university had not taught me to recognize literary quality in any
> form of which the original mold was not Greek or Roman or Hebrew.
>
> MARY AUSTIN[1]

> I think very well of my way.
>
> GERTRUDE STEIN[2]

It is important to emphasize that the formal experiments of turn-of-the-century women writers reflect no essential "female" attitudes toward form or structure. While some of the patterns that I have discussed—the concentric shape of *The Country of the Pointed Firs* or the thirty-nine-part structure of *The Awakening*—may echo women's experiences either as they have been socially constructed for a particular group at a particular time or as they have been affected by biology, it does not follow that only women can or do produce such forms nor that they do so, when they do so, because they "must" as women. They do so, in my view, because they subscribe to a particular theory of art which says that they are free to do what they wish as individuals. Not surprisingly, what they wish to do as individuals on occasion is to capture formally some of the rhythms and structures experienced in their own lives as women. On other occasions, different goals surface. The patterns of multiplicity or simultaneity in *The Goodness of St. Rocque* and of deliberate generic conflation in *Of One Blood*, for instance, may suggest gender-bound associations but not necessarily. Moreover, artistically ambitious women writers at the turn of the century often worked in and valued conventional, inherited, "linear," western narrative forms, particularly the novel and short story, both of which came to them not exclusively yet nevertheless primarily out of privileged white male tradition.

It is therefore not my argument that women determined to be artists at the turn of the century in the United States were adverse to writing like men, or at least like the men selected out by them and others as great literary artists. To the contrary, as I will develop more in Chapter 8, many of them highly esteemed the work of particular male predecessors—Flaubert, Tolstoi, Thackeray, Balzac. Jewett for one (consciously at least) lamented her inability to create effective conventional plots and at one point named as her best book *The Tory Lover* (1901)—surely her most conventional and worst long narrative. Dunbar-Nelson spent years trying to write novels and get them published. Hopkins succeeded in *Contending Forces* in producing a conventionally structured novel. Chopin did likewise in important respects in *The Awakening*. It is not that artistically ambitious women writers at the turn into the twentieth century disdained conventional inherited narrative forms—as the expert manipulations of Edith Wharton or Nella Larsen attest. Rather, what stands out about a significant number of the writers that I am talking about is their relative failure with conventional form, even if they professed to admire it, compared with their greater success at experimental structures or at radical adaptations of existing high-culture narrative patterns. This does not amount to any essentialist argument about gender and genre. Think of the experiments of Toomer and Faulkner, both men, in the 1920s. Instead, what it amounts to is an argument about certain turn-of-the-century American women writers and, as the modern west constructs the term, art. I am saying that serious women writers of this period, whether as generators of new forms or as idiosyncratic manipulators of old ones, display as a group a fundamental, shared, and yet highly diverse conception of themselves as "artists"—as makers, in the modern high-culture, western definition of elite art valued in the twentieth century, of original forms.

Perhaps nowhere is this determination to define oneself as a serious high-culture artist more striking than in the work of Mary Austin and Gertrude Stein. Their experiments with form and language emphatically assert their originality and independence—their desire, even, to explode or circumvent fundamental structures of white patriarchal consciousness itself. Indeed, it may be that at the turn of the century only Sui Sin Far, the subject of the chapter after this one, went further: claiming not the right to remake the molds but to speak at all.

Mary Austin declares in her autobiography, *Earth Horizon* (1932), that she learned to write through contact with Native American culture and art. Speaking of herself in the third person, she states:

> She had begun the study of Indian verse, strange and meaningful; of Indian wisdom, of Indian art. The Paiutes were basket-makers; the finest of their sort. What Mary drew from them was their naked craft, the subtle sympathies of twig and root and bark; she consorted with them; she laid herself open to the influences of the wild, the thing done, accomplished. She entered into their lives, the life of the campody, the strange secret life of the tribe, the struggle of Whiteness with Darkness, the struggle of the individual soul with the Friend-of-the-Soul-of-Man. She learned what it meant; how to prevail; how to measure her strength against it. Learning that, she learned to write.[3]

Similarly, Stein said that her writing truly began not under the tutelage of literary masters, though James and Flaubert obviously affected her earliest work, but because of the influence of Cézanne, an artist whose medium was not even language.[4]

What both writers are doing in these statements about influence and origins is radically separating themselves from mainstream white western literary tradition, a maneuver to be different that shows up flamboyantly in their lives as well. Claiming genius—defining herself as having no forebears just like herself—each divorced herself dramatically from conventional mores. Stein dressed mannishly, cropped her hair close, lived with another woman, and got fatter and fatter. Austin piled her hair high with exotic combs (or let it hang wildly down her shoulders), went into trances, spoke of the I-Mary within, and wore outrageously vivid gowns at her public readings. In fact, it is surprising that these two figures have not been considered together. Operating on opposite sides of the Atlantic, each presented herself to the world as a complete original and a sage, a kind of modern-day Sibyl who lived her life as she pleased and created art in brilliant defiance of traditional white western literary theory and practice.

In one way these rebellions were utterly conventional. To be an original, to defy and surpass the accomplishments of one's predecessors, is probably, as Harold Bloom has argued, one of the distinguishing features of elite western art in the modern period—that is, of high-culture art by men, or people acting like them (Austin and Stein, for example). Yet it may be that at another level Austin and Stein's rebellions, their efforts truly to innovate, do not simply mirror traditional male artists' quests for supremacy. Although their work sharply contrasts on the surface, both writers seek in their most experimental writing not only to create narrative located outside of conventional white western notions of form. They also attempt to give expression to alternative linguistic and narrative rhythms and patterns—in Austin's case liquid and seductive, in Stein's startling and disorienting—that reach back, finally, to what we might conceptualize as a mother tongue: a body-generated rhythm and way of speaking that can be thought of as preceding the head-discourse of authoritative white fathers.

For both Austin and Stein, the initial task is to dislodge the reader. Where Jewett, Dunbar-Nelson, Chopin, and Hopkins play with form in challenging but, it could be said, not fundamentally disturbing ways (this may not be true of Hopkins's *Of One Blood*), clearly Austin and especially Stein wish to unsettle their readers. Whatever one's personal opinion is of the writing of Stein, for example, and there is certainly no American writer whose work provokes more controversy than hers (in itself a measure of her success by one standard), it is safe to say that for everyone the immediate effect of reading her mature experimental work is incomprehension, not knowing where we are or how to operate. Stein makes us start over. We cannot rely on what we have been taught about language, literature, reading, and hence, in literate culture, even thinking itself. We are confronted with familiar linguistic units—we *should* understand what is going on—but we find ourselves on strange new terrain. The rhythms and rules come from some place other than the long, learned tradition of great white masters systematically presented to generation after generation in the west as the authors of ''literature.''

Similarly but more subtly, Austin in *The Land of Little Rain* (1903), her most innovative work, radically relocates us (by ''us'' I mean western-educated literature consumers). She opens her book by explicitly announcing that her authorities will not be whites, men or women, but Native Americans. Their language—their way of naming—will be her guide; and the place to which she will take us, the Land of Little Rain, exists far beyond the edges of established white civilization. That place is a ''Country of Lost Borders,'' a place where ''not the law, but the land sets the limit,''[5] and it is profoundly alternative: unbounded, cyclic, apparently barren but actually rich with life, and fundamentally differently structured. "This is the country of three seasons," not four, we learn almost immediately (*LLR*, p. 5). Austin's unbordered territory geographically and literarily represents a space beyond or, at the very least, on the edge of white patriarchal control. It is not characterized by plot as we have learned to expect in mainstream western narrative tradition, and it finds its best expression in the art not of a white person nor of a man but of a Native American woman, the basketmaker, Seyavi. In short, although Mary Austin is often compared with Thoreau and Muir, and important connections do exist, she herself both in what she says and in how she says it points instead in *The Land of Little Rain* to her distance from white male predecessors, whether in the parodic title of her seventh sketch, "My Neighbor's Field," or in her explicit announcement that she will *not* give us a Bret Harte tale in "Jimville: A Bret Harte Town." It is her break from inherited white civilized literary tradition, her choice in favor of Native, unbordered, plotless art, that motivates *The Land of Little Rain*.

Stein's rebellion against the past displays an equally obvious reaction against inherited western narrative form. Inspired by the way Cézanne foregrounded paint and the painted surface to collapse the premise of traditional western illusionistic painting, the idea that the canvas is a kind of window opening onto deep "real" space,[6] Stein foregrounds language. She, like Cézanne, makes her medium her subject and thus disjoints her audience's learned expectations about art, meaning, form, and referentiality. As Richard Kostelanetz points out, "The reader's mind is forced out of its customary perceptual procedures."[7] When we read work by Stein, we often don't know what to make of either the individual word or the overall configuration of words, the controlling form. Customary, logical, western, linguistic arrangements producing "meaning" by accepted, agreed-upon rules either of grammar or of narrative do not operate in Stein's mature experimental work. The result is that the very question of meaning as we have been taught to understand literature to have meaning is itself called into question.

Therefore, for many readers what Stein offers at her most experimental are simply constellations of words—patterns, rhythms—employed not to evoke meaning outside the text but to exist in and of themselves, without external reference. As Kostelanetz expresses it, such passages in Stein's work might "be characterized as 'acoherent' with respect to traditional kinds of linguistic coherence, much as the epithet 'atonal music' has been used to distinguish new ways of organizing sound from traditional diatonic tonalities. As the 'meaning' of such passages lies wholly within language, rather than beyond it, this prose need not be 'interpreted' in terms of other meanings. What you read is all there is."[8] For other readers, as I will explain shortly, Stein's work even at its seemingly most abstract probably does have referential meaning, though the references are highly encoded, often to disguise lesbian subject matter. Whichever view of Stein is taken, however, there is agreement on this: Her progression from *QED* (1903) through *The Making of Americans* (1903–6) and *Three Lives* (1905–6) to *Tender Buttons* (1912–14) charts a dramatic, radical movement away from traditional western linear narrative form. As Kostelanetz states with simplicity, her mature work is marked by an "absence of linear focus."[9]

Austin's most innovative work also rejects conventional linear architecture. Al-

though she wrote a number of novels, her more experimental and formally unconventional books such as *The Land of Little Rain* or *Lost Borders* (1909), in the
opinion of both Austin and her critics, represent her more accomplished and lasting
achievements. (It is relevant here that the novel widely regarded as her best, *A
Woman of Genius* [1912], contains in its opening pages the declaration: "If you are
looking for anything ordinarily called plot, you will be disappointed.")[10] Writing
about the work of the painter Diego Rivera, Austin calls attention to its "patterns
of communality,"[11] a phrase that might well describe her own aesthetic in a book
such as *The Land of Little Rain*. Austin sees in Rivera's work what she aims for in
her own: formal as well as conceptual realization of a basic physical-spiritual integration. One way of saying this is that both Austin and Stein try to realize in their
experimental works a kind of sacred ceremony, a felt experience leading into a deep
natural state of harmony that instead of transcending body, as most western mystical
tradition attempts to do, stays rooted in it. As Lisa Ruddick explains of Stein's
Tender Buttons, it signals "a collapse of the mind-body dualism." In her work
"Stein is concerned to recover and honor the continuity *between* thinking and body,
between an adult self that has consciousness and a social role, and an infant self
that lives in the flesh."[12]

Certainly such continuity lies at the heart of Mary Austin's attraction to Native
American art. In her view "the Indian has sought incessantly for the precise values
in his body and soul of what is presaged to him in the sun and the cloud and the
rain. . . . Art for him is a logical necessity, and there is no art without the inclusion
of the body."[13] A mural by Diego Rivera, which Austin first experienced after being
profoundly moved by a modern dance based on Aztec material, suggests a physical
experience to her. "We began at the beginning of Diego's work," she explains,
"and traced it foot by foot, seeing how the artist had worked his way into it, how
it had grown upon him, filled him out until it ballooned about him like a cloud."
Austin's description of the painting as something growing simultaneously upon and
in the artist, coming from both outside and inside flesh, till it engulfs its creator in
a sort of billowy sky-womb, applies perfectly to the aesthetic of her own narrative,
The Land of Little Rain. She reports weeping in response to Rivera's work, which
she explicitly identifies as affecting her as a woman: "I was down in touch with
what I had known so long, where I had so long wanted to be, next to reality; the
things I had long missed from American life; the thing every woman misses from
American life; tenderness, the strength of tenderness, compassion, surrender." Austin then directly connects her own most recent work (the book *The American
Rhythm*): "I told him what it made me feel about my work; that I, too, had done
what I tried to do; that my work on the American Rhythm was good; that it was
sound; that I was not disappointed in it."[14]

As Austin's language suggests (her desire for "tenderness, the strength of tenderness, compassion, surrender"), her need for art to be physical, to hold the body
as well as the spirit, contains powerful erotic longing. Particularly, her need suggests
the ferocious hunger of the infant, in this case the daughter, for the unconditional
and intensely physical love of the mother from which Austin, as a middle-class
white Protestant woman, felt amputated. (Indeed, for both Austin and Stein, radical
formal experimentation seems to have been one way to use their art to recover the

mother, the first and total lover, with whom they craved union.) In Austin's case, the gulf between her and her mother was a source of conscious grief. Much as Charlotte Perkins Gilman, whom Austin met and liked,[15] describes being able to touch and be hugged by her mother only in the dark of night, Mary Austin could recall only bitter rebuffs. She recounts in *Earth Horizon* how her bereaved mother pushed her away at her father's funeral, and how on a different occasion her mother said that she wished it had been Mary instead of her other daughter, Jennie, who died in childhood. When the author's mother learned that Mary's only child, Ruth, was retarded, the stern Methodist woman declared, according to Austin: "I don't know what you've done, daughter, to have such a judgment upon you." Summarizing their relationship, Austin stated simply but with great pain, "Mary and her mother missed each other."[16]

Given this personal history, it is not surprising that so much of the energy of Austin's experimental work collects in images and structures of merging and that she places at the heart of *The Land of Little Rain* a healing grand/mother, the Native American artist, Seyavi. Historically, this pattern connects with other serious turn-of-the-century women writers' yearning to establish or sustain bonds with a strong, empowering maternal past: Harper's restoration of Iola Leroy's mother, Jewett's return to Mrs. Todd, Dunbar-Nelson's celebration of the Wizened One, Hopkins's transportation of the text to Candace in Africa. Personally, the pattern speaks to Austin's childhood deprivation. Affected on both levels—and of course the historical and the personal are not really separate, as the parallel personal experiences of Gilman and Austin make obvious—Austin found in Native American lifeways and art a healing vision. In her view Native American art and culture offered a lived concept of integrated form standing outside of and therefore alternative to the white patriarchal thought structures that, she believed, sought to assail and conquer consciousness rather than dare enter into it.

The central aesthetic question of *The Land of Little Rain* can be easily stated. Similar to *The Goodness of St. Rocque* in this respect, Austin's book asks: How can a text lead modern western readers into a place, a consciousness, which we can progress through, but more importantly we need simply to quit progressing, quit straining and searching, in order to know? How does a writer construct a narrative to tell us formally as well as conceptually to be still—to give over, merge, stop struggling?

It is true that it is quite possible to read *The Land of Little Rain* linearly. The text moves us as readers from ignorance of the land through growing knowledge of it to a celebration in the last sketch, "The Little Town of the Grape Vines," of a human ethic based on harmony with the environment rather than dominance of it. However, operating simultaneously with this linear movement, much as two large formal patterns inhabit Jewett's *Country of the Pointed Firs*, is a more significant, powerful antilinear organizing principle that takes its form not from inherited western literary tradition but from the earth and from Native American art, particularly the baskets of Seyavi.

Repetition is the key element in this form. Though we find in *The Land of Little Rain* all kinds of different "stories"—of water trails, pocket hunters, Indian people, winds, buzzards, Mexican American towns—the design of the parts and of the whole is always the same. The book constantly reiterates the simple construct of push/ pull, ebb/flow, shrink/expand that Austin considered the pulse, the constant, cyclic, unaccented rhythm of the earth itself. This basic formal principle was borrowed, of course, rather than invented by Austin. If we think of *The Land of Little Rain* as autobiography, which is certainly one of the ways in which it functions, the observation of Gretchen Bataille and Kathleen Mullen Sands that linear structure is often not important in Native American women's narrative is revealing. "There is a sense in most Indian women's autobiographies of the connectedness of all things, of personal life flow, and episodes are often not sequential but linked thematically to establish a pattern of character developing through the response to private experience."[17] Austin herself argued in the early 1920s that the problem with white American literature was its derivativeness from English intellectual tradition. American poets, she believed, needed to move behind the imported European trochee, what she identified as a "*lub*-dub, *lub*-dub" pattern of imposed hierarchy and dichotomy, to the rhythm of "unaccented" unified consciousness that the land, as she saw it, gives rise to. This "American rhythm" she describes as unaccented, undichotomized. It is the "dub-dub, dub-dub, dub-dub" commonly heard "in the plazas of Zuni and Oraibi."[18]

This aesthetic of repetition that Austin found in the earth and in Native American art may very well have appealed to her with such force because of the misery, from her point of view, of her relationship with her mother. As Joan Lidoff, thinking about women's narrative, explains: "The process which first creates meaning in both love and language is repetition. In the repetitive process of mother-infant mirroring, of feeding, of gazes, of emotional response, and later in the repetitive shaping of the recursive babbling that creates language's patterns, the infant's sense of self is formed."[19] Because Austin was estranged even as a child from her mother and never secure in her sense of being totally, unequivocally loved, it is very probable that a large part of her strong pull toward Native American lifeways and art was activated by her yearning as a white woman from a repressive Protestant background for the kind of love and integrated awareness of the universe that she felt cut off from.

But whatever brought her to her attraction to Indian perspectives and art, as an adult Austin was clear about her need for art to nurture and sustain. Surveying white American poetry in the 1920s, she found it impoverished by its ignorance of Native American art:

All of this time there was an American race singing in tune with the beloved environment, to the measures of life-sustaining gestures, taking the material of their songs out of the common human occasions, out of the democratic experience and the profound desire of man to assimilate himself to the Allness as it is displayed to him in all the peacock splendor of the American continent.

She explains that the Native American songs which her book tries to re-express into English come out of a consciousness and concept of form vastly different from that of Anglo-America. "Mold or rhythm-pattern" in Indian song, she says, "exists only as a point of rest for the verse to flow into and out of as a mountain stream flows in and out of ripple-linked pools."[20]

Taught by the earth and by Native American art, Austin in *The Land of Little*

Rain can be thought of as attempting to ground her narrative in what the contemporary Cherokee poet, Awiakta, defines as

> the Indian mode of thought. This mode begins with the heart of a matter and webs outward through myriad life-strands to a parameter of conclusion.
>
> Within that parameter is an allowance for the natural flow of variables. This combination of interconnection plus constancy in the midst of change mirrors the process of Mother Nature herself.
>
> Since this Indian mode is virtually inverse to the standard Western method, which reasons from a collection of facts to a conclusion,[21]

Awiakta explains, non-Indian readers need to open themselves to a fundamentally different way of knowing. This is true of Austin's *Land of Little Rain* (and to a lesser extent some of her subsequent volumes such as *Lost Borders*). In *The Land of Little Rain* we do not encounter, to borrow again from Awiakta, "the linear, Western, masculine mode of thought [which] has been . . . intent on conquering nature."[22] We enter instead a composition created out of principles of flow, repetition, web, and to repeat Awiakta's words, interconnection plus constancy in the midst of change.

In its largest nonlinear design, *The Land of Little Rain* refuses to participate in the most conventional western paradigm of narrative, which, as Paula Gunn Allen puts it, "is structured to create the illusion of change in the characters occurring over a period of time as a result of conflict and crisis." Austin's design comes closer to embodying traditional Native American values which generate narratives that "possess a circular structure, incorporating event within event, piling meaning upon meaning, until the accretion finally results in a story."[23]

To the extent that it is repetitive, fluid, and aggregative, Austin's narrative guides western-trained readers to see things we have not been taught to see, to find life where we have not assumed it to be. The earth, for example, becomes language. In "Water Trails of the Ceriso," we learn to read strange squiggly lines in the dust. We are taught to decipher and comprehend elaborate surface patterns and deep underlying meanings where, prior to being initiated into this borderless space, we would have thought there was only blankness, silence. Specifically, we learn that all of the squiggles connect at the waterhole. All of life—trails/tracks/language— gathers around the simple principle of thirst being relieved.

Geographically, that place where thirst is relieved, where everything comes together, is—as in the work of Jewett or Hopkins—a depression or cavity in the earth, a place Austin describes as the final destination of "wild creatures" who journey "down" to drink. Sexually charged, Austin's spring hides between folds in the earth that are bordered by lush vegetation: "Where the rim of the Ceriso breaks away to the lower country, there is a perpetual rill of fresh sweet drink in the midst of lush grass and watercress" (*LLR*, p. 18). Recalling Jewett's pennyroyal plot and anticipating the erotic iconography of Cather's Panther Canyon in *The Song of the Lark*, Austin's imagery of a secret life-giving cavity in the earth, shrunken in the desert to a small pocket under a ledge where all trails converge and lose themselves, repeats throughout her book. We meet this pattern of centrifugal pull and fusion in the circling scavengers that will descend, in the Pocket Hunter's uncontrollable return to the veins in the earth, in Winnenap's journey back and down to the land of his birth. Most important, we meet this pattern in the art of Seyavi: the bowls she makes.

Seyavi's art is erotic and religious. It is a celebration and enactment of merged creative and procreative desire. Austin tells us: "Before Seyavi made baskets for the satisfaction of desire,—for that is a house-bred theory of art that makes anything more of it,—she danced and dressed her hair." Wearing "the white flower of twining (clematis)" and with her "blood pricked to the mating fever," Seyavi sings of herself as the flower; and this erotic ritual prepares for the making of art: "So sang Seyavi of the campoodie before she made baskets" (*LLR*, p. 107).

The importance of Seyavi's art for Austin is that it comes out of women's lives, is not intellectualized, is technically superb, expresses eros, and captures in its circular form the essential connectedness of human and natural pattern: "Every Indian woman is an artist,—sees, feels, creates, but does not philosophize about her processes. Seyavi's bowls are wonders of technical precision, inside and out, the palm finds no fault with them, but the subtlest appeal is in the sense that warns us of humanness in the way the design spreads into the flare of the bowl." This art articulates a concept of time fundamentally different from that of white western civilization with its incessant emphasis on forward-moving progression. Austin explains that Seyavi and her art "lived next to the earth and were saturated with the same elements" and then states, without a paragraph break, that "the Paiute fashion of counting time appeals to me more than any other calendar. They . . . count forward and back by the progress of the season; the time of *taboose*, before the trout begin to leap, the end of the piñon harvest, about the beginning of deep snows. So they get nearer the sense of the season, which runs early or late according as the rains are forward or delayed." But this earthbound concept of time needs explaining only to people unfamiliar with Indian women's art. "If you had ever owned one of Seyavi's golden russet cooking bowls with the pattern of plumed quail," Austin concludes, "you would understand all this without saying anything" (*LLR*, pp. 106–7).

Seyavi's aesthetic as Austin describes it—earthbound, erotic, generated by women, productive of multiple pieces, each of which is different and yet the same, and expressive of an elastic concept of time—is the aesthetic of *The Land of Little Rain*. Coming out of Austin's understanding of Indian art, in combination with nineteenth-century western sketch tradition, the book, more than anything else, resembles a collection of Seyavi's bowls. Each individual narrative unit represents a variation on the same form. As is true of the earth, the source of both Austin's and Seyavi's art, there exists both endless subtle difference and profound sameness, repetition. We can move the units, arrange the bowls in any order, and the result varies yet remains the same. Whether we look at one bowl or fourteen (the number of narrative units Austin assembles in her book), we come away with the same message. All of the pieces tell us that we are part of the earth; our patterns are its; its harmony ours.

Therefore, when we finish reading, it may be that we return with new eyes to Austin's dedication of *The Land of Little Rain*:

TO EVE
"The Comfortress of Unsuccess."
(*LLR*, p. v)

For with these words Mary Austin, a white woman about to try to write out of Native American values, celebrates the stigmatized first transgressor of the tradition into which she was born. That transgressor, like Austin, was a mother and sexual (as is Seyavi); and Austin glorifies her as the presiding spirit over an alternative ethic of anti-Progress succor ("The Comfortress of Unsuccess"). What Austin's cryptic dedication tells us is that we are embarking on forbidden territory, on the buried or left-out story of western tradition: the unwritten female space. From the point of view of western culture, we are heading in *The Land of Little Rain* into the anti-story, the content and form of not-Adam.

Adamic art appears in *The Land of Little Rain*. Much as Jewett weaves into *The Country of the Pointed Firs* a glimpse of the masculine text, the confused "Little-page," that she has not followed as a model, so Austin gives us a peek at the white masculine patterns that she is writing against. In "The Pocket Hunter," the only sketch devoted to a white man, the speaker repeatedly tells us that she cannot speak his language. "I could never get the run of miner's talk," she says. Later, of ore-hunting, she warns: "Remember that I can never be depended on to get the terms right" (*LLR*, pp. 45, 46). She then explains: "When I could get him away from 'leads' and 'strikes' and 'contacts' "—away, that is, from the language for which Austin has no use—he was "full of fascinating small talk about the ebb and flood of creeks, the piñon crop on Black Mountain, and the wolves of Mesquite Valley" (*LLR*, p. 49). Austin likes the Pocket Hunter. He is a misfit, a white man who, whether he admits it or not, has merged with the earth despite his notion that he is conquering it. She therefore ignores his silly masculine language and slyly relocates him in spite of himself in feminized space. He may talk impenetrable male lingo, but we meet him in female territory: He is cooking supper in a place made sweet by "Diana's sage" and "a young white moon" (*LLR*, p. 43).

Austin's Pocket Hunter is subversive. In what may be the wittiest jab in the book, she tells us that her social stray—a white man who is gentle (he owns no gun), domestic, and at home in the wild—carries his "belongings done up in green canvas bags, the veritable 'green bags' of English novels" (*LLR*, p. 51). That is, this Pocket Hunter, like Austin herself in this particular book, has thrown out the conventional forms themselves—the novels that are supposed to fill the English-bags/bags-of-English—and has instead stuffed into the narrative containers the real paraphernalia of life, material which pooches the empty forms out into very different patterns than the ones dictated by dominant literary practices in the west. Obviously the Pocket Hunter, a vagabond figure hovering in the margin of both the white masculine and the "civilized" worlds, stands in for Austin. "He had made the Grand Tour," we are told, "and had brought nothing away from it but the green canvas bags, which he conceived would fit his needs, and an ambition" (*LLR*, p. 52). So Mary Austin has made the grand tour and brought away, in place of the tidy, squared-up containers of white western literary tradition, loose, marvelously empty bags in which she can put whatever narrative she pleases. And an ambition.

Austin reinforces her refusal to tell the usual white story in the sketch immediately following "The Pocket Hunter," "Shoshone Land." In conventional white masculine dramatic structure, the execution of Winnenap would almost certainly define the sensational climax of the story—the "point" of telling about him at all.

But in Austin's piece his death at the hands of the tribe is a detail, almost an afterthought. The pattern of her narrative does not follow predictable white narrative structure. Moreover, the fact that she knows that she is not following conventional structure, indeed is actively choosing against it, and wants us to know that, is the obvious point of "Jimville: A Bret Harte Town," the piece that comes next.

Both the subtitle and the first line of "Jimville" mention by name the tradition Austin is not writing in: that of Bret Harte. She certainly *could* write like Harte. The following dialog à la Harte from "Jimville" is about mining and murder:

> Says Three Finger, relating the history of the Mariposa [Mine], "I took it off'n Tom Beatty, cheap, after his brother Bill was shot."
> Says Bill Jenkins, "What was the matter of him?"
> "Who? Bill? Abe Johnson shot him; he was fooling around Johnson's wife, an' Tom sold me the mine dirt cheap."
> "Why didn't he work it himself?"
> "Him? Oh, he was laying for Abe and calculated to have to leave the country pretty quick."
> "Huh!" says Jim Jenkins, and the tale flows smoothly on. (*LLR*, pp. 76–77).

Maybe it does—but if it does, it does so in somebody else's book. Mary Austin strands her patch of Hartean dialog and moves to other things. As she says elsewhere in the sketch of a different piece of potential plot: "If it had been in mediaeval times you would have had a legend or a ballad. Bret Harte would have given you a tale. You see in me a mere recorder, for I know what is best for you; you shall blow out this bubble from your own breath" (*LLR*, p. 73).

Refusing in *The Land of Little Rain* to pour her material into conventional western molds—whether medieval legends or Bret Harte tales—Austin, like Sarah Orne Jewett and Alice Dunbar-Nelson, adapts the sketch tradition, a marginal, formal tradition shaped largely by women, to give us an antimasculine version even of very masculine territory. Her strategy appears in "The Pocket Hunter," "Shoshone Land," and "Jimville: A Bret Harte Town," and then, most heretically perhaps, in "My Neighbor's Field."

Taken from *Walden*, the most famous book about nature in white American literature, the title "My Neighbor's Field" immediately calls contrast into focus. Austin's book grows out of fourteen sketches that create a coherent whole less because they fit into a logically ordered superstructure than because they breathe with a rhythm, a structural pattern of repetition, that emanates from the earth itself. Formally Austin's book takes Europeanized readers out of themselves, out of a learned tradition of endless disunification for-the-sake-of-struggle-for-the-sake-of-synthesis that will inevitably result only in more disunification. Whereas *Walden* is imbued with that paradigm, *The Land of Little Rain* records a journey that moves through no diagrammatic trauma of spirit. There is no divorce from physical reality, alienation, and then rebirth. Instead of a structure based on that model of physical and spiritual disunion which produces the familiar western narrative/dramatic pattern of successively higher peaks finally cresting in one overriding, cathartic climax somewhere between the middle and the end of a piece (what Paula Gunn Allen succinctly identifies as "the western plot structure of conflict-crisis-resolution"),[24] Austin creates a structure of no large climaxes: no big peaks and valleys. "My

Neighbor's Field'' invites us to think of Thoreau, Austin's literary neighbor, but
then leads us away from him. Even literally, the sketch moves from white masculine
individualism toward female community. Carefully situated in *The Land of Little
Rain*, "My Neighbor's Field" begins right after "Jimville: A Bret Harte Town"
and ends at the mesa trail that leads to Seyavi.

Constructed out of Native American and nineteenth-century narrative sketch
principles, both of which defy the dominant white western aesthetic of climax-driven
linear plot and honor in its place a sense of self and creation that is both corporate
and connected, *The Land of Little Rain* ends with what may be Mary Austin's most
audacious—and brilliant—literary act. She springs at the heart of white patriarchy.

The Anglican prayerbook has Jesus say: "Come away, ye who are weary and
downtrodden, and I will refresh you." Mary Austin has the last line of *The Land
of Little Rain* say: "Come away, you who are obsessed with your own importance
in the scheme of things, and have got nothing you did not sweat for, come away by
the brown valleys and full-bosomed hills to the even-breathing days, to the kindli-
ness, earthiness, ease of El Pueblo de Las Uvas" (*LLR*, p. 171). Thus Austin,
student of Seyavi, appropriates the most privileged, sacred language of the white
fathers to rewrite the Son's words in the Mother Earth. Those words call us into,
rather than away from, the flesh—the full-bosomed hills and even-breathing days.
Most important, this rewrite of the august, Anglican Book of Common Prayer does
not end in English. The last words of *The Land of Little Rain*, it is crucial to notice,
are Spanish.

Where Austin's experimental prose rocks and caresses, Stein's jolts and disconcerts.
Her search to recover the mother—in Austin, the Mother Earth, the mother artist,
the mother tongue of the land—is not gentle and earthbound. It is typically fierce,
cryptic, and emphatically intellectual.

Stein drenches us in words: thick, dense, piled repetitively on top of each other;
or stark, isolated, standing alone yet positioned provocatively next to each other.
But in any case, words. Language itself. In place of story—shaped, meaningful,
narrative development—we are confronted with simple obvious words (Stein is not
interested in showy erudite diction) so plentiful, so insistent, and so seemingly
unmediated that language itself becomes subject, and that subject becomes virtually
a physical experience. As Lisa Ruddick says: Stein "immerses us in the material
feel of words."[25] We are saturated, surrounded, steeped, and stuffed. Denied traditional plot, we get in its place an overwhelming, sensuous experience of language
that, try as our brains must, at least initially has to be met as a body not a head
experience. As Sherwood Anderson put it: "She is laying word against word, re-
lating sound to sound, feeling for the taste, the smell, the rhythm of the individual
word."[26]

What this amounts to, bizarre as it may sound at first, is Sarah Orne Jewett's
delicious, physical women's language realized. Words not in the head but on the
tongue, in the belly. Simple, unliterary, decontextualized—whether on cakes and
pies or on published pages—the words we get in Stein at her most arcane are
ironically what Jewett offers at her most down-home (the Bowden reunion): words
to be licked, chewed, gobbled, savored, swallowed, embodied. Of course, the

alinear narratives of Jewett and Stein are in many ways diametrically opposed. While Jewett, like Dunbar-Nelson and Austin, beckons us in discursively, Stein, self-consciously difficult, puts us off. We have to struggle to read Stein's work. She makes things very hard. Beneath the differences, however, it is possible to argue that there is a yearning for a mother tongue in Stein's mature work—a reach for language outside or beyond the control of white patriarchal authority—as powerful as there is in the writing of all of the other figures I have discussed.

Brilliantly arguing that it is interpretable, Lisa Ruddick finds in *Tender Buttons*, the work that first fully realized Stein's mature experimentation, a system of coded writing. Pointing out that *Tender Buttons* was written in 1912, the year Stein and her brother quit living together and she entered into the long-term erotic and nurturing relationship with Alice Toklas that would sustain her throughout the rest of her career, Ruddick observes that Stein's work after 1912 is marked by a new kind of writing, dense, cryptic, difficult, but *not* meaningless. Its function in large part is to explore the forbidden terrain of lesbian love and consciousness.[27]

Reading with penetrating imagination, Ruddick lets Stein's language fall apart, combine, and recombine in every direction until the strange secret code that she believes governs *Tender Buttons* starts to crack and yield possible meaning. She pauses, for example, with Stein's section

MILK
Climb up in sight climb in the whole utter needles and a guess a whole guess is hanging. Hanging hanging.[28]

Ruddick analyzes a portion of these words in relation to the antipatriarchal thematic that she finds animating *Tender Buttons*:

MILK
Climb up in sight climb in the whole utter. . . . Hanging hanging.
The poem envisions a climb into the udder, or the mother's breast. The title, "MILK," and the references to something "hanging" help to make us hear "utter" as "udder." The sentence contains another pun: "climb in the hole," or the womb. And it's just conceivable to me that the last words, "hanging hanging" are meant to suggest, among other things: killing killing. Stein hangs hanging, does away with sacrifice [patriarchy's mechanism for controlling women's power], by recovering the udder that sacrifice erased.

Yet there's no such thing as an unmediated return to the mother's body. The word "udder" is, after all, spelled "utter." For we can only recover the udder by utterance, by putting words together in particular ways. Once we are adults, there's no getting back to the womb, except in and through advanced mental processes—language, thinking. Stein's poem uses the word (or the syllables) "in-sight." It's about a kind of wisdom, not a drifting back to infancy.[29]

Ruddick's perceptions make Stein's language continue to unfold with possibilities, for once we learn how to negotiate Stein's code, we might argue that "advanced mental processes—language, thinking" are not in fact the only route to (w)holeness implied by Stein's words. Another way for an adult woman to get back to the womb, back to the antithesis of patriarchal control—to a place we might think of as matrisexuality ("MILK")—can be found in the "in sight climb" (insight climb/in-site-climb) of lesbian love-making.

The small section "MILK" can be used as one illustration of both method and argument in *Tender Buttons*. Celebrating breasts ("MILK," utter/udder) and total immersion within another ("climb in the whole") within a totally female context ("MILK"), Stein's words emphasize physical experiences of enwombment and intense sensory awareness (the climbing-in images and the word "needles"), which are simultaneously open-ended and endless: The section stops with the word "hanging" repeated three times. These images create a verbal portrait of love-making between women: nonphallic, boundariless, matrisexual. Read thus, Stein's words in "MILK," to combine Ruddick's and my readings, fuse descriptions of writing, nursing, lesbian sex, and an end to patriarchal violence to suggest, I would argue, the possibility of a gynocentric aesthetic. That is, "MILK" plays with language to force into coalescence themes of breaking silence, staying connected to the nurturing *and* the erotic energy of the Mother, and making art. (Certainly it cannot be accidental that the next passage in *Tender Buttons* is "EGGS.")

What even this one small section, "MILK," suggests is that there exists at the heart of *Tender Buttons*, and probably of much of Stein's other mature experimental writing as well, a search, carefully disguised and encoded, for an alternative voice to express alternative intellectual, erotic, and emotional possibilities for women. That those possibilities originate in western culture—the repressive power of institutionalized heterosexuality notwithstanding—in the same-sex erotic bond of mother and daughter is repeatedly implied in *Tender Buttons*. As Ruddick points out, "At the center of *Tender Buttons*, there's a nostalgia for the intensely oral bond an infant shares with its mother." In "Stein's work in the decade from the time she began to write seriously to *Tender Buttons*," Ruddick continues, there is a "slow unearthing of her archaic longing for her own mother"; yet, at the same time, "Stein's longing was not in fact for the mother she had lost at fourteen, but for what we would now call the pre-Oedipal mother, the mother of infancy."[30] This yearning for maternal connection was not unique. It echoes Austin's gravitation toward Seyavi or Hopkins's need to find Candace. Both personally and culturally, it corresponds with the widespread longing among twentieth-century western women to recover traditional mother-daughter intimacy and wholeness.

Yet an important difference also exists. As a lesbian in what seems to have been a very strong and supportive relationship, Stein was enabled in her art, unlike most of the other writers I am discussing, to explore the taboo erotic dimensions of the daughter's yearning for the mother, feelings profoundly threatening to patriarchal control of women and therefore forbidden, labeled deviant and depraved, by institutionalized heterosexuality. Consider Stein's very title: *Tender Buttons*. The words identify women's world, the world of nurturance and domesticity, as erotic. They force us to ask: What are the tender buttons, the delicious firm things, the highly sensitive-to-the-touch triggers, that Stein intends as the controlling metaphor of her densely encoded prose poem or poeticized prose (even naming Stein's genre is difficult)? Nipples? Clitorises? Should we read "tender" as soft and tasty? Certainly the word evokes eating, chewing, sucking. Or does it mean painful? Or maybe we should read tender as tend/her? And if so, tend her what or how? Whatever we decide, the point is that radical confusion is what Stein confronts us with from the beginning, and it is radical confusion in the service of a subversive erotic argument.

Her title, like the literary work that will follow, enjambs and deconstructs simple, familiar terms to explode established patriarchal and heterosexual associations and assumptions in order to offer in their place, in deeply encoded writing, the possibility of an alternative, lesbian eros and world view. From the first words of *Tender Buttons*, the title, Stein cryptically makes the ordinary erotic and in so doing challenges us to crack her code (''EGGS''), read her mind, see what she is up to.

Which, of course, is the problem. Catharine Stimpson asks in an essay title, ''Gertrude Stein: Why Do We Hate Her?'' One answer is because her work is so difficult. And this is not simply a matter of readers being lazy and not wanting to apply themselves. It is a matter, to paraphrase Audre Lorde, of whether or not the master's house can be dismantled by using the master's tools.[31]

The issue of Stein's difficulty is serious. One way to explain her method in her mature experimental work is to say, as critics often do, that we should not try to decipher logical meaning where there is none; Stein ''paints'' with words and the sheer physical experience of them—their texture, sound, rhythm, appearance—is what she offers. She is not really difficult if we suspend our learned notions about how writing operates. The other way to explain Stein's art, as Lisa Ruddick does so persuasively and as I have pursued here, is to say that Stein had to make her writing difficult—she could only talk in code—because her subject matter was so dangerous.

The problem with either explanation is that Stein's experimentation, her alogical word-painting or her writing in code, whichever one assumes it to be, does not defy patriarchal principles of elite art but participates in them. No matter how much one talks about language as a physical, immersing experience in Stein's work, one is never allowed to forget that behind that experience of language—watching us sweat and struggle or leap and shout—is the designer, the genius who set the experience up for us, the Almighty Author, Gertrude Stein. In other words, if the purpose of Stein's experimentation is to make us lose ourselves in words, the method defeats the purpose; we are always aware of Gertrude Stein. Or if the purpose is to speak in code, that too is a failure. The code is so difficult (clearly it has to be complicated to avoid being easily cracked) that Stein's system reproduces rather than undermines western patriarchy because it is so totally complicit in its high-culture literary strategies of textual formidableness, authorial authority, and privileged language control.

The late twentieth-century French theorist Xaviere Gauthier wrestles with the issue of women's voice:

> Women are, in fact, caught in a very real contradiction. Throughout the course of history, they have been mute, and it is doubtless by virtue of this mutism that men have been able to speak and write. As long as women remain silent, they will be outside the historical process. But, if they begin to speak and write *as men do*, they will enter history subdued and alienated; it is a history that, logically speaking, their speech should disrupt.
>
> If, however, ''replete'' words (*mots pleins*) belong to men, how can women speak ''otherwise,'' unless, perhaps, we can *make audible* that which agitates within us, suffers silently in the *holes of discourse*, in the unsaid, or in the non-sense.[32]

This may very well describe Stein's dilemma—and solution. Writing nonsense full of sense may be one way of circumventing patriarchal control. Certainly it is true that Stein avoids reproducing what Gauthier, in words that recall Awiakta's, identifies as conventional civilized discourse, "the linear, grammatical, linguistic system that orders the symbolic, the superego, the law. It is a system based entirely upon one fundamental signifier, the phallus."[33] But the question is: Does Stein's solution—as may be logically inevitable for any solution attempted within patriarchy, and yet we know of no place outside of it—defy certain white, western, high-culture, patriarchal norms, those of linear, grammatical discourse, only to fall into the trap of others—textual inaccessibility and authorial omnipotence? If so, can we really consider her voice "alternative"?

A second question that must be asked of both Stein and Austin may be even more difficult.

What does it mean for an educated, privileged, white woman to attempt to participate in an aesthetic developed by or modeled on values of people who are oppressed by the very white western society whose privileges the white woman enjoys? What are the ethics of advantaged white women adapting other people's cultural perspectives to their own personal ends, as Austin does in a number of her works and as Stein, it can be argued, does both in her use of African American material in the story "Melanctha" and in her work as a whole insofar as she mimics the fascination with "primitivism" of avant garde western painters?

The issue clearly applies to Austin. At the end of *Earth Horizon,* she thinks about the appeal for her of Diego Rivera's art and says: "It was a relief to discover that there was no Nordic taint in Diego Rivera. There was Moorish blood, a little Jewish, perhaps, Spanish and Indian. Especially the Indian; poised, centered, at home with his work. A great painter; a great man."[34] With its turn-of-the-century race-theory rhetoric, this statement has to make a modern reader cringe. Ideas of racial and ethnic "taint" and "blood" have always been used to promote racist agendas. Certainly Austin's conceptualization of Rivera in terms of pints and cups of racial and ethnic heritage, even though she is trying to be complimentary, participates in racism. How do we interpret her praise for his work because he was not "white"? Does it suggest a genuine desire for new leadership? A recognition of Rivera's articulation of values preceding white western imperialist domination? Surely it underscores what Austin, at her most experimental, was reaching for as a white woman artist: an aesthetic not only outside the control of the white man, as she knew it in the English and Anglo-American literary traditions, but actively opposed to and preceding it. Does that resolve the issue, though?

In the history of modernism the appropriation by white artists of the cultural perspectives of people of color has almost always been racist and exploitative. One "brilliant" white colonial after another—Picasso, Van Gogh, D. H. Lawrence—has displayed "exotic" and by no accident almost always erotic and female images of brown- and black-skinned people to celebrate the supposed fact that dark-skinned human beings (especially women) are closer to nature, freer, and "simpler" than their neurotic white brothers and sisters lost in the cold, dying north. Imperialism and racism collaborate in such an outlook. Modernism is rooted in repeated raids by the twentieth-century west, for its own psychic and artistic purposes, on cultures it has defined as less "civilized" or more "primitive"—cultures characterized, it is maintained, by a fused physical/spiritual consciousness, a perfect integration of inside and outside and of past, present, and future, which the modern, alienated west has lost. Museums, canvases, texts, and lecture halls in the west and north have been filled with plunder from the east and south. Indeed, it may be that any attempt by a white person in the twentieth century to participate intellectually in the cultures of nonwhite peoples is by definition corrupt, given the pervasively discriminatory construction of race, class, culture, and nationality in the modern world.

If that is not true, however, if it is possible for a member of the dominant group honestly to cross cultural boundaries, then Mary Austin may have succeeded better than most. She was hardly perfect in her relationships with Native Americans. She aggressed on individuals, as her 1902 letter to Grant Overton, itself demeaningly rendered in dialect, reveals: "Says my friend Kern River Jim, 'What for you learn them Injun songs? You can't sing um. You go learn songs in a book, that's good enough for you.' "[35] Beyond doubt, Austin intruded herself on people, violated their privacy, and used their friendship. At the same time, though, her belief in Native American art was not a phase or "period" in her career, but suffused her adult life. She tried to open herself up to Native American, Mexican, and Mexican American cultures and art, and although she did borrow from Indian cultures intellectually and spiritually to serve her own ends, she also campaigned for Indian rights and worked hard to understand Native American lifeways and values.[36] She did not assume it would or should be easy for her to enter into the lives and belief systems of other people.

For instance, although Austin was often cited by white journalists as an "authority" on Indians, she rejected the label even as she affirmed her immigrant relationship to Native American values. She explains in *The American Rhythm:*

> I have naturally a mimetic temperament which drives me toward the understanding of life by living it. If I wished to know what went into the patterns of the basket makers, I gathered willows in the moon of white butterflies and fern stems when these were ripest. I soaked the fibers in running water, turning them as the light turned, and did my ineffectual best to sit on the ground scraping them flat with an obsidian blade, holding the extra fibers between my toes. I made singing medicine as I was taught, and surprised the Friend-of-the-Soul-of-Man between the rattles and the drums. Now and then in the midst of these processes I felt myself caught up in the collective mind, carried with it toward states of super-consciousness that escape the exactitudes of the ethnologist as the life of the flower escapes between the presses of the herbalist. So that when I say that I am not, have never been, nor offered myself, as an authority on things Amerindian, I do not wish to have it understood that I may not, at times, have succeeded in being Indian.[37]

Histrionic as she was, "being Indian" was something Austin took seriously. She was racist.[38] At the same time, however, I think, her interest in Indians was for the most part a genuine attempt to participate in the values of a culture she believed more life-supporting than the one into which she was born.

Gertrude Stein's turn to nonwhite material was different. Her grotesque stereotypes of black people in the story "Melanctha" in *Three Lives,* as well as the casual, gratuitous use of the term *nigger* elsewhere in her work, suggest that she enthusiastically and carelessly shared in the racist project of white modernism early in the twentieth century—its projection onto people of color, and especially women, of the west's own repressed and often prurient sexual fantasies and desires.

The racism of "Melanctha" is pervasive. Black people in this work are stupid, hypersexual, immature, and fundamentally Other in their feelings about human life. The opening page is enough to make the point. Melanctha's friend Rose Johnson is "sullen, childish, [and] cowardly." Having just given birth, she "grumbled and fussed and howled and made herself to be an abomination and like a simple beast." Although her baby was born healthy,

> Rose Johnson was careless and negligent and selfish, and when Melanctha had to leave for a few days, the baby died. Rose Johnson had liked the baby well enough and perhaps she just forgot it for awhile, anyway the child was dead and Rose and Sam her husband were very sorry but then these things came so often in the negro world in Bridgepoint, that they neither of them thought about it very long.[39]

"Melanctha" reflects the standard schizophrenia of much white racism. It is a story set in an imaginary world of casual sex, razor fights, and "big black virile negroes" that nevertheless overflows with dreamy-headed assumptions about the "warm broad glow of negro sunshine," the "earth-born, boundless joy of negroes," and the "simple, promiscuous unmorality of the black people."[40]

Usually ignored in the criticism about Stein, this racism in "Melanctha" matters not only because it is offensive and extensive, in themselves sufficient reasons for reacting strongly, but also because, by Stein's own admission, this story marked "the beginning of her revolutionary work."[41] What does it mean that she began her own liberation as a white woman writer by creating a sexist, racist portrait of a black woman?

The standard explanation of "Melanctha" is that it is Stein's disguised retelling of the lesbian love story that she expressed in *Q.E.D.* but could not publish because of its volatile content. The explanation makes partial sense. Translating the lesbian love conflict of *Q.E.D.* into a heterosexual story in "Melanctha," or more properly, translating the love triangle made up of a man and a woman competing for a woman in *Q.E.D.* into a totally heterosexual love triangle in "Melanctha," does to some degree effectively allow Stein to retell yet disguise her original narrative. But why the change from white characters to black?

The black world of Stein's imagination in "Melanctha"—and it is important to remember that this world is not based on significant knowledge but on fantasy and prejudice[42]—is a very particularly conceived place: dangerous, ostracized, freely sexual, adult yet not involved with family responsibilities and children, and generally antisocial if judged by mainstream middle-class, dominant-culture norms. This fictitious black world, in other words, is Stein's way—having turned the story heterosexual—of keeping it, in code, lesbian, and of making it fall outside dominant-culture sexual mores. The problem is that she does this by dealing wholesale in racist stereotypes. She imagines black people not as human beings but as convenient objectifications. Specifically, she uses black people, and particularly the black female character Melanctha, as men have always used women and as white men in particular have used black women: to play out her own erotic fantasies. She does exactly what black women writers such as Frances Harper or Pauline Hopkins accused white women of doing; she negotiates (in secret) a small part of her own freedom as a white woman by indulging actively in the oppression of black women. She hypersexualizes them, thus feeding into the racist stereotype of the all-sexual black woman, in order to talk about her own sexuality without getting caught.

In one way Stein's tracing of her revolutionary impulses as an artist back to "Melanctha" accurately signals her debt to African American culture and art. At a deep, creative level her fascination with African American life in "Melanctha" and her lifelong fascination with formal and verbal experimentation probably were connected. Although Stein did not dwell on her identity as a Jew, it may have affected her attitude toward mainstream American hegemony and smugness more than she admitted. In any case, much like the black characters she imagines in "Melanctha," Stein rebelled against respectable, middle-class, white cultural and aesthetic expectations. The African American presence that Toni Morrison has labeled "the ghost in the machine" surfaces powerfully in Stein's art. It shows up in her verbal and formal audacity, her irreverence, her enthusiasm for improvisation, and her signifying on words themselves—in short, in her constant refusal to play artistically (and personally as well) by the Man's rules.

Yet does this change much? Perhaps the most pressing question is why the racism of "Melanctha" has received so little attention in Stein criticism, including feminist criticism. One explanation may be that if her racism is taken seriously, it has to be recognized as part of her modernism. We have to admit that the two, from "Melanctha" on, cannot be separated in Stein's work. To be sure, the blatant racism and class condescension of *Three Lives* appear to get left behind in Stein's career. But do they really, or do they just appear to disappear because the conventional realism of that early work disappears? The critical reluctance to deal fully with Stein's racism may come from the unarticulated recognition that if it is addressed, then we have to raise a very large and probably disillusioning question. What is the true nature of Stein's "revolution" as an artist? What does any revolution consist of if it begins in the blatant racism of "Melanctha," goes on to mimic modernist painting strategies based on "primitive" models that the west has appropriated from "less civilized" parts of the world, and culminates in writing that reifies rather than deconstructs a high-culture, western, patriarchal aesthetic of textual inaccessibility and authorial omnipotence? Is Stein really a revolutionary? Or does she simply use the appearance of revolution to advance herself in the existing, privileged order?

7 Audacious Words: Sui Sin Far's *Mrs. Spring Fragrance*

They tell me that if I wish to succeed in literature in America I should dress in Chinese costume, carry a fan in my hand, wear a pair of scarlet beaded slippers, live in New York, and come of high birth. Instead of making myself familiar with the Chinese-Americans around me, I should discourse on my spirit acquaintance with Chinese ancestors and quote in between the "Good mornings" and "How d'ye dos" of editors,

> "Confucius, Confucius, how great is Confucius.
> Before Confucius, there never was Confucius.
> After Confucius, there never came Confucius,"
> etc., etc., etc.

or something like that, both illuminating and obscuring, don't you know. They forget, or perhaps they are not aware that the old Chinese sage taught "The way of sincerity is the way of heaven."

Sui Sin Far[1]

The issue of negotiating cultures and subcultures was a constant, lived issue for Sui Sin Far. She was the first person of Chinese ancestry to publish stories in the United States that were centered in the Chinese American community and focused on Chinese American experiences. She had no literary models, no published female forebears like herself to guide and empower her; and she wrote at a time of intensified, virulent anti-Chinese sentiment in the United States. That Sui Sin Far invented herself—created her own voice—out of such deep silencing and systematic racist repression was one of the triumphs of American literature at the turn of the century.

What little we know about Sui Sin Far comes largely from her autobiographical essay in the *Independent* in 1909, "Leaves from the Mental Portfolio of an Eurasian."[2] Born in 1865 and named Edith Maud Eaton, she was the daughter of a Chinese mother and an English father. As the oldest daughter of fourteen children, she and her family, which was poor, lived in England, Canada, and the United States. Her father, who attempted to support his family as an artist, came from an economically comfortable family from which he was, at least in part because of his marriage, estranged. Her mother had been born in China but was removed from her home when very young; she left China when she married. Sui Sin Far did not marry.

She supported herself by working as a stenographer (like Hopkins), a reporter, and a fiction writer, as did her sister, Winnifred Eaton, who claimed that her ancestry was Japanese and, publishing under the name Onoto Watanna, specialized in romantic stories with Japanese settings. Sui Sin Far, in contrast, acknowledged her Chinese heritage and identified with Chinese America even though her physical appearance would have made it possible for her to pass as white had she wished. She traveled and lived in the northern United States, Canada, and the Caribbean, settling for ten years in Seattle; and her published work appeared from the early 1890s to the teens in such periodicals as the *Independent, Out West, Century, Delineator, Good Housekeeping, Youth's Companion,* and the *New York Evening Post.*[3] In 1912, two years before her death, thirty-seven of her stories were collected in her only published book, *Mrs. Spring Fragrance.*

In addition to providing most of the facts that we have about Sui Sin Far's life, "Leaves from the Mental Portfolio of an Eurasian" offers an invaluable glimpse into the author's sense of her own formation as an artist in an inhospitable world. If Mary Austin and Gertrude Stein's struggles as writers centered on the issue of how to say what they needed to say, Sui Sin Far's struggle centered on being able to speak at all. Primary themes in the essay focus on memories of racist and racist/sexist abuse and discrimination, tremendous pride in her mother, and recollections of her own determination even as a little girl to fight back and speak out against racial hatred.

"Leaves" opens with vignettes of white people's meanness and bigotry. Two English nannies whisper about Sui Sin Far's being Chinese. A schoolgirl cries out to a friend: "I wouldn't speak to Sui if I were you. Her mamma is Chinese." A white-haired old man at a tea party studies her like a bug under glass: "Ah, indeed! . . . Who would have thought it at first glance. Yet now I see the difference between her and other children. What a peculiar coloring! Her mother's eyes and hair and her father's features, I presume. Very interesting little creature!" ("Leaves," pp. 125–26). These anecdotes show not only racial prejudice but also the author's outrage and retaliation, even as a child. A boy in the street hurls slurs at her and her brother, "Chinky, Chinky, Chinaman, yellow-face, pig-tail, rat-eater," and on the heels of her brother's retort, "Better than you," she records her own screaming response, "I'd rather be Chinese than anything else in the world" ("Leaves," p. 126). Naming the cruelties, actually repeating the ugly language, *and* her own resistance to it, defines the opening act—rhetorical, political—of Sui Sin Far's self portrait. She defies the stereotype of the passive, impassive, fragile, inscrutable "Oriental." She refuses to take on the identity assigned her by racist whites. Instead, anticipating her spiritual great granddaughter Maxine Hong Kingston by three-quarters of a century, she creates herself as a fighter.

Sui Sin Far frequently ties such images of fighting in "Leaves" to her love and admiration for her mother. She reports how she and her brother, scratched and bruised from a confrontation with violent white children,

> crawl home, and report to our mother that we have "won the battle."
> "Are you sure?" asks my mother doubtfully.
> "Of course. They ran from us. They were frightened," returns my brother.

My mother smiles with satisfaction.
"Do you hear?" she asks my father. ("Leaves," p. 126)

This maternal pride in her children's self-defense echoes in a later contrast that Sui Sin Far draws between her parents: "My mother takes a great interest in our battles, and usually cheers us on. . . . As to my father, peace is his motto, and he deems it wisest to be blind and deaf to many things" ("Leaves," p. 127). Sui Sin Far follows her mother. Although she expresses no overt animosity toward her father in "Leaves," peace is not her motto. She does not consider it wisest to be blind and deaf to the white people who insult and revile her.

Among the more dramatic instances of this refusal to suffer abuse in silence is an experience during a dinner Sui Sin Far attends in a midwestern town where she is employed as a stenographer. Her employer, unaware that she is Asian, casually remarks over his meal: "Somehow or other . . . I cannot reconcile myself to the thought that the Chinese are humans like ourselves. They may have immortal souls, but their faces seem to be so utterly devoid of expression that I cannot help but doubt." A fellow diner, the town clerk, chimes in: "Souls. . . . Their bodies are enough for me. A Chinaman is, in my eyes, more repulsive than a nigger." As the conversation continues ("I wouldn't have one in my house," declares Sui Sin Far's landlady), Sui Sin Far fights her temptation to hide:

A miserable, cowardly feeling keeps me silent. . . If I declare what I am, every person in the place will hear about it the next day. The population is in the main made up of working folks with strong prejudices against my mother's countrymen. The prospect before me is not an enviable one—if I speak. I have no longer an ambition to die at the stake for the sake of demonstrating the greatness and nobleness of the Chinese people.

But she cannot remain silent. Her boss asks, "What makes Miss Far so quiet?," and she lifts her eyes with great effort to stare into his: "Mr. K, . . . the Chinese people may have no souls, no expression on their faces, be altogether beyond the pale of civilization, but whatever they are, I want you to understand that I am—I am a Chinese" ("Leaves," p. 129). Speaking up, this passage says, is extremely difficult. Sui Sin Far is not a fighter because resistance comes easily for her. She thinks back on the "attacks of nervous sickness" she suffered as a child, and says: "In the light of the present I know that the cross of the Eurasian bore too heavily upon my childish shoulders" ("Leaves," p. 127). Racism literally made her sick as a child, and no doubt ruined her health as an adult. But being quiet, for Sui Sin Far, is not an acceptable alternative. For her, as for Frances Ellen Harper or Pauline Hopkins, the imperative to break silence has to take precedence over the seduction of remaining quiet.

Being sexual prey also forms a constant part of Sui Sin Far's world. Working in the West Indies, she becomes the target of white men's advances when it becomes known that she is "not all white." Although most of these encounters, she claims, simply amuse her, it is revealing that the one on which she spends time as a writer in "Leaves" clearly does not. She reports in detail the insulting come-on of a "big, blond, handsome" naval officer who sends his card up to her room (she assumes he has some news story for her as a reporter). He lounges on the hotel veranda when she appears and responds to her sharp statement that she is in a hurry:

> "Oh, you don't really mean that," he answers, with another silly and offensive laugh. "There's always plenty of time for good times. That's what I am here for. I saw you at the races the other day and twice at King's House. My ship will be here——weeks."
>
> "Do you wish that noted?" I ask.
>
> "Oh, no! Why—I came just because I had an idea that you might like to know me. I would like to know you. You look such a nice little body. Say, wouldn't you like to go out for a sail this lovely night? I will tell you all about the sweet little Chinese girls I met when we were in Hong Kong. They're not so shy!" ("Leaves," p. 130)

Sui Sin Far breaks the narrative at this point. She draws seven dots across a white space on the page and resumes her story far away in eastern Canada. In the resumption, however, she is sick, severely underweight, and worried about making enough money from her writing to support herself. That is, the break on the page and the switch in focus say as much as or more than a direct comment from the author might. As a woman of color in racist territories—whether the United States, the West Indies, or Canada—Sui Sin Far speaks out at severe risk to her physical well-being. While she presents her story as one of triumphant survival, and it certainly is that, it is also a story of painful rootlessness and loneliness—of constantly being on the move—and of sickness, sexual threats, endless searching, and debilitating fighting.

Mainly what Sui Sin Far searches for in "Leaves," as in her fiction, is an identity that is both Chinese and western. Clearly, she cherishes her mother's combination of cultures: "She sings us the songs she learned at her English school. She tells us tales of China" ("Leaves," p. 128). But Sui Sin Far is not her mother; she is not a Chinese émigré. Nor is she her father, completely a westerner. She feels different from both.

> I do not confide in my father and mother. They would not understand. How could they? He is English, she is Chinese. I am different to both of them—a stranger, tho [sic] their own child. "What are we?" I ask my brother. "It doesn't matter, sissy," he responds. But it does. ("Leaves," p. 128)

White people reject her because she is part Chinese; Chinese people reject her because she is part Caucasian ("Leaves," p. 129). As a child she reads voraciously about China; as an adult she wishes she could speak and understand Chinese but she does not know how ("Leaves," pp. 128, 131). The last words of "Leaves" contain an overt plea for tolerance and then, in a return to the essay's ubiquitous imagery of battle and resistance, the hope that she will be allowed to survive: "I give my right hand to the Occidentals and my left to the Orientals, hoping that between them they will not utterly destroy the insignificant 'connecting link.' And that's all" ("Leaves," p. 132).

Mrs. Spring Fragrance transforms into fiction many of the conflicts and tensions that Sui Sin Far knew personally. The book embodies her effort as an artist to explain in some of its full complexity what it means to be Chinese American. As Amy Ling points out, the goal was pioneering: "No one before her had written so sympathetically and so extensively about the Chinese in America, and never before from this far inside."⁴ Part of Sui Sin Far's purpose as a writer, like Harper or Gilman or Hopkins, was clearly political. Although her stories at times deal in clichés, they also counter stereotypes with realistically drawn portraits of Chinese, Chinese American, and Caucasian American people, and many of the pieces explicitly address issues of racial discrimination, exploitation, and abuse. In addition, the volume celebrates some of the ordinary joys and pleasures in the lives of Chinese Americans, dramatizes acts of heroism, kindness, and compassion within the Chinese American community, and satirizes pomposity and vanity in whomever they appear.

Composed out of previously published stories, *Mrs. Spring Fragrance* is divided in two parts: seventeen stories under the heading "MRS. SPRING FRAGRANCE" and twenty under the heading "TALES OF CHINESE CHILDREN." The two halves work together to develop for different audiences a number of shared themes, such as admiration for acts of loyalty and sacrifice or of outrage at racial bigotry. But they are also highly separable because of their distinct audiences. In general, the children's stories teach readily apparent morals and explain the world, often in animal fables. In contrast, the "MRS. SPRING FRAGRANCE"stories, which will be my concern, have more complicated moral contours and fall into an implicit two-part structure. The first eight stories concentrate on interactions between Chinese Americans and white Americans, particularly women. The last nine stories focus more exclusively on life and issues within the Chinese American community; if white people are present, they are usually on the periphery as the enemy or the problem, or they appear primarily as representatives of the bigger context. One effect of this two-part grouping is to create a subtle but pervasive argument or premise. Sui Sin Far's structure seems to say that in order to focus on and understand Chinese American experiences within the community itself, the issue of the dominant culture's power and interference, especially that of emancipated white women, must be confronted first.

The premise has historical validity. The principal white people carrying moral uplift and Christianity into America's Chinatowns at the end of the nineteenth century and early in the twentieth were women, missionaries and reformers committed to "saving" Asians in the United States, who were mostly men, from lives of sin, drug addiction, and despair. The Chinese Exclusion Act of 1882 and its renewals had effectively stranded large numbers of Chinese men in the United States. If they returned to China, they could not reenter the States, yet if they stayed they had no hope of reunion with the wives and children whom they had left in their homeland and who were now barred by law from entering the U.S. Ghettoized in Chinatowns and exploited economically as cheap labor, the men were condemned by the legal and social structure to lifelong bachelorhood (racial intermarriage was illegal, and at the turn of the century only 5 percent of the Chinese in California, for example, were women). The morality and welfare of these men and of the Chinese American families that did exist became a "cause" for philanthropic white women, especially churchwomen, who ran missions in the Chinatowns. On the historical level, then,

Sui Sin Far's attention to white women's interference and influence, conscious and unconscious, in the Chinese community was well founded.[5]

However, the fact that she does not talk about churchwomen but about secular, apparently unaffiliated white women, and especially white feminists, was probably more personal. As a liberated, self-sufficient Chinese American woman at the turn of the century—she worked, traveled, lived alone, and supported herself financially—Sui Sin Far obviously resented white feminists' presumption of authority when it came to defining women's issues. As I will examine later, a major theme in the first half of *Mrs. Spring Fragrance* is criticism not only of white racism but specifically of the arrogance and ethnocentricity of white feminism.

Although well disguised, the beginning of *Mrs. Spring Fragrance* is autobiographical and defiant. Sui Fin Far opens the book by writing about writing. In stories that appear light and frothy but that in fact mount a serious argument, she takes on Anglo-American literary tradition at its very pinnacle—Tennyson—and lays claim to the Chinese American woman's right to write.

In the first story, "Mrs. Spring Fragrance," we meet the young, happily married Chinese American couple, Mr. and Mrs. Spring Fragrance. He is busy trying to make sense of lines he overhears his wife quoting from "a beautiful American poem written by a noble American named Tennyson. . .":

> 'Tis better to have loved and lost,
> Than never to have loved at all.[6]

She is busy matchmaking for a young friend who wants to follow the American custom of marrying for love rather than the Chinese custom of arranged marriages. At first, the literary joke lands on the Spring Fragrances. She doesn't realize that Tennyson is English not American. He doesn't understand what the two celebrated lines of English poetry mean. We find ourselves in the presence of a familiar cliché—ignorant, laughable foreigners struggling to understand what is completely obvious to "us," the enlightened insiders. As the story goes on, however, the butt of the joke starts to shift. The laugh begins to fall not on them but on the lines of poetry and the very idea of separate national traditions on which the joke is based. As we repeatedly hear Tennyson identified as American, we must begin to wonder what the English/American distinction means anyway. What makes Tennyson "English" and not "American," really? The poetry actually is—as Mary Austin would totally agree—all in the same tradition: Distinctions essential to separating British and mainstream white American literary lines are miniscule when looked at globally. Indeed, *is* white American literature different from British if considered from an Asian American point of view? How?

Even more heretical, Mr. Spring Fragrance decides that Tennyson's lines are dumb. (Tennyson dumb? That's like calling Milton boring.) " 'Tis better to have loved and lost,/ Than never to have loved at all" expresses a ridiculous sentiment in his view. It is not better to have loved and lost than never to have loved at all, Mr. Spring Fragrance insists:

"The truth of the teaching! . . . There is no truth in it whatever. It is disobedient to reason. Is it not better to have what you do not love than to love what you do not have?''. . . He turned away to muse upon the unwisdom of the American way of looking at things. (*MSF,* p. 5)

Sui Sin Far is having fun with Mr. Spring Fragrance, whom she makes hot-headed and obstinate. But she is also having serious fun with us. She is forcing us to think about American literature and sentimentality from a place outside white western consciousness. When we do that, mainstream American literature (which really *is* Anglo, of course) clearly emerges as the product of just one ethnic point of view. The Tennyson joke, very early in *Mrs. Spring Fragrance,* starts undermining, inch by inch, our monolithic confidence about what American literature is, what it says, and who writes it.

Against this shift in perspective Sui Sin Far introduces the first and most important writer in her book: not a man and not a white person but an Asian American woman. Her subject, only thinly satirically veiled, is her right to think for herself independent of two particular kinds of people: white women and Asian men.

Away on a trip, Mrs. Spring Fragrance sends her husband this pretty piece of writing:

> GREAT AND HONORED MAN,—Greeting from your plum blossom, who is desirous of hiding herself from the sun of your presence for a week of seven days more. My honorable cousin is preparing for the Fifth Moon Festival, and wishes me to compound for the occasion some American "fudge," for which delectable sweet, made by my clumsy hands, you have sometimes shown a slight prejudice. I am enjoying a most agreeable visit, and American friends, as also our own, strive benevolently for the accomplishment of my pleasure. Mrs. Samuel Smith, an American lady, known to my cousin, asked for my accompaniment to a maniloquent lecture the other evening. The subject was "America, the Protector of China!" It was most exhilarating, and the effect of so much expression of benevolence leads me to beg of you to forget to remember that the barber charges you one dollar for a shave while he humbly submits to the American man a bill of fifteen cents. And murmur no more because your honored elder brother, on a visit to this country, is detained under the roof-tree of this great Government instead of under your own humble roof. Console him with the reflection that he is protected under the wing of the Eagle, the Emblem of Liberty. What is the loss of ten hundred years or ten thousand times ten dollars compared with the happiness of knowing oneself so securely sheltered? All of this I have learned from Mrs. Samuel Smith, who is as brilliant and great of mind as one of your own superior sex. (*MSF,* pp. 8–9)

This letter, as Amy Ling points out, allows Sui Sin Far subtly "to protest not only the arrogance of Americans toward Chinese but also of husbands toward wives." As Ling puts it, Mrs. Spring Fragrance uses the occasion to draw

> a parallel between her misguided friend, who thought she would find this pompous lecture edifying, and her know-it-all husband, who is always critical of her actions. In other words, racism and sexism are rooted in the same error: the belief that one is innately superior to another. As a Chinese American woman, Mrs. Spring Fragrance must endure the superior attitudes of white people in general and of Chinese American men as well.[7]

It can certainly be said that in the character of Mrs. Spring Fragrance, as her letter illustrates, Sui Sin Far deflates the most common stereotype of the Chinese

American wife, that of the docile, housebound, domestic ornament, only to play into the hands of another, that of the ever-cheerful manipulative busybody. But it is also important to notice that she shows in a figure usually dismissed as trivial and laughable (or simply irritating) the engines of resistance. That is, she herself manipulates the stereotype of manipulativeness to serve her own serious political agenda. She deals with the form at her disposal (the lovely Chinese wife) much as Mrs. Spring Fragrance deals with the form at hers (the lovely, wifely letter). Subversively.

Placed at the front of the book, this writing within the writing in Sui Sin Far's text accomplishes two important tasks. It identifies Mrs. Spring Fragrance's struggle for independence from the two groups who feel entitled to tell her what to think, white women and Asian men. And it teaches us how to approach the art of *Mrs. Spring Fragrance*. The woman writer within the woman's writing—Mrs. Spring Fragrance within Sui Sin Far's text—crafts a lovely, properly humble, and even in places stereotypically "Chinesified" description of her experiences that is in fact full of attack. Just barely beneath the surface of this sweet, dutiful document she places pointed, independent opinion and criticism. Clearly this letter, appearing in the volume's initial story, offers a sly model of the method of the whole. "Nice" as Sui Sin Far's book appears, it—like the pretty composition by the woman writer in the volume's opening piece—contains a strong, independent, critical voice that is not going to be controlled either by officious white women or by superior Asian men.

Having laid her groundwork with jokes and hints in the first story, Sui Sin Far comes out in the open in her second, "The Inferior Woman." Mrs. Spring Fragrance announces that she will become an author. She muses: "Many American women wrote books. Why should not a Chinese? She would write a book about Americans for her Chinese women friends. The American people were so interesting and mysterious" (*MSF*, p. 22). Even more blatantly turning on its head the white stereotype of "mysterious," exotic Asians, she exclaims: "Ah, these Americans! These mysterious, inscrutable, incomprehensible Americans! Had I the divine right of learning I would put them into an immortal book!" (*MSF*, p. 31). Assured by her husband that one does not need the divine right of learning to write books in America, Mrs. Spring Fragrance is delighted and begs him to wait a minute. Wary, he "eyed her for a moment with suspicion," but she unruffles him:

> "As I have told you, O Great Man . . . I desire to write an immortal book, and now that I have learned from you that it is not necessary to acquire the 'divine right of learning' in order to accomplish things, I will begin the work without delay. My first subject will be 'The Inferior Woman of America.' Please advise me how I shall best inform myself concerning her." (*MSF*, pp. 32–33)

(Mr. Spring Fragrance, always secure in his superior wisdom, is only too glad to accommodate.) At the end of the story Mrs. Spring Fragrance bluntly reiterates: "The American woman writes books about the Chinese. Why not a Chinese woman write books about the Americans?" (*MSF*, p. 41).[8]

This story asserts the Chinese American woman's right to write and names her two major subjects from Sui Sin Far's point of view: Americans and The Inferior

Woman. Each has multiple meanings. Mrs. Spring Fragrance plans to write about Americans, by which she means white Americans. But behind her, Sui Sin Far is already writing not only about white Americans but also about Chinese Americans, such as Mrs. Spring Fragrance herself—thus expanding and rewriting the definition of "Americans" even as her protagonist audaciously decides to make some of them, members of the dominant race, her subject. Likewise the literary topic of The Inferior Woman can mean more than one thing. To Mrs. Spring Fragrance the Inferior Woman in America is the white New Woman of the working class who is "inferior" in the eyes of white feminists of the middle and upper-middle class. To Sui Sin Far standing behind Mrs. Spring Fragrance, the Inferior Woman is both the white working-class New Woman considered "inferior" by snobbish middle-class white feminists, *and* the Chinese American woman such as Mrs. Spring Fragrance (and Sui Sin Far herself), who is widely considered "inferior" by the dominant culture. In short, the simple image of the title "The Inferior Woman" gets complicated. Who is Inferior and who is Superior grow murky. And that is Sui Sin Far's point, of course, in this story about the importance of an Asian American woman being able to inscribe her own story: to define America and American from her point of view and to name her experiences and herself for herself and for others.

The tragedy of not having that power consumes Sui Sin Far's third story, "The Widsom of the New." The story completes the book's opening focus on speech, silence, and authority. If the first two pieces in *Mrs. Spring Fragrance* are playful, even funny, this one is deadly serious. It is about female voicelessness and ends in death.

Pau Lin, after staying behind in China for seven years, comes with her son to the United States to join her husband, Wou Sankwei, who has been befriended by a benevolent older white woman who has helped Americanize him. One of his best friends is the white woman's niece, a young artist named Adah Charlton. She is an emancipated, modern American woman, and their friendship, innocent and completely normal in their eyes, enrages and humiliates Pau Lin, whose jealousy Sui Sin Far makes completely understandable. From a traditional Chinese point of view, there is no such thing as innocent friendship between a married man and a single young woman. Pau Lin can only interpret her husband and Adah's relationship as a manifestation of "the wisdom of the new," which robs her of her right as a married woman to her husband's companionship and affection. Sui Sin Far brilliantly describes the unthinking privilege of Adah Charlton, who is completely oblivious to the Chinese woman's misery: "Secure in the difference of race, in the love of many friends, and in the happiness of her chosen work, no suspicion whatever crossed her mind that the woman whose husband was her aunt's protégé tasted everything bitter because of her" (*MSF*, p. 66). Adah senses too late that her closeness to Wou Sankwei threatens his wife. Meanwhile, Wou Sankwei never takes his wife's unhappiness seriously. At the end of the story, Pau Lin murders her child to keep him from entering the American school that would alter him as America has altered his father.

This story records the pain of the Chinese woman in America who is silenced both in the dominant culture and within the Chinese American community. Dismissed by her husband, she is heard too late by the white woman artist, who paradoxically represents both the focus of Pau Lin's problem and the only person who, albeit belatedly, understands her situation. The story suggests that understanding across the language barrier is possible for a new generation of women; Adah Charlton finally realizes what Pau Lin is feeling. But it also says that such understanding may come too late. In the meantime, deep, permanent damage is taking place. The collusion of Adah's aunt and Wou Sankwei in an Americanization that does not extend to women produces tragedy. Indeed, the person most responsible is Adah's aunt, Mrs. Dean, the philanthropic white woman who sets the situation up and then, in effect, disappears. Her ethnocentric benevolence is not simply misguided. It leads to death. Literally unable to speak and be heard except by her husband, who ignores her, Pau Lin can articulate her resistance only through violence.

A major problem in this story, as in others in *Mrs. Spring Fragrance*, is Sui Sin Far's idealization of Chinese men. Wou Sankwei's overnight reform into a sensitive, understanding husband who contritely forgives his wife for the murder of their son is not believable. The characterization suggests that Sui Sin Far is as romantic and out-of-touch in her perspective on Chinese men as the do-gooder white women she attacks in her stories. If Chinese men are so miraculously forgiving and caring, why do Chinese women in Sui Sin Far's fiction—or in real life—have any problems?[9]

How aware of it she was we cannot say, but Sui Sin Far's dilemma as a writer is not hard to imagine. It is a dilemma constantly faced by women of color in the United States. At the turn of the century the dominant culture was filled with vicious, racist stereotypes of Chinese men. To admit any flaws in them beyond the most minor foibles was to give the racist script credibility. Yet to say that they had no significant flaws was to cooperate in Chinese women's oppression. Sui Sin Far's negotiation of this minefield was not always successful. Ironically, it can be argued that her own "Americanization"—her distance from the day-to-day lives of Chinese women in the United States—in combination with her desire to counteract racist stereotypes of Chinese men as tyrants and brutes led her to exaggerate in the opposite direction. Too often she presents unrealistically ideal male characters and, therefore, an inaccurately "benevolent" view of gender relations in the Chinese community.

However, if the argument of Wou Sankwei's story in "The Wisdom of the New" is hard to accept, the meaning of Pau Lin's is not. As a story about creativity, silencing, and death, "The Wisdom of the New" is also about art. Denied voice, Pau Lin murders her son, her most wonderful creation; she renders herself barren, without offspring. It is more than accidental here, I think, that Sui Sin Far, in her acknowledgment to *Mrs. Spring Fragrance*, speaks with great tenderness of her stories as her "children" whom she sent "out into the world," her "dear ones" who have been allowed to live in magazines and are now returning to her "to be grouped together within this volume" (*MSF*, p. vii). If we extend this metaphor, we can think not only of Sui Sin Far's art as her children, the products of her flesh and blood that are mercifully allowed to live and come home to her, but also, conversely, of Pau Lin's child as her art, the product of her flesh and blood that, cruelly, is allowed to live only if it is so transformed and deformed that it turns against rather than expresses its creator. That is, the murder of the child in "The Wisdom of the New," in addition to signifying a real death, represents as well the murder of Chinese women's art in America. Using a white American woman artist as foil, Adah Charlton, the story speaks of the deathly, "barren," deeply unnatural silence into which potential artists like Pau Lin have been plunged by a racist, sexist culture.

Voice and voicelessness, speech and silence, who has the authority to name and shape the Chinese American woman's experiences and who does not—these are the issues that open *Mrs. Spring Fragrance*. Sui Sin Far's method is cautious and indirect. As people in risky situations often must, she uses humor and allegory to suggest her meaning, to assert her claim to authority in a hostile environment. Assert it she does, however, and the volume's subsequent stories branch out in various directions. The remaining stories in the first half of the "MRS. SPRING FRA-GRANCE" section continue to examine relationships between Chinese Americans and Caucasian Americans and to concentrate on women's experiences.

In "Its Wavering Image" a young woman of mixed Asian and white parentage embraces her Chinese ancestry and cultural identity after being exploited and be-trayed by a young white newspaperman who prints information that she gave him confidentially about the Chinese community. "The Gift of Little Me" praises the devotion of a white American woman who lives and works in Chinatown as a schoolteacher and is wrongfully accused of kidnapping a Chinese baby. "The Story of One White Woman Who Married a Chinese" develops openly Sui Sin Far's criticism of white middle-class feminism, portraying it as a culturally and class-biased ideology that is arrogant and authoritarian in its ethnocentricity (in fact, the story identifies white middle-class feminism as a male rather than a female political project). Its sequel, "Her Chinese Husband," also flies in the face of stereotypes. Painting a very positive picture of a Chinese American man, it shows that a young white woman enjoys more true freedom, as well as an undemeaning dependence, in her marriage to him than she did in her earlier marriage to a supposedly eman-cipated white American man. Rather than expect her to masculinize herself, as her first husband had demanded, the young woman's Chinese husband respects and shares with her values and activities that are denigrated in the dominant culture as feminine: cooking, sewing, being with children, talking about feelings. Sexual pas-sion, frequently the pretext for the sexual domination and exploitation of women in hierarchical heterosexual society, does not constitute the center of their relationship. Instead, at the heart of their bond is a genuine emotional compatibility and rapport. The last story in this first section, "The Americanizing of Pau Tsu," reiterates the theme of "The Wisdom of the New," but does not end in death. Both the Ameri-canized Chinese husband and his friend, the modern young white woman, come to realize how their friendship wounds and renders invisible the Chinese wife who is not included in it.[10]

The nine stories that complete the "MRS. SPRING FRAGRANCE" section of the book also deal with discrimination and Anglo-Asian conflicts and problems, but they generally focus on relationships among Chinese Americans. "The Chinese Lily" celebrates the loyalty of a brother to his sister and the heroic sacrifice made for her by the woman he loves. "The God of Restoration" shows the betrayal of trust between cousins in America and supports the traditional Chinese idea that romantic love is not sufficient reason to ignore family duties. "The Smuggling of

Tie Co'' and ''Tian Shan's Kindred Spirit'' are both love stories set against the backdrop of illegal border crossings and the threat of deportation. In one story a young woman dressed as a man sacrifices herself to protect the smuggler she secretly loves; in the other a young woman (also dressed as a man) gets herself caught by border police in order to be deported with the man she loves. ''The Sing Song Woman'' shows the generous friendship of an unrespectable woman for another woman. ''The Three Souls of Ah So Nan'' illustrates the wisdom of not following traditional customs if no one is hurt by the deviation. ''The Prize China Baby'' tells of a poor and powerless woman's decision to enter her child in a mission contest in an effort to gain control over her life and keep her baby, whom her husband plans to give away. ''Lin John'' records a brother's labor to make enough money to buy his sister out of concubinage, only to learn that she has no desire to be liberated. ''In the Land of the Free' relates in depressing detail a Chinese couple's fight to get their baby out of a United States government immigration detention orphanage.

Thematically, these stories present a range of issues and perspectives. Some address white manipulation and exploitation of Chinese people in the United States. Others show friendships between white people and Chinese people. Still others show friendships, but the emphasis falls on how problematic such bonds are. Certain stories celebrate immigrant life in the United States (the Spring Fragrances' happiness), and certain stories dramatize a strong yearning to return to China—to leave North America forever. There is rage at U.S. government policies in the fiction. There is hope that the Chinese family can survive the pressures of dissolution in the New World. There is also hope that the family will adapt and change in some ways. Contempt for stereotypes is a frequent theme—and yet often rising out of that contempt are characterizations of Chinese men that, ironically, err in the opposite direction. Frequently there is anger at middle-class white feminism. Just as frequently, there is pride in Chinese American women's own strength and courageous self-definitions.

Perhaps most fascinating, however, are *Mrs. Spring Fragrance*'s images of female cross-dressing, rebellion, and secret, subversive writing that invite us to reflect on Sui Sin Far's own story as the first woman of Chinese heritage in the United States to publicly and successfully make writing about Chinese American experiences her life's work. Composed of many pieces, the panorama of *Mrs. Spring Fragrance* is sweeping and evocative. The book constantly shifts its focus rather than concentrate in depth on one individual's experience. What Sui Sin Far offers is a collection of lives, not an intensive anatomy of one life.

Because *Mrs. Spring Fragrance* does not fall generically within the most preferred category of modern western fiction, the novel, the question has been raised as to how successful Sui Sin Far was as an artist. S. E. Solberg develops the idea that she

> was trapped by experience and inclination into working within a sub-genre of American prose; what, for lack of a better term, we might call Chinatown Tales. Such classification by subject matter (Chinatown, or more broadly, the Chinese in America) breaks down an established literary form, the novel, into sub-genres defined by content, not form or stylistic skill. Eaton, by choosing to identify with and write

about the Chinese, found herself alone in an essentially formless field. . . . [She] did manage to dip into . . . deeper currents beneath the surface color [of Chinatown], but no matter what she saw and understood, there was no acceptable form to shape it to. Had she been physically stronger and had a more sophisticated literary apprenticeship, she might have been able to create that new form. As it was, she was defeated. . . . When she turned her hand to fiction the possible was limited by the acceptable. . . . She never acquired the control of style necessary to deal with her subjects in depth and length. What she wrote were chiefly sketches, vignettes. . . . [She was] trapped in the stylistic conventions of the time."[11]

It may be that Sui Sin Far was trapped. Possibly she published only short fiction because she was not able to write novels. Since her sister did write novels with Japanese settings and did well publishing them, perhaps Sui Sin Far was forced to stick to short fiction because of the bigotry in the United States against Chinese at the turn of the century. We might theorize that the reading public could be counted on to digest a story here and there about Chinese Americans but not a long novel, and therefore Sui Sin Far was severely limited as an artist by the market, or the publishers' concept of it.[12]

It is also possible, however, to argue that Sui Sin Far succeeded at what she attempted—that she did not share the midtwentieth-century bias against short fiction, sketches, and vignettes as inferior "sub-genres" of the novel. We can hypothesize, in other words, that she found in the literary tradition of short fiction and the sketch—a primarily feminine tradition also used to great advantage by Sarah Orne Jewett, Alice Dunbar-Nelson, and Mary Austin, as well as by men such as W. E. B. Du Bois and Sherwood Anderson—formal possibilities that enabled rather than stunted her. Houston Baker argues of the Harlem Renaissance that as long as we continue to ask, "Why did it fail?," our analyses can be predicted to prove failure, when in fact, if the Harlem Renaissance is approached on its own terms rather than on those of white modernism, tremendous success emerges as the reality.[13] The same can be said of Sui Sin Far. If we approach her as a writer who succeeded rather than failed at what she did—if we do not judge her automatically by aesthetic criteria that are appropriate to white modernism but probably not to her, such as textual opacity and intellectual ambiguity—what do we see?

It seems to me that Sui Sin Far found in the short story and sketch, and then in the collecting of those forms into *Mrs. Spring Fragrance*, a way of expressing a variety of Chinese American experiences and issues. As I have pointed out, unifying themes certainly exist: the clash between Anglo and Chinese values and customs; the institutionalization of anti-Chinese racism in the United States; the irrelevance and even destructiveness of white feminism to the Chinese community; the heroism and courage of Chinese women; the power of whites who exploit and demean Chinese people but also of some who admire and respect Chinese values; the need for Chinese Americans, especially children, to remember and honor the ways of their ancestors; the wisdom and beauty of traditional Chinese stories; the need in some situations to abandon traditional ways. However, it may not be the thickness of this thematic fabric, finally, that makes *Mrs. Spring Fragrance* as interesting as its breadth of perspective. What the short story and sketch forms allow Sui Sin Far to do is to present many different people's stories, with the cumulative effect in

Mrs. Spring Fragrance of giving us a glimpse into a community bound together by shared traditions and problems but composed of individual lives, no one more important than another. The genre that Sandra Zagarell names "the narrative of community," although it does not fit exactly, applies usefully here. Unlike the conventional western novel, which usually privileges the story of one individual's life, *Mrs. Spring Fragrance*, as a collection of stories, focuses on many individuals' lives. Occupying its center is not, as in standard western long narratives, the all-important individual, but rather the configuration of figures who make up a group.[14]

Did Sui Sin Far "intend" the collective or communal form I have been describing? It seems safe to assume that it was she who arranged the book into its two-part structure and further organized the first half thematically. Still, we know that she did not compose the parts of *Mrs. Spring Fragrance* for the volume, but collected already published pieces into the book. And doesn't that method of composition generally preclude the possibility of meaningful, coherent form governing the whole?

People, especially women and poor people, have been making coherent, meaningfully unified art—new original wholes—out of existing, collected, "found" pieces, whether of food, fabric, or plants, for as long as we know. It is only a recent and very specific notion of literary art that finds all fiction not patterned on the grand western novel springing Athena-like from its author's mind minor and disappointing. Sui Sin Far, like Jewett and Dunbar-Nelson, may very well have wished that she could write a big, impressive novel. It is reported that she had a novel in manuscript at the time of her death.[15] In any case, I think that we can say that she, again like Jewett and Dunbar-Nelson and Austin too, did succeed at something else. Amy Ling draws a loose parallel between *Mrs. Spring Fragrance* and *Winesburg, Ohio*, and the comparison is a good one. My argument is that Sui Sin Far did not flounder in a formless field. Instead, like Jewett before her and Anderson after her, she manipulated to her advantage the tradition of regional and sketch fiction that she inherited primarily from women to offer not a long narrative about one individual but a multifaceted, collective narrative about a group of people and a network of issues. We can and should speculate on what Sui Sin Far might have accomplished as an artist if her life had been easier and longer. At the same time, we need to recognize that *Mrs. Spring Fragrance* is an important, highly original, coherent work of fiction in and of itself. It is impressive in its thematic range, its carefully controlled anger (a necessity given the racist climate in which Sui Sin Far wrote), and its political honesty, especially about feminism. It is also, I think, extremely successful in its formal challenge to the dominant western bias in favor of the individual-focused novel as the only or best way to tell people's stories.

On these issues of art, voice, and form in *Mrs. Spring Fragrance*, I have deliberately saved until last what are for me the two most complicated and perhaps unanswerable questions about Sui Sin Far and her work.

First, what do we make of the material reality of the volume: the literal encoding of difference into every page of the book—the very paper on which Sui Sin Far's words appear? As Amy Ling describes the book:

> The pages are gray-green, lightly imprinted with a Chinese-style painting of a crested bird on a branch of bamboo, a flowering branch of plum and the Chinese characters

for Happiness, Prosperity, and Longevity vertically descending along the right side. Eaton's stories, some appropriately charming and lively, others, however, striking ironic, even bitter, notes, are printed on these delicately decorated sheets.[16]

Did Sui Sin Far like this paper? Was she consulted? Or did she resent the infusion of femininity and Orientalism, the two collapsed into one visual statement on every page of her book? Although the novels by Sui Sin Far's sister are also printed on decorated paper, no other text that I am referring to in this study, though many of them have illustrations, bears the literal, page-by-page marking of difference that *Mrs. Spring Fragrance* does. How do we read this?

It has been my assumption throughout that artists choose their forms, whether out of conscious reaction to conventional expectations or out of less-than-conscious but nonetheless purposeful desires to manipulate existing forms and adapt them to their own needs and ends. Sui Sin Far's book rattles my assumption. Although I do think that the book's internal design and the author's use of the short story and sketch tradition can fruitfully be considered within a framework of choice, it is not at all clear whether the most obvious and inescapable formal choice of the book—its insistently "Orientalized," hyperfeminized pages—came from the author or the publisher.

Since a book's format and production are usually the province of publishers, the decorated paper in *Mrs. Spring Fragrance* was probably not Sui Sin Far's idea. But that still leaves the question of what she thought of it. We could reason from her autobiographical essay and from her stories that she hated the paper because it renders her work exotic and unserious. Her published words—her creations—have to compete on every page with the background noise of stereotypic Orientalization. But we could argue just as logically that she loved the paper. It brings to the narrow, unimaginative form of the conventional western book a constant reminder of difference, of other languages—literally, Chinese characters and beautiful images from nature—that the west works hard to eradicate. It is even possible that the whole issue as an issue did not provoke much or any reaction from her—that it is more of an issue for us than it was for her. The point is that we cannot say. Talking about the art of Sui Sin Far, like talking about her life, must at this time remain open to a considerable degree of inconclusiveness.

Which brings me to my second and last hard question: how to understand the author's name, something that we can usually leave beyond interrogation. Contemporary criticism is indecisive over whether to call her Edith Eaton or Sui Sin Far; some readers use one name, some the other, and some interchange. I consistently use Sui Sin Far because that is the name she published under and that is how she refers to herself in her autobiographical essay. More important, there is the question of what Sui Sin Far means—and to whom. The words translated mean "Water Fragrant Flower or Narcissus"[17]; and Sui Sin Far, calling one of her characters in *Mrs. Spring Fragrance* "Sin Far," tells us that the name means "Pure Flower, or Chinese Lily" (*MSF*, p. 281). Yet two words in the pseudonym Sui Sin Far, if it is a pseudonym (in her autobiographical essay she has people address her by that name as a child),[18] have clear meanings in English: sin and far. While these two words may be camouflaged for western readers to whom the whole name looks convincingly eastern, they can leap out at a person from China, to whom the name may not look very Chinese at all.[19]

The custom in China is to give people positive names. While the various flower translations of the words *Sui Sin Far* conform to that tradition, the English words *sin* and *far* certainly do not. Add to them the meaning of *sui* in Latin, ''of herself,'' and a cryptic phrase made up of western words hovers within the Anglicized Chinese name. The phrase might read, ''Of sin far herself.'' If Sui Sin Far chose this name as a penname, did she build hidden levels into it? Is the name her first way of stating her subject as an artist, her audacity as a woman of Chinese ancestry in the west to sin far from what is expected of her, to break the commandment of silence imposed on her as an Asian woman?

Whatever we conclude, the name demands that we read it, that we see in it simultaneous Chinese and English possibilities. As such it is the perfect introduction to the author's work. Sui Sin Far's subject is not Chinese experience, not American experience, but Chinese American experience: a new, doubled (like her name) awareness/reality that is both beautiful—the lily—and outcast and disobedient— the sinning far. (Recall Austin's comfortress Eve.) The author's deceptively simple name on the cover and first pages of the flamboyantly Orientalized volume, *Mrs. Spring Fragrance*, suggests that writing in code may have been as essential for Sui Sin Far as it was for Frances Ellen Harper or Gertrude Stein.

8 Art: Willa Cather, the Woman Writer as Artist, and Humishuma

> The lover is as well done as he could be when a woman writes in the man's character,—it must always, I believe, be something of a masquerade . . . and you could almost have done it as yourself—a woman could love her in the same protecting way—a woman could even care enough to wish to take her away from such a life, by some means or other.
>
> SARAH ORNE JEWETT TO WILLA CATHER[1]

> Very often the words are merely the punctuation of thought; rather, the crests of the long waves of inter-communicative silences.
>
> MARY AUSTIN[2]

As is obvious by now, I am sure, when Willa Cather made the heroine of *The Song of the Lark* (1915) an artist, she was not making an unusual choice. In fiction by women at the turn of the century, the figure of the woman artist appears almost obsessively. Iola Leroy wants to be a writer, as does the protagonist of "The Yellow Wallpaper." The narrator of *The Country of the Pointed Firs* is a writer. The heroine of Edith Wharton's first novel, *The Touchstone* (1900), is a famous author. A principal character in Hopkins's *Contending Forces* is named for the poet Sappho, and the heroine in *Of One Blood* is a singer. The main female character of Ellen Glasgow's first novel, *The Descendant* (1900), is a painter; the protagonist of Kate Chopin's *The Awakening* is a would-be painter, and the supporting character Mademoiselle Reisz an accomplished musician. The heroine of Austin's *A Woman of Genius* (1912) is an actress. The title character of Sui Sin Far's *Mrs. Spring Fragrance* wishes to write. The heroine of Jessie Redmon Fauset's first novel, *There is Confusion* (1924), is a dancer, and the protagonist of her second, *Plum Bun* (1929), a painter. The heroine of Anzia Yezierska's "My Own People" in *Hungry Hearts* (1920) is a writer, and the main character of her last published novel, *All I Could Never Be* (1932), is a famous author. The protagonist of Edith Summers Kelley's *Weeds* (1923) sketches and draws. Clearly, writing about the woman artist—and my list here contains only literal examples and not all of those—compelled not only Willa Cather but almost all serious turn-of-the-century women writers.

Why?

Although the nineteenth century saw American women enter the literary marketplace in unprecedented numbers, for the most part they did so as money-making professionals rather than as artists. They did not conceive of themselves as creators expected and expecting themselves to reenvision or at the very least to explore and press against the boundaries of received western aesthetic tradition.[3] In contrast, many women coming into full possession of or launching careers in the 1890s and the following two decades defined themselves not simply as hard-working professionals but as artists. Black women sought to establish for themselves a tradition in published fiction that built on black male and selected white models but that nevertheless articulated from their own points of view the complex reality of being American, black, and female. Other women of color such as Sui Sin Far or the Native American author Humishuma likewise worked, with even fewer models, to find their own voices in fiction. Many white women writers tried to divorce themselves from the tradition of the domestic novelist that, with few exceptions (in their view), contained and trivialized women fiction writers in the United States for most of the nineteenth century.

To grasp how new, how groundbreaking and even dangerous the project seemed to many writers at the time, the silence of Harper's and Gilman's would-be artists at the very beginning of the period might well serve as symbol—or omen. Although Iola wishes to write, racism prevents her. Although the narrator of "The Yellow Wallpaper" does write, she has no audience. To these two examples can be added the would-be or actual artist-heroines of Wharton, Hopkins, Chopin, Dunbar-Nelson, Sui Sin Far, Glasgow, Fauset, Larsen, and Kelley—a number of whom end up literally dead: Wharton's Margaret Aubyn, Hopkins's Dianthe Lusk, Chopin's Edna Pontellier, Dunbar-Nelson's troubadour in "A Carnival Jangle," Larsen's Clare Kendry. Certainly the silencing of fictitious women artists evokes, as their authors doubtless intended at some level, the long history of silencing out of which their creators believed that their own voices were breaking—and into which, it might be feared, women's voices could once again subside. As a matter of fact, of course, the struggle of the woman writer in America to make art was not new at the turn of the century, any more than the portrayal of that struggle in fiction was unprecedented. Behind *Iola Leroy* and "The Yellow Wallpaper" stood major fictions about women and art. Harriet E. Wilson's *Our Nig* in 1859 had depicted Frado with her mouth literally blocked by a powerful white woman. Elizabeth Stuart Phelps's *The Story of Avis* in 1877 had shown a woman artist completely crushed by domestic obligations. What was new at the turn of the century were the number of women writers confronting the issues, the wealth of fiction they created about them, and the range of artistic freedom and experimentation that their struggles released.

Cather's position in this historical drama was typical. She published her first short story in 1892, the year that *Iola Leroy* came out, and her last novel in 1940, long after many of the women writers in this book had died and almost all of the rest had quit publishing. One way to understand her career is through her struggle as a white middle-class woman to create herself as an artist, as a creative woman who was not connected to popular nineteenth-century women writers yet was connected to a world of traditional women's values, who was not a disciple of male masters such as Henry James yet was considered their equal. As Sharon O'Brien has laid out in brilliant detail in *Willa Cather: The Emerging Voice*, this lifelong struggle, most intense from 1892 to 1912, particularly underlies the story of Willa

Cather's development as a writer in the years that led up to her debut as a novelist in 1912 when she published *Alexander's Bridge*.[4]

O'Brien explains how Cather's determination to gain self-definition and freedom as an artist had, well before *The Song of the Lark* was published in 1915, driven her through a long and often deeply self-alienating process of rejecting almost all women precursors. Her aspiration to be taken seriously as an artist had inspired in her, as in other turn-of-the-century women committed to art as their goal, a strong and frequently outspoken—indeed, often belligerent—identification with the acknowledged great writers of western tradition, who were almost all male. While this alignment in many cases generated profound self-conflict, its motivation is not mysterious. Identification with the "masters" of western literary tradition reflected ambitious women writers' desire not to be written off as second-rate or, equally devastating, curtailed in what it was assumed they could do. As much of my discussion has already detailed, most serious turn-of-the-century women writers who were determined to establish themselves as artists sought to create a public image of themselves as independent, self-directed creators emphatically not bound by historical assumptions based on gender and, for women of color, on race as well.

This resolve of turn-of-the-century women writers to define themselves, rather than *be* defined, was fundamental to their conception of themselves as artists. If Alice Dunbar-Nelson refused to comply with the white American expectation that black authors stick to dialect, then twenty years later Jessie Redmon Fauset was equally adamant about not contributing to racist agendas by writing only sexual dramas and thereby participating in the dominant culture's 1920s preoccupation with black "exoticism" and sensuality. White women also rebelled against pigeonholing. Wishing to resist definition as sentimental domestic writers, they visibly separated themselves from popular feminine tradition. Asked for an interview for the 1903 volume, *Women Authors of Our Day in Their Homes*, Edith Wharton flatly declined, to the compiler's obvious irritation; and Gertrude Atherton, who loved to shock, declared: "But I have no home. . . . The necessity to settle down would, I think, actually affect my brain. . . . Freedom is, or at least should be, essential to any artist." Lest we miss her antidomestic brief, Atherton adds, "Freedom is to be found only through an open mind and a wide and varying horizon."[5]

Along with this refusal of artistically ambitious turn-of-the-century American women writers to identify with the popular white women writers who had dominated the fiction market in the United States throughout most of the nineteenth century was their choice, fully shared by Cather, not to identify with white male American predecessors. Instead, they looked to Europe and Great Britain for their models and mentors. As if to emphasize their independence—their newness on the American scene and their status as artists—they distanced themselves from U.S. literary tradition, connecting themselves instead to an international artistic community. There were important exceptions, of course: Jewett and Harper's respect for Stowe, Wharton's obvious admiration for Hawthorne and James, Hopkins's published tribute to Lydia Maria Child.[6] (Lateral admiration such as Cather's for Jewett or Fauset's for Wharton falls in a different category.) But the generalization holds that ambitious turn-of-the-century American women writers who placed themselves historically did not as a rule invoke American authors as their most important models and mentors.

Kate Chopin, for example, although enamored of Whitman (as was Cather), was most impressed as a young woman, in the words of her biographer Per Seyersted, by her reading of "such authors as Dante, Cervantes, Corneille, Racine, Moliere, Mme. de Staël, Chateaubriand, Goethe, Coleridge, Jane Austen, Charlotte Brontë, and Longfellow." As an adult she so admired George Sand that she named her only daughter, Leila, for a character in Sand's work, and the author she cited as the most powerful example of what she wished to achieve was Maupassant. Discovering him in the 1880s, she said of his daring manipulation of form: "Here was life, not fiction; for where were the plots, the old fashioned mechanism and stage trapping that in a vague, unthinking way I had fancied were essential to the art of story making. Here was a man who had escaped from tradition and authority, who had entered into himself and looked out upon life through his own being and with his own eyes."[7] Chopin's words implicitly reject formulaic midnineteenth-century women's fiction in the United States at the same time that they shed light not only on her impulse toward formal innovation but also on that of other women writers of the period such as Jewett, Dunbar-Nelson, Austin, and Cather.

To teach herself to be a novelist in the 1890s, Ellen Glasgow likewise turned to the continent and to England. Greatly admiring British women such as the Brontës and George Eliot, and wishing very much to secure an English audience for her own work, she read Balzac, Flaubert, and Maupassant avidly. She rejected James as a model (as Cather would after her), and she named *War and Peace* as the book she admired above all others.[8] Similarly, Sarah Orne Jewett, for all her association with American sketch and local color tradition, looked across the Atlantic for inspiration. She kept pinned above her writing desk two maxims from Flaubert: "Ecrire la vie ordinaire comme on écrit l'histoire"; and "Ce n'est pas de faire rire, ni de faire pleurer, ni de vous mettre à fureur, mais d'agir à la façon de la nature, c'est à dire de faire rêver."[9] According to Cather, Jewett, who applied the term "great" to almost no one, made exceptions of Flaubert and Tolstoi, and the last author she was reading before she died was Conrad.[10]

Although Jessie Redmon Fauset explicitly named W. E. B. Du Bois and Edith Wharton as "models" for aspiring writers, she placed them in the company of four Englishmen: Shaw, Galsworthy, Conrad, and Pater. In 1923 she admonished teachers to introduce students to these writers as stylists to imitate.[11] Likewise Wharton's own list of models and mentors, as they show up in her book-length discussion of literary art, *The Writing of Fiction* (1924), is emphatically not American. Except for a mention of *The Scarlet Letter* and several references to Henry James, the writers about whom she talks are Balzac, Stendhal, Tolstoi, Austen, Thackeray, Eliot, Dickens, Scott, Flaubert, Dostoievsky, the Brontës, Turgenev, Conrad, Kipling, and Proust.

Given this context, it should come as no surprise that the writers that Willa Cather keeps coming back to in her collection *Not Under Forty* (1936) are also British and European. Except for substantial essays on Katherine Mansfield and Jewett, the former a contemporary and not American and the latter an author whom she knew personally and did greatly admire, the literary world she invokes is made up primarily of Balzac, Flaubert, Stendhal, Dumas, Merimee, Hardy, Conrad, Turgenev, Tolstoi, Proust, and Mann.

Reinforcing this widespread identification with British and European models is the conscious articulation of high ambition that shows up repeatedly in the lives and work of artistically aspirant turn-of-the-century women writers, including Cather. Alice Dunbar-Nelson declared that she not only aimed to surpass George Washington Cable as a Southern writer, but she also wished to write the best novel ever written.[12] Glasgow openly admitted her desire to be famous—toying at the same time with the idea that neglect might be the real sign of greatness.[13] Larsen wrote from Spain while on a Guggenheim fellowship: "I do so want to be famous."[14] Chopin chafed at not being taken seriously by those around her, complaining after the appearance of her fourth book: "How hard it is for one's acquaintances and friends to realize that one's books are to be taken seriously."[15] Yezierska protested in disgust to a Hollywood producer: "I'm not a *professional* writer. I am ———." (Certainly "artist" is the missing term.)[16] Stein situated herself among avant garde painters and artists. Sui Sin Far made jokes about Tennyson. Edith Wharton took it upon herself to criticize the great George Eliot, thus placing herself among those entitled to do so. Hopkins drew with ease on Milton and Shakespeare.[17] Willa Cather, fitting right in, volubly distinguished herself from what she labeled rather contemptuously the "commercial novel-maker."[18]

A picture emerges of a group of writers who were ambitious, generally committed to an elite international standard, and insistent on their right to equal status with even the most privileged "masters" in the world of art. Although, as their individual struggles often attest, there was another and less felicitous side to this optimistic picture, the public image announced a self-confident—indeed, self-important—break with the past. Artistically ambitious American women writers were determined to be categorized with the great artists of European and English tradition, most of whom were male.

In one way, of course, this taste in mentors simply reflected the fact that male and foreign models were more plentiful—there were more to choose from. At the same time, however, it cannot be denied that the maleness of these women authors' avowed literary models calls attention to a strong theme among a number of them of antifeminine identification as writers. Consciously in some cases and unconsciously in others, the majority placed themselves in a literary tradition quite unlike the one carved out by midnineteenth-century white women fiction writers in America, who conceptualized their work as domestic, primarily money-making, and formally formulaic. Ambitious turn-of-the-century women writers did not identify with such midcentury writers as E. D. E. N. Southworth, Augusta Evans, and Maria Susanna Cummins. They were, as Mary Austin explains in her autobiography, the people her mother read: "Lydia Maria Child . . . Augusta Evans . . . Maria Cummins . . . and the over-saccharine Jennie June," along with " 'Godey's Lady's Book,' which provided a great deal of serious if somewhat condescending advice on what 'pure young womanhood' ought to know." Austin describes herself as outgrowing these books of her mother's. She progressed "through the adolescent period, with early American novels, 'Queechy,' 'The Wide Wide World,' 'The Lamplighter.' You went along that path to 'Beulah' and 'St. Elmo,' and the first thing you knew you were at 'Jane Eyre'—how you adored Rochester! and then you were at Jane Austen!"[19]

Having arrived at Austen, turn-of-the-century women writers who aspired to be artists were not interested in turning back. In general, they identified with literarily elite, mostly male writers whose work came out of the modern high western tradition of art not as business but as vocation—as an intellectually daring and passionate calling that drew on the deepest creative powers within a human being. Like distinguished female social scientists of the period,[20] these women writers rejected the definition of female intellect as separate and inferior, by "nature" soft, intuitive, and fundamentally unsuited for rigorous, independent, creative thought. Constantly threatened by mounting reactionary attempts to categorize people ever more rigidly by gender and, for women of color, by race as well, they insisted on their equality, or at the very least their potential equality, with the "greats" of recent western literary tradition.

To be sure, in earlier periods individual American women had dreamed of being taken seriously as artists: Anne Bradstreet, Phillis Wheatley, Emily Dickinson, Constance Fenimore Woolson. The difference is that by the end of the nineteenth century that ambition was not freak. Mary Austin, referring to herself in the third person in her autobiography, observes that there had transpired a "slow progression of woman's mastery over her own talent which it has been the business of Mary's generation to initiate on a scale of social significance." Austin attaches this historical development to the struggle that "any number of American women . . . went through in the disentangling of their natural endowment from the givingness of women, from their tendency to see in the exactitudes of professional technique only another oddity of the male mind."[21] Convinced that the "exactitudes of professional technique" are *not* solely the property of men—an "oddity of the male mind"—and refusing to sacrifice her talent to the feminine occupation of "givingness"—of caring for other individuals such as a husband or dependent family members—Austin quite accurately saw herself and her peers as part of a new historical moment.

White women at the middle of the nineteenth century had by their own accounts found in novel writing a profession compatible with Victorian ideology. They could work at home, out of the public eye, remain close to the nursery, sickroom, parlor, or kitchen. They could make money without physically challenging the idea that woman's first duty was to the family; they could exercise intellect and imagination, even exert considerable influence, without (so the official publicity maintained) violating the fundamental nineteenth-century white middle-class ideal, and for many women practical reality as well, that woman's place was in the home.[22] Nineteenth-century black women writers often said that they wrote because political conditions *forced* them to; slavery and its aftermath made the act of telling the truth about African American experiences a necessity, whether one felt qualified to make art or not. In contrast, most artistically ambitious women writers early in the twentieth century did not write, or say they wrote, because it was the easiest way to make or supplement the family's living or because politics forced them to (though politics, especially for women of color, continued to play a major role). Almost without exception, they wrote instead like ambitious male authors in the west before them. They wrote because they "needed" to write, felt driven to write—even, in many cases, because they craved fame.

Contempt for the domestic-writers tradition was overt by the turn of the century. Engaged as early as 1891 in the crucial feminist task of challenging how—upon what grounds—a national literature is decided, literary historian Helen Gray Cone argues for the importance of Margaret Fuller as the forebear of modern American women artists. Even though her corpus was small and its quality uneven, Fuller was daring and original. Cone states that Fuller's

> mission was "to free, arouse, dilate." Those who immediately responded were few; and as the circle of her influence has widened through their lives, the source of the original impulse has been unnamed and forgotten. But if we are disposed to rank a fragmentary greatness above a narrow perfection, to value loftiness of aim more than the complete attainment of an inferior object, we must set Margaret Fuller, despite all errors of judgment, all faults of style, very high among the "Writing Women" of America.[23]

Cone goes on to announce that "the distinctly woman's novel,—that is, the novel designed expressly for feminine readers, such as 'The Wide, Wide World,' and 'The Lamplighter,' . . . has become nearly extinct at the very time when women are supplying a larger proportion of fiction than ever before."[24] Twenty-six years later Edith Wharton would still be emphasizing this point about modern women writers' distance from the nineteenth-century domestic novel by having the heroine of her radically unsentimental novel, *Summer* (1917), kill time by winding her handwork around a battered but no longer read copy of *The Lamplighter* (1854).

As Sharon O'Brien explains, the way that Cather dealt with the issue of predecessors early in her career was by attacking, often viciously, what she regarded as "feminine" art. In the 1890s she conceded that authors such as George Eliot and George Sand, Jane Austen and Charlotte Brontë, succeeded as artists, as did Sappho centuries ago, but she maintained nevertheless that women in general made terrible writers. She declared in a review in 1895: "Sometimes I wonder why God ever trusts talent in the hands of women, they usually make such an infernal mess of it. I think He must do it as a sort of ghastly joke." Again in 1897 she pronounced: "I have not a great deal of faith in women in literature. As a rule, if I see the announcement of a new book by a woman, I—well, I take one by a man instead. . . . I have noticed that the great masters of letters are men, and I prefer to take no chances when I read."[25] Even as late as 1918, inclusion in Grant Overton's *The Women Who Make Our Novels* gave Cather pause. She wrote to her editor at Houghton Mifflin that the honor classed her among the "authorines."[26]

Moving away from sweeping contempt for women, and with it her complicated disavowal of crucial "feminine" parts of herself, without which she would never be able fully to realize her own art, constituted the arduous task of Willa Cather's long apprenticeship as a fiction writer.[27] O'Brien argues with great persuasion that Sarah Orne Jewett became a key figure in helping Cather resolve the tension that she as a white middle-class woman felt between the identities of woman and artist, the former associated for her with domesticity, nurturance, and private relationality, the latter with public ambition, rule-breaking, and daring individualism. Jewett's famous advice that Cather should quit her editorial job at *McClure's Magazine* and devote herself full time to fiction-writing changed Cather's life.[28] But even more so, O'Brien argues, the example that the older writer set of identifying with many traditional feminine values and yet producing exquisite original writing inspired

Cather to locate her own voice not in opposition to but conjunction with her experiences as a woman. Testifying to Jewett's importance to her emergence as an artist,
Cather dedicated *O Pioneers!*, her first novel about a woman and the first that she
herself liked, to Sarah Orne Jewett.

There is, I want to suggest, a strong connection between Cather's need to reconcile the terms *woman* and *artist* and her lifelong experimentation with form. After
the publication of her first novel, *Alexander's Bridge* (1912), a book about a brilliant
man's failure at his job of building bridges, that is, of connecting places otherwise
hopelessly separated,[29] Cather repeatedly returned to the twin tasks of experimenting
with narrative form and plumbing the intricate relationship among gender, art, sexuality, form, and cultural context. In her second novel, *O Pioneers!*, she succeeded
at creating alternative narrative form and telling the story of a woman (covertly
exploring same-sex romantic attraction as well). Having launched her novel-writing
career with these two, short, highly intertextual fictions about gender and creativity
(even the names of her protagonists talk back and forth: Alexander in the first novel,
Alexandra in the second), Cather then risked a novel directly about a woman artist,
The Song of the Lark.

The Song of the Lark finds its climax in one woman artist's epiphanal compre-
hension of her own art form deep in a canyon in the Arizona desert. The imagery
surrounding Thea Kronborg's trip into this desert brings to mind similar journeys
down into secret, healing places in nature in *The Country of the Pointed Firs, The
Awakening, The Land of Little Rain,* and *Of One Blood.* Thea moves down from
Flagstaff on a road that "dropped and dropped' to the land of Panther Canyon.[30]
There, she descends even deeper to a wild, domestic kingdom where she comes into
a profound spiritual and physical communion with the earth itself and with the spirits
of Native American women artists who long ago walked the water trails of the
canyon.

Celebrating female self-sufficiency, descent, continuity, and art-making, Thea's
journey down into Panther Canyon represents a return of the rigorously trained,
professional, and therefore "masculinized" western woman artist to the starting
place of all human art, which Cather defines as primordial, female, and inseparable
from the earth itself. Like the narrators' experiences in *The Country of the Pointed
Firs* and *The Land of Little Rain* or Manuela's in *The Goodness of St. Rocque,*
Thea's experience of the canyon is one of reconnecting with the erotic, primal,
creative energy of women that western civilization, and especially high-culture art
in the west, have systematically divorced women from—the ancient earth arts: in
Jewett, herbal healing; in Austin, basketmaking; in Dunbar-Nelson, fortunetelling;
in Cather, potting. Thea goes down into the canyon, a fierce opening in the earth
that holds "a gentler cañon within a wilder one," a softer, secret, protected place
within the bigger opening, "hollow (like a great fold in the rock),'' and there she
"nests" (*SOL*, pp. 370–71). The sexual imagery identifies this place as female and
erotic even before Cather's artist, in a ritual of ecstatic purification, stands naked
in the pool of water at the canyon's base—wetness exists at the deepest place in
this opening—and feels the presence of the ancient Indian women potters who came
before her.

Alone, deep in the earth, Thea understands in a flash the connectedness of earth,
flesh, womb, sexuality, art, and form:

Something flashed through her mind that made her draw herself up and stand still until the water had quite dried upon her flushed skin. The stream and the broken pottery: what was any art but an effort to make a sheath, a mould in which to imprison for a moment the shining, elusive element which is life itself—life hurrying past us and running away, too strong to stop, too sweet to lose? The Indian women had held it in their jars. In the sculpture she had seen in the Art Institute, it had been caught in a flash of arrested motion. In singing, one made a vessel of one's throat and nostrils and held it on one's breath, caught the stream in a scale of natural intervals. (*SOL*, p. 378)

The repetition of circular and container forms here—jars, sheaths, vessels, pools, throats—recalls Thea's nest in the fold in the rock far above, her womb-room in this wild, homey canyon, and also identifies Cather's own favorite form as an artist, the nesting or sheathing of story within story. The White Mulberry section held within *O Pioneers!*, the Lena Lingard story placed within Jim Burden's version of *My Ántonia*, the Tom Outland narrative set deep in *The Professor's House*—Cather loved to break linear development by curving the line, so to speak, into a sheath, or hollow place, holding within itself, like jars within jars, other rounded forms.[31] That Thea has her revelation in space inhabited by the spirits of Indian women is not accidental. For Cather, like Austin, Native American art offered a model of holistic, nonwestern form that she, as a woman attempting, paradoxically, both to write herself into high western tradition and to remain alternative to it, found powerful.

The reality that Thea discovers in Panther Canyon exists outside white, western, male-centered, Protestant work-ethic time:

All her life she had been hurrying and sputtering, as if she had been born behind time and had been trying to catch up. Now, she reflected, as she drew herself out long upon the rugs [in her room in her cliff house], it was as if she were waiting for something to catch up with her. She had got to a place where she was out of the stream of meaningless activity and undirected effort. (*SOL*, pp. 372–73)

This safe, wild zone lies even beyond the control of speech. Thea holds "incomplete conceptions in her mind—almost in her hands. . . . They had something to do with fragrance and colour and sound, but almost nothing to do with words" (*SOL*, p. 373). Art becomes totally sensuous, Thea herself a vessel: "She could become a mere receptacle for heat, or become a colour, like the bright lizards that darted about on the hot stones outside her door; or she could become a continuous repetition of sound, like the cicadas" (*SOL*, p. 373).

In Panther Canyon individualism evaporates for Thea. As Paula Gunn Allen, talking about differences between Indian and western perspectives, explains:

Chronological time structuring is useful in promoting and supporting an industrial time sense. The idea that everything has a starting point and an ending point reflects accurately the process by which industry produces goods. . . . Chronological organization also supports allied western beliefs that the individual is separate from the environment, that man is separate from God, that life is an isolated business, and that the person who controls the events around him is a hero. (*Woman* seldom—indeed virtually never—is addressed or referred to in western theological or philosophical speculations.)

This western outlook," Allen emphasizes, "includes a strong belief in individualism as well as the belief that time operates external to the internal workings of human and other beings," and it "contrasts sharply with a ceremonial time sense that assumes the individual as a moving event shaped by and shaping human and non-human surroundings."[32] Locating her woman artist outside modern western chronology, Cather states: "Thea's bath came to have a ceremonial gravity. The atmosphere of the cañon was ritualistic" (*SOL*, p. 378). Gradually Thea heals. In the womb of the earth her mother, in the presence of Native American foremother artists, in ceremonial oneness with her own naked woman's body and potent sensuality, Thea—her very name a feminization of the Greek word for god—believes again in her power to make art. Transported out of hard-driving white western linear time with its relentless ethic of individualism into a time-space of enfoldment and fusion, Thea can imagine form, can experience it with her whole body, capable of holding art worth making.

All of her life Cather would return, metaphorically, to Panther Canyon. Never, however, would she find it again as she did in *The Song of the Lark*. In *The Professor's House* the space has been taken over by white men who plunder and put up for sale the sacred art of Indians; and the white artist, turned into a dutiful academic who closes himself up with lifeless, beheaded female forms (literally dummies), lacks vitality. Likewise Jim Burden's story as a writer in *My Ántonia*— and Jim both is and isn't Cather—records the failure of the white western male artist to connect with life, the earth, and the flesh, all of which find embodiment in the woman Ántonia.

But even in *The Song of the Lark* the story of becoming an artist is more complicated than I have suggested, for Thea's experience in Panther Canyon only begins with her epiphanal bath. It ends with the information that the white man she has fallen in love with and plans to marry is a liar. He is already married.

Male heterosexual treachery haunts Cather's work. Although the popular view of her fiction usually holds that hers is a pacific, even asexual world, it is actually full of heterosexual violence. The murder in *O Pioneers!*, the attempted rape in *My Ántonia*, the sadism of Ivy Peters in *A Lost Lady*, the imagined murder of "Eve" in *The Professor's House*, the infanticide and wife abuse in *Death Comes for the Archbishop*, the systematic sexual predation and rape plot in *Sapphira and the Slave Girl*—Cather's work contains image after image of deadly male heterosexual aggression. What Thea has to deal with in *The Song of the Lark* is comparatively minor. All she has to get over is the illusion that she can love and trust a man. This man does not physically rape, beat, imprison, or kill her; indeed, he caresses and shelters her. He loves her. However, precisely that love, luscious in the freedom of Panther Canyon, becomes dangerous and destructive outside that haven because Fred Ottenburg has already committed himself to another woman.

That woman is shallow, proprietary, and mean-spirited; and the strong similarity between her and Jim Burden's wife is telling. It reminds us that Fred Ottenburg and Jim Burden are not simply victims: They *chose* these women. Privileged heterosexual white men like distant, self-centered women. They choose to bind themselves to narrow, greedy, cold wives who may seem to oppress them but who in fact are not even in their lives—they are simply vague, irritating figures way off on the margin. In the foreground, as Cather sees it, is the fact that the powerful female sexuality of a Thea or an Ántonia, attractive as it might be to play with either on vacation (Fred) or on paper (Jim), is far too threatening for a civilized white male to live with full time.

In many ways Cather's manipulation of narrative form connects with these issues of sexuality and socially constructed gender. Of course, in a career as long and varied as Cather's, no one issue or even set of issues marches simplistically through the work from beginning to end. Cather's interests shift many times; she writes of different situations, kinds of people, problems, and experiences. Yet throughout her work, receiving varying degrees of emphasis and appearing at various times, she returns repeatedly to a nexus of issues that interlocks male violence, the dangerousness of heterosexuality, the need of women to find and establish deep and often sexually charged relationships with each other, the creation of art by women, the value of multicultural contexts, and the search for form. Most important to me here in Cather's lifelong effort to forge art that would articulate her deepest concerns was her repeated need to explore in conjunction three of these issues: the power of same-sex love, the integrity and vitality of art created by people not dominated by a white western aesthetic, and the liberating possibilities of formal innovation.

All three of these concerns appear vividly in *My Ántonia*. Admittedly, in this early novel, a book with one author who writes and loves in secret (Jim Burden) and the other a public figure who delivers Jim's manuscript to us (the "I" of the introduction), same-sex love is carefully transposed into the attraction of Jim for Ántonia. But this heterosexuality is paper thin.[33] As a boy Jim is centered in the world of his grandmother. As a young man he loves Ántonia, yet for no good reason refuses to act on that love (the excuse of class carries us only so far). As an adult he is miserable in his heterosexual marriage. Cather's homoerotic subtext pushes against the surface of *My Ántonia*. Arriving in Nebraska at the age of ten, which is about when Cather herself arrived, Jim becomes a main character in the secret love story of Jim and "Tony." As these nicknames suggest, Cather's story is not simply about missed love between a man and a woman because of class and cowardice. It is also and covertly about missed love between two people of the same sex because that love cannot even be named. Indeed, the consequence of this un-naming is what we first meet in the novel: an impotent artist—a speechless writer. "Jim," unable to tell his story, can finish it only when he meets the "I" of Cather's introduction; his story literally cannot get told until it passes through a woman. As Jewett wrote to Cather in another context, but the observation applies well to the layering of disguises, authors, and lovers in *My Ántonia*: "It is always hard to write about the things near to your heart, from a kind of self-preservation you distort them and disguise them.[34]

When Jim's story does appear, we are told, significantly, that "it hasn't any form."[35] Actually, as Susan Rosowski points out, *My Ántonia* has a strong design. It is simply that it is unconventional. The book "consists of two major movements, followed by fusion: first, awakening to experience (Part I) and moving outward by its physicality (Part II), then awakening to ideas (Part III) and returning by them (Part IV); finally, fusing the two as symbol (Part V). By turning back upon itself,

the pattern forms circles of expanding meaning.'' Judith Fryer also points out that
Jim's statement about his manuscript having no form

> means that it does not have the usual form: plot, conflict, the development of char-
> acter, the Aristotelian form of beginning, middle and end. The parts of *My Ántonia*
> have a semi-independent existence of their own, like separate stories, like the separate
> squares of hemmed fabric that are pieced together to make a quilt, like the separate
> rooms of a frame house on a western prairie; together, they do form a whole.[36]

Constructed on principles of separate set-scenes and circularity (as Rosowski observes, the book begins and ends in the same place, childhood)[37] and drawing its
most powerful, memorable images from nature—the bug in Ántonia's hair, the plow
against the sky, the cave out of which Ántonia's children tumble—Cather's book,
with its strong evocations of a primordial Earth Mother, relies on an aesthetic of
simplification that participates in the modernist project of seeking alternatives to the
dominant high-culture western tradition in art.[38]

Cather's technique in *My Ántonia,* as critics have remarked, parallels modernist
painters' visual abstracting: Planes and lines and blocks of color, rather than pho-
tographic detail, form the text.[39] Cather names this aesthetic in her text by embodying it in two ''primitive'' artists, Mr. Shimerda, an impoverished Eastern European
immigrant who plays the fiddle, and Blind d'Arnault, an African American pianist.
These two men are Cather's models. (It is significant, of course, that they are men—
though at the same time men, by virtue of their ethnicity and race, who are not
members of the dominant class.) They manipulate high-culture instruments—the
violin, the piano—to make breathtaking, alternative music, dazzlingly simple yet
complex art (like Cather's novel), that violates and dissolves the strict intellectual
and emotional boundaries of inherited, elaborate, high-culture western art.

Indeed, the form of *My Ántonia,* much like the structure of *The Awakening,*
contains what Toni Morrison labels ''the ghost in the machine'': the powerful influence of African American culture and art on white art. Cather was born in Virginia, where she spent the first ten years of her life; and as she herself admitted, she
was deeply affected as an artist by the black people she knew as a child. In her last
novel, *Sapphira and the Slave Girl,* to which I will return, she explicitly acknowl-
edges this influence. Yet Cather's racism made her ambivalent about her debt. As
her picture of Blind d'Arnault shows, in *My Ántonia* she simultaneously celebrates
and insults the black genius that she cannot keep out of her work. (One of the
important facts about the black pianist is that he does not *have* to be in the book.
He seems to materialize out of nowhere, to pop into the text as if by his own will.)
Blind d'Arnault, in other words, is the literal, unbidden, but irrepressible signifier
of the formal ''ghost in the machine'' in *My Ántonia.*[40]

Cather's search for new or radically modified narrative forms and, inseparably,
for ways to talk in code about same-sex love continued after *My Ántonia,* with two
of the most important books in this inquiry surely being *The Professor's House* and
Death Comes for the Archbishop. Cather signals her experimentation with form in
The Professor's House, with its nesting of Tom Outland's story inside the professor's, by placing on her title page the image: ''A turquoise set in silver, wasn't
it? . . . Yes, a turquoise set in dull silver.''[41] Speaking of the form of her later book,

Death Comes for the Archbishop, Cather explained (in the words I used to open my chapter on Jewett): "I am amused that so many of the reviews of this book begin with the statement: 'This book is hard to classify.' Then why bother? Many more assert vehemently that it is not a novel. Myself, I prefer to call it a narrative."[42]

The Professor's House and *Death Comes for the Archbishop* clearly show the intimate interrelation of Cather's sexual, formal, and cross-cultural agendas. The books experiment with narrative patterns and rhythms that depart significantly from traditional, mainstream, western notions of pacing and structure: the Tom Outland section stuck in *The Professor's House;* the unregimented and hence unclassifiable narrative flow in *Death Comes for the Archbishop.* Simultaneously, they secretly celebrate same-sex love, placing against backdrops of heterosexual jealousy and violence loving relationships between highly domesticated, nonviolent men, who clearly could be or are, under the skin, women. Professor St. Peter feels secure only in his blatantly feminized world—his study is literally a sewing room. The all-male mesa world of the man he loves, Tom Outland, ostensibly one of Cather's most masculine characters, is also virtually a parody of domesticity, with its stereotypic familial roles, home-cooked meals, and quiet chats around the campfire. Likewise in *Death Comes for the Archbishop* the two men, who are deeply in love with each other, lead lives embedded in shared domestic rituals. In fact, as priests, they have publicly pledged themselves to the traditionally "feminine" values of self-sacrifice, nurturance, and obedience. It is simply an added detail that they literally wear skirts.

Providing intellectual or spiritual context for these novels' overt employment of unconventional narrative form and covert exploration of same-sex love is Cather's attempt to evoke the beauty and integrity of aesthetic worlds developed beyond the boundaries of Anglo patriarchy by Native Americans. That imagined Native American context is prehistoric in *The Professor's House* and contemporary in *Death Comes for the Archbishop,* in which Cather makes a point of praising Navajo and Hopi art, as well as all Indians' respect for nature and for the many various forms of life on earth.[43] Thoroughly modernist in this appeal to what she regards as the "primitive" but attractive cultural values of Native Americans, Cather in both novels is able to derail both gender and genre. In these two mature, experimental novels, reinforced as they are by sets of human values created outside the boundaries of white patriarchy, she is able to offer in anticonventional narrative containers stories about both the pain and the potential of love that is not heterosexual.

The problem is, as in the case of Stein, Cather's racism. The Indians in *The Song of the Lark* and *The Professor's House* are dead, the favorite white version of Indians, of course, while their descendants in *Death Comes for the Archbishop* appear as romanticized decorative details. The characterization of Blind d'Arnault in *My Ántonia,* as Blanche Gelfant has pointed out,[44] is totally stereotypic. The novel describes him as having "the soft, amiable Negro voice, like those I remembered from early childhood, with the note of docile subservience in it. He had the Negro head, too; almost no head at all; nothing behind the ears but folds of neck under close-clipped wool.[45] The values of Hispanic people in *Death Comes for the Archbishop,* as E. A. Mares has stated and Mary Austin complained when the book came out, are dismissed in favor of sympathy with two foreign priests busy building a French cathedral on Mexican and Indian land.[46] Again and again, Cather's racism and ethnocentricity undercut her attempt to create art somehow outside of or at least in dialog with inherited, conventional, white western narrative tradition.

The issue becomes completely inescapable in Cather's last novel, *Sapphira and the Slave Girl*, which may explain why the book is so seldom discussed. The novel makes totally untenable the usual comfortable view of Cather as a writer of broad and inclusive sympathies and imagination. Cather can put herself inside the experiences of Eastern European immigrants, French Americans, or Canadians, people in many ways quite unlike herself. But when it comes to Americans of other races, such as Indians, Asians, Chicanos, or blacks, her racism blinds her.[47]

Published at the end of Cather's career (1940), *Sapphira* is one of the most important books she wrote. In it she attempts to go back to the original story of her life as an artist. The book tells how a young black woman, Nancy Till, escapes from slavery, and specifically from the sexual envy and rage of her aging white mistress, Sapphira Colbert, who plots to have the young woman raped. The escape occurs because Nancy is secretly aided by Sapphira's grown daughter, Rachel Blake, a character drawn directly from Cather's own maternal grandmother, Rachel Siebert Boak, whose maiden name the author respelled as Sibert and took as her own middle name.

Clearly, Cather intends this story to pay tribute to the heroic women, black and white, who empowered her as a writer. In the epilogue she depicts herself as a five-year-old witnessing Nancy's reunion with her mother, from whom she has been separated for twenty-five years. This reunion takes place in the bedroom of the little girl's own mother, the daughter of Rachel Blake, and Cather admitted after the publication of the novel that its epilogue was true and described the "greatest event of her Virginia years."[48] Interpreted biographically, this important scene, Sharon O'Brien argues,

> evokes the harmonious bond between mothers and daughters in an exclusively female world. The setting for the reunion—the mother's bedroom—is the private space of warmth, informality, and harmony. The powerful image of mother-daughter unity expressed in the embrace [of Nancy and her mother] is apparent also in the bond between Willa Cather and her mother: here they share a common purpose. Virginia Cather is the caring mother concerned with pleasing her daughter, not the repressive mother concerned with her daughter's pleasing Southern men.[49]

As O'Brien's reference to Virginia Cather's repressive heterosexuality suggests, Willa Cather differed greatly from her mother in many ways, not the least of which was sexually. Nevertheless, Cather memorializes in *Sapphira* not only the reunion of Nancy and her mother but also, symbolically, of herself and her own mother.

As a chronicle of Cather's journey back in memory, past Nebraska, to the true origins of her artistic gift, and as a tribute to the black and white mothers and daughters who shaped her artistic vision, *Sapphira and the Slave Girl* is biographically a significant work. In her last novel, Cather implies that her own story of freedom and rule-breaking—of bravely defying and leaving the world of domineering heterosexual white women like Sapphira who insist that everything must be done their way—began when she heard the story of Nancy: when she heard the story of a black woman's escape and a white daughter's rebellious collaboration. Equally important, the book identifies a white woman as the true mastermind of racist rape mythology: Sapphira. Laying responsibility for the threatened sexual violation of a black woman on a heterosexual white woman, the book concludes Cather's lifelong examination of male heterosexual sexual violence with a sharp twist of the screw.

None of my intellectualizing, however, erases the book's racism. Its images of blacks participate wholeheartedly in the standard stereotypes of the early twentieth century and particularly the 1930s (the decade of *Gone With the Wind* [1936], it should be remembered). Cather refers casually to "the emotional darkies,"[50] never calls the cook anything but "fat Lizzie," always describes the black butler as scuttling and shuffling, continues to catalog black head shapes like she did twenty years before in *My Ántonia* (in *Sapphira* she offers, "His head was full behind the ears, shaped more like a melon lying down than a peanut standing on end" [*SSG*, p. 109]), remarks matter-of-factly on the "foolish, dreamy, nigger side" of a character's nature (*SSG*, p. 178), and seriously presents the ancient black woman Jezebel, a character she seems to intend as a figure comparable in mythic stature to Augusta in *The Professor's House*, as a cannibal.[51]

In addition to these images and descriptions is the mind-boggling fact that no slave in *Sapphira and the Slave Girl* hates slavery. Nancy wishes for freedom only after being driven to it by Sapphira's rape plot, and even then her desire is competely personal. Black people in the book have no political or philosophical objections to slavery. White people, including Cather as the narrator, occasionally question and criticize the institution, but black people, evidently, do not share their viewpoints, much less have revolutionary political positions of their own. Indeed, when freedom comes, Cather's black characters want to remain on white plantations and farms as white people's dependents. Apparently, a lifetime of observation and experience had done nothing to deconstruct the sentimental racist myths of her Virginia girlhood.

But most disturbing of all is Cather's appropriation of Nancy's story. Appearing to celebrate black and white women's shared struggle, and particularly the heroism of a black woman, the novel in fact steals the black woman's story to give it to white women. At the center of the book is not Nancy Till as an agent in her own drama but Sapphira, Rachel, and vicariously Willa Cather as Nancy's manipulators. Sapphira is gloriously realized in the text. Bitter, ruthless, yet often magnificent in her pride and cynicism, she may not be likable, but she is grand. Her power and individuality, as the word "Sappho" buried in her New Testament name hints, are very real. In contrast, Nancy, like all the other black characters in the book, is vague, stereotypic, a pawn. She exists not as a fictionalized human being but as Cather's solipsistic, racist projection.

One of the brilliant achievements of *My Ántonia*, and it is repeated in *A Lost Lady*, is Cather's subtle exposure of her heterosexual male narrator's attempt to take over and rewrite a strong, threatening woman's story in terms that suit his own image of her. In those novels Cather simultaneously shows the man's need to distort and, through extremely skillful narrative maneuvering on her part, manages to give a sense of the "real" woman and the "real" story being denied and avoided by the threatened man.[52] Those women, however, are white. When it comes to women of color, whether Indian women in Arizona or black women in Virginia, Cather does not subvert but instead becomes Jim Burden and Niel Herbert. There is, in contrast to the novels told by those men, no Cather behind the Cather to imply some fuller, more real account of dark-skinned women's lives in *The Song of the Lark* or *Sapphira and the Slave Girl*. The women of color in those novels have no text within the text to liberate them, even partially, from the romanticizations and lies imposed upon them.

The appropriation of Nancy's story to tell her own, the choice to celebrate dead Indian women artists rather than to see living ones, the general invisibility of Mexican women on a landscape daily cultivated by them—throughout her career Cather silenced women of color even as she attempted, as in *The Song of the Lark* or *Sapphira and the Slave Girl*, to praise and honor them. Her vision and sympathies had rigid boundaries. Perhaps, like her characters Jim Burden and Niel Herbert, she did not want to admit that people unlike herself, in this case women of color, were as strong or stronger than she, as self-sufficient and independent of her definitions of them as she wished to be of most people's definitions of her. Cather understood how the fear of displacement operated in white men such as Jim and Niel, and she wrote against it, allowing their subjects—Ántonia Shimerda, Marian Forrester—to escape their control and, between the lines, to tell their own stories, inscribe their own identities, in spite of the men who would confine them. Indian woman, black women, and Mexican women did not enjoy the same privilege in Cather's novels. As Cather is praised for her groundbreaking portraits of strong women, it is imperative that we remember that those women are white.

Appropriation and silencing were real. It is one of the tragedies of American literary history that during the same period that Mary Austin, Pauline Hopkins, and Willa Cather were incorporating Indian material into such works as *The Land of Little Rain, Winona, The Song of the Lark, The Professor's House,* and *Death Comes for the Archbishop*, the novel usually cited as the first by a Native American woman, Humishuma or Mourning Dove of the Okanogan people of eastern Washington, appeared and went virtually unnoticed.

Cogewea; The Half Blood, published in 1927, the same year that *Death Comes for the Archbishop* came out, shows the struggle of Cogewea, a firey young woman of mixed Okanogan and Anglo parentage, to mediate between her Indian and white heritages. The novel's foregrounded plot is simple. Loved by a young ranch-hand who is also of mixed heritage and is therefore at home in both the Indian and white worlds, Cogewea foolishly falls in love and runs away with an exploitative, racist white man despite her grandmother's strong warnings and, finally, outright prohibition. When at the end of the story Cogewea is alone with this man far from the ranch, she, like the heroine of Fauset's *The Sleeper Wakes*, finds herself brutally confronted with the full force of his racist misogyny. He does not plan to marry her; he does plan to steal the $1,000 he got her to withdraw from the bank; he does not have any reservations about using the system to back him up. He boasts: ''The law is of the white man's make, interpreted by the white man, made to talk by the white man's money. With a comparatively small amount of this which you have so generously bestowed upon me, I can make the law talk! You have no witnesses! It would be my word against yours; a white gentleman's against an Injun squaw's."[53] When this man abandons Cogewea, it is a good thing. The book ends with her realizing that she should have listened to her grandmother's instructive tales.

Those tales, folded into the narrative of *Cogewea*, differ dramatically in tone, style, and content from the novelistic context that holds them. Three times Cogewea's grandmother, her Stemteema, prepares herself to speak by smoking the sacred pipe and then tells her granddaughter a tale passed on from their ancestors. Each tale warns of the treachery of white men. The second two specifically focus on a white man's sexual exploitation and betrayal of an Indian woman. Gathered by Humishuma for her book or known beforehand, these tales come from her oral literary heritage; the Stemteema's stories are not invented by the author but, rather, transcribed. Therefore, the form of *Cogewea* itself, in a very real sense, manifests or embodies the book's basic question: how to embrace within a modern westernized context the traditional truths and lifeways of generations of Native American foremothers.

However, what Humishuma's answer to that question really was we cannot say, at least at this time. Indeed, the story of the composition and publication of *Cogewea*, if put in a novel, would probably be dismissed as incredible.

In contrast to the other writers in this book, Humishuma had little formal education. Born in 1888, she grew up in a small community in what is now Washington state and then on the Flathead Reservation. She attended school formally for perhaps four years as a child and apparently acquired a little more schooling later on at some points. The formative event for her as an artist was witnessing the federally ordered round-up and evacuation of the buffalo on her reservation in 1912. Cogewea describes the event in the novel:

> It was pitiful to see the animals fight so desperately for freedom. Although I participated in a way, it brought a dimness to my eyes. They seemed to realize that they were leaving their native haunts for all time. To the Indian, they were the last link connecting him with the past, and when one of the animals burst through the car, falling to the tracks and breaking its neck, I saw some of the older people shedding silent tears. (*CMB*, p. 148).

As Alanna Kathleen Brown explains in a brief profile of Humishuma: "It was this 1912 event that spurred Mourning Dove to write a novel for her people, for herself, and for the Euro-Americans who understood so little about those they had conquered."[54]

She began that novel around 1912 and then in 1914 shared her manuscript with Lucullus Virgil McWhorter, a white man deeply involved in championing Indian rights; he added some quotations and some notes, did some editing, and submitted the manuscript to several publishers for Humishuma. At least in part because of the war, it is thought, no publisher picked the novel up, and this prewar manuscript appears to be lost. After the war, as Brown explains, the book became even more difficult to place because "there was a mania for war stories and the Western romance itself had changed." McWhorter therefore decided to add more political and ethnographic material to the manuscript, but he did not show Humishuma these changes. Now, as Brown puts it, the novel "had two writers with separate purposes. Mourning Dove's story focused on the spiritual struggles of her generation and the blatant racism of the times. McWhorter's sections added extensive ethnographic commentary to the novel" and large patches of explicit political polemic against federal corruption and Christian hypocrisy.[55]

The result was a book that, when it finally saw publication in 1927, made Humishuma write to McWhorter:

> I had just got through going over the book *Cogewea*, and am surprised at the changes that you made. I think they are fine, and you made a tasty dressing like a cook would do, with a fine meal. I sure was interested in the book, and hubby read it over and also all the rest of the family neglected their housework till they read it cover to cover. I feel like it was someone elses book and not mine at all. In fact the finishing touches are put there by you, and I have never seen it.[56]

Humishuma wrote *Cogewea* at night in tents and shacks after laboring for up to ten hours a day as a migrant worker. She waited nearly fifteen years to see her novel in print. Her reward was to have a book so altered that she could not even recognize it as her own.

The terrible irony of Humishuma's story as an artist is that her voice as a novelist was muffled, perhaps even hopelessly buried, not by an "enemy" but by a benevolent, silencing, white "friend" (not unlike the benevolent white friends Sui Sin Far includes in *Mrs. Spring Fragrance*). McWhorter did not spend his days in hard physical labor, making his living as a migrant farm worker, but instead exercised his privilege as an elite white male by correcting and managing (appropriating) the story of his dark-skinned colleague. No doubt McWhorter was well intentioned.[57] Nevertheless, he virtually obliterated Humishuma as a writer. Unless manuscripts are found, the extent to which *Cogewea* is his and the extent to which it is hers cannot with certainty be determined. We simply cannot talk about this text as we can those of the other writers in this book, no matter how constrained or compromised they were.

Stated simply, what McWhorter did was rewrite Humishuma. He took over her story to make it his—much as Cather did Nancy's.

Humishuma's story tells a truth about race, class, colonialism, and female authorship in the United States that it has been in the interest of mainstream writers, critics, and literary historians to ignore and deny.

Toward the end of *The Song of the Lark* Thea Kronborg, tense, exhausted, driven, paces her hotel room worrying about how she will get the sleep she needs to be in top form the next day to sing.

> While she was undressing—Thérèse was brushing out her *Sieglinde* wig in the trunk-room—she went on chiding herself bitterly. "And how am I ever going to sleep in this state?" she kept asking herself. "If I don't sleep, I'll be perfectly worthless to-morrow. I'll go down there to-morrow and make a fool of myself. If I'd let that laundry alone with whatever nigger has stolen it—*Why* did I undertake to reform the management of this hotel to-night?" . . . Suddenly she checked herself. "What *am* I doing this for? I can't move into another hotel to-night. I'll keep this up till morning. I shan't sleep a wink." (*SOL*, p. 563).

The casual eruption of ''nigger'' here must arrest us. It is insufficient simply to note the racism, write it off to history, and continue unchanged with celebrating Cather's novel as one of the great modern narratives about ''the woman artist.'' As this passage makes inescapable, the book is not about ''the'' woman artist. It is about one very particular, highly privileged woman artist, the elite white woman artist, whose success depends on the paid services of working-class white women (Thérèse in the trunk room) and whose accomplishments are achieved as a privilege of race.[58]

Almost all of the experience open to Thea is open to her because she is white. For example, the very freedom of travel that takes her to Panther Canyon would be extremely difficult, probably impossible, for a black heroine. Furthermore, the singing roles that Thea is able to fill would have been closed to women of color. Although the black artist Marie Selika could sing in Europe at the turn of the century, she could not, as Thea could, perform major roles in the United States at that time.[59] Most fundamental, however, is the fact that Thea's life as an artist is made possible by the labor of women of color. Her success is built on the backs of black women. The people washing her underclothes in the hotel laundry many stories beneath her pacing feet are, as the historian Jacqueline Jones makes clear in her discussion of African American women and work, women.[60] Invisible, all but written out the text except for this petulant outburst on Thea's part, African American women, buried in the basement of this novel as well as in the basement of the hotel in which Cather's artist fights insomnia and rages at their presumed dishonesty, are the people who make the white woman artist's world possible. They do her dirty work and, unnamed and unseen, receive in return her abuse. That Cather implicitly names but in no way attends to this power dynamic and its meaning is the issue.

Plots:
Jessie Fauset and Edith Wharton

For Jessie Redmon Fauset and Edith Wharton, appearing conventional as artists and being deeply involved with issues confronting women, including women artists, were totally compatible positions. They—like Harper in *Iola Leroy,* Hopkins in *Contending Forces,* Chopin in *The Awakening,* or Austin in a number of her novels but most notably *A Woman of Genius*—set out not to undo but instead to own the full-length high-culture western novel. Instead of attempting to make it over, they took it on. Moved in.

By the early 1920s Jessie Redmon Fauset had been publishing short fiction for more than a decade and serving officially as the literary editor of the *Crisis* for several years (unofficially she had been its literary editor for longer than that). So when she offered advice to would-be writers and teachers of writing in the black community in 1923, she spoke from experience. Stressing the importance of practice and models, she asked: "Do our colored pupils read the great writers and stylists? Are they ever shown the prose of Shaw, Galsworthy, Mrs. Wharton, Du Bois or Conrad, or that old master of exquisite phrase and imaginative incident—Walter Pater?"[1] Fauset's list is telling. Noticeably missing is any white male American author. Not Hawthorne, James, or Emerson but Wharton and Du Bois, in Jessie Fauset's judgment early in the 1920s, constitute the "great writers and stylists" from the United States that she hoped aspiring young African American writers would read and emulate.

Why Fauset named W. E. B. Du Bois needs little explanation. Intellectual, activist, and artist, he was Fauset's friend, supporter, and then colleague and boss in the years that they worked together on the *Crisis,* the official publication of the National Association for the Advancement of Colored People, Du Bois as editor in chief and Fauset as literary editor from 1919 to 1926. Even more important, Du Bois provided a powerful model of fused political and artistic energy and of the artist as aesthetic pioneer (his brilliant *Souls of Black Folk* in 1903 first attracted Fauset to him).[2] His example deeply inspired and encouraged his young friend and co-worker and could, her recommendation of his work implies, do the same for other aspiring African American writers.

But what did Edith Wharton have to offer a Jessie Redmon Fauset? Fauset was twenty years younger than Wharton; African American; a member of a large family, including sisters; self-supporting all of her life; and single until the age of forty-seven. Major differences, clearly, separate the two writers.

Yet as Fauset's naming Edith Wharton in 1923 suggests, there also exist strong parallels and affinities. Each writer published her first full-length novel late in life; Wharton was forty, Fauset forty-two. At least consciously, each identified more closely with her father than with her mother. For both, the encouragement and friendship of a brilliant, established, older man, in Wharton's case Henry James, in Fauset's W. E. B. Du Bois, played an important role in their development as artists. Each was born into the upper stratum of her particular ethnic group, and the mixed blessing of that elite birthright—Wharton's Old New York upbringing, Fauset's Old Philadelphia heritage—both enabled and limited the author's work. Each writer was unusually well educated. Wharton's private tutoring meant that she was introduced at an early age to the several languages that would allow her to read widely and deeply throughout her life. Fauset attended Cornell University, from which she graduated Phi Beta Kappa in 1905, and later she enrolled in the University of Pennsylvania, from which she earned the Master of Arts in French in 1919.

Because of their extraordinary educations, for each woman access to the great texts of western civilization was virtually unlimited. Personally, both became well known not simply for what they wrote but also for the intellectual elegance and vitality of their company. During the 1920s each created in her home a kind of *salon* where artists and friends could meet and relax. (One principle for Fauset, it is important to mention, was that most of the guests at her private gatherings were black; she was not interested in opening her house to the white literati whom she considered sightseers swarming though the Harlem literary scene during the Roaring Twenties.)[3] French was the favorite second language of both authors; each found propaganda or outright protest fiction unpalatable; both were consummate essayists; neither had any children; each could be bitingly outspoken when need be[4]; for each the proletarian 1930s posed insurmountable career obstacles.

To be sure, the most obvious reason for Fauset to place Wharton on her list of six models in 1923 is the fact that, at the time, if one wished to include a living woman writer, Wharton was the logical one to include. She was the author of critically acclaimed best-sellers; she had won a Pulitzer Prize in 1921 for *The Age of Innocence*; in 1923 she was the first woman to receive an honorary degree from Yale University. In listing Wharton, Fauset was simply naming the most famous and most critically respected living American woman writer of the day.

At the same time, however, the similarities in Wharton and Fauset's backgrounds and outlook suggest to me meaningful links between the two figures. Other equally important literary connections can and should be made. My coupling of Wharton and Fauset does not mean that the literary connections between Wharton and Cather, or Fauset and Larsen—or any number of other possibilities—matter less. It simply means that I am interested here in following Fauset's lead, which like at least one review of her work, plus the publicity on her first novel, associates her with Edith Wharton.[5]

Perhaps the most striking similarity between Jessie Fauset and Edith Wharton was their independence. (Certainly their independence *as* women writers—their refusal to behave as many critics have assumed they should as writing women, and in Fauset's case as a black writer as well—has caught the attention of critics.)[6] Born into the leisure class, Edith Wharton was not expected to ''do'' anything with her life except become a well-bred wife, mother, and hostess. Yet she turned herself into a famous, prolific artist. If for Jessie Redmon Fauset, an African American woman of comparably privileged birth and education, the script was different, it was nevertheless equally fixed and prescribed. The standard expectation for a woman of her background and upbringing was twofold: to marry well (for example, a minister or a physician) and be socially active as her husband's helpmate, or to become a teacher, the only profession truly open to black women at the turn of the century, and contribute energetically to race work and the club movement.[7] Remaining single until she was close to fifty, Fauset, who did not care for teaching even though she was forced to do it almost all of her life, dared to be an artist. Moreover, she decided to be one who broke from tradition as an African American woman in two important ways. First, the point of view of her fiction was completely secular. Second, she did not subordinate sex to race. As Deborah E. McDowell argues, Fauset refused to make the untenable choice between race and gender constantly forced on black women in the United States.[8] Instead, she insisted on the equal importance of sex and race as systems of oppression and silencing in African American women's lives.

If it is possible to compare Fauset and Wharton in terms of their similar advantages in class privilege and education or in terms of their remarkable personal successes in defiantly breaking with tradition, it is also the case that, although exhilarating, the struggle to become a writer was for each quite difficult.

As Cynthia Griffin Wolff argues in *A Feast of Words: The Triumph of Edith Wharton,* the transformation of the lonely, insecure child Edith Newbold Jones into the confident, prodigious author Edith Wharton was long and arduous. It is a matter of record that in the 1890s Wharton suffered bouts of acute and debilitating depression, which she was able to end only by seeking medical attention and by establishing an independent identity for herself as a publishing writer. She had to overcome the deep prejudice of her class, and in particular of her family, against a woman's creating a productive, public career for herself as an artist. Additionally, her interests and those of her husband, instead of growing closer and more compatible, only diverged as the marriage she had made at twenty-three in 1885 (and which she would finally terminate in divorce in 1913) crept depressingly forward. As a privileged white woman of tremendous but frustrated talent at the close of the nineteenth century, Wharton, like the heroine of ''The Yellow Wallpaper''—though with the crucial differences that she did not have to deal with motherhood and that her story would have a happy ending—had to wrest her right to write from a world—external and internalized—that assumed she would be silent.

The black community did not assume that Jessie Fauset would be silent. Though upper middle class by birth, Fauset as a young African American woman at the turn of the century was certainly not expected by her family and community to be invisible, idle, and merely decorative. Although required to be well mannered and modest, as a woman of color she was spared that part of the Victorian ethic of The Lady that demanded removal from the remunerative work world and therefore in a capitalist society no, or almost no, public identity. For example, at the age of eighteen in 1900, which was the year in which Wharton's first novel, *The Touchstone,* appeared, Fauset would have been able to see around her any number of impressive, articulate, outspoken black women of her own class. They were teaching school, organizing church and community projects, writing for the *Colored American Magazine* and other less widely circulated black periodicals and newspapers, laboring in women's clubs to combat lynching, disenfranchisement, and rising segregation, and, like many middle-class white women (it is important to remember that Wharton was not middle but upper class), campaigning for women's suffrage and for temperance.[9] The expectation was not that a Jessie Fauset would retire from the world—a luxury (or punishment) reserved mainly for privileged white women— but that she would work in it—within limits to be sure, as a teacher, church worker, and clubwoman, but nonetheless in it. The problem for Fauset, therefore, was almost the flipside of what it was for Wharton: not how to find courage in a life of imposed leisure and endless entertaining, visiting, and traveling to work (write), but how to find both time and courage in a life of work for the leisure required to make art (to write).

Almost a quarter of a century apart, Edith Wharton and Jessie Fauset launched their novel-writing careers with books about women artists, Wharton's *The Touchstone* (1900) and Fauset's *There Is Confusion* (1924). The two novels differ greatly. Wharton's book is short, explicitly about a writer, and formally unadventurous. Fauset's is full-length, concerned with a dancer, and formally ambitious. Even more fundamentally, as I will go on to explain, the contrasting racial contexts of Wharton's and Fauset's worlds produce significantly different issues for their imagined women artists.

But *The Touchstone* and *There Is Confusion* also share at least one strong common theme: intense anxiety and anger about the conflict for a woman between art and heterosexual desire. In *The Song of the Lark* Willa Cather is able to spring Thea Kronborg out of the clutches of Frederick Ottenburg. Thea falls in love with Fred; Cather makes him a liar and a cad; Thea is free to resume her life as an artist. In contrast, escaping the sexual power of men is not that easy for Fauset and Wharton, and the reason is simple. One's own sexuality, and not that of some imagined Other, is at stake. In both their novels, the conflict between art and sexuality sits at the center like a barely concealed private nightmare, though in *There Is Confusion* the issue is even more complicated because racism renders it not simply personal but also communal.

The fears in *The Touchstone* are clearly personal. Wharton's woman writer is almost a parody of the ugly, unlovable, sexually pathetic, intellectual woman. Stephen Glennard, about to violate and exploit the famous author Margaret Aubyn after her death, thinks back: "He saw her again as she had looked at their first meeting, the poor woman of genius with her long pale face and short-sighted eyes, softened a little by the grace of youth and inexperience, but so incapable even then of any hold upon the pulses. When she spoke, indeed, she was wonderful." But a wonderful voice is no substitute for sex appeal. "Later, when to be loved by her had been a state to touch any man's imagination, the physical reluctance had, inexplicably, so overborne the intellectual attraction, that the years had been, to both of them, an agony of conflicting impulses."[10] Not surprisingly, there is a lot of distancing in this novel. Ludicrously incapable of making herself attractive,

Margaret Aubyn is *not* Edith Wharton, the real woman writer behind the scenes wants to make clear. With one-liners such as "Genius is of small use to a woman who does not know how to do her hair" (*T*, p. 19), Wharton is commenting on Glennard, to be sure; but she is also, I think, desperately trying to ensure her own distance from Margaret. Edith Wharton, we are being told implicitly, knows how to do her hair.

The anger that accompanies Wharton's anxiety in *The Touchstone* gets translated very directly into revenge. Margaret, dead, tortures Glennard. Haunting him until he confesses that he has misused and wronged her, Wharton's woman artist achieves a kind of posthumous triumph over Glennard, who, presumably, represents the ordinary heterosexual white male in America and, hence, dominant, conventional male sexual attitudes and tastes in the United States. Literally his offense is the sale of Margaret's letters, but finally that offense is only a convenience for Wharton. Logically, she cannot hold Glennard accountable for not loving Margaret, since love is not reasonable to begin with—*and,* it must be remembered, Wharton herself has made Margaret unlovable. Nevertheless, not loving Margaret is what Wharton holds against Glennard. Otherwise, why include his rejection of her? Why not have him sell the letters of some woman he once loved but now does not? Why tell us about his sexual aversion to Margaret, unless that is part of what we charge against him? The punishment of Glennard occurs not simply because he sold the letters, though that act precipitates the climax and resolution of Wharton's story, but because his entire relationship with Margaret Aubyn was a crime, an abuse and violation.

Yet the story of the woman artist that Wharton tells in *The Touchstone* is not entirely one of fear and anger. Counterbalancing the novel's charge of deep heterosexual violation—the woman artist in this book is rejected as a woman and prostituted as an artist—is a strong fantasy of love and support between women. Alexa Glennard sides with Margaret against her husband; the two women, even though Margaret is dead, bond. Alexa befriends Margaret, takes up her case, loves and supports her. That is, the woman artist in the end is not abandoned but supported in *The Touchstone,* and that support comes from another woman.

Usually ignored in the criticism, this theme of women supporting each other in Edith Wharton's work—either mothering each other or putting sisterly love before heterosexual desire, or both—reappears throughout her career. We see it in Alexa's bond with Margaret, Gerty Farish's caring for Lily Bart in *The House of Mirth,* Justine Brent's devotion to Bessy Amherst in *The Fruit of the Tree,* Ellen Olenska's sacrifice for May Welland in *The Age of Innocence.* Almost always a minor theme, indeed virtually overwhelmed in most of Wharton's books, this need of women for each other usually conflicts directly with women's heterosexual desire. In *The Reef* and *The Mother's Recompense,* for instance, the conflict between the two kinds of love occupies the center of both narratives. Likewise the twin needs to make art and to satisfy heterosexual desire, in the few texts Wharton dares to think about the two together, cannot both be met. In *The Age of Innocence,* for example, Ellen Olenska, clearly an artist figure, cannot have both love and the freedom to be creative. She must choose one or the other.[11]

How do we read this almost constant thwarting of women's dreams and desires in Wharton's work? Edith Wharton achieved her own success, it could be argued, by refusing to be bound by the rules governing respectable heterosexual desire. She had a secret affair with Morton Fullerton while she was still married. When it became clear that her relationship with her husband, Teddy, was hopeless, she secured a divorce despite the objections of his family. Ellen Glasgow's famous statement, ''I have had as much love and more romance than most women, and I have not had to stroke some man the right way to win my bread or the wrong way to win my freedom,' ''[12] might well have been the mature Edith Wharton's. Unlike the tragic heroine of *The Touchstone*—surely a vision of what Wharton was determined would *not* happen to her—Edith Wharton did not die prematurely, remain ignorant about her own erotic capacities, or following her death, get exploited and exposed by a man she loved. Like Margaret Aubyn, however, Wharton did wrestle, as many of her letters to Fullerton disclose, with terrible feelings of rejection and powerlessness because of her experience of female heterosexual passion in a world constructed to privilege men.[13] While she did not suffer Margaret's fate, she did know, as she shows in her fiction again and again, that heterosexual desire, given the structure of modern western society, was dangerous for women.

One way of conceptualizing Edith Wharton's fiction is that it repeatedly breaks down thematically among the competing needs of her middle- and upper-class heterosexual white women for community with women, an erotic relationship with a man, and the freedom to express personal autonomy, to be independent as an adult human being. Perhaps Wharton's failure to reconcile those needs reflects her own lack of imagination. Hopelessly bound by class herself, the argument could run, she simply could not envision how women like herself could have women friends, heterosexual love, and freedom.

However, I do not find that argument compelling. More likely than a failure of imagination, or a jealous refusal to give her fictitious women what she herself, at least at times, did enjoy, I think that Wharton's pessimism about American women's lives probably does reflect deep personal fears. No doubt she wrote about women entrapped and defeated because, as *The Touchstone* shows, she feared those fates for herself. But I also think that Wharton's pessimism was highly rational and reflected her understanding of American culture as one in which, historically, women's needs have been systematically denied. As I argue at length in *Edith Wharton's Argument with America*, the fact that Wharton from *The Touchstone* in 1900 through *The Gods Arrive* in 1932 shows it impossible for the women she imagines to have personal freedom, a love relationship with a man, and meaningful, supportive friendships with other women—one might have one, or two, but never all three—does not speak to her cynicism, her pathological fear of happiness, or her hatred of women. It speaks, rather, to her realistic analysis of mainstream modern America as a culture that pretends to, but does not really, offer women equality with men.[14]

This fear and anger about male control of female sexuality and creativity, which was expressed by both Wharton and Fauset, to whom I will return shortly, also surfaces dramatically in short fiction by María Cristina Mena.

Born in 1893, Mena is thought to be the first woman of Mexican heritage to publish fiction in the United States in English. Though she published no novels, novellas, or collections of stories at the turn of the century, which is why she is not one of the central figures in this study, it is highly significant that she launched her career as a writer during the years I am discussing. The period from the 1890s to the late 1920s saw women in the United States from every major racial and ethnic group publish fiction. Not only were white women and black women able to build on predecessors' successes in extraordinary ways, but also women from racial and ethnic groups that before had been completely or almost completely silenced in the world of published literature in English were able to begin careers as authors. Sui Sin Far, Onoto Watanna, Humishuma, Zitkala-Ša, Anzia Yezierska, and Mary Antin all began publishing in the late nineteenth or early twentieth century. Added to this group of pathbreakers was María Cristina Mena, whose most powerful story, "The Vine-Leaf," published in the *Century Magazine* in 1914, clearly shares her peers' concern with issues of silencing, sexual violation, violence, and male control of art in the modern west.

Set in Mexico, "The Vine-Leaf" is about sexuality, art, medicine, textual erasure, and murder. Told long after the fact by a famous, old male physician to one of his female patients to demonstrate his ability to keep women's secrets, the story is really about violent female resistance to being made the object of the male artist's gaze—the naked subject on his canvas. Old Dr. Malsufrido tells how a veiled woman came to him when he was very young and asked him to remove a blemish on her body. Though he can hear this woman, he is not allowed to see her face as he surgically removes from her back a dark wine-red blemish in the shape of a vine-leaf. Years later the doctor visits a friend, a *marqués* who gives him a tour of the "curiosities" he has accumulated, most of which "recalled scenes of horror, for he had a morbid fancy."[15] Among these "curiosities" is a large portrait of a nude woman painted by the well-known artist Andrade, who was murdered while completing the canvas. On the nude's back is the red vine-leaf. Where her face should be, the canvas has been defaced. At this point, the *marqués'* elegant wife enters the room. Although the doctor keeps her secret, she is, of course, the woman on the canvas, the woman from whose back he removed the vine-leaf years ago, the woman who murdered the male painter and who scraped her own face from the canvas.

At a glance Mena's deft story—like Dunbar-Nelson's deceptively clever fiction—seems nothing more than a successful little thriller, a good piece of formulaic surprise-ending writing that holds our attention and rewards our suspicions at its end. But the gender configuration of the plot, together with that of the narrative frame, says that there is more to the tale then simple mystery-for-its-own-sake. Mena's story is about a woman totally objectified, acted upon, and owned by men— a woman disrobed, painted, carved, secretly displayed, and domestically hoarded. Yet the thrill for the reader is not in this voyeuristic ownership and control by men, the hackneyed pornographic plot in the background of Mena's story. The fascination of "The Vine-Leaf" lies in the viewed woman's revenge on and countercontrol of the men who would control her. She kills the painter, directs the surgeon's knife, and marries the owner of the canvas that might incriminate her. Most exciting, in this story about women and art, what Mena's protagonist does is literally erase both her face from the male artist's canvas and his signature—the red vine-leaf (a bloody reminder of Eden?)—from her flesh.

Mena's heroine is ostensibly owned by men. Certainly she is surrounded by them narratively—the narrator, the painter, the husband. But in fact she has wrested from her situation of supposed powerlessness considerable power. Striking in its parallels with "The Yellow Wallpaper," in which the sexual politics of male medicine, the issue of women's relationship to art, and the hypersexualization of female flesh are also central themes, "The Vine-Leaf" shows a woman outdoing men at their own game of violence and sexual control. It is a horror story. Mena's heroine is dangerous and ruthless. But she is also triumphant; she successfully manipulates the system of male authority (aesthetic, scientific, domestic) to gain the most freedom she can for herself as a woman. The doctor may think this story shows his female patient that she can trust a man (him). In fact, it shows that a woman—at least the woman in this story—must trust only herself. As a revenge story about women and art, Mena's heroine takes back from the male artist the face of his female nude. (Ironically the full-page illustration in *Century* accompanying the story lavishly lingers on the nude.) He may put the body on canvas, but it will have no face—no eyes, no mouth, no pretense of individual identity.

The story that Fauset tells about the woman artist in *There Is Confusion* deals with many similar issues of control, freedom, and sexual conflict. Published in 1924, Fauset's novel had behind it important precedents in African American fiction by women. In *Iola Leroy* Frances Ellen Harper thinks about the woman artist when she has Iola wish to write. In *Contending Forces* Pauline Hopkins tells some of the secret story of "Sappho," and in *Of One Blood* she foregrounds the tragedy of the brilliant singer, Dianthe. In *The Goodness of St. Rocque* Alice Dunbar-Nelson shows us the murder of the cross-dressed woman troubadour. Fauset's story about Joanna Marshall's ambition to make art, though different from these precursors, grows out of them and in significant ways shares with them far more than it shares with a book such as Wharton's *The Touchstone*.

The major difference is context. For Wharton the story of the woman artist exists against the dynamic of the heterosexual couple; that is, both the context and the issue for Wharton's white woman artist is the heterosexual couple, as, for example, the nuclear family is for Charlotte Perkins Gilman, Kate Chopin, and Elizabeth Stuart Phelps in "The Yellow Wallpaper," *The Awakening*, and *The Story of Avis*. In contrast, Fauset's story of Joanna is set against not simply a couple or a single family but a whole community. Three stories structure *There Is Confusion*: Joanna Marshall's ambition to be an artist; Peter Bye's struggle to find himself as a middle-class black man; and Maggie Ellersley's fight against class discrimination within the black community. Joanna's story exists as part of a group story. It does receive the most emphasis of Fauset's three plots; clearly it is the one closest to her and hardest for her to work out. Nevertheless, Joanna's story is only one of several—part of a braided narrative, one strand of three. It can be singled out, as can the other two, but the important point asserted by *There Is Confusion* both structurally and thematically is that the woman artist's story is one element in a shared whole bigger than itself. It represents just one line that finally must be thought about not individually, as Margaret Aubyn's story can, but in relation to the life and welfare of the group.

This inseparability of Joanna's story from the group story inspires Fauset, gives her the opportunity to express racial pride and to argue for black women's freedom as part of a whole people's struggle for freedom. Harder for her to face, however, is the fact that the inseparability of personal and communal issues for black women at many points angers and depresses her. Throughout Fauset's career, conflicts between individual and group desires and needs complicate her heroines' lives in ways undreamed of, much less experienced by, privileged white authors such as Edith Wharton.

Despite its title, *There Is Confusion* is unconfused about many things, especially when it comes to the African American woman artist. Specifically, the novel asserts that as an artist Joanna Marshall enjoys strong support in the black community and has behind her a long heritage of accomplished black women. Fauset's heroine finds herself from an early age encouraged to excel, particularly by her father, Joel, whose pride in his smart, ambitious daughter bears no trace of jealousy or condescension. Indeed, it is from him that Joanna first demands, and receives, stories about "great" African Americans. As Fauset says of Joel Marshall in another context: "Perhaps a man of another race might have stopped to consider such a proposition [of employment] coming from the lips of a young and dainty girl. . . . But colored men of old Joel's type are obsessed with the idea of a progressing younger generation. 'They must advance,' thinks the older man, 'I must do all in my power to help them. This is my contribution to mine own.' "[16] He tells Joanna about "Douglass and Vesey and Turner" and emphasizes that "there were great women, too, Harriet Tubman, Phillis Wheatley, Sojourner Truth, women who had been slaves, he explained to her, but had won their way to fame and freedom through their efforts" (*C*, p. 14). As a child Joanna spends her Sunday afternoons reading "notable women of color" (*C*, p. 72), and the first living artist she meets is a woman, Madame Caldwell, "a great colored singer, a beautiful woman, [who] sang an Easter anthem in church, lifting up a golden voice among the tall white lilies. Afterwards she went home with Mr. and Mrs. Marshall and stayed to dinner. Joanna never moved her eyes from her during the ride home" (*C*, pp. 14–15). Long before she is grown, Joanna Marshall knows that black women can be artists.

Fauset is also clear about the kind of art black women may create: any kind they wish. She argues repeatedly that it is Joanna's right as a dancer to represent not black America but America. Like Alice Dunbar-Nelson, Jessie Fauset fiercely resented efforts to limit and circumscribe black artists' territory. All of American culture belongs to Fauset's heroine as much as it does to anyone else, indeed probably more so. A friend advises Joanna:

> "Better stick to your own Janna, and build up colored art."
> "Why, I am," cried Joanna astonished. "You don't think I want to forsake—
> us. Not at all. But I want to show *us* to the world. I am colored, of course, but American first. Why shouldn't I speak to all America?" (*C*, p. 76)

And *for* all America as well. Joanna refuses to bow to racist expectations. One white manager puts the case more crudely than most when he says,

> "Couldn't make any money out of you. America doesn't want to see a colored dancer in the role of a *premiere danseuse*. How's that accent, Bertully [Joanna's agent]? She wants you to be absurd, grotesque. Of course," tentatively, "you couldn't

consider being corked up—you're brown but you're too light as you are—and doing a break-down?'' (*C*, p. 148)

The answer is no, she couldn't. And neither, of course, could her creator. It is ironic that the manuscript of *There Is Confusion* was rejected by the first publisher Fauset approached because ''white readers just don't expect Negroes to be like this.''[17] Even Fauset's arguments within the text could not counteract the stereotypic racist expectations she knew were out there.

Joanna triumphs as an artist when she lands the role of America in the Dance of the Nations at the District Line Theater in New York. Replacing the white woman who had danced the lead, Joanna performs the role exquisitely behind a mask—which soon gets dropped.

> On the first night on which the new ''America'' was introduced, an inveterate theater-goer in the first row of the orchestra insisted on encoring her. Joanna returned, bowed and bowed, was encored. Somehow the habitué guessed the truth. ''Pull off your mask America,'' he shouted. The house took it up. ''Let's see your face, America!''

To this demand that she show her true face, ''America'' complies:

> There was a moment's silence, a moment's tenseness. Then Joanna smiled and spoke. ''I hardly need to tell you that there is no one in the audience more American than I am. My great-grandfather fought in the Revolution, my uncle fought in the Civil War and my brother is 'over there' right now.'' (*C*, p. 232)

All of Joanna's pride and anger, and surely Fauset's as well, gather into this calm, center-stage, face-to-face declaration that she, not in spite of being a black woman, but because she is a black woman, *is* America.

Equally strong is Fauset's belief that all of western culture belongs to the black artist no less than to the white. Unlike a Gertrude Stein or Mary Austin, restless to break the bonds of high western aesthetic authority, Jessie Fauset as a black artist, a person frequently assumed by a racist culture to stand outside of and irrelevant to European tradition, was insistent on black Americans' right to lay claim to that tradition as part of their heritage in exactly the same way that white Americans claimed it as part of theirs. If Harriet Tubman and Sojourner Truth are Joanna's heroines, so is Joan of Arc (*C*, p. 14). Throughout the novel Fauset's heroine draws on European art. She sings from an old Italian song, quotes poetry by Goethe, thinks of a German story, hums Tschaikowsky (*C*, pp. 105, 166, 195, 278). It is extremely important that Joanna's most vital inspiration as a dancer comes from black children's street dancing (*C*, pp. 47–48, 229–30); her most deeply felt, original, creative springs are African American. Nevertheless, Fauset maintains in *There Is Confusion* that the black American artist is heir to *all* art, which means in this book European and Euro-American, as well as African and African American, aesthetic traditions. Just as Du Bois in *The Souls of Black Folk* juxtaposes snatches of canonical western poetry and of African American spirituals, forcibly bringing the two together as equals, complements, and contrasts, so Fauset makes Joanna as a dancer expertly trained and literate in high-culture European technique and repertoire and at the same time totally at home with and involved in black American vernacular dance. The two traditions, though very different, are not antihetical, this book says. And both belong to the black woman artist.

Despite these strong, firm convictions, however, fears and doubts plague Fauset in *There Is Confusion*. A number of questions keep reappearing. Can one be an ambitious high-culture artist in the west and remain human? Is it possible for the black woman artist to have both her art and a love relationship with a man? How does the ambitious black woman artist choose between building up the ego of the black man, systematically demoralized in a racist society, and focusing on herself?

Fauset has answers, each more depressing than the last. The pursuit of a high-culture artistic career dehumanizes. The black woman artist cannot have both a career and a love relationship with a man. The black woman artist must subordinate her own needs to the greater imperative of building up the ego of the black man. Where confusion enters is not intellectually but emotionally—the anger Fauset has to quell, the longings she has to deny—as she works out these answers she believes to be inescapable. Similar to Mena's ''The Vine-Leaf'' in this important respect, Fauset's novel is full of suppressed fury.

There Is Confusion ends with Joanna Marshall abandoning her dream of an artistic career to devote her life to being a supportive wife and mother. It is an extremely conservative—and depressing—conclusion.[18] Yet this conclusion has been embedded in the novel from the beginning. If Joanna wishes to become a decent human being, she *must* become a different sort of person from the one we meet early on; she must give up her ambition. Throughout most of the novel Joanna is ruthless in that ambition, which is how she must behave as a black female artist in order to gain even the most slippery foothold in the world of the performing arts. But precisely the heartlessness that makes her successful as an artist—to the extent that she is successful—condemns her as a person. Fauset hates acknowledging that reality: Her characterization of Joanna is highly ambivalent—sympathetic at some points and extremely detached and critical at others. It is as if she resists the conclusion she feels she must write, which may be why the ending feels abrupt or false even though its seeds have been planted all along.

As Joanna is forced to admit late in the book, racism creates obstacles for her that are undreamed of by aspiring young white artists. She makes the acquaintance of a number of white contemporaries:

> To her astonishment she found herself in a setting where people, without being considered ''different,'' ''high-brow,'' ''affected,''—and not greatly caring if they were—talked, breathed, lived for and submerged themselves and others, too, in their calling. She met girls not as old as she, who had already ''arrived'' in their chosen profession; incredibly young editors, artists—exponents of new and inexplicable schools of drawing,—women with causes,—birth-control, single tax, psychiatry,—teachers of dancing, radical high school teachers. . . .
>
> For a while she was puzzled, a little ashamed when she realized that so many of these women had outstripped her so early; some of them were poor, some had responsibilities. There were not many of these last. It was a long time before the solution occurred to her and when it did the result was her first real rebellion against the stupidity of prejudice.
>
> These women had not been compelled to endure her long, heartrending struggle against color. Those who had had means had been able to plunge immediately into the sea of preparation; they had had their choice of teachers; as soon as they were equipped they had been able to approach the guardians of literary and artistic portals. Joanna thought of her many futile efforts with Bertully. . . . Sometimes she felt like

a battle-scarred veteran among all these successful, happy, chattering people. . . .
(*C*, pp. 234–35)

To succeed as their equal—or even their subordinate—Joanna must be twice as accomplished as white women. She has no choice but to drive herself monomaniacally to perfect her craft, pursue openings, beat out the competition. As a black woman, her situation is even worse than a black man's: "The big theatrical trusts refused her absolutely—one had even said frankly: 'We'll try a colored man in a white company but we won't have any colored women' " (*C*, p. 275). These realities do not create a nice human being.

The dilemma that Fauset struggles with in *There Is Confusion*, and then throughout her career as a novelist, is basic. In order to survive at all in the art world, an environment both racist and sexist, Joanna must be ruthless and utterly self-centered. In order to be part of the black community, she must think of the group, must be willing to put other people's needs before her own. She must be able to give and to receive love, which involves compromise, sacrifice, and often self-denial. This choice—between making art or being a loving, embraced member of the black community—is unbearable. It translates most directly into having her art or having a relationship with a man. Joanna alternately pronounces that she will live without love (*C*, p. 95) and fantasizes having it all: "Through her mind was floating a series of little detached pictures. She saw a glittering stage, Peter, herself, some little children. She felt a hazy, nebulous, mystical joy" (*C*, p. 101). A pretty picture. In fact, Joanna can have either the stage—and given the double bias against her as a black woman, the best she can hope for are high-class vaudeville roles (*C*, p. 275)—or she can have love, marriage, and a family. The latter choice, which Fauset backs, *is* conservative and *is* disappointing. But given the alternatives that she says America constructs, what is the choice? Joanna can center herself in the white world—as a second-class performer, bear in mind—and remain a hard, driven, selfish person who arrogantly sets herself up above Maggie Ellersley and Peter Bye and whose plot spins off individualistically on its own self-absorbed trajectory. Or she can make a choice in favor of staying within the black community, a choice that encourages rather than discourages the giving, feeling parts of her personality and, significantly, keeps her plot line tangled with Maggie's and Peter's.

This theme of art dehumanizing the black woman artist and cutting her off from the black community, especially from sisters and mothers, is so strong and persistent in Fauset's fiction that it very likely articulates her own deepest fears as an African American woman trying both to stay connected to her heritage and community and to succeed as a publishing artist in a commercial and intellectual world dominated and controlled by whites. The protagonist or strongest central character of each of Fauset's four novels is a black woman who physically or emotionally (or both) cuts herself off from her mother—a rupture which, according to Fauset, constitutes becoming "white." The division appears literally in *Plum Bun* and *Comedy: American Style,* in which Angela Murray and Olivia Blanchard pass, and metaphorically in *There Is Confusion* and *The Chinaberry Tree,* in which Joanna Marshall and Laurentine Strange (whose last name comments on her choice) either renounce or disapprove of their mothers' lives.

Often the pattern is reinforced by the heroine disowning her sister. In *There Is Confusion* Joanna viciously deceives and cuts her future sister-in-law, Maggie Ellersley. In *Plum Bun* Angela disavows her biological sister, Virginia, and then turns her back on Virginia's surrogate, Rachel Powell. In *The Chinaberry Tree* Laurentine abuses her maternal cousin, Melissa. That the last of these mother-denying characters in Fauset's novel-publishing career, Olivia in *Comedy: American Style*, does not pay enough attention to her half-sister even to betray or abuse her signals her total alienation. Unlike her predecessors (and perhaps explaining why Fauset would publish no more novels), Olivia Blanchard is unredeemable. No reunion of this hideously whitened black woman with either mother or sister is imaginable. (As Carolyn Wedin Sylvander points out, Fauset encodes the word "blanched" into her character's name.)[19] Olivia Blanchard has permanently cut herself off from her race, which in Fauset's novel means she has alienated herself from life. The book ends without mother-daughter restoration, or its stand-in, sister-sister reunion. The mother Olivia disowned is dead, and the daughter she deformed and betrayed is the prisoner of a white man. Although mitigated slightly by the marriage of Christopher and Phebe, the conclusion of *Comedy: American Style* shows us exile, whiteness, silence, living death.

The drama of mother-daughter separation at the heart of Fauset's novels expresses a profound division that almost certainly emerged from the author's own struggle to resolve the clash between competing communal and individualistic ideologies pressing on her as a middle-class black woman artist, and no doubt on other black women artists as well, at the beginning of the twentieth century. For Frances Harper, a black woman writing at the close of the nineteenth century, the issue was simple. The modern division between mother and daughter is aberrant and deadly: Iola and her mother yearn for and must find each other. Rooted in slavery, their separation is externally imposed, part of a white plot to destroy the black family, and their reunion signifies unconflicted wholeness, hope, and community. It is crucial that Iola never chose, but instead was forced, to leave her mother. Hence Harper's communal conclusion seems to flow out of rather than to be superimposed upon her narrative. (This is also true of Hopkins's *Contending Forces*.) The end of *Iola Leroy* celebrates the literal reunion of the daughter with her mother. Against that backdrop Iola's personal goals of having a family and finding meaningful, rewarding work and the black community's corporate goals of combatting racism and achieving uplift gracefully merge.

Though Edith Wharton argues a totally different position, for her, a privileged white woman publishing at the beginning of the twentieth century, the issue of mother-daughter separation also was in many ways clear-cut. Especially in Wharton's early novels, the mothers of her most interesting, rebellious young women—Lily Bart in *The House of Mirth*, Undine Spragg in *The Custom of the Country*, Charity Royall in *Summer*—represent a world that should be left behind, a heritage that is confining and suffocating. (The exception proving the rule is Ellen Olenska, who follows in her mother's footsteps; but then her mother was deviant to begin with, not behaving as her culture and class expected her to.) Symbolizing an impoverished past for women—whether it is the spiritual poverty of Lily's mother or the literal misery of Charity's—most of Wharton's mothers before the 1920s personify a negative legacy from which the daughters rightly rebel. Pain and sadness do mark the rupture. Lily, for example, misses her mother, and Charity desperately tries to find hers. But reunion is not possible, or desirable. Lily's mother, we are led to believe, was weak and offered her daughter little support or guidance. Charity's mother, in the only image we have of her, is a filthy, cruelly deformed corpse. In Wharton's novels, especially before the 1920s, daughters must sometimes, for their own good, leave their mothers actually or emotionally, difficult as the break might be.

This argument gets stated in the extreme in *Summer*, where it literally becomes Charity's job to bury her mother. She must try to make the abused body less ugly; watch as the lifeless form is lowered into the earth and covered from sight; endure a sleepless night on the floor of a shack, lying "as her dead mother's body had lain"[20]; and face the fact that she has no choice but to leave her birthplace, the mountain, and separate forever from her mother's world. Yet the link Wharton draws between this burial and Charity's future suggests that even their extreme separation may not be enough to save Charity from her mother's misery. Listening to the minister intone her wedding service, Charity Royall can hear only the burial service of her mother. The two rites merge. Her mother's fate and her own marriage become one and the same. This terrible scene says that patriarchal marriage, no matter how kindly the patriarch, is finally lethal. It is to participate, over and over, in the death of the mother; it is to be taken against one's will into a relationship marked by violence, incest, and living death.[21]

But what does remaining connected to the mother mean? Gazing at Charity over her mother's corpse is her second self, the woman she would be if she had not left the mountain, if she had remained with her mother. This other self lounges against a table, grumbling when asked to light a candle to illuminate the room where the tortured maternal form lies twisted on the floor: "One arm was flung above her head, one leg drawn up under a torn skirt that left the other bare to the knee: a swollen glistening leg with a ragged stocking rolled down about the ankle. The woman lay on her back, her eyes staring up unblinkingly" (*S*, p. 184). Remarks pass.

> There was a silence; then the young woman who had been lolling against the table suddenly parted the group, and stood in front of Charity. She was healthier and robuster looking than the others, and her weather-beaten face had a certain sullen beauty.
>
> "Who's the girl? Who brought her here?" she said, fixing her eyes mistrustfully on the young man who had rebuked her for not having a candle ready.
>
> Mr. Miles [the minister] spoke. "I brought her; she is Mary Hyatt's daughter."
>
> "What? Her too?" the girl sneered; and the young man turned on her with an oath. "Shut your mouth, damn you, or get out of here," he said; then he relapsed into his former apathy, and dropped down on the bench, leaning his head against the wall. (*S*, p. 185)

The horror of who she might have been had she stayed with her mother—this bitter, hopeless sister—makes Charity's loss of maternal connection seem good and necessary. Her mother and her mother's world do not offer strength, nor even life. (In much of the fiction Wharton wrote after the First World War, she reversed this position, favoring the values and life choices of her middle-aged mothers over those of their postwar daughters[22]; the basic issue of mother-daughter alienation, however, remained.) It is significant that in *The Touchstone* we are told Margaret Aubyn titled a book for the Demeter-Persephone myth: *Pomegranate Seed* (*T*, p. 79). Yearning for mother-daughter restoration and communion was, without doubt, as strong in Wharton as it was in Harper or Jewett. But, to her, finding it was almost impossible.

For Fauset, caught somewhere between the worlds of Harper and Wharton, this issue of mother-daughter separation was virtually insoluble. The problem was largely political. As an artist, Fauset had to live in the white world, had no choice but to separate herself from her mother's life. The white world, as Deobrah E. McDowell points out in a superb introduction to *Plum Bun*, was where the publishers, editors, and reviewers were.[23] To create—to express herself as an artist—Jessie Fauset had to pass over into that territory, learn its rules, play its games, adopt its values. Her preoccupation with "passing" in her fiction, like that of other turn-of-the-century black women writers,[24] was not simply deference to a conventional theme in African American literature. It was one way of talking about her own impossible situation as a black woman writer in a publishing world controlled by whites. As an artist, the black woman writer constantly had to "pass," to cross over into and negotiate the white world, whether she wanted to or not. She had to leave her mother. What did that mean? What would that do to her as a woman? As a human being?

Not to pass, that is, to stay firmly identified as African American but nevertheless to enter the white world of art training, production, and sale, leads, at least in *There Is Confusion*, to silence—oblivion—as an artist. Yet to pass, as in *Plum Bun*, is to enjoy success as an artist at the cost of betraying one's sister. In sharp contrast to Edith Wharton, but in complete harmony with Frances Harper, Jessie Fauset, as a black woman writer, cherished and valued the world of her maternal forebears. The mothers in Fauset's novels offer strong, positive, communally oriented models of how to live. The women who bear and raise Joanna, Angela, Laurentine, and Olivia are competent, confident women. But they function in a world of the past. The issue for Fauset is how does a young black woman in the present remain connected to that strong traditional black maternal world *and* launch herself into mainstream white-dominated modern American life? *Plum Bun*'s conclusion tries to solve the dilemma. Angela will sometimes pass, and sometimes not, and she will have everything: art, husband, family, security in the black community, acceptance in the white world. How she will manage this ideal integration of worlds, however, is completely vague.

What *Plum Bun* pictures is not any solution but the pain and danger of passing: the destructiveness of the white world for the black woman artist. Embodied in the handsome, sexy, deceitful young white man Roger Fielding, the epitome of ruling-class America in Fauset's novel, the white world welcomes Angela by seducing, betraying, and then ignoring her. As a parable of what it means for the black woman artist to pass, the maneuver demanded of her in order to make art, *Plum Bun* is chilling: Angela's act of leaving her mother, of entering the white world of art training and production, becomes an act of prostitution. Yet how else—the question haunts Fauset's fiction—is the black woman to make art? The painter Rachel Powell in *Plum Bun* does have both her career and a strong bond with her mother. However, she does not, as far as we know, have a man in her life, and her story is not the one that Fauset struggles with centrally. The situation that compels Fauset is that of the black woman artist such as Joanna Marshall or Angela Murray who wants to succeed in the mainstream twentieth-century art world, which is controlled by white people; to stay rooted in the black community; and to have a personal life that includes both a love relationship with a black man and the possibility of children. Except for the vague fairy-tale conclusion to *Plum Bun*, itself a contradiction given the novel's assault on fairy-tale illusions, Fauset never resolves the issue. Like Edith Wharton, she was a realist. She could record the facts, not remake them.

Quite possibly the most powerful expression of Fauset's struggle with these issues is formal. Structurally *There Is Confusion*, as mentioned earlier, seeks to develop a shared—a braided—story rather than a singularly individualistic one. Published five years later, *Plum Bun* (1929), as Deborah McDowell brilliantly argues, does not simply talk about passing, but itself passes: "Inherently self-reflexive, the novel, like the protagonist whose story it tells, is passing. It 'passes' for just another novel of passing (a popular genre among the writers of the Harlem Renaissance) and for the age-old fairy tale and romance. While white skin is Angela's mask, these familiar genres and their conventions are the narrative's mask."[25] Posing as a love story, *Plum Bun* is the opposite—an economic novel as unsentimental in its analysis of sexual politics as any that Edith Wharton wrote. In addition, the novel chooses not to indulge racist demands for salacious fiction full of violence, sex, and caricatured low-life. Beginning with its title, as McDowell points out, it plays sophisticatedly with covert sexual jokes, innuendo, and *double entendres*[26]; and its violence, low-key but no less vicious for that, significantly is white not black: Roger's fistless pummeling of Angela. (It is a mark of his privilege that he does not even have to touch her to beat her.) As McDowell so persuasively concludes of the novel:

> We can say, then, that *Plum Bun* has the hull but not the core of literary conservatism and convention. Like Angela's it is the case of mistaken identity. It passes for conservative, employing "outworn" and "safe" literary materials while, simulta-neously, remaining suspicious of them. The novel moves toward dismantling the fantasy of racial passing, but more importantly, it moves toward de-idealizing ro-mantic love and criticizing those literary and cultural structures that reinforce and promote that idealization.[27]

While Fauset's next novel, *The Chinaberry Tree* (1931), is probably her most conventional formally, her last book, *Comedy: American Style* (1933), as its title announces, focuses on form. Its Table of Contents takes the bones of genre and juts them through the narrative surface:

This announced dramatic structure broadcasts the ritual power of Fauset's story by identifying her form as that of one of the oldest western narrative models, classical drama, which Fauset uses in this last, grim, bitter novel to dismantle the American Dream.[28] She opens the book with a changeling tale, staple not only of classical drama but also of folk and oral literatures throughout the world, and hence an ideal (because so fundamental) form to contain Fauset's revisionist myth of the fundamental, racist, American plot. Early on Olivia's mother says of her unfeeling, unnaturally cold and hard child: " 'I'm just wondering, Lee, how she can be the child of either one of us.' " Olivia's father replies, "She's a changeling.' . . . Thereafter to themselves they frequently referred to her as 'C.' "[29]

"C" is not a name and not even a word. It is a broken circle. It is a curved line seeking itself but unable to close. Used to describe the child Olivia, it also describes the shape of Fauset's novel. The book ends with Olivia Blanchard, a "confirmed Negro-hater" (*CAS*, p. 23) who has caused the literal death of her son and the living death of her daughter, exiled but hovering on the margin of life in France. Pale and withered, she resembles the wicked witch of fairy tale—banished to a cold, lonely, barren world where, significantly, she can neither speak the language nor be understood. Engulfed in silence and solitude, Olivia, obsessed all her life with passing, has finally and permanently passed. She is now totally "white." She is completely alienated, lost.

Opening with this changeling story, Fauset's last novel churns up frightening questions: Who is Olivia? Is she a black woman at all? Is she *really* white? Where does this monstrous mother come from? Self-hating and destructive, surely Olivia is a woman the white world creates and imposes on black America—slips in like a switched baby in the night to grow up and kill and maim the next generation. Hugh Gloster said more than forty years ago that Fauset's characterization of Olivia offers "the most penetrating study of color mania in American fiction" and is an "analysis of psychopathic Aryanism."[30] Fauset's first three novels end with heroines on the threshold of motherhood. Her last crosses over, and the particular portrait of a black mother that Fauset chooses to provide is terrifying. This last fairy tale, in a career that like Edith Wharton's was full of allusions to and experiments with fairy-tale themes and forms,[31] pictures the white witch: She eats her mate, kills her children, and loathes blackness. A highly symbolic text, *Comedy: American Style* is, to follow Fauset's brilliant inversion of expectations and generic formulae, the ultimate dark comedy. A white comedy.

What does it mean to say that Wharton and Fauset are conventional as artists, that they manipulate genre but do so subtly—in ostensible harmony with, rather than opposition to, tradition?

Charlotte Perkins Gilman in *The Man-Made World* in 1911 asked about gender and genre: "What are the facts as to the relation of men and woman to art? And what, in especial, has been the effect upon art of a solely masculine expression?"[32] Perfectly reflecting the historical period by emphasizing a major difference between "art" (what women have been allowed to do) and "Art" (what men have reserved for themselves), Gilman declares of the "primitive arts" of women such as "pottery, basketry, leatherwork, needlework, weaving," beadwork, quilting, and the like:

"Much of this is strong and beautiful, but its time is long past"; it "is not Art with a large A, the Art which requires Artists, among whom are so few women of note." High art, Gilman emphasizes, has been the province primarily of men in the civilized, androcentric west (she subtitles her book *Our Androcentric Culture*), and not surprisingly it therefore displays the gender of its creators: "the advantages—and disadvantages—of maleness, of those dominant characteristics, desire, combat, self-expression." The exclusion of women from the production of high art has meant that the western novel in particular, Gilman says, has privileged plots that are by definition masculine. The form of the novel itself, she argues, reflects maleness.[33]

A major problem with Gilman's argument, like that of many of her descendants, is that it does not account for the fact that women have been architects and practitioners of the novel from the beginning. Indeed, unlike formal high-culture drama in the west or elite poetry (although what do we know about Sappho—who was she and what did her art look like?), the novel as we know it is historically the creation of both sexes. Moreover, from its earliest incarnations the genre has encompassed the unruly as well as the orderly, the cyclic and repetitious as well as the pointedly climactic, and both women and men have experimented with it in different ways. As M. M. Bakhtin has argued, the form of the novel itself may very well be anti-canonical since it "is plasticity itself."[34] Anything can be done with it, and it still remains the novel.

Yet is that true? *Can* anything be done with it and it still remains the novel? If so, why is there such confusion and even argument about so calm and polite a text as *The Country of the Pointed Firs*? Why did reviewers have trouble calling *Death Comes for the Archbishop* a novel? Moreover, even if it is granted that the genre is profoundly plastic and has been created and recreated throughout its history by both men and women, does that mean it is gender-free?

A self-contradictory position may be most logical. Of course, the novel is not gendered. Of course, it is. Let me use Wharton to illustrate. She, like most of the writers I am discussing, staunchly acted on the belief that successful high-culture art transcends the temporal, the personal, the merely individual. In her career Edith Wharton defied the idea that women and men, if they are truly artists (by which is meant, in the modern western sense of the term, genius, innovator, inventor), write differently from each other because of gender or that form itself is gendered. Precisely that kind of essentialism was what Wharton and Cather and Fauset and Dunbar-Nelson and Helen Gray Cone—and the list goes on—rebelled against, and it is why they insisted that women must have full access to the realm of high art, inhabited largely by men and almost exclusively by white people, where freedom and transcendence were said to exist.[35]

Yet this notion presumes that freedom and transcendence exist in one place and not another—that they are properties of space from which most women have been excluded. Therefore, to enter that space, women must work doubly hard, and women of color, trebly hard. Whether it is "really" so or not, this concept underlines the fact that people, including artists themselves (consider Gilman's generalizations), have routinely conceived of art, art-making, and art forms as gendered. Art, like everything else in life, exists within human culture, and human culture, in all known constructions of it, is gendered. Replying in 1907 to Robert Grant's comments on the construction of her early novel *The Fruit of the Tree*, Wharton herself wrote:

> The fact is that I am beginning to see exactly where my weakest point is.—I conceive my subjects like a man—that is, rather more architectonically & dramatically than most women—& then execute them like a woman; or rather, I sacrifice to my desire for construction & breadth, the small incidental effects that women have always excelled in, the episodical characterisation, I mean. The worst of it is that this fault is congenital, & not the result of an ambition to do big things. As soon as I look at a subject from the novel-angle I see it in its relation to a larger whole, in all its remotest connotations; & I can't help trying to take them in, at the cost of the smaller realism that I arrive at, I think, better in my short stories. This is the reason why I have always obscurely felt that I didn't know how to write a novel. I feel it more clearly after each attempt, because it is in such sharp contrast to the sense of authority with which I take hold of a short story.—I think it ought to be a warning to stop; but, alas, I see things more & more from the novel-angle, so that I'm enclosed in a vicious circle from which I suspect silence to be the only escape.[36]

At least in this early letter, Wharton easily relies on casual gender stereotypes about the act of writing and about the challenge of creating fictive form.

On the one hand, it seems obvious that no form nor part of the process of making form inherently has gender.[37] Biology, itself a socially constructed system, does not determine art. On the other hand, however, permission to create in given ways, as Wharton's letter suggests, often is highly gender-inflected and, given racist pre-scriptions, race-bound as well. What Edith Wharton wishes to do, according to her self-description, is write big, sweeping narratives—large, "masculine" creations. What she feels most comfortable doing (although certainly we have to ask how much her letter reflects what she thinks she *should* be saying as a new woman novelist with very high ambitions as an artist, her protests to the contrary notwith-standing) is writing short stories—close, "feminine" work, the kind of narratives women have "authority" over. As Gilman notes, the world of high art in the west has not welcomed women as a group. One response to that discrimination at the turn of the century, I have been arguing throughout this book, was to try new forms, to rebel against racist and sexist categories by writing differently from how most women or most people of color in the nineteenth century had been writing or had been assumed to be writing, and thus defiantly to assert oneself as an "artist"—as *un*conventional. Another response, that of Wharton and Fauset, as well as a number of others in this book in some or all of their work, was not to rebel but to appropriate, remodel, take on the high-culture western novel as it had been crafted by the great English and European masters, primarily white men, and claim it as their own.

Wharton was more successful at writing herself into that great tradition than any other American at the time. She published such beautifully crafted traditional novels that, in the eyes of young upstarts in the 1920s such as Hemingway and Fitzgerald, she became the very symbol of high-culture, old-fashioned, outdated novel-mak-ing—the precursor to topple, the master to displace. The story of Fitzgerald's need to fortify himself with alcohol before meeting Edith Wharton in her *salon* is leg-endary,[38] and Wharton herself joked about her reputation for being old-fashioned when she received younger authors' praise in the 1920s. She wrote to William

Gerhardie in 1922: "I am so accustomed nowadays to being regarded as a deplorable example of what people used to read in the Dark Ages before the 'tranche de vie' had been rediscovered, that my very letter-paper blushes as I thank a novelist of your generation for his praise." She said to Fitzgerald of *The Great Gatsby* in 1925 (before they met): "I am touched at your sending me a copy, for I feel that to your generation, which has taken such a flying leap into the future, I must represent the literary equivalent of tufted furniture and gas chandeliers."[39] That Edith Wharton had achieved what she wished in being regarded as a superb traditional novelist— one not swayed by experimental fads and modernist gimmickry—is clear in her statement to a friend about *The Mother's Recompense* (1925): "It *is*, of course, what an English reviewer (I forget in what paper) reviewing it jointly with Mrs. Woolf's latest [*Mrs. Dalloway*], calls it: an old-fashioned novel. I was not trying to follow the new methods, as May Sinclair so pantingly & anxiously does."[40] Wharton's success at writing herself into the old-fashioned high tradition marks one of the great literary achievements of the period.

Jessie Redmon Fauset's relative lack of success is just as important, and certainly just as interesting. As McDowell argues of *Plum Bun* and I would extend to *There Is Confusion* and *Comedy: American Style* as well, Fauset's long fiction looks totally conventional but actually is not. Her novels exist in tension with themselves. They want to be utterly traditional yet they fight with tradition. The result, in contrast to the almost overly controlled fiction of Wharton, is unstable fiction, highly imperfect and often frustrating books that in their very instability and, at times, ponderousness speak to the complexity of Fauset's ambivalence about the novel itself as a form capable of carrying what she needs it to. All of Fauset's books attempt too much: too much plot, too much description, too much concept. Consequently, they frequently lose life under their heavy load. But that is precisely the point. It seems to me that Fauset tries but finally fails to compress her vision into the well-made, cleanly focused, protagonist-antagonist, realistic novel. And that failure, for me, points to her books' true power. Often they are more compelling subtextually than textually, more vital in their covert, almost too well-disguised implications—for example, *Plum Bun*'s trope on passing or *Comedy: American Style*'s brilliant fusion of changeling, American Dream (Nightmare), and fairy-tale witch plots—than in their overt rhetorical and narrative aspects. Had Fauset been able to start writing novels as a younger woman; had her career as a novelist not coincided so directly in the 1920s with the exploitative pressure on black artists to be exotic and flam-boyant, which she understandably loathed and rebelled against; had her education been a little less fine, strange as that sounds, or her class a little less elevated; had she been free to write full time—might she have dared to pull her buried plots closer to the surface and forsaken the prosaic and everyday a little more in favor of the parabolic as an artist?

But my question may miss the mark. What Fauset's novels, neglected for far too long, do offer is subtle and complex. Early in her first novel she takes what feels like a long and unnecessary detour into an elaborate genealogy that names all of the ancestors of Peter Bye, the young man Fauset's woman artist will eventually marry. In fact, the narrative loop is no detour at all. It is a direct line back to two symbolic figures. One is the black man, Caezer, who asks which name is his in the

Bye Bible so that he can cross it out—so that he can record in the west's most sacred text his resistance to false naming and to white manipulation of black men. The other is the black woman, Judy Bye, whose response is the opposite. Laboriously, personally, without help from anyone else, she writes her own name JUDY in the Bible. She inscribes her own original, self-articulating presence in the text that will move down from generation to generation. In other words, the first act of authorship in Fauset's first act of authorship as a novelist is that of an uneducated slave woman who insists on writing her own name into history. In a novel largely about a modern black woman's terrible struggle to make art in a racist world and yet retain what it means to be human, the image speaks.

10 Slow Starvation: Hunger and Hatred in Anzia Yezierska, Ellen Glasgow, and Edith Summers Kelley

Why worry? Nobody knows how writing is written, the writers least of all!
GERTRUDE STEIN TO ANZIA YEZIERSKA[1]

It was easy for Stein to say. Neglect was not a problem for her, and neither was fame. She could afford to ask, "Why worry?"

Such confidence did not plague Anzia Yezierska, Ellen Glasgow, or Edith Summers Kelley. For each, as for many of the writers in this book, the act of writing tapped and produced tremendous insecurities. Yezierska obsessively revised, rewrote, and reworked her material—never satisfied, never secure in her art. Glasgow vacillated between agreeing that the first twenty-five years of her career were undistinguished and then complaining bitterly about neglect and lack of recognition. Kelley, like a figure out of a story by Charlotte Perkins Gilman, watched poverty and the exhausting demands of motherhood eat away at her talent. For these three writers—although extremely different from each other in basic ways—authorship was anything but easy, joyful, exuberant. It had its happy moments, of course. But it was mainly full of agonizing isolation and struggle, deep doubts and disappointments.

Anzia Yezierska loved romanticizing her development as an artist. In interviews, correspondence, autobiography, and fiction she encouraged a popular fairy-tale image of herself as a kind of American Cinderella: a poor, uneducated, spontaneous talent who burst miraculously out of the dirt and oppression of New York's Lower East Side to pour out her heart in raw, undisciplined prose. In response to the Houghton Mifflin publicity department's request for information, for example, Yezierska reported that a university department head had said to her:

"A writer?" the woman stared at me. "My dear child—you might as well want to be dean of the university. There are native-born writers who do not earn their salt. What chance is there for you with your immigrant English?"

"If I can't get a chance to learn the American English, I'll write in 'immigrant English,' " I answered, "—but write I must."

And without guide or compass I plunged into the sea of the short story and have
been earning a living writing before I had a chance to learn American English.''[2]

This version of Yezierska's entrance into authorship was enthusiastically embraced by contemporary promoters. After she marched unannounced into his office,
the syndicated columnist Dr. Frank Crane, who wrote for the huge Hearst chain,
devoted a column to the author in 1920, exclaiming: ''Here was a person. . . . Here
was an East Side Jewess that has struggled and suffered in the desperate battle for
life amid the swarms of New York. . . . Why? Because she wanted to—write. And
that, ladies and gentlemen, is all there is to genius. An undying flame, an unquench-
able hope, an inviolable belief that you are God's stenographer.''[3] Echoing Crane's
portrait, Burton Rascoe wrote in *The Bookman* in 1922: ''Miss Yezierska is an
extremely emotional, acutely sensitive woman with almost no mental discipline or
training and only a meager education, who has somehow managed in the stories of
hers that I have read to give life and vividness and drama to her pictures of the
ghetto.''[4]

Partially, this portrait is accurate. As Yezierska's daughter, Louise Levitas Henriksen, states repeatedly in her superb biography of her mother, *Anzia Yezierska: A
Writer's Life,* Yezierska lived and wrote from the heart. Both as a person and as a
writer, she was impulsive, intense, always passionate. But at the same time, as
Henriksen also points out, Yezierska was educated and highly disciplined—indeed,
she was a fanatical reviser and compulsive worker. It is true that she grew up in
extreme poverty in the ghetto, labored in sweatshops, and had to struggle fiercely
against the expectation that she would settle for scant education and the usual
Orthodox Jewish path of devoting her life to being a wife and mother. Nevertheless,
Yezierska the writer did not burst unmediated from the ghetto into the publishing
world. For six years she worked during the day and went to night school to study
English. Receiving a scholarship, she graduated with a degree in domestic science
from the Teachers College of Columbia University in 1904. In 1918, following an
intimate but unconsummated relationship with John Dewey, who encouraged her
writing, she took a creative writing course at Columbia. Anzia Yezierska's self-
image as an untutored, spontaneous voice direct from the ghetto, an image eagerly
picked up and repeated by others and certainly not disputed by her, was not literally
true.

There are truths besides the literal, however. Although Yezierska was educated,
how did she *feel*? Did she feel that English and what she had learned about published,
elite literature were part of her, were in her gut as her childhood was—or did she
spin the fairy tale of herself as unvarnished, unmediated, because that was how she
felt? And how she wished to write? It may be that Yezierska's image and even
practice of rawness as a writer (not to mention as a person) were in part deliberately
assumed, or preserved, to keep her different, special, interesting. Much as Mary
Austin or Gertrude Stein or, emerging a little later than Yezierska in the 1920s,
Zora Neale Hurston realized the commercial value of self-dramatization in the modern marketplace, so it may be that to some degree Yezierska knew that it was good
business to play up her miraculousness. Yet I doubt that her image of untutored
genius was totally or even mostly calculated. Under Yezierska's publicity-conscious
attachment to the myth of her spontaneous emergence as a writer was tremendous

fear that acquired technique would kill her talent, silence her. Not unlike Jessie Fauset, Yezierska knew that to succeed as a writer she had to pass deep into the dominant culture, which meant for her, as an Eastern European immigrant and Jew, immersing herself in the scrubbed, hush-toned, degree-deferring white Anglo-Saxon Protestant intellectual and literary establishment. To complicate things, this move was not wholly unappealing. Throughout her life Yezierska was drawn to white Anglo-Saxon Protestant models and mentors: John Dewey, Clifford Smyth, Mary Austin, Amy Lowell, Zona Gale, Dorothy Canfield Fisher. What she perceived as their coolness and restraint in speech, body language, lifestyle, and art she passionately admired and envied, even as, at some deep and hard-to-acknowledge level, she also despised their world. Emphasizing and even exaggerating the supposed miraculousness of her emergence as an artist—her art's alleged eruption out of pure undisciplined passion—was one way of staving off dissolution, complete co-optation and assimilation as a working-class or even underclass Jewish artist forced—but also wanting—to adopt certain middle-class values at the same time that she was rightly terrified of losing her vitality, her voice, in the polite parlor of bourgeois aesthetics.

In short, for Yezierska it was not simply that middle-class work habits and aesthetic principles were repellent but necessary. To write, she truly needed and desired the cleanness, quiet, privacy, and autonomy commonly associated with middle-class elite authorship in the west. Yet that very stillness and control threatened her creativity: the loud, impolite, out-of-control art she wanted to make. How to combine the clarity and precision of disciplined form with the chaos and anarchy of passionately felt emotion and thought—in art, in life—obsessed Anzia Yezierska. She stripped her life almost savagely of friends, family, possessions, domesticity, even clothes, and then tried desperately to fill it back up. As Henriksen describes it, Yezierska lived in spaces that she designed to be spartan but into which she almost compulsively reintroduced mess and dirt; and she dressed in a virtual uniform. She encased her voluptuous body in a plain tailored suit, blue when she was young, gray as she aged, which simultaneously contained and, of course, failed to contain her enormous physical power. She lived in places as different as Hollywood, small-town Vermont, and New York City, but never, biography and autobiography suggest, felt at home. In her life as in her art, trying to impose form and control without losing life defined a constant struggle for Anzia Yezierska.

Her early story "My Own People," included in her 1920 collection *Hungry Hearts and Other Stories,* dramatizes this conflict. In the story the young writer Sophie Sapinsky meticulously establishes private writing space in the ghetto by renting a room of her own, solitary and well separated from the distracting demands of other people's lives. Among other things, this room symbolizes bourgeois art. To get to her space Sophie must walk down a narrow, dark corridor to the place farthest from the street and its messy throng of pushcarts, peddlers, dirty children, and haggling housewives. Once ensconced in this luxurious separate space (in reality a dark, tiny cell on a filthy airshaft with "a narrow window [that] looked out into the bottom of a chimney-like pit, where lay the accumulated refuse from a score of crowded kitchens''),[5] Sophie attempts to write. She cannot. She rereads her grand Emersonian titles—"Believe in Yourself," "The Quest of the Ideal"—and despairs. Her words are dead. She writhes with a "wild, blind hunger to release the dumbness that choked her" (*HH*, p. 228) and agonizes: "The intensity of experience, the surge of emotion that had been hers when she wrote—where were they? The words had failed to catch the life-beat—had failed to register the passion she had poured into them. . . . Choked with discouragement, the cry broke from her, 'O—God—God help me! I feel—I see, but it all dies in me—dumb!' " (*HH*, p. 229).

These images of starvation, choking, and dumbness become violent as Sophie barricades herself in her room:

> "But it *is* in me!" With clenched fist she smote her bosom. "It must be in me! I believe in it! I got to get it out—even if it tears my flesh in pieces—even if it kills me! . . .
> "I'll push on—on—I'll not eat—I'll not sleep—I'll not move from this spot till I get it to say on the paper what I got in my heart!" (*HH*, pp. 229, 230)

Unlike Jewett's writer glued to her schoolhouse desk in *The Country of the Pointed Firs*, Sophie is able to make her confinement work. "Slowly the dead words seemed to begin to breathe" (*HH*, p. 230). But then—just as the embalmed words start to move—real life bursts in on Sophie, and the intruder is no boring old man named Littlepage. It is the young writer's sunken-eyed, needy, talkative neighbor: Hanneh Breineh.

Sophie tries to ignore Hanneh. She concentrates on her lofty art as Hanneh rattles in her ear, in a scene, on Yezierska's part, of dazzling formal and conceptual control. "Resolved not to listen to the intruder," Sophie mentally dissects the niceties of various Emersonian titles for her essay while her neighbor, in an avalanche of words, pours out the pain of having to send her underage daughter out each day to work in a sweatshop so that the family can eat. Yezierska's juxtaposition of cool, elegant, cerebrated, inherited white male written tradition (Emerson) and hot, violent, spontaneous, inherited female Jewish oral tradition (Hanneh Breineh) perfectly captures the antithetical worlds that Sophie, the immigrant Jewish woman writer, struggles to reconcile. Hanneh's explosion into Emersonian space and her defiant claiming of it as her own literally act out the authorial problem for Yezierska: how to connect (much less fuse) the conflicting worlds of impeccably controlled, intellectual, white Anglo-Saxon Protestant patriarchal art, on the one hand, and of vibrantly uninhibited, luxuriously emotional, maternal Jewish oral tradition, on the other. As Hanneh Breineh announces to Sophie early in the story, whether the young woman likes it or not: "I'll treat you like a mother!" [*HH*, p. 227]).

Ironically, Yezierska's solution in "My Own People," as is also the case in *Bread Givers*, depends on the Jewish father. (I say ironically because Yezierska could celebrate in fiction the relationship that she could never work out in life: her bond with her Old World Orthodox father.) Hanneh's invasion of Sophie's space leads to a sacred meal provided by the old man Shmendrik, who feeds Sophie, Hanneh, and Hanneh's starving children. Putting "his hands over the heads of the children in silent benediction," Shmendrik miraculously produces a "cake and nuts and raisins and even a bottle of wine" (*HH*, p. 238). A "sacrificial solemnity" falls over the group; Hanneh pours the wine "with almost religious fervor"; and no one eats until "the ritual was completed." This ritual consists of Shmendrik saluting Hanneh—"Hanneh Breineh—you drink from my Sabbath wine-glass!"; the two of them clinking their glasses; and Hanneh, after bestowing blessings on Shmendrik and Sophie, lifting the cup to her lips and drinking (*HH*, pp. 240–41). At this point, "the spell was broken" and everyone plunges into the food.

The complete antithesis of the private, solitary communion depicted in *The Awakening*, this ritual in "My Own People" pulls Sophie into a group much as the food at the Bowden reunion pulls Jewett's woman writer into, rather than away from, relationships and community. In this case the group is an impromptu family made up of Shmendrik, Hanneh, and a large number of swirling, dirty, hungry children. The communal ceremony breaks in on Sophie's isolation, disrupts her tidy, writerly regimen, first to immerse her in family and celebrate the nourishment to be received from traditional patriarchal culture, and then to drench her in the life-steeped words of a loud, physical, this-worldly Jewish mother. That voice, literally, frees Sophie's. A powerful figure far closer to Dunbar-Nelson's Praline Woman or her Wisened One than to the silent, long-suffering Victorian mother of Anglo mythology, a depressing version of whom appears in Glasgow's *Barren Ground*, Hanneh makes language come alive in exactly the way that Sophie, bent in frustration over her crumpled pages, wishes to but cannot. Hanneh shrieks at her children: "Gluttons—wolves—thieves! . . . I should only live to bury you all in one day!" (*HH*, p. 237). Or she lovingly toasts Sophie: "May you yet marry yourself from our basement to a millionaire!" (*HH*, p. 241). In either case, Yezierska's blocked writer studies Hanneh Breineh, "this ragged wreck of a woman":

> "Ach, if I could only write like Hanneh Breineh talks!" thought Sophie. "Her words dance with a thousand colors. Like a rainbow it flows from her lips." Sentences from her own essays marched before her, stiff and wooden. How clumsy, how unreal, were her most labored phrases compared to Hanneh Breineh's spontaneity. Fascinated, she listened to Hanneh Breineh, drinking her words as a thirst-perishing man drinks water. Every bubbling phrase filled her with a drunken rapture to create.
>
> "Up till now I was only trying to write from my head. It wasn't real—it wasn't life. Hanneh Breineh is real. Hanneh Breineh is life." (*HH*, pp. 242–43)

Having begun with Emerson, Sophie graduates to Hanneh Breineh.

Near the end of "My Own People," however, Sophie's voicelessness temporarily returns. Charity inspectors invade the tenement to upbraid the impoverished celebrants for their audacity in consuming cake and raisins and nuts and wine; and in the face of this intimidating bourgeois rhetoric, Sophie is once more, as she was when the story began, struck dumb: "Sophie's throat strained with passionate protest, but no words came to her release" (*HH*, p. 246). First, Shmendrik speaks and, after him, Hanneh. As a result Sophie, empowered by these two, bursts into brilliant, enraged voice (*HH*, pp. 247–48), and the story ends with her gloriously verbal: "The barriers burst. Something in her began pouring itself out. She felt for her pencil—paper—and began to write." Words rush out of her all night, and "My Own People" closes at dawn. "Sophie looked up: 'Ach! At last it writes itself in me!' she whispered triumphantly. 'It's not me—it's their cries—my own people— crying in me! Hanneh Breineh, Shmendrik, they will not be stilled in me, till all America stops to listen' " (*HH*, p. 249).

At story's end, Sophie may live in her private room, but that privacy has been fundamentally altered. Her space and the community's space, the space of Hanneh Breineh, Shmendrik, and the many children, connect and interchange. Because Sophie has gone out into their world to eat, they have come into hers and she has speech, words that live, writing that is not dead.

How to achieve for herself the integration of worlds imaginatively won in "My Own People" tormented Yezierska for most, if not all, of her life. Writing was the center of her existence; she let nothing come before her art. She wrote constantly and revised fanatically (her daughter recalls in her biography how her one day each week with her mother, Saturday, was frequently devoted to unrelieved concentration on Yezierska's manuscripts); yet Yezierska rarely felt satisfied about her career. She changed publishers often because she was sure, as she told them repeatedly, that they were not promoting her work properly. She found it impossible to live and write in the Lower East Side, where her subject matter was, yet when she tried to build a life for herself elsewhere, she felt creatively empty.

Given these conflicts, it is not surprising that clashing ethics and aesthetics constantly inform her fiction. Orthodox patriarchal erudition and privilege crash up against this-worldly Jewish maternal wisdom, passion, and vitality. Cool Anglo control, whether of writing or of living, vies with intense, messy immersion in language and life. Tidy middle-class individualism wars with jostling working-class spatial overlap and layering, whether of territory or of ego. Given to extremes and often to stereotypes, Yezierska's fiction, especially that written in her prime during the late teens and 1920s, is almost never calm. At its most successful it exists in a state, to borrow from physics, of unstable equilibrium. Formally and conceptually her best work succeeds because it achieves neither resolution nor integration of competing ideas and aesthetics but temporary, precarious cohabitation. Sophie must live both in her room and out of it; the people in the tenement simultaneously feel entitled to go into her room and reluctant to do so. Pushed too far in one direction—allowed to have too much "spontaneous," colorful, from-the-gut writing—and Yezierska's fiction explodes into bathos. Pushed too far in the other direction—given too much smoothing out of language and form—and her fiction waters down into nondescript polite prose. (This kind of oversmoothness is partly what keeps her later novel, *All I Could Never Be* [1932], from matching *Bread Givers*.) Like a mixture of volatile chemical compounds that do not want to share the same space, much less blend, her fiction at its most vibrant holds together without harmony, without true stability, elements that want to diverge.

The achievement of *Bread Givers* (1925) stems directly from this impulse to forcibly combine clashing elements—to lock Emerson and Hanneh Breineh in the same room and see what their children look like. At several points Louise Levitas Henriksen characterizes her mother as "a born rule breaker,"[6] and the concept certainly describes her art. *Bread Givers* by conventional standards is a mess. It is a hodgepodge of realism, folk tale, fairy tale, melodrama, polemic, exposé, and Horatio Alger how-to myth. The book does not at all behave the way a nice middle-class novel should.

But it works. And what makes it work, I believe, is precisely its generic instability, its coherence achieved not in spite of but out of its internal unresolved tensions.

Like a number of the other long narratives I have discussed—*The Country of the Pointed Firs, The Awakening, The Land of Little Rain*—*Bread Givers* has both a strong through line and an alinear, or even antilinear, overall shape. The novel's plot line charts Sara Smolinsky's move from poverty to economic security, from childhood to adulthood, from ignorance to education, from rebellion against her father to acceptance of him. To describe it only in that way, however, is to imply a formal and conceptual easiness that the book does not display. *Bread Givers* develops by jerks. Generically it vacillates among forms and progresses according to a principle of narrative patchwork rather than of sustained, sequential flow.

Discrete narrative episodes protrude in *Bread Givers*: the love stories of Sara's three sisters, which take up the first third of the book; the disastrous relocation of Sara's parents from New York City to Elizabeth, New Jersey; Sara's experience of living on her own and going to college; or her miraculous engagement to the perfect man followed by her surprise reconciliation with her father. The novel is in some ways so chaotic that the first third might be described as folk tale, the center as realism, and the end as fairy tale, though elements of all three appear everywhere.

Running through *Bread Givers* from beginning to end, however, is the strong, formal influence of oral tradition. Following one of the most familiar patterns in western folklore, the first three stories actually constitute one story: The same thing happens each time with different characters.[7] Bessie loves a manufacturer and is forced by her father to marry a fish peddler. Mashah loves a pianist and is forced by her father to marry a phony diamond salesman. Fania loves a poet and is forced by her father to marry a gambler. Three times the same narrative repeats (the number itself is talismanic in western folk literature): An ogre father forces his helpless daughter to give up a good man in favor of a bad or disgusting one. Although told realistically (no "Once upon a time" appears to crudely give form away), the strong, buried genre of the novel's first third, with its repetition of exactly the same story three times, obviously comes more directly from folk or peasant tradition than from high, polished, modern novel tradition, with its premium on narrative variety, innovation, and originality.

If Yezierska's next move at first seems a dramatic switch in form, actually it is not. Although the Elizabeth, New Jersey, grocery story section is painfully realistic, it also draws heavily on folk and oral literary traditions. Change a store for a horse and the episode perfectly conforms to the classic horse-trade yarn of nineteenth-century American vernacular literature, which is simply a historically specific variant on folk and oral swindle tales the world over.

Such folk and oral forms come and go throughout *Bread Givers* at both the surface and the substructure level. In the midst of one of the most realistic scenes in the novel, Sara's unsuccessful attempt on a bitterly cold night to stay warm in her unheated tenement room, fantasy, even fairy tale, erupts totally unexpectedly into the text: Sara's mother appears out of nowhere with a featherbed and a jar of pickled herring, only to disappear just as abruptly back into the night. Likewise the closing section of the novel contains major surprises—violations not simply of credibility but of genre. In light of the gritty realism of much of the novel—its powerful evocations of real hunger, real dirt, real exhaustion, real violence, and real struggle (think of Sara's furious fight to get even one piece of meat in her watery stew in the cheap cafeteria, or her argument with the college dean that it is preposterous to require physical education of a person who spends hours every day working in a sweatshop as an ironer)—the resolution of *Bread Givers* reads like a fairy tale. Into the text step a wicked stepmother (Reb Smolinsky's second wife), Prince Charming (Hugo Seelig), and a happily-ever-after fastforward wrap-up: Sara and Hugo will marry, and Reb, his tyranny forgiven by his daughter, will live with them.

Maybe it is possible to defend the book's conclusion as realistic; nice men like Hugo do exist, and rebellious daughters do grow up and accept their parents. But *how* do these things come to pass in Yezierska's novel? Process is almost nonexistent; things just happen. They fall out of the sky—as in fairy tales. Hugo, like the earlier vision of Sara's mother in the night, arrives out of nowhere, as does the daughter's ability to accept her father. In sharp contrast, other important developments in the novel receive detailed motivation and causality: Sara's decision to leave home, her determination to get an education, her sisters' capitulations to their father's will, Sara's final parting with her mother as the old woman is dying. Two totally different generic orders coexist and swirl around in *Bread Givers*, one deriving from folk- and fairy-tale tradition and depending on patterns of magical repetition, transformation, and change, the other coming out of the realistic novel tradition and depending on accurate representation of credible psychological motivation, probable causation, and believable descriptions of physical environment and human behavior. Like Pauline Hopkins in *Of One Blood,* Yezierska in *Bread Givers* contradicts, conflates, and confuses conventional high-culture white western generic expectations to create her own new de-formed form.

In the creative writing course that Anzia Yezierska took at Columbia University seven years before the publication of *Bread Givers*, her story "The Fat of the Land" (which would be chosen in 1920 by the influential editor of *The Best Short Stories* series, Edward J. O'Brien, as the best short story of 1919) met some sharp criticism. As Henriksen reports: " 'It's not a story,' the teacher and students agreed. 'It has no plot.' 'Over-emotional.' 'Feeling without form.' " Yezierska defended her creation: " 'If the method I evolved is unconventional, lacking in form, so much the better. . . . I care nothing for the ready-made mental garments of the writer who has been fitted by colleges and short story classes.' "[8] In part Yezierska is lying. Of course, she cared about forms taught in colleges and short story classes. Why else did she take the class at Columbia? But there is also great truth in her expressed disdain for conventional, polite, taught form, as a work such as *Bread Givers* shows. Her lifelong obsession as an artist focused on making words live, breathe, and move on the printed page—the challenge she dramatized at the outset of her career in "My Own People." Inextricable from that struggle with language was the question of how to create forms that would contain and order but not crush and academize. In other words, at the level of form as well as of language, Yezierska labored to realize in print the vitality of oral tradition. Just as she was totally unwilling to elevate the speech of the people she wrote about, so her fiction formally holds onto folk- and fairy-tale patterns—pushcart and kitchen table aesthetic. Mothers don't show up miraculously in the dead of night? Three sisters don't have exactly the same thing happen to each of them? Perfect husbands don't appear out of nowhere? Of course they do, all the time. Maybe not in the stories university-trained writers tell. But are those the only stories—the only forms to put in a book about real life?

Capturing real life was also the issue for Ellen Glasgow, who wrestled with class as tenaciously as did Anzia Yezierska, but at the opposite end of the social scale. If Yezierska had to struggle to break into WASP America, Ellen Glasgow had to try to break out. She knew that in order to tell the truth about the South she had to refuse to follow in the tradition of Southern white sentimental prose, "the romantic delusion," as she would put it late in life.[9] She would have to write unpretty, complicated, fierce fiction—not the delicate imaginings of a Lady, which she as the daughter of solid upper-middle-class Virginia parents had been raised to epitomize. How to achieve that goal was the question.

Like many other artistically ambitious women writers at the turn into the twentieth century—Alice Dunbar-Nelson, Edith Wharton, Jessie Fauset, Willa Cather, Anzia Yezierska, Nella Larsen—Ellen Glasgow found it extremely difficult to integrate her identity in terms of gender, race, class, and the ambition to make art. For Glasgow the conservatism of her region (she lived virtually all of her life in the house where she grew up in Richmond, Virginia) plus the force of institutionalized heterosexuality, especially given the strength of her attachment to her privileged class standing, gathered and gained devastating reinforcement in the limiting but alluring (for her) white ideal of the Southern Lady. Stated simply, that ideal repressed anger, particularly anger against white men. But anger against white men, beginning with her father, was the primary, driving force of Ellen Glasgow's life as a woman.

For the white Southern Lady, overt rebellion against the authority of white men of one's own or a higher class was strictly forbidden. As the historian Anne Firor Scott explains, the white ideal of the Southern Lady required women to be "meek, mild, quiet outside their homes, self-abnegating, kind to all, and to accept their husbands as lord and master."[10] Resistance to this code, like resistance to white men's power, including its expression in sexual abuse and physical violence, was conveniently rendered taboo by the ideal itself. Enmeshed, Glasgow both lived within and despised this Southern ethos. She adored the mother who personified the Southern Lady—and, deep down, hated her. She constantly involved herself in heterosexual relationships—yet repeatedly made sure she did not end up in one for life (i.e., married). This tortuous, buried anger at the feminine ideal assigned her by her region, class, and race compromised almost all of Glasgow's work. With the clear exception of *Barren Ground* (1925), most of what she wrote during her long and prolific career from the late 1890s to the early 1940s (she published eighteen novels, and a nineteenth came out posthumously) sublimates and disguises her true fury in novels about everything except what she felt most keenly: her own experience as a woman.

Glasgow's solution to her conflict was much the same as that of many other Southern white New Women at the turn of the century. For most of her career, she directed her personal anger, which the ideal of the Lady proscribed, into the socially accepted channel of public reform. Scott describes how progressive-minded middle-

and upper-middle-class white New Women in the South at the turn of the century joined together to work for moderate change in the social sector: limitation of child labor, temperance, compulsory education, prison reform.[11] True to her class and culture, Ellen Glasgow, who herself became active in antivivisectionist work and the suffrage campaign, threw herself into competent but formulaic Progressive Era problem novels, historical sagas, and pseudo-exposé fictions. One after another, objectified fictionalized attacks on social problems poured from Glasgow's pen for the first twenty-five years of her career, with *Virginia* (1913) the only novel coming close to revealing anything personal about the author. She could be a Lady, totally private about her own situation, and yet voice anger—deflected, rechanneled, camouflaged, but nonetheless anger. She could write impassioned novels, yet at the same time, if she was careful to keep the subject matter impersonal, she could live peacefully within a conservative political subculture and, perhaps more important, private emotional subculture, as a Lady.

Abetting this strategy was the fact that, like so many other women writers at the time, Glasgow associated high art with men and yet was determined to be an artist. Consequently, not only because of the confining ideal of the Lady but also because of her ambition to be an artist with—as Charlotte Perkins Gilman put it—a capital A, Glasgow spent her life as a fiction writer who, with rare exception, denied, buried, hid, or projected and transferred her true feelings as a woman. As Linda Wagner explains in *Ellen Glasgow: Beyond Convention*, it took Glasgow "twenty years to be comfortable writing about a female protagonist." Her early novels include strong female characters whom the author invariably removes to the background and then condemns to conventionality. Wagner persuasively theorizes that this avoidance of female protagonists and reductive treatment of female unconventionality reflect Glasgow's belief that, for most readers, men are superior to women and the corollary gender-bound premise that "certain kinds of activities are more valuable than others, just as certain kinds of knowledge—philosophy, science, history—are also more valuable." Wagner summarizes:

> Characters in her early novels don't garden or cook, though Glasgow's notebooks are full of recipes; they discuss free will, Malthus, and John Stuart Mill. When critics guessed that Glasgow's anonymous first novel, *The Descendant* [1897], had been written by Harold Frederic, author of *The Damnation of Theron Ware* [1896], Glasgow was delighted. She may have been a woman writer, but during the 1890's she was a woman writer trying desperately to pretend that she was, in fact, a liberal, well-educated man.[12]

This desire to be classed among male artists never really left Glasgow, even after her partial self-confrontation in *Virginia* in 1913 and then her more complete disavowal of disguise in *Barren Ground* in 1925. A major part of Dorinda Oakley's "triumph" as a farmer in *Barren Ground* consists of being admired by another farmer as if she were a man.[13] As Wagner points out, *Vein of Iron*, published a decade after *Barren Ground*, retreats dramatically from self-portraiture into a conventional split protagonist: "The isolated philosopher-artist is pictured as male; the person searching for love is female." This split argues that Glasgow continued to see "her own role in life, as woman and as writer, as paradoxical."[14] Likewise, as Wagner observes with great insight, the title alone of Glasgow's posthumously published autobiography, *The Woman Within* (1954), reiterates the bitter irresolution of gender and art that haunted her throughout her career.[15]

Yet in *Barren Ground* Glasgow did face this dilemma fully. Before it, *Virginia*, by exploring the waste and stunting of a woman's life in traditional, privileged, Southern white society, helped Glasgow move toward open and honest expression of her private anger as a woman. With her mother and beloved sister Cary dead (this sister's death in 1911 probably moved Glasgow to write *Virginia*), Glasgow could in 1913, at the age of forty, at last attack the crippling ideal that all three of them had been taught to embody. Still, this early novel wobbles, as Anne Goodwyn Jones points out: "In *Virginia*, Ellen Glasgow started out to define and embalm the southern lady of the 1880s. She ended up almost enshrining her."[16] Because the ideal was so very closely associated with two people she loved, and because she was so invested in it herself, Glasgow lost perspective in *Virginia*. If she pities her heroine, she also feels protective and defensive; the novel's sentimental conclusion ends up colluding in the very ethic that she ostensibly regrets.

Barren Ground is different. Published twelve years after *Virginia*, it is a hard, tough novel, simultaneously very personal and, in most ways, clear-sighted.

Glasgow knew that *Barren Ground* was special. She stated when the novel came out, "It is the best book I have written,"[17] and she never wavered in that high opinion. In 1931 she called *Barren Ground* "the one of my books I like best." In 1932 she declared it "the truest novel ever written. Not true to locality only—I don't mean that—but to life and to the inevitable change and fall of the years. That book deserves to live. It is a perfectly honest interpretation of experience, without illusion, without evasion . . ." (Glasgow's ellipsis).[18] Glasgow says in her book about her own writing, *A Certain Measure*, that *Barren Ground* marked a turning point in her career. Calling attention to the book's form, she explains that the novel captures a "universal rhythm more fluid than any material texture" and that the handling of time in the book reflects nature (the seasons) rather than some artificial, superimposed authorial scheme. Reflecting on her fascination with narrative theory, she explains that she always read everything she could about the making of fiction, and like Fauset, she has advice for beginners. They should study technique and the principles of construction thoroughly so that they can then consciously forget all that they have learned. The best writing, Glasgow concludes, comes from letting one's knowledge seep underground to operate unconsciously, spontaneously, organically.[19]

Glasgow specifically links this theory of organic composition to *Barren Ground*. Dorinda Oakley came to her, she explains, immediately after the completion of *Life and Gabriella* (1915), her upbeat, falsely cheerful, New Woman novel written on the heels of *Virginia*; but Glasgow "pushed her back." She avoided Dorinda. However, the character refused to go away. She was "buried, but alive, for a decade, when she emerged from the yeasty medium with hard round limbs and the bloom of health on her cheeks." According to Glasgow, this character differed fundamentally from the "anemic offspring of the brain" that any author knows how to force onto the page. She came out of Glasgow herself; nothing about her was unknown or unknowable; she was tied to her author "by a living nerve."[20]

The form of *Barren Ground* reflects this special, intimate relationship that Glasgow always described when speaking of the novel. Not that she, any more than

Edith Wharton or Jessie Fauset, was interested in faddish, self-conscious experimentation. After meeting Gertrude Stein, Glasgow recorded contemptuously in her private notebook: "Gertrude Stein—a wise overgrown child, as obvious as an infant. Likes obvious things. Barnum discovered that people are always willing to pay for the pleasure of being fooled. 'Alice, Alice, Gert is eating chocolate!' "[21] Nevertheless, *Barren Ground* is formally innovative. The book does not so much feel built, as do most of Glasgow's books, as it feels grown. Most Glasgow novels display highly cerebrated, even graphable architecture. The absolute opposite of a text such as *Bread Givers*, they are almost formulaic in their structural conventionality and orderliness, right down to their frequently very schematic Tables of Contents, some of which seem literally to construct logical arguments.[22] In contrast, *Barren Ground*, taking its very name from the organic world that Glasgow repeatedly evoked in descriptions of the novel and of her process of creating it, seems formed by principles more dense and interlapping.

The famous image of the tangled bank at the end of Charles Darwin's *The Origin of Species*, especially given Glasgow's passion for and wide reading in Darwin's work, provides a useful way of describing this felt structure in *Barren Ground*.[23] Although the book moves from one place in Dorinda's life to another—a large and dramatic sweep in terms of the changes in the heroine's circumstances and consciousness (she grows from a vulnerable adolescent into a tough, independent woman)—the real terrain of the novel is psychological, the complexly multidirectional labyrinth of Dorinda's emotions and decisions. This dramatic field is not linear but matrixed and tangled. It is as if Glasgow, like Darwin, keeps us walking around in crisscrossing paths on one small, but representative, dense space. What fills *Barren Ground* is detail: microscopic attention to Dorinda's interior struggle to survive. Glasgow is neither the social historian nor the satirist in *Barren Ground* that she is in most of her other fiction; instead, she is a naturalist. Like Darwin, she studies closely—with passionate care and attention to detail—one tangled bank, Dorinda Oakley's emotional life. We encounter some of the same things over and over, such as Dorinda's announcement that she is done with love; and despite glimpses of a larger world (New York), we never really move far in this book (the novel begins and ends at Old Farm). The bank contains the world. To know one piece of nature well is, for Darwin, to know the whole. To know Dorinda well is, for Glasgow, to know the whole.

And what we know is rage. The power of *Barren Ground* comes from the way that Glasgow confronts her own anger—her fury at heterosexuality itself—and imagines how that rage can liberate rather than imprison and incapacitate a woman. That is, the charge frequently made that Glasgow was a feminist who hated men is, in my opinion, largely true.[24] The challenge, I would say, is not to deny that fact but to understand it—to ask why Glasgow felt as she did, how she used her anger or was used by it, and where it finally led her as an artist.

Barren Ground links male violence, heterosexuality, and the real or potential destruction of women.

Appearing early in the novel, the drunkard father of the book's principal male character, Jason Greylock, exists to symbolize the inherited white male power structure in the South. He offers a horrifying glimpse of the privileged white heterosexual patriarch, conveniently released by alcohol from any inhibitions he might otherwise have and therefore naked—raw—in his exercise of power. Old Doctor Greylock lurches around his broken-down Big House at night, where he perpetuates slavery by keeping a black woman and their "illegitimate" children dependent on him, and brandishes "a horsewhip, looking in every room and closet for something to flog" (*BG*, p. 93). This is Jason's birthright. This is the paternal role, that of demonic despot at Five Oaks, that he inherits, and with it the long history of unleashed white male sexual exploitation and violence which it signifies.

Yet the problem is not simply that a powerful white man (no matter how weak on the surface, as in Jason's case) victimizes women. Worse for Glasgow is the fact that women's own sexuality traps them. Dorinda comes from a long line of women prey to their own heterosexual desire. Her great aunt and namesake Dorinda threw herself in the millpond when she could not have the man she loved. This great aunt's sister Abigail "went deranged about some man she hadn't seen but a few times, and they had to put her away in a room with barred windows" (*BG*, p. 88). Dorinda tries to dismiss these sexually possessed ancestresses as harmless "witches" (*BG*, p. 92), but their curse is real. Heterosexual desire destroys women in *Barren Ground*. Think of Dorinda's mother or of the storekeeper's wife, Rose Emily Pedlar, both of whose lives are simply slow exercises in death. Also, there is Jason Greylock's wife, who is so tortured by visions of white male violence that she finally kills herself. Stated politically: getting beyond institutionalized heterosexuality without the overt option of lesbianism represents the difficult but crucial survival act for Glasgow's heroine in *Barren Ground*—as it no doubt was for Glasgow in her own life.

The answer Glasgow imagines in *Barren Ground* is art. Dorinda Oakley, having renounced heterosexual passion, attends a concert for the first time in her life, and the experience is blatantly erotic.

> With the flight of wings, ecstasy quivered over her, while sound and colour were transformed into rhythms of feeling. Pure sensation held and tortured her. She felt the music playing on her nerves as the wind plays on a harp; she felt it shatter her nerves like broken string, and sweep on, crashing, ploughing through the labyrinth of her soul. Down there, in the deep below the depths of her being, she felt it tearing her vitals. Down there, in the buried jungle, where her thoughts had never penetrated, she felt it destroying the hidden roots of her life. In this darkness there was no colour; there was no glimmer of twilight; there was only the maze of inarticulate agony. . . . [Glasgow's ellipsis].
>
> Now it was dying away. Now it was returning. Something that she had thought dead was coming to life again. Something that she had buried out of sight under the earth was pushing upward in anguish. Something that she had defeated was marching as a conqueror over her life. Suddenly she was pierced by a thousand splinters of crystal sound. Little quivers of light ran over her. Beads of pain broke out on her forehead and her lips. She clenched her hands together, and forced her body back into her chair. "I've got to stand it. No matter what it does to me, I've got to stand it." (*BG*, p. 204)

Much as Cather announces Thea Kronborg's deepest revelation as an artist in *The Song of the Lark* by evoking a lesbian erotic, so Glasgow, deep in *Barren Ground*, marks Dorinda's awakening as an artist in this scene of searing heterosexual passion.

The violence of this scene communicates Glasgow's belief that real art and its creation are painful and frightening. Even more radical, however, the scene shows Dorinda achieving heterosexual ecstacy without a man. Although Dorinda's erotic climax occurs in a couple, she literally touches and is touched by no other person. She and the music are the lovers. Subverting the ancient patriarchal image of a sexy female (the muse) arousing a heterosexual male artist, Glasgow writes a passionate heterosexual scene showing the violent, erotic seduction of the woman artist by art itself—ethereal yet excrutiatingly physical (and, interestingly, completely nonverbal). Made love to by art, Dorinda becomes the artist, the creator she is capable of being; and her medium, like Cather's Alexandra Bergson in *O Pioneers!* or Jewett's Almira Todd in *The Country of the Pointed Firs*, will be the earth itself. Immediately following the concert, she decides to return to Old Farm.

The art Dorinda creates there is matrifocal. Her mother greets her return with the simple, epiphanal words: "So you've come, daughter" (*BG*, p. 224). The earth becomes a sentient presence—"The old feeling that the land thought and felt, that it possessed a secret personal life of its own, brushed her mood as it sped lightly by" (*BG*, p. 233)—and the central focus, the all-consuming main product of the farm, is milk. Cows, walking udders, obsess Dorinda. She insists that they be milked only by women, and making her special labor force all-female, she transforms Old Farm into a new, or perhaps very old, separate all-female kingdom at its inner core. A woman in man's clothing (Dorinda defiantly wears overalls), Glasgow's artist literally takes over male space, her father's territory, and redefines it as female. Livestock, inner-sanctum workers, and boss all exist and function without significant contact with males.

Glasgow's vision of this new Old Farm evokes Gilman's fantasy of female self-sufficiency and power in *Herland* (1915), and before that, the mythic matriarchies of Jewett, Hopkins, and Cather in *The Country of the Pointed Firs, Of One Blood, and O Pioneers!*, as well as the cryptic utterance of Stein's "MILK" in *Tender Buttons* and the supernatural vision of Dunbar-Nelson's Mistress of the Cards in *The Goodness of St. Rocque*. In different ways, all of these texts participate in a shared dream of matrifocal and sororal reconstitution of human reality. When Dorinda's mother is killed off by Dorinda's brother, forcing him to run away and leave the father's land totally in the hands of the daughter, the central couple at Old Farm, the two people who make the earth flourish and take care of each other, is female. Their very names yoke classical and organic images: Dorinda Oakley and Fluvanna Green, daughter of Aunt Mehitable, the most respected midwife and conjure woman in the region.

But their relationship, like Cather's handling of Nancy's story in *Sapphira and the Slave Girl*, presents problems. Perhaps because she lived in the South all of her life, rather than simply carrying the region with her as a romantic memory from childhood, Glasgow, unlike Cather, consciously wished to write against the kind of stereotypic romanticizing and buffooning of black people that she disliked in much Southern white fiction. She stated in *A Certain Measure* that even in her earliest books she had intended "to avoid the romantic delusion, so prevalent in fiction at the turn of the century, that the South was inhabited exclusively by aristocrats and picturesque Negroes, who afforded what used to be called 'comic relief' in the novel.''[25] In *Barren Ground* she clearly speaks out against such racist attitudes. She has Jason concede early in the novel that black people ''are the best farmers about here. The negro who owns his ten or twelve acres is a better manager than the poor white with twice the number'' (*BG*, p. 27). She has Dorinda late in the novel wish that her husband, Nathan (who dies), ''wouldn't say 'niggers.' That scornful label was already archaic, except among the poorest of the 'poor white class' at Pedlar's Mill'' (*BG*, p. 234). She obviously intends Aunt Mehitable as a credible and admired, even if minor, character whose wisdom as a midwife and power as a conjure woman should be taken seriously.

Still, *Barren Ground*, like much of Glasgow's work, is damaged by blindness and condescension on the subject of race. Describing several black men, Glasgow easily generalizes about their ''expression of wistful resignation which was characteristic less of an individual than of a race'' (*BG*, p. 63). She states sweepingly about the thoughts and ''instincts'' of African Americans in the area of Virginia that she fictionalizes: ''In spite of the influence of Aunt Mehitable Green they had not yet learned to think as a race, and the individual negro still attached himself instinctively to the superior powers'' (*BG*, p.. 240). She makes black Southerners but not white ones speak in dialect (recall Alice Dunbar-Nelson's resistance to just this double standard). At the end of the novel she indulges freely in stereotypes about the untrustworthiness and carelessness of black workers (*BG*, pp. 250, 362)— forgetting entirely, it seems, her own earlier praise for African Americans' skill and industry as farmers or her important distinctions about how hard people work depending on whether they are employees or owners of their own enterprise.

Precisely this kind of contradiction mars Glasgow's conception of the relationship between Dorinda and Fluvanna. Glasgow seems to intend their close companionship as an example of strong female partnership. With Fluvanna by her side, Dorinda is able to achieve—gloriously—the independence from men, literal and emotional, that she has struggled toward throughout most of the novel. The two women immerse themselves in the work of the farm, caring about every detail of its management and thrilling to every success. They spend their days in mutual labor and their evenings in shared conversation. What Glasgow never questions in this idyllic (from her point of view) sisterhood is the tremendous imbalance of power built into the completely unequal relationship.

Adrienne Rich's poem ''Education of a Novelist'' is about Ellen Glasgow. In the poem Rich addresses the tragedy—for Glasgow, but far more so for black women—of the kind of benevolent racism that could allow a white writer to dislike the word *nigger* and wish to honor the wisdom of a black midwife and conjure woman and yet, simultaneously, to participate blithely in the exploitation of black people. In *Barren Ground* Glasgow consigns to cheerful subservience and dependence on a white woman the character Fluvanna, just as in real life, as Rich points out, she consigned to illiteracy Lizzie Jones, the black woman who not only raised her but also nurtured, if not bequeathed, her gift as a fiction-maker.[26] Just as Glasgow tried to rebel against the repressive white ideal of the Southern Lady but was able to move only so far out of the orbit into which she was born, so she tried to rebel against certain racist attitudes of her time and region but was able to go only so far out of the system of values that she inherited. Her ambition to rebel, and the degree to which she succeeded, against both race and class should not be underrated or, from an easy, arrogant, late twentieth-century point of view, held in contempt. Rich's poem may say most when it cautions against white hypocrisy and its all too convenient displacement of guilt: "It's not enough/ using your words to damn you, Ellen:/ they could have been my own."[27] At the same time, it is imperative to recognize the damage done to Glasgow's art by her class privilege and racism. In terms of race, what could have been one of the most groundbreaking insights in *Barren Ground*—the complexity of the relationship between Dorinda and Fluvanna—goes unexamined in a book about, ironically, female anger and empowerment. The same kind of racism that ten years earlier vitiated Charlotte Perkins Gilman's utopian vision in *Herland* undercuts Glasgow's feminist dream world in *Barren Ground*. Except from the point of view of the white woman in charge, the improvement represented, finally, by replacing a white male overseer with a white female one is minor, if important at all.

A sense of failure haunted Glasgow. Two years before her death, she stated in *A Certain Measure* (1943), self-pityingly to be sure but nonetheless accurately: "Few persistent novelists, I suppose, have ever received in one lifetime so generous a measure of benevolent neglect."[28] One reason for the neglect that Glasgow felt in her lifetime and that critics such as C. Hugh Holman, Linda Wagner, and Julius Raper have sought to remedy since,[29] is the extreme unevenness of her career, the fact that of the many novels she wrote only one, *Barren Ground*, unquestionably stands out. Very late in her life, she wrote to a friend abut the act of writing: "What is the meaning of it? . . . For more than forty years I was driven by some inner scourge to commit an act which appears to me, now, as useless as murder."[30]

Why this violent metaphor? Writing, for Glasgow as an old woman, makes her think of torture and killing. The gestation metaphor that appears so reassuringly in *A Certain Measure* to describe Dorinda Oakley's genesis might apply to the creative act some of the time apparently, but its other face is lethal—or, worse, vacant. A battle between belief in the value of art, in the value of creative production, and despair and cynicism about life, including art, wracked Ellen Glasgow. She was caught between worlds as desperately as Anzia Yezierska or Jessie Fauset. As her biographer, E. Stanly Godbold, Jr., observes: "Ellen herself was one day an old fashioned Southern girl and the next day a modern intellectual in total rebellion against the traditions of her past. In all of her life she was not able to shed either role, nor was she able to reconcile them."[31] Revealingly, the working title under which she started her autobiography was *The Autobiography of an Exile*.[32] The feelings of alienation and resentment that appear on the surface in this early title simply go underground in her more cryptic and therefore slightly less naked published title, *The Woman Within*.

What makes *Barren Ground* powerful is that it truly records the conflicting feelings, many of them violent, that Glasgow had about being a creative woman. At the close of the novel, Dorinda seethes with resentment at the emotional deprivation she has been forced to accept:

> The only thing that made life worth living was the love that she had never known and the happiness that she had missed. (*BG*, p. 447)

Nothing mattered but the things of which life had cheated her. (*BG*, p. 447)

The work of thirty years was nothing. . . . Success, achievement, victory over fate, all these things were nothing beside that imperishable illusion. Love was the only thing that made life desirable, and love was irrevocably lost to her. (*BG*, p. 449)

The word *barren* in Glasgow's title; the images of dead babies in the novel (recall the game Rose Emily's children play as the novel opens, the nightmare of infanticide that drives Jason's wife to suicide, and the pregnancy Dorinda loses); the gulf between Dorinda and her mother, which is partially but never fully closed: *Barren Ground* is about deep female loss and pain—emotional, erotic, and procreative.

Glasgow says that Dorinda's harmony with the earth will relieve this terrible hunger, redeem the losses. In words that could have been written by Jewett or Austin or Cather, she ends her novel with triumphant images celebrating Dorinda's "living communion with the earth under her feet. While the soil endured, while the seasons bloomed and dropped, while the ancient, beneficent ritual of sowing and reaping moved in the fields, she knew that she could never despair of contentment" (*BG*, pp. 449–50). I believe Glasgow here. But I also know/remember/anticipate that just two inches over on the tangled bank despair is still alive. And anger—not detached, elegant, satiric wit, such as appears in the best of Glasgow's subsequent novels, but hot rage, fury, desire for revenge, and bitter resentment. The creativity that Glasgow celebrates is finally a grim, furious creativity. Giving up on heterosexual erotic passion may be liberating for Glasgow, but it is also painful and hardening. Cynicism as well as freedom is its harvest.

Published two years before *Barren Ground*, Edith Summers Kelley's *Weeds* (1923) met good reviews and terrible sales. Therefore, like its heroine and its author, it sank into oblivion until its fortuitous recovery in the 1970s by Matthew J. Bruccoli.

As a novel about a woman artist, *Weeds* dramatizes issues about gender and art against the unlikely backdrop of a Kentucky dirt farm, where a poor white woman is doomed by economics and constant childbearing and childrearing never to develop her gift as an artist. Kelley's Judith Pippinger faces a bitter double conflict between motherhood and art and heterosexual desire and freedom. Also, far removed from avant garde intellectualizing and posturing, the novel shows a totally isolated white woman's need to break radically from a nineteenth-century domestic aesthetic. Judith Pippinger needs to create the kind of complex, provocative, and even threatening art historically considered in the west to be the province solely of elite white men, or their occasional freak female imitator.

Weeds' directness produces its strength. Early in the novel, Kelley provides an image of Judith Pippinger refusing as a baby to stay on the quilt where she is supposed to lie: "She soon passed the boundaries of the quilt, then of the kitchen, and began bruising her temples by pitching head first from the rather high doorstep."[33] Getting off the quilt, out of the kitchen, and free of the house propel Kelley's heroine from infancy on. As an adult, she is able to admire the quilts other women make and give her (*W*, p. 104). But she has no desire to try her own hand at women's art. When she was growing up, she never bothered to collect and box the feminine treasures hoarded by her sisters—bits of lace and velvet, stray glass beads and buttons, locks of hair, pretty romantic pictures (*W*, pp. 28–29). Her sister talks about domestic novels, but Judith (and clearly Kelley behind her) is not interested: "Lizzie May named several novels by such purveyors of roseate fiction as Bertha M. Clay, Mary Jane Holmes and Laura Jean Libbey, which in ragged paper covers had found their way into the Pippinger home. 'Yes, but in them books it allus ends when they git married,' Judith reminded her. 'They never tell what happens after. All they say is that they lived happy ever after' " (*W*, p. 120).

Kelley's artist emphatically identifies not with domesticity but with the outdoors and with the freer, more physically active life allowed men in her rural environment. Pronounced "more a boy'n a gal" by her father (*W*, p. 34), she would rather spend time with him shoeing horses than with her sisters and the contents of their treasure boxes. She likes to ride hard and speak her mind. As she is told admiringly by the man she will end up marrying, Jerry Blackford: "You're the on'y woman I know that's got a man's ways, Judy. You hain't spiled" (*W*, p. 103). This woman artist's preference for male company and prerogatives is not learned; it is, Kelley says as soon as she shows the infant Judith creeping over the boundaries of the quilt, part of this woman's instinctual "nature" as a human being. Judith chooses the freer, the riskier, the more open and exploratory territory of men, the territory beyond the quilt, because that territory calls her as a human being. It speaks to her *human* nature, her artist's soul, which is neither male nor female, as society would like to have it, with quilts and pies for one group and tomes and galleries for the other, but simply—actually, complexly—human. Put another way, Kelley shows that in a world in which human is defined as male, it follows that a woman wishing to be human must often act like a man, must reject the socially constructed world of femininity, including feminine art, in order to know herself.

That art is strange and unsettling. Judith makes pictures of people that exaggerate and redefine features (*W*, pp. 25–26). She sees beautiful forms and patterns where others see nothing or only ugliness: " 'Land, hain't that a nice pattern this platter is burned into, Elly!' exclaimed Judith, examining a small platter which she had just picked up from the table. 'Look here at all the nice squares an' di'monds—an' all jes as even!' "(*W*, p. 27)—to which her sister responds crossly that the platter is ruined and Judith is to blame. Stains on the wallpaper, in an echo of Gilman, intrigue Judith (*W*, p. 301), and cloud pictures fascinate her even more, "for in them there was infinite variety and change." She can see turreted castles and "great trees with weirdly twisted limbs" or "a peaceful valley with a river winding through it, a little steep-roofed house on the river bank and a church spire in the distance." These scenes give way to distorted faces: "droll, exaggerated faces such as she had tried to draw when she was a little girl at school, faces with bulbous noses and bulging foreheads, faces half animal, half human, crafty faces with little fox eyes, great flabby faces like Aunt Maggie Slatten's" (*W*, p. 328). Although she can make pretty pictures, the sketching she prefers reproduces and participates in this world of the grotesque and the stylized: "She would amuse herself by sketching faces, some human, some animal, some half and half, as she had used to do when she was a little girl at school. Luella, looking over her shoulder, was scandalized" (*W*, p. 211; cf. p. 122).

Judith does not draw for approval or money. She has no desire to satisfy any conventional inherited nineteenth-century feminine aesthetic commited to conformity, decorativeness, and easy accessibility. Asked why she does what she does, she gives as a child the classic response of the elite western (male) artist from the Romantic period forward. She says, in rural Kentucky dialect: "Cuz I had to" (*W*, p. 26). Totally unsophisticated, Judith claims as her own the modern western credo of the high-culture artist. She makes art because of her burning need to express her own unique, individual vision.

But this woman artist in *Weeds* starves. Motherhood, poverty, overwork, loneliness, and isolation exhaust and emaciate her. Her children, born and unborn, seem to devour her very flesh. Following childbirth, she lies for days as if dead, "half unconscious, scarcely moving a finger, hardly lifting an eyelash," and revival from this near-death state is difficult. " 'The girl must have nourishment,' said Dr. MacTaggert. 'Milk' " (*W*, p. 210). The prescription is literal. Judith's physical strength has been so sapped that she needs to start over like a baby, with milk, to build up her body. The doctor's advice is also figurative, however. Trapped in deadening domesticity and poverty, isolated from the outside world and people who might understand the strange images that spring from her imagination, the soul of Kelley's woman artist is starving. Her spirit lies weak from lack of nourishment.

She gets no food. Judith's body mends, and she finds a way to work out her relationship with her husband so that they will not continue to live in bitter rage and hatred. But her life as an artist, such as it is, does not survive. It dies—indeed, never really gets a chance to develop and mature.

Weeds ends with a scene of female communion with the earth that at first resembles scenes offered by Jewett, Austin, Cather, and Glasgow. The future looks all right. Judith gazes on the turkeys in the yard and the dog and the cat sleeping on the porch: "Standing wrapped in the growing twilight she felt herself like those humbler creatures an outgrowth of the soil, its life her life even as theirs. Quiet, peace and calm, these things belonged to them, a part of their heritage. These things in less measure her own life had to offer. These things at last she was ready to accept." Then, like her drawings, this conventional image—this pretty picture of human and natural harmony—gives way to the truth: "Like a dog tied by a strong chain, what had she to gain by continually pulling at the leash? What hope was there in rebellion for her or hers?" Beaten, she thinks: "Peace was better than struggle, peace and a decent acquiescence before the things which had to be." Judith lectures herself into resignation:

> She told herself again that she was through with struggle and question. . . . She would go on for her allotted time bearing and nursing babies and rearing them as best she could. And when her time of child bearing was over she would go back to the field, like the other women, and set tobacco and worm and top tobacco, shuck corn and plant potatoes. Already people were beginning to call her "Aunt Judy." Some day she would be too old to work in the field and would sit all day in the kitchen in winter and on the porch in summer shelling beans or stripping corn from the cob. She would be "granmammy" then. (*W*, p. 331)

Far from comforting, this resignation means that the artist in Judith is dead. The rebellious, passionate, creative, *un*resigned part of her has finally, been killed—as is immediately confirmed in the news brought to Judith at this point in the text that Jabez, her only kindred soul, is dead.

Fellow "crazy" and artist (a fiddler), the old man Jabez understood Judith. "Together she and Uncle Jabez would notice all sorts of things; and they would point them out to each other and laugh and wonder and enjoy the beauty and strangeness of the world" (W, p. 170). She asks him the question that is really the question of her own life, with the gender and the art form altered: " 'Which would have meant more to you,' she asked, 'the fiddle or the woman?' He came and sat down on the step beside her. 'I reckon the fiddle, Judy. The world's chuck full o' wimmin; but a man hain't got but one set o' gifts' " (W, p. 311). The abrupt death of this man at the end of Weeds completely undercuts Judith's thoughts about peace being better than struggle. Such peace may be physically and psychically imperative. There is a limit to how much struggle against insuperable odds a woman, like a dog, can stand; at some point struggle must end to end the torture. But that does not mean that the peace gained is good, is better than the struggle. The peace is not good. It is Jabez dead; the leashed dog defeated; Judith beaten.

If the story about the woman artist that Edith Summers Kelley tells is bitter, it was also real. As Matthew J. Bruccoli and Charlotte Goodman explain, [34] although Kelley was college-educated, had influential literary friends such as Upton Sinclair and Sinclair Lewis (to whom she was engaged briefly as a young woman), and lived for a time in New York and then in Helicon, the socialist experimental community in New Jersey, she and her common law sculptor husband spent most of their lives in great poverty, trying to eke out a living as farmers first in Kentucky, then in New Jersey, and finally in southern California. One venture after another failed, and although Kelley was better off than her character Judith in that she and her family could move, it was not until old age that she enjoyed any economic security. Before that, Kelley—who wrote to a friend, "I put a great deal of myself into Judy"[35]— lived in shacks and dilapidated housing, trying to write while doing strenuous farm work and keeping house for five people, three of them children. As she wrote to Alfred Harcourt when she submitted the manuscript of Weeds to Harcourt, Brace in 1923: "It has been a terrible task to write the book underneath the same roof with three irrepressible children who had nobody to care for them but me." Requesting an advance a few months later so that her husband could quit working in a slaughterhouse and return to chicken-farming, she explained:

> By making this change in our way of living, I could get at the work of revising the book more promptly, could get it done earlier and make a better job of it, because my husband would be near at hand to keep the children out of the way while I worked. Indeed I hardly see how I can revise the book unless he is at home; for the writing of the book under the circumstances in which we live was a supreme effort which I now feel incapable of repeating.[36]

Other than Weeds, Kelley wrote short stories, essays, poetry, and a second novel, The Devil's Hand, which she was not able to publish during her lifetime. Issued posthumously in the 1970s, the novel did not satisfy Kelley herself. It is about two women farmers in southern California, and though very interesting, it does not equal her first novel in the clarity of either its passion or its vision. In 1925, Kelley forecast in a letter to her friend and supporter Upton Sinclair: "I'm afraid it won't be in many respects so good a book as 'Weeds' "; and she recognized in another letter: "One trouble was that I tried to work at it when conditions were so unfavorable that I simply couldn't give it my best efforts or even my second best.''[37] Although she continued to write, she was unable to publish anything after *Weeds* appeared in 1923, despite the fact that she lived for thirty-three more years. As the one clear achievement of her life as an artist, *Weeds,* like Gilman's "The Yellow Wallpaper" or Hopkins's *Of One Blood* two and three decades earlier, is about the defeat of the woman artist in modern America.

The careers of Yezierska, Glasgow, and Kelley raise hard issues. That Yezierska, growing up in poverty on the Lower East Side at the turn of the century, or Kelley, living in shacks or sunbaked tents in southern California and writing *Weeds* in moments stolen from hard physical labor and childrearing, managed to write at all, as I have also said of others in this book, represents a triumph against tremendous, negative odds. The same recognition is due to Ellen Glasgow who turned herself into a prolific author of serious fiction despite the expectation that she do little but be decorative and, as she put it, stroke some man the right way. Such hard-won successes, even when short-lived or limited, emphasize how hospitable, comparatively, the first two and a half decades of the twentieth century were for serious women writers in the United States.

Another face to put on this story, however, is not positive. Yezierska wrote constantly—built her entire life around her art—but only in *Bread Givers* and a handful of short stories, critics agree, did she realize her talent fully. Glasgow wrote all of her life, putting nothing before her art, and though prolific lived with constant anxiety about the quality of her work, which was often compared invidiously to that of other women such as Wharton or Cather. Although not everyone will agree with me that *Barren Ground* alone stands out in her work, all do agree that of her many books only a very few truly reflect her real gift. Likewise Kelley took herself completely seriously as an artist, continuing to write after *Weeds,* but that book was her only published novel and it disappeared almost as soon as it appeared. Failure or the feeling of failure, or both, haunted all three of these writers, who in most other respects could not be more different from each other. What sense, if any, is there to be made of their lives as artists?

One answer is that there is no common denominator. For different reasons these different writers endured difficult struggles as artists, which resulted in more failure than success for each. For Yezierska the major obstacles were one thing, for Glasgow another, for Kelley another, and we could add to this threesome other writers already discussed, and the obstacle for each of them would be yet something else. This possibility that the differences outweigh the similarities, that each writer's unique experience is more important than any perceived (invented) commonalities, is quite plausible. It may very well be that beyond the broadest outline, generalizations about women writers' careers at the turn of the century, if the field is at all heterogeneous, break down, and that the breakdown is good. It prevents us from creating neat, reductive patterns that simply replace old stereotypes with new ones and that conveniently serve, as tidy interpretation must, to exclude and ignore what does not fit. Indeed, part of what my title *Conflicting Stories* means is this: diversity is a unifying feature of the period.

Yet perhaps it can also be said that the struggles of Yezierska, Glasgow, and

Kelley—so utterly different on the surface—do share a common thread. Artists in the high western tradition in the Romantic and modern periods are supposed to suffer. Pain is part of the code. Yezierska's acute sense of alienation; Glasgow's terrible anxiety and self-doubts[38]; Kelley's life in shacks and tumbled down houses—are these totally unrelated miseries or are they manifestations of, among other things, these women's successful arrival, to use Gilman's shorthand, as Artists? In the modern period, a writer for whom success and productivity come easily is suspect. Edith Wharton, for example, was long belittled on these grounds. Her art seemed to come too effortlessly and certainly it came too often. Hence she could not really be an artist (just a technician), or so it was implied in the 1920s by young men rebelling against her and then in the criticism for years afterward. Much the same charge has been leveled at Jessie Fauset. How could the author of such polite, well-mannered fiction be an artist? Pain, anxiety, suffering—these are the signs of art-in-the-making and therefore of the true artist in the modern west.

What does such an ideology mean for women? Since around the middle of the nineteenth century in the United States, for many middle- and upper-class women—which is to say women most likely to have the educations and opportunities to become writers—escaping imposed ideologies of gender that valorize suffering has constituted one of the crucial acts of sexual liberation. What does it mean, then, to struggle for liberation from one ideology of valorized pain and suffering only to become trapped in another? Might it, for some women such as Glasgow, lead to the probability of stasis? Can the codes of the self-sacrificing Lady (or Wife or Mother) and of the suffering Artist get lost in each other for certain women in self-destructive ways that do not exist for men? It might very well be that the aspiration to be an elite artist in the modern west has posed for some women (perhaps for all?) a trap that has led them to romanticize the very feelings of exile and incapacitating difference and failure that they have simultaneously been trying to free themselves from as women.

11 Jumping Out the Window: Nella Larsen's *Passing* and the End of an Era

Opposition is the life of an enterprise; criticism tells you that you are doing something.

Pauline Hopkins[1]

Often the 1920s are separated from the decades that preceded. The Roaring Twenties. The Harlem Renaissance. The Jazz Age. The Lost Generation. But how different were the 1920s for American women writers?

Certainly there were changes. The passage of the Nineteenth Amendment in 1920 conferred on all American women the right to vote for the first time in the nation's history. The end of World War One brought to a close a period in which thousands of women had held well-paying, traditionally male jobs. Sexual mores relaxed. In terms of literature, a number of new authors emerged: among men, Ernest Hemingway, F. Scott Fitzgerald, Claude McKay, Jean Toomer, Langston Hughes, William Faulkner; among women Anzia Yezierska, Edith Summers Kelley, Nella Larsen, Helen Hull, Zora Neale Hurston. The 1920s, as many scholars stress, can be seen as an important new epoch in American culture, the true beginning of what we now recognize as the modern period.[2]

However, the 1920s can also be understood as the continuation and culmination of decades of change at the turn of the century, especially if the social and literary history of women rather than of men define one's focus. The passage of the Nineteenth Amendment did represent a major victory, but that victory, as historians now point out, may be most significant as a pivot in women's political struggles at the turn of the century rather than as the end of them.[3] Similarly, the jobs that women lost when soldiers returned at the end of the war were jobs that they held in the first place not simply because men vacated them, but also because, since the 1890s, more and more women of every sort had been entering the paid workforce.[4] Even the new sexual openness of the 1920s reflected not simply a postwar revolution but also the culmination of changes in American culture strongly in evidence for one or two decades before 1920.

What, then, of the new authors most commonly thought of as twenties writers— Hemingway, Fitzgerald, Hughes, Toomer, Faulkner? They might very well represent a new development. If we are talking about male American writers, isolating the decade of the 1920s makes sense. A group of significant, interesting, and, not coincidentally, highly self-consciously male writers emerged in the postwar decade, initiating in their view, as well as in that of many critics at the time and of most scholars since, a new era in American writing.

If, however, we are talking about women writers, does isolating the 1920s make good sense? When we think of the twenties, the prose writers who come into view are Edith Wharton, Gertrude Stein, Jessie Fauset, Alice Dunbar-Nelson, Willa Cather, Ellen Glasgow—all of whose careers began and in most cases thrived both before and during the twenties—plus new figures such as Anzia Yezierska, Zora Neale Hurston, Edith Summers Kelley, Helen Hull, Humishuma, and Nella Larsen. What this suggests is that using the 1920s to mark out a new period in the history of American women writers invents a break where there was for the most part continuity. It artificially divides in two the careers of Glasgow, Wharton, Fauset, Cather, Stein, Austin, and Dunbar-Nelson, all of whom began writing in the early years of the twentieth century, or even in the 1890s, and then continued publishing in the 1920s. It strands new writers such as Kelley, Yezierska, Humishuma, and Larsen by cutting them off from the tradition of turn-of-the-century realistic social fiction by women out of which they sprang.

It is true that the career patterns of certain women writers seem to reinforce the usefulness of 1920 as a literary historical dividing line. Dunbar-Nelson, for example, published fiction in the 1890s, continued writing but brought out relatively little for the next twenty years, and then made a place for herself in the 1920s as a poet and journalist.[5] But the overall picture reveals various patterns. Depending on our preferences and taste, we might say that Austin's career crested in the 1900s; Stein, Glasgow, and Fauset's in the 1920s; Wharton's in the teens; and Cather's in the teens and late twenties. Moreover, no matter how we view these careers, the common denominator is that all of them spanned the teens and twenties, and most continued from the late 1890s or early 1900s *through* the twenties. To speak of the 1920s as a meaningfully separate decade in American literary history may be a good way of conceptualizing certain phenomena such as the Harlem Renaissance or the expatriate culture of "Lost Generation" artists in Paris, although even these, scholars now argue, may have had stronger, deeper roots in prewar attitudes and developments than has often been observed.[6] But it is not very useful when talking about American women fiction writers in general. It has the effect of chopping off as separate the last quarter, third, or half of many women writers' careers and then, more often than not, placing those fragments—plus the careers of young women emerging in the twenties—in an alien social and aesthetic context defined by interests and issues not of women but of men, all of them young and most of them highly preoccupied with male sexual performance and anxiety. In that context the mature work of artists such as Wharton, Fauset, Glasgow, and Cather, as well as the new work by women such as Yezierska, Kelley, and Larsen, except for a flash here and there, gets labeled "old-fashioned," archaic, out-of-step. It is not accidental, of course, that the most famous of these emerging women artists in the 1920s, Zora Neale Hurston, is usually not even thought of as a twenties writer. She is best known, and it makes sense, as a 1930s author. In general, the 1920s were not the beginning but the end of an era for American women writers. Zora Neale Hurston, characteristically nonconformist and a tough, adaptive fighter, lived through that end and resurfaced—recreated herself—in the thirties and forties. Nella Larsen, like Anzia Yezierska and Edith Summers Kelley, did not.

To end this book with Zora Neale Hurston and Nella Larsen is to end with two very different figures. Hurston went on to publish her best and most famous work in the late 1930s. Strictly speaking, she falls beyond the boundaries of this book, which is why I have excluded her until now, when she appears as a kind of surprise—a position she no doubt would like. In contrast, Larsen wrote two brilliant and in many ways summational fictions at the very end of the period I am looking at, in the late 1920s, and then fell silent for the rest of her life.

Zora Neale Hurston spent her life exploding categories. She was one of the stars of the Harlem Renaissance, yet she laughed at its pretensions. She needed money for her work, so she stroked the vanity of the white, self-appointed guru of black primitivism, Charlotte Mason, calling her "godmother" and writing her adoring letters. She voted Republican after the New Deal and denounced the Supreme Court's landmark 1954 antisegregation ruling as an insult to black people and to black institutions.[7] Conformity and predictability were not traits Hurston cultivated.

As an artist, she was equally independent. In the integration-conscious twenties, she wrote about self-sufficient black communities. In the grim social-activist thirties, she published a celebratory novel about a self-reliant black woman. At her death in 1960, she left behind a long, unfinished manuscript about Herod the Great. Flamboyant, opinionated, idiosyncratic: It is no wonder that Zora Neale Hurston so often appears in the criticism as a strange and exciting "original," a figure without significant predecessors or peers, a kind of black Athena sprung miraculously from the brow of the Harlem Renaissance. In fact, although Hurston would vastly prefer the miraculous version, she was in important ways thoroughly a product of the turn of the century.

As most of the careers described in this book illustrate, being an original—breaking the mold—was one of the primary, driving impulses of artistically ambitious American women writers as a group at the turn into the twentieth century. Frances Ellen Harper, Charlotte Perkins Gilman, Alice Dunbar-Nelson, Kate Chopin, Pauline Hopkins, Gertrude Stein, Sui Sin Far, Ellen Glasgow, Humishuma, Anzia Yezierska, Edith Wharton, Jessie Redmon Fauset all invented themselves. What they were expected to be, especially in terms of standard expectations grounded in assumptions about gender, class, culture, and race, and what they decided to be—artists—were two very different things. If Hurston was unusually flamboyant and theatrical about creating herself, she was no more so than Stein or Yezierska. If she was adamantly opposed to obeying prescriptions about what she should or should not as a black artist do, she was no more so than Dunbar-Nelson or Hopkins or Fauset. She did not, in other words, spring out of nowhere. Highly ambitious, college-educated, determined to succeed, she sprang out of the same complicated, individualistic, pervasively feminist, and yet racist and self-fracturing cultural milieu that produced the other artistically ambitious American women writers that I have been discussing.

Born in 1891 (although she often gave the date as 1901 or later), [8] Hurston began publishing fiction in the mid-1920s. Although the volume of her writing in that decade is slight—some short stories, a play, some essays, and *The Eatonville Anthology*—it does reveal her early interest in formal experimentation. Hurston published a number of structurally conventional short stories such as "Spunk" (1925), "Muttsey" (1926), and "Sweat" (1926), all of which focus on fierce adult heterosexual conflict, or what Sandra M. Gilbert and Susan Gubar identify in *No Man's Land: The Place of the Woman Writer in the Twentieth Century* as the great modernist thematic of the battle of the sexes. These stories rely on vividly drawn main characters, strong central conflicts, and pronounced dramatic climaxes.

But Hurston also played with form in the twenties, as *The Eatonville Anthology* strikingly illustrates. Published in 1926 in three installments in the *Messenger,* the work is a collection of fourteen sketches apparently arranged randomly and bound together by place, Eatonville. As her biographer, Robert E. Hemenway, explains, *The Eatonville Anthology* mixes well-known folklore and original material. Some sketches are retellings of familiar folk tales or anecdotes, while others come from Hurston's individual memories and inventions. The effect of the whole

> is the literary equivalent of Hurston's memorable performances at parties. The reader has the impression of sitting in a corner listening to anecdotes. . . . The fourteen parts have no thematic, structural, or imagistic relationship beyond their general identification with Eatonville in a bygone age: "back in the good old days before the World War when things were very simple in Eatonville." . . . The anthology succeeds despite its lack of form. [9]

Another way to look at *The Eatonville Anthology* is to say that it, like *The Country of the Pointed Firs, The Goodness of St. Rocque,* or *The Land of Little Rain,* does not lack form as much as it chooses against conventional, preferred, high-culture, western fictive form. Although shorter than Jewett's, Dunbar-Nelson's, or Austin's works, Hurston's "anthology" also relies on place as a unifier and experiments with structuring principles that fall outside the usual western high-culture dependence on individual-focused, climactic, linear narrative. Resembling *Mrs. Spring Fragrance, The Eatonville Anthology* coheres communally, is held together by its collective focus. Hurston's approach is more hieroglyphic than Sui Sin Far's. Rather than full-blown stories, the collection gives us only vignettes, sketches, and jokes—just enough to etch the individual or the relationship, and then we are on to the next section. Some pieces have titles, others do not; length varies from section to section; twelve units are about people, two about animals. Variety and asymmetry, in other words, govern the internal workings of *The Eatonville Anthology,* which is polyrhythmic and unstandardized. The work deliberately ignores basic learned western concepts of linear narrative drive, unity, and uniformity.

This does not mean, however, that *The Eatonville Anthology* is incoherent. To say that the work departs from traditional high-culture western narrative practice is not to say that it lacks form. While working as a folklorist in the American South in the 1920s, Hurston, in a letter to Langston Hughes two years after the publication of *The Eatonville Anthology,* described "5 general laws" that she believed inspired the aesthetic of much African American folk art:

1. The Negro's outstanding characteristic is drama. . . . Note gesture in place of words.
2. Negro is lacking in reverence. Note number of stories in which god, church and heaven are treated lightly.
3. *Angularity* in everything, sculpture, dancing, abrupt story telling.
4. Redundance. Examples: low down, cap'n high sheriff, top-superior, the number of times—usually three—that a feature is repeated in a story. Repetition of a single, simple strain in music.
5. Restrained ferocity in everything. . . .

From this empirical aesthetic can be extracted the basic principles of *The Eatonville Anthology*: gesture in place of words; irreverence; abrupt storytelling; redundance; restrained ferocity. Underlying the fiction's apparent formlessness is a strong adherence to African American oral and folk tradition as Hurston understood them. Her role as teller—as generator of the narrative with its irreverence, abruptness, redundance, and restrained ferocity—is one of the basic unifiers of the collection. From its opening sketch to its last line—"Stepped on a tin, mah story ends"[11]— we never forget that this is a told piece, a tale to be heard. As it was for Yezierska, one principal challenge for Hurston was to capture and celebrate in high art the oral tradition from which she sprang.

Another basic unifier of the anthology operates so subtly, as Hurston no doubt intended, that we are probably unaware of it except unconsciously. Each selection, with two exceptions, opens with a person's name. In order:

Mrs. Tony Roberts. . . .
Jim Merchant. . . .
Becky Moore. . . .
Sykes Jones'. . . .
Old Man Anderson. . . .
Coon Taylor. . . .
Joe Lindsay. . . .
Sewell. . . .
Mrs. Clarke. . . .
Mrs. McDuffy. . . .
Back in the good old days before the World War. . . .
Daisy Taylor. . . .
Sister Cal'line Potts. . . .
Once 'way back yonder before the stars fell.[12] . . .

Certainly there is pattern here. If we take away the two openings that do not begin with a person's name, we have twelve names (a deliberate play on the African American rhetorical device of the dozens?), half of them women's, half of them men's. Hurston does not communicate this balance in any obvious, simplistic way; polarity—dualism—is not what structures *The Eatonville Anthology*. Rather, it is an intricate, interwoven, fundamental balance, in this case of gender, that runs through the piece, conveying itself to us subtly, subliminally, randomly. Form does not descend onto *The Eatonville Anthology* from outside and above. It grows improvisationally out of the "telling."

Nella Larsen was less experimental structurally. Her two novels, *Quicksand*

(1928) and *Passing* (1929), present themselves as elegant, beautifully crafted, conventional turn-of-the-century books, similar generically to the long fiction of Fauset, Wharton, or Chopin. Conceptually rather than formally, Larsen's novels declare their author's rebellion as an artist.

Quicksand lashes out at what Larsen saw as the standard options available to an attractive, young, middle-class, African American woman in the early twentieth century. The book opens with a luxurious portrait of Larsen's heroine:

> Helga Crane sat alone in her room, which at that hour, eight in the evening, was in soft gloom. Only a single reading lamp, dimmed by a great black and red shade, made a pool of light on the blue Chinese carpet, on the bright covers of the books which she had taken down from their long shelves, on the white pages of the opened one selected, on the shining brass bowl crowded with many-colored nasturtiums beside her on the low table, and on the oriental silk which covered the stool at her slim feet.[13]

The scene is so perfect—so picturesque and artistic—that we are not surprised to have Larsen open the second paragraph by announcing that she knows she has been giving us a posed shot: "An observer would have thought her well fitted to that framing of light and shade" (*Q*, p. 2). This initial framing of Helga becomes an important trope. First in Naxos, then in Harlem, then in Denmark, Helga Crane struggles to step out of the frames others design for her.

At Naxos, Larsen's version of Tuskegee Institute, which evokes turn-of-the-century black uplift culture in general, Helga is framed, closed in by stifling bourgeois respectability, appearing most obviously in the compulsive orderliness and sexual repression of her environment. Free of Naxos, Helga finds Harlem in the long run not much better. From her point of view, its obsessive focus on race and protest (her friend Anne "revels" in an "orgy of protest," according to Helga) only masks a fundamental hypocrisy: Anne "hated white people with a deep and burning hatred. . . . But she aped their clothes, their manners, and their gracious ways of living. While proclaiming loudly the undiluted good of all things Negro, she yet disliked the songs, the dances, and the softly blurred speech of the race" (*Q*, p. 48). Despairing of both middle-class African American worlds available to her, Naxos and Harlem, Helga goes to Denmark—where Larsen takes on white modernism.

In Denmark Helga is literally turned into white people's "primitive" art object, the human canvas on which they work out their racist colonialist fantasies. Her hosts insist on buying her strange, flashy clothes. Decked out in large shiny earrings and "glittering shoe-buckles," Helga "felt like a veritable savage as they made their leisurely way across the pavement from the shop to the waiting motor." Pedestrians "stopped to stare at the queer dark creature, strange to their city" (*Q*, p. 69). This elaborate creation of Helga as an exotic, a vividly sensual "primitive," is primarily undertaken to catch the eye of one person: the avant garde painter Axel Olsen, whom Larsen perfectly describes as "brilliant, bored, elegant, urbane, cynical, worldly" (*Q*, p. 77). Larsen takes the full measure of white modernism's racism when she has this celebrated white artist, whose job it is to frame subjects, casually tell Helga "in his assured, despotic way": " 'You have the warm impulsive nature of the women of Africa, but, my lovely, you have, I fear, the soul of a prostitute. You sell yourself to the highest buyer. I should of course be happy that it is I. And I am.' He stopped, contemplating her, lost apparently, for the second, in pleasant thoughts of the future" (*Q*, p. 87). As Cheryl Wall states: "Only the spell of racial mythology could lead a man to mistake such insults for gallantry. Olsen knows nothing of African women, but that does not shake his belief in their exotic primitivism.[14]

Zora Neale Hurston also commented on jaded white fantasies and projections. In "Isis" (1924), her affectionate story about a child such as she herself had been (or remembered being)[15]—feisty, creative, an inveterate rule-breaker—the little girl Isis moves easily between the traditional, rural, African American world of her grandmother and the fast-paced, joy-starved world of sophisticated white people driving past her house on their way to luxury hotels. In the former she is a troublemaker, loved but feared for what she will do next. In the latter she is a little icon, a precious, personified abstraction. The child's vitality provokes this closing reflection by an elegant, world-weary, white woman passing through Isis's life: "She looked hungrily ahead of her and spoke into space rather than to anyone in the car. 'I would like just a little of her sunshine to soak into my soul. I would like that alot.' "[16]

The question is: How do we read "Isis"—or its author? What was Zora Neale Hurston's opinion of the mania of white modernism for the primitive? As Mary Helen Washington observes, Hurston could be exasperating in her participation in demeaning popular stereotypes, that of the "happy darky," for instance, "who sings and dances for white folks, for money and for joy," or that of "the educated black person who is, underneath the thin veneer of civilization, still a 'heathen,' "[17] "Isis," in fictional form, projects onto a child named for the Egyptian goddess of fertility a stereotype of untamed black soul—ancient, fecund, irrepressible—supposedly lurking just below the surface in black people, or certain black people. It is a stereotype that Hurston herself, in her theatrical entrances and irreverent pronouncements, repeatedly seemed to embody, at least in the view of whites such as Charlotte Mason. Was Hurston projecting a sincere self-portrait? Or was she acting—skillfully manipulating racial stereotypes to her own advantage, letting people think whatever they chose while she enjoyed herself and took their money, without which she could not pursue her life's work?

Quite possibly, both interpretations are correct: Hurston sincerely participated in modernism's fascination with primitivism, and she acted her part for ulterior reasons. To survive as a black woman artist in a world economically controlled by whites, as writers such as Harper and Hopkins had learned earlier, required extraordinary talent, hard work, luck, and probably most important, incredible mental balance between the irreconcilable opposites of hard-line resistance to the status quo, on the one hand, and flexibility or the ability to adapt, on the other. The way Hurston worked this puzzle out, especially in terms of the white rage for black primitivism, is itself often confusing. In "Isis" she seems genuinely to believe in the existence of a joyfully wild and spontaneous African creative genius, the eruption of Isis—powerful, ancient, prewestern—into modern America in the body of a black girl-child. But she also toys with, mocks, pities, and undercuts, as well as takes seriously, white people's envy of "Isis the Joyful."[18] The conclusion of the story is brilliantly ambiguous. Hurston has the color-hungry white woman greedily hug the little black girl, regally clad in her grandmother's flaming red tablecloth, as the car in which they ride roars through the Florida countryside en route to a luxury hotel in Orlando where the only black people allowed will be menial laborers such as kitchen help and waiters: that is, grown-up, paid caretakers and displayers of fancy tablecloths. The white woman's wistful "I would like just a little of her sunshine to soak into my soul. I would like that alot" can be read sympathetically as Hurston's agreement that there exists a whole world of consciousness from which modern white civilization has tragically cut itself off. Or it can be read sardonically as Hurston's comment on white privilege and self-indulgence; the white woman's words reek of self-pity and ignorance. Either way, the conclusion of this story forces readers to think about the hubris of the casual white modernist longing (felt most keenly in Hurston's story while blasting through the countryside in a speeding automobile) to appropriate and take into oneself the "sunny," "natural," supposedly less complicated experience of dark-skinned, poor, "primitive" people like— outrageously—the artist Zora Neale Hurston.

Echoing some of the concerns of *The Eatonville Anthology*, *Quicksand*, and "Isis," Larsen's *Passing* talks in code about the deep, secret self-division and terror accompanying the determination of women, and particularly black women, to create themselves as artists at the turn into the twentieth century. Larsen's own story as an artist, as I will suggest at the end of this chapter, was very complicated. It is not surprising that when she published *Passing* in 1929 (she was thirty-eight at the time), she offered what may be the most subtle and frightening book about a woman writer in the whole period.

Passing opens with a woman's writing. It is on "Italian paper," "almost illegible," "out of place," "alien," "mysterious," and "slightly furtive." It is also, however, "in some peculiar, determined way a little flaunting. Purple ink. Foreign paper of extraordinary size" (*P*, p. 143). The author of this barely legible yet assertive writing in Larsen's last novel is profoundly conflicted. She is self-determined and daring. She is also almost totally self-alienated. Clare Kendry has passed so deeply and completely into the world of powerful white men, epitomized by the racist she has married, that in order to participate at all in the life of the African American community from which she came she must sneak around, lie, and construct an elaborate double life.

No less self-alienated is the bourgeois black woman who desires, fears, and finally kills Clare Kendry. To her chagrin, Irene Redfield finds Clare's voice (for which we might read, figuratively, her capacity to make art—to speak in her purple ink on oversized pages) irresistible. Irene upbraids herself: "What was it about Clare's voice that was so appealing, so very seductive?" (*P*, p. 165). Irene disapproves of Clare. But she also experiences envy and frustration: "In spite of her determined selfishness the woman before her was yet capable of heights and depths of feeling that she, Irene Redfield, had never known. Indeed, never cared to know" (*P*, p. 195). Clare is "selfish, willful, and disturbing" (*P*, p. 202). She confronts Irene: "Can't you realize that I'm not like you a bit? Why, to get the things I want badly enough, I'd do anything, hurt anybody, throw anything away. Really, 'Rene, I'm not safe" (*P*, p. 210). Irene fears, with good cause: "If Clare was freed, anything might happen" (*P*, p. 236).

Clearly, Irene and Clare are doubles. Clare represents for Irene the dangerous side of herself—foreign, outlawed—that she as a respectable middle-class black woman has successfully denied. Clare is sexual, daring, creative. She has moved out of African American bourgeois culture; she roams free of its demands for conformity and social service and endless attention to familial and community uplift.

But where has this "freedom" taken Clare? Her life as a white woman is hollow and self-destructive; it represents a pact with self-loathing, a project in self-erasure. Her true self is so unknown to the white man she has married and with whom she has had a child that she lives daily with his racist and hideously ironic nickname for her, "Nig." To tell him why the appellation is particularly offensive would be to lose the position of "freedom" she has created for herself. To remain silent is to acquiesce in the system of self-degradation that she has bought into.

As a parable about the modern African American woman writer, *Passing* is complex and depressing. Clare in her hypocrisy and cowardice is not, finally, attractive. Her silencing results as much from her own decision to deny her black heritage as it does from any outside forces, of which, Larsen takes care to explain very early in the novel, there have been a number. Clare was brutalized as a child by her drunkard white father and, upon his death, forced to live with racist white aunts. Thus alienated in childhood from the black community that, to the child's way of thinking, had abandoned her to racist whites, Clare as an adult gains her revenge on both worlds by passing. Seen in this way, her story is tragic. *Passing* presents Clare as the victim of internalized racism.

Yet Clare has also *chosen* to alienate herself from black American culture. She is not simply a victim but a willing agent in her own alienation, cynically determined to have it both ways. She wishes to remain in her lucrative white marriage and at the same time play at being African American on the sly. From this point of view, her dishonesty and cowardice—not some abstract victimization—keep her mute, erased, the author of foreign, furtive, barely legible writing.

Complicating these conflicting possibilities even further, Larsen allows us to know Clare's story only through another woman no less conflicted, dishonest, or cowardly than Clare. Dutiful, repressed, correct, Irene clearly *needs* Clare dead. The black woman artist is too frightening, threatening, and sexual—too unsafe— for the conventional bourgeois black woman, in Larsen's view, to embrace. Irene secretly desires union with Clare. As Deborah McDowell argues, there is a strong lesbian pull in this novel.[19] Irene's loathing and fear of Clare are so intense that they immediately point to their opposite: love and desire, a passionate longing for fusion. But Irene can no more face or live with the forbidden sexual longings within herself than she can tolerate the threat Clare represents to her tidy, hyperheterosexual family life. She pushes Clare out the window.

Or does Clare jump? We cannot say. We can surmise either possibility—or, paradoxically, in this novel about split and conflicting identities and possibilities— both. If Clare and Irene, finally, are alienated parts of one potentially whole identity, to say that Clare jumped is the same as to say that Irene pushed her, and vice versa. In either case, Larsen's story about the black woman artist in *Passing* ends in permanent silence. The divisions between respectable middle-class feminine status and the woman artist, between heterosexual and lesbian desire, and between acceptance in white and black America are unbridgeable.

How different were the stories of the real women I have been discussing?

In many cases, despite public images of change and freedom, the reality for turn-of-the-century women who wished to succeed as serious artists was one of bitter struggle. For almost all of them, a basic struggle centered on the difficulty of putting together who one was as a woman—whether black or white or Asian American or Native American, heterosexual or lesbian—with the ambition to be an artist in an elevated tradition that had either entirely or for the most part written them out.

Surely some strength was drawn by many of them from comparisons they could make among themselves, whether negative or positive. If there were relatively few women artists in the past to invoke as models—for most Austen, Eliot, Wheatley, Sand, de Staël, and the Brontës exhausted the list—there were many in the present. Kate Chopin expressed admiration for the work of Jewett, and so did Willa Cather. Pauline Hopkins warmly praised Frances Ellen Harper. Jessie Fauset named Edith Wharton among the authors especially worth studying. Dunbar-Nelson praised Larsen's work. Even when a connection amounted to envy or rivalry, it still represented connection—evidence of other women like oneself. If the success of Wharton and Cather gnawed at Ellen Glasgow, for example, it also defined one major context in which Glasgow could see herself. Likewise the mercurial relationship between Mary Austin and Willa Cather was the result of keen competition, a sign of shared territory, as could probably be said of Nella Larsen's tie to Jessie Fauset, the older and more established author. Similarly, Wharton's famous criticism of Jewett as a New England writer who looked at the region through rose-colored glasses probably reflects more accurately on Wharton's competitiveness than on Jewett's work. The point is that even the less than harmonious relationships, in some cases personal, in others not, speak to a felt context, an awareness of self as part of a group of women artists.

This group, it is important to emphasize, was never a "community." Ambitious turn-of-the-century women writers tended to work through problems individually, partly because of the era's intense emphasis on individualism, an option in some ways newly opened up to women, and partly because of the particular model of the artist to which most aspired and which by definition implied solitary struggle. In a sense each writer was alone. The issue of defining oneself as an artist was the shared yet highly idiosyncratic issue with which a number of women writers as individuals struggled. Those struggles ended in some cases in brilliant success, in others in highly compromised or aborted achievement, in still others in crushing discouragement and failure.

Of Frances Ellen Harper, Charlotte Perkins Gilman, Sarah Orne Jewett, Gertrude Stein, Mary Austin, Willa Cather, and Edith Wharton, it can probably be said that, even if their lives were not easy, they did to a significant degree find themselves able to realize their ambitions on their own terms, in their own lifetimes.

Not publicly declaring themselves artists—though certainly, as their fictions show, secretly identifying as such—Frances Ellen Harper and Charlotte Perkins Gilman had the satisfaction of acquiring during their lifetimes the kinds of activist literary reputations that they desired and worked hard to achieve. Antedating the period in many of her accomplishments, Harper drew large audiences when she spoke, was recognized as the most important African American poet between Wheatley and Dunbar, and saw her novel go into second and third editions. Gilman found publishers and a market for numerous volumes of discursive prose on the woman question and was able to create her own journal, the *Forerunner,* as an outlet for much of her fiction. She placed other stories, despite the initial rejection of "The Yellow Wallpaper," in established publications and found herself recognized in her own life as the foremost white feminist theorist of her generation in the United States.

Likewise Sarah Orne Jewett, Gertrude Stein, and Mary Austin were able to construct their lives in ways that permitted development of their art. Jewett, encouraged first by her supportive father and then by a network of lifelong friendships with women, particularly Annie Fields, had the good fortune to be born into comfortable economic circumstances that allowed her to devote herself full time to writing. Psychologically empowered by an established tradition of women regionalists, which would come to include people such as Rose Terry Cooke, Alice Cary, and Mary Wilkins Freeman, Jewett began publishing in her twenties. Well before the close of the nineteenth century she had earned a reputation as one of the nation's accomplished stylists, regionalists, and realists. Long before her death she saw her work widely admired and appreciated.

Eccentric where Jewett was conventional, Stein and Austin created for themselves radically nonconformist lives that simultaneously facilitated and reflected their needs as artists to break rules. Moving as far away as possible from the literary worlds of Boston and New York—Stein heading east to Paris, Austin west to New Mexico and California—they deliberately engaged different cultures: Stein immersed herself in the world of modernist painters in Europe; Austin plunged into Native American, Mexican, and Mexican American art and heritage. Out of these encounters they created books that gained them reputations as innovators and visionaries, which is exactly what they wanted. Flamboyant as both were, even negative criticism, and Stein especially believed this, confirmed success. If people did not understand or like the finished work, it proved that the challenge had been authentic, the risk real. Although the young womanhood of each was difficult, and Austin always felt that she was not fully appreciated, both Stein and Austin had the satisfaction of seeing their mature work talked and argued about.

For Willa Cather, as Sharon O'Brien has explained, the challenge of finding a way to write as a woman and to produce the kind of extraordinary art to which she aspired was especially intense. Her struggle to become a novelist was intricately entangled with the problem of accepting her lesbianism, as well as with the more general difficulty of reconciling gender with her ambition to be an artist. Jewett had thrived in a pre-Freudian era in which intimate relationships between women were accepted as normal; Stein had escaped to the Left Bank where nontraditional personal styles were the rule, not the exception; Dunbar-Nelson had worked out a bisexual life for herself. For Cather as a lesbian trying to live and write in early twentieth-century America, which was in the first throes of defining women-identified women as sick, the risk of embarking on novel-writing full time, which meant revealing herself in one way or another, was very great. Yet once she took the risk, which she did partly at the urging of Jewett, her career blossomed. Although she did not publish a novel until she was almost forty years old, she went on to publish many books over the course of her life and her critical reputation was extremely high. Asked at a 1929 symposium to name the leading American fiction writers of the day, thirty-two "outstanding critics" present, in the words of Fred Lewis Pattee, placed "independently, two women, Willa Cather and Edith Wharton," at the top of the list.[20]

Wharton's handicap (and asset as well), like Ellen Glasgow's, Jessie Redmon Fauset's, and Nella Larsen's, was class. In contrast to middle-class white women such as Austin and Cather, who were brought up in the American Midwest and expected to learn to take care of themselves, including economically, Wharton and Glasgow were the products of conservative upper-middle- and upper-class white families that defined work as unladylike and then held up ladylikeness as the sole goal of a respectable woman's life.

As Linda Wagner explains of Ellen Glasgow: "The conflict [was] between having to be aggressive in order to write, and passive in order to exist," a conflict that "was intensified by living in the South," the most conservative part of the country.[21] The struggle between the lady Glasgow was brought up to be—always agreeable, intellectually timid, dependent on white men—and the writer she wanted to be—daring, avant garde, independent—never left her. Her output was prodigious—almost twenty novels plus a number of other volumes. Nevertheless, although several of her books attracted high and lasting praise—*Barren Ground* (1925), most of all—Glasgow did not in her own eyes achieve the greatness she craved, the stature of Cather or Wharton. At the end of her life she felt defeated.

Also coming from a suffocatingly elite class, but a more liberal region, the Northeast, Wharton successfully freed herself from the feelings of failure that Glasgow was never able to escape. She had inhibiting class attitudes and, as Cynthia Griffin Wolff details, fundamental family relationships to work out, particularly with her mother, before she could fully realize her talent as a writer. But she did realize that talent. She was blessed with money and access to people in important places; and she overcame her personal obstacles very successfully, as the title of Wolff's analytical biography, *A Feast of Words: The Triumph of Edith Wharton,* announces. Edith Wharton, like Cather, Fauset, and many other women writers before and since (suggesting that this may be a norm rather than an exception for women), did not start as a novelist until relatively late in life, publishing her first full-length novel at the age of forty. But she then went on to publish prolifically over the span of her long fiction-writing career, which ran from the early 1890s into the early 1930s. Her career brought Edith Wharton a lot of money and extraordinary critical as well as popular acclaim.

The struggle of Jessie Fauset is both similar and different. Similar is the fact that class was an issue for Fauset; different is the fact that her struggle was played out not only in terms of class and gender but also of race. Too black for the white literary world, which despite the Harlem Renaissance remained largely ignorant of, if not hostile to, African American writers in general, and women in particular, Fauset, who was not focused on pleasing white people anyway—she just wanted to please enough editors, publishers, and reviewers to get and stay in print—was occasionally accused of not being black enough by members of the black literary community because of the middle-class focus of her work. Alain Locke at one point labeled her style "mid-Victorian,"[22] and the degree to which that stereotype, largely unchallenged until very recently, undermined Fauset's career is hard to establish. Certainly her privileged Philadelphia background limited her vision. But her background also strengthened her. It enabled her to create a significant body of published fiction between the early teens and the early 1930s. It enabled her as well to serve as the literary editor of the *Crisis* from 1919 to 1926 and as the promoter of many other black writers such as Countee Cullen, Langston Hughes, and Claude McKay throughout the Harlem Renaissance.[23]

After 1933 Jessie Redmon Fauset published no more novels, and very little else, although she lived until 1961. Reasons given for this silence are vague: the Great Depression, the marriage she made in the late 1920s, the gradual decline of her health as she grew older.[24] A further possibility is that the stresses she encountered even when she was successful were so complex that, to continue the struggle, even though she is reported to have wanted to write more,[25] may simply have been impossible. The conflicts she had to reconcile during the teens and twenties were multiple. She wrote out of a tradition, as Deborah E. McDowell has argued,[26] that expected black women writers to "represent" the race—that is, to depict morally and especially sexually, unimpeachable African American heroines to counteract the racist denigration of black women in the culture at large. At the same time she was criticized for being too timid, too "Victorian." She had to please white publishers to get into print, yet she somehow had to remain true to her own refusal to deal in stereotypes and caricature. She had to write about what she knew, which was black middle-class life, at a time when it was increasingly unfashionable to write sympathetically about bourgeois issues. (Probably one of the deepest biases of the liberal literary establishment—across the boards—is its aversion to literature about itself.) That Jessie Fauset accomplished as much as she did, given the obstacles she had to negotiate, is impressive.

Other turn-of-the-century writers were not as successful. The careers of Glasgow and Fauset, women who struggled in private with tensions imposed upon them by their positions in the culture, look almost carefree compared with the rejections and disappointments that Chopin, Hopkins, Dunbar-Nelson, Sui Sin Far, Humishuma, Yezierska, Kelley, and Larsen faced.

As is well known, Kate Chopin's assumption that she could write freely about whatever she wished, including and especially female sexuality, resulted in such hostility toward *The Awakening* that the reviews were devastating. The book was called unhealthy and morbid, its theme sordid, and the behavior of its main character totally incomprehensible.[27] This condemnation virtually paralyzed Chopin's creativity. Although she wrote a few more pieces, the rejections they incurred only further crushed her resolve, and *The Awakening* was the last major work of her career, which rapidly fell into oblivion.

Pauline Hopkins's career seems to have been destroyed not only by hostility but also and perhaps even more devastatingly by indifference and abandonment. As part of the editorial staff of the *Colored American Magazine* from 1900 to 1904, she successfully created an outlet for her own work as well as for that of other black writers, and her output was prodigious. During her years at the magazine, *Contending Forces* came out, and she serialized three novels in the magazine, ran her own stories and articles in every issue, and handled all the normal duties of literary editorship. Perhaps the first bad omen appeared in the magazine's inability after the publication of *Contending Forces* to underwrite further any separate novel publication. But the real blow came in 1904 with the magazine's secret purchase by Booker T. Washington, followed by the removal of its editorial offices from Boston New York. Although Hopkins made the move, she left the staff soon thereafter. From sources presently available, the facts of her life from this point on are difficult to establish, even though she lived until 1930. What is clear is that after four years of astonishingly vigorous productivity at the beginning of the twentieth century she published very little else.

The frustrations and obstacles that Alice Dunbar-Nelson faced were both similar and different. Like Hopkins, as a black woman Alice Ruth Moore, a woman in her twenties in the 1890s, faced limited outlets for her work. Added to this was the young writer's refusal to conform: her belief that she should not be restricted to race writing or, when writing about African Americans, be required to write in prescribed ways, using dialect, focusing on the tragic mulatto theme, and sprinkling stock plantation characters throughout her work. Consequently, like Jessie Fauset, she was not sufficiently "black" for the white press, which had clear notions of how blacks should write. Yet as the publication of Hopkins's *Contending Forces* illustrates, the resources of the black publishing world early in the twentieth century were extremely limited.

In addition, Dunbar-Nelson's marriage to Paul Laurence Dunbar may have compounded her problems, even though they lived together only from 1898 to 1902. Although their agreement had been that they would both continue their careers, Dunbar's needs, in the opinion of Ora Williams, took precedence, with the young wife taking dictation and typing, caring for her husband when he was sick, and supporting him emotionally as he struggled with the alcoholism he had developed as the result of bad medical advice. Simultaneously she argued with him not to give in as a writer to what she felt were white racist demands.[28] But Alice Dunbar could also be quite unsupportive, as Gloria T. Hull explains in *Color, Sex, and Poetry*,[29] and the stresses of this two-artist marriage in racist America, when one career would be hard enough to sustain, were no doubt very great, with unhappy consequences for both people. Although Dunbar-Nelson tried to reeenter the fiction market later in life—indeed, her dying wish was for her unpublished novel *The Lofty Oak* to be published—the combination of racist expectations in the dominant culture, the need to earn a living, the break that her first marriage caused in her development as an artist (much as this marriage to Dunbar also helped her professionally), and in the opinion of Hull, her insistence on separating the material in her fiction from the racial circumstances of her life seem to have created insurmountable, destructive pressures on her career as a fiction writer. She did continue to write and publish. In addition to compiling two anthologies, she published poems and a number of essays, plus a few short stories, during the first thirty years of the twentieth century. She also established a distinguished record as a journalist, wrote several plays, and produced out of her experience an invaluable personal narrative, as her recently edited diary illustrates.[30] But the promise of her early fiction—elegant and gemlike— was never realized.

For Anzia Yezierska becoming a writer meant defying centuries of Orthodox Jewish tradition, which reserved intellectual work for men. Remaining a writer meant surviving severe loneliness, guilt, and anxiety as she tried to bridge the two worlds that made her art possible yet tore her apart. She was determined to hold onto her ethnic identity. At the same time her Orthodox heritage taught her that as a woman she should not aspire to be an artist; and life in the ghetto made time and space in which to write impossible. Whisked off to Hollywood in the 1920s to compete in a slick world of popular professional writers, Yezierska suffered acute feelings of alienation. Her autobiography expresses her fury at one of the perfectly groomed, powerful, Anglo men she met in California: "You're so utterly beyond the sweat of struggle. Your voice flows so evenly when you talk. On the lecture platform, you look so cold in the heart and clear in the head." At another point she tells how some of these prosperous white men jokingly argue over who "made" her—"I discovered her first," says one; "Don't forget I published her first story," says another—like greedy sweatshop bosses.[31]

As she watched her work transformed into a parody of itself for the screen (joke writers were brought in to lighten up her material), the question for Yezierska became very clear: "What is the difference between a potbellied boss who exploits the labor of helpless workers and an author who grows rich writing of the poor?"[32] Yezierska lived to write; yet sickening guilt, self-doubt, and fears about exploitation plagued her. She could not write in the ghetto; she could not write out of it. After the publication of her novel *All I Could Never Be* in 1932, she published no more books except for her autobiography in 1950, even though she lived until 1970.

Nella Larsen's silence after the publication of *Quicksand* and *Passing* in 1928 and 1929 was equally profound. In 1930 her career stood poised on the edge of stupendous success. In that year she became the first African American woman to receive a Guggenheim fellowship to write fiction. But her career ended abruptly in the early 1930s. One set of problems involved charges of plagiarism and an ugly divorce. Although she was defended by the editor of *Forum* where her story accused of plagiarism appeared in 1930, Larsen was, as Mary Helen Washington puts it, "devastated by the criticism." Then her divorce three years later brought her into the news again, this time as a jealous, allegedly suicidal wife. Quite possibly the two scandals, on top of her insecurity and internalized anger as a woman of color fully at home neither in white nor black America, broke her creativity. As Washington says, the "two events of public shame, plus a fragile and vulnerable personality, a sense of oddness that made her seem strange even to her friends, and a deep-seated ambivalence about her racial status combined to reinforce her sense of herself as the Outsider and may finally have pushed her into a life of obscurity."[33] It is also likely, as Thadious Davis argues, that Larsen's obsession with elite subject matter and her fiercely production- and fame-focused motivation as a writer, neither of which made sense in the straitened thirties, dried up her career.[34] Whatever the combination of reasons, Larsen did not continue to publish, although she lived until 1963.[35]

The stories of Sui Sin Far and Humishuma are stories of fierce, heroic struggle. As Sui Sin Far explains in her autobiographical essay, she constantly had to combat racism in her personal life and the expectation that she would as a fiction writer produce nothing but pretty, exotic fluff. The brevity of her publishing career, the sickness she records in her essay, and her early death all suggest how extremely difficult her pioneering was. Likewise Humishuma's determination to write met almost insurmountable obstacles. Producing her novel under extremely difficult conditions, she finally saw it published only to realize that it had been so radically altered by her well-meaning but nevertheless proprietary white "friend" that she could barely recognize her own book. Humishuma did go on to publish *Coyote Stories* in 1933, a collection of traditional Okanogan tales rendered in English. Also, she was determined to write another novel, and this time without anyone's "help." But we do not know if she succeeded, for no manuscript has been discovered.[36]

Edith Summers Kelley, like Humishuma, wrote under exhausting, inhospitable physical conditions, struggling against poverty and the debilitating demands of full-time motherhood and hard domestic labor. Even as she wrote and revised *Weeds,* she knew that the circumstances of her life kept her from doing the kind of work she was capable of; and her inability to find a publisher for her only other novel, *The Devil's Hand,* which came out posthumously, only confirmed her analysis. After *Weeds* in 1923, her career, in effect, ended.

One important construct that emerges from these career sketches is the existence of a historical break at the end of the 1920s or early in the thirties. By the very early 1930s the period that had witnessed the work of so many outstanding turn-of-the-century American women writers was over. Some had been dead for more than a decade: Jewett, Chopin, Harper, Sui Sin Far. Others would write a few more things, often along the lines of memoirs, but their major work was done: Gilman, Wharton, Glasgow, Cather, Yezierska, Dunbar-Nelson, Austin, Stein, Fauset. Others had disappeared into silence or were in the process of doing so: Hopkins, Kelley, Larsen, Humishuma. The Great Depression and the changes in literary values and opportunities that came with it, the advancing age of many of the authors, the critical establishment's increasing disinterest in women writers, the dominant culture's unremitting racism, and the demise of vigorous women's movements in the United States all contributed to this end.

A second important conclusion to draw from these sketches is the fact that it was significantly more difficult to be a woman of color or an ethnically identified immigrant woman and to aspire to be an artist at the turn of the century than to be a white, American-born woman with the same aspiration. Among the stories of most intense struggle and outright tragedy, those of women of color outnumber those of white women. Racism at the turn of the century, it is safe to say, was the most powerful negative force operating in the lives of the women writers I have grouped. In the society at large poverty was a pervasively destructive force. We can only guess at the women of every background who never laid pencil to paper, indeed, never learned to read and write.[37] However, within the group of writers I am discussing—a grouping that presupposes literacy and if not a room, then at least a table of one's own, and therefore, by those criteria at least, middle-class status (though perhaps Humishuma's struggle undermines that categorization)—racism and ethnic discrimination presented the most difficult problems.

For women of color trying to be artists, it seems clear that the psychologically most burdensome problem was the experience of profound self-division: the feeling of being simultaneously part of two cultures that were at a fundamental level in conflict. Black women such as Harper, Hopkins, Dunbar-Nelson, Fauset, and Larsen, and Asian American and Indian women such as Sui Sin Far and Humishuma, knew that they had to be accepted by the white literary establishment. That world finally determined who would get into and stay in print.[38] Yet for many if not all of the writers I have mentioned, it was not even that simple—a matter of "having to" succeed in that world. They also wanted to. It was, as W. E. B. Du Bois argues in *The Souls of Black Folk* and Jessie Fauset eloquently articulates in *There Is Confusion,* their world too. Entering their fiction in the tradition that had produced Shakespeare and Pater, Tennyson and Proust was the right of Dunbar-Nelson and Fauset and Sui Sin Far every bit as much as it was of any other citizen of the modern world. At the same time, how to exercise that right was often unclear. Western literary tradition was interconnectedly misogynist and racist. How to lay claim to a place in a fundamentally hostile tradition *and* stay rooted in one's own subculture— which contained its own gender issues—was the schizophrenic challenge that plagued many women writers at the turn of the century, as it has since.

Further exacerbating this tension for some of these writers was the issue of class. It segregated writers like Fauset and Larsen from the majority of the black community (as it did Wharton from the majority of the white community, but the meaning of that separation is different). Especially during the Harlem Renaissance, when powerful white "literati" and patrons like Carl Van Vechten and Charlotte Mason were only too happy to cultivate and exploit black friendships, and when certain artists like Larsen were in turn only too willing to dissociate themselves from the "lower classes," the intersection of racism and class discrimination had, in the end, a dehydrating effect. Larsen, for example, in the opinion of Thadious Davis, subverted her talent to her obsession with class privilege and with "making it" in an elite world of interracial mutual aggrandizement—even as she criticized such values in *Passing.* It was probably inevitable that once the New Negro movement of the 1920s fell into decline, her career would too.[39]

No less complex were the pitfalls and contradictions that Yezierska faced. As an immigrant Jewish woman she confronted profound divisions. As a Jew she was trying to be part of a national literary tradition that was anti-Semitic. As a feminist she was trying to stay attached to an Old World heritage that was misogynist. As a person raised in the working class she was trying to make a place for herself in an elite occupation. Reconciling these allegiances was in many ways impossible. Discovering how to integrate various parts of herself that were in fundamental conflict became Yezierska's lifelong challenge, as it seems to have been for Sui Sin Far as an immigrant woman facing equally fierce ethnic and racist biases.

A sense of conflicting cultures plagued many white American-born women writers at the turn of the century as well. From Jewett to Cather the issue recurs of how to operate successfully in modern urban America, a culture defined and controlled by mainstream white "masculine" values of individualistic, marketplace aggression and competition, and at the same time stay attached to the values of relationality and nurturing that many white women associated with white middle-class women's culture of the nineteenth century. Even for writers such as Wharton and Gilman, seemingly delighted to be free of nineteenth-century domestic ideology, intense conflict about what it meant to invade traditionally male territory, to cut oneself off from a maternalized past, surfaces. Think of how terrible modern motherlessness looks in Wharton's *Custom of the Country,* for example, or of how Gilman longs for a world of mothers in *Herland.* There is throughout the period a yearning, a passionately felt need, somehow to reconcile middle- and upper-class white women's maternal past and their supposedly liberated, which is to say masculinized, present.

Cutting across all of the lines of race, class, culture, and ethnicity, this sense of splitting, of trying to bridge and connect worlds, runs through the period. Especially in fictions about women artists—from Harper's and Gilman's stories in 1892 to Larsen's *Passing* in 1929—issues of separation and loss tormented women writers at the turn into the twentieth century. But these dislocations and divisions also created tremendous strength and artistic empowerment. Negotiating the conflicts—struggling with the myriad contradictions and antitheses—seems to have released enormous artistic energy, both conceptually and, perhaps even more important, formally. Out of their individual struggles to assert their right to make art, women writers at the turn into the twentieth century created a collection not only of important stories but also of unusually original and vocal forms as they looked for new ways to articulate new, and old, truths.

NOTES

Preface

1. See Elaine Showalter, "Women Who Write Are Women," *New York Times Book Review* (Dec. 16, 1984), 31ff.

2. I develop this point at more length in "Crossing the Color Line: White Feminist Criticism and Black Women Writers," paper presented to the Modern Language Association, 1986. See also Deborah E. McDowell's criticism of white feminist criticism in "New Directions for Black Feminist Criticism," *The New Feminist Criticism: Essays on Women, Literature, and Theory*, ed. Elaine Showalter (New York: Pantheon, 1985), pp. 186–99; Audre Lorde's rebuke of white scholars in "Age, Race, Class, and Sex: Women Redefining Difference," *Sister Outsider* (Trumansburg, NY: The Crossing Press, 1984), pp. 114–15; and Merle Woo's direct charge to white women in "Letter to Ma," *This Bridge Called My Back: Writings by Radical Women of Color*, eds. Cherríe Moraga and Gloria Anzaldúa (Watertown, Mass.: Persephone Press, 1981), pp. 140–47.

3. Nina Baym, "Melodramas of Be-Set Manhood: How Theories of American Fiction Exclude Women Authors," *American Quarterly* 33 (Summer 1981), 123–39.

4. That women fiction writers before Wharton and Cather should be taken seriously, an argument now widely and persuasively mounted by many scholars, apparently remains difficult to accept for many American literary critics, whether they agree with the escapist thesis or not. See, e.g., Samuel Chase Coale, *In Hawthorne's Shadow: American Romance from Melville to Mailer* (Lexington: UP of Kentucky, 1985), or Allen F. Stein, *After the Vows Were Spoken: Marriage in American Literary Realism* (Columbus: Ohio State UP, 1984).

Chapter 1

1. See, e.g., Richard Chase, *The American Novel and Its Tradition* (Garden City, NY: Doubleday, 1957); Leslie Fiedler, *Love and Death in the American Novel* (New York: Criterion, 1960); and R. W. B. Lewis, *The American Adam* (Chicago: U of Chicago P, 1955). For analysis of the critical biases and some of the historical errors informing this portrait of American literature, see Nina Baym, "Melodramas of Be-Set Manhood: How Theories of American Fiction Exclude Women Authors," *American Quarterly* 33 (Summer 1981), 123–39, and *Novels, Readers, and Reviewers: Responses to Fiction in Antebellum America* (Ithaca, NY: Cornell UP, 1984). For discussion of some of the historical forces in the twentieth century that have produced this masculine intellectual map-making, see Paul Lauter, "Race and Gender in the Shaping of the American Literary Canon: A Case Study from the Twenties," *Feminist Studies* 9 (Fall 1983), 435–64; Alfred Habegger, *Gender, Fantasy, and Realism in American Literature* (New York: Columbia UP, 1982); and Jane Tompkins, *Sensational Designs: The Cultural Work of American Fiction, 1790–1860* (New York: Oxford UP, 1985).

2. Eileen S. Kraditor, *The Ideas of the Woman Suffrage Movement, 1890–1920* (New York: Columbia UP, 1965; rpt. Doubleday, 1971), p. 44 (emphasis added).

3. Recent titles alone in women's history emphasize this point. For example, Kraditor's

book, cited above; Mari Jo Buhle, *Women and American Socialism, 1870–1920* (Urbana: U of Illinois P, 1981); Margery W. Davies, *Woman's Place Is at the Typewriter: Office Work and Office Workers, 1870–1930* (Philadelphia: Temple UP, 1982); Margaret S. Marsh, *Anarchist Women, 1870–1920* (Philadelphia: Temple UP, 1981); Ruth Rosen, *The Lost Sisterhood: Prostitution in America, 1900–1918* (Baltimore: The Johns Hopkins UP, 1982); Beverly Guy-Sheftall, *Daughters of Sorrow: Attitudes Toward Black Women, 1880–1920* (Brooklyn: Carlson Publishing, 1990); and Dorothy Salem, *To Better Our World: Black Women in Organized Reform, 1890–1920* (Brooklyn: Carlson Publishing, 1990).

4. William H. Chafe, *The American Woman: Her Changing Social, Economic, and Political Role, 1920–1970* (New York: Oxford UP, 1972), p. 89.

5. I will return to this in more detail in Chapter 2. For excellent historical treatment of African American women's campaign for suffrage as an essential step in realizing racial as well as sexual equality, plus discussion of white suffragists' repeated betrayal of black suffragists, see Paula Giddings, *When and Where I Enter: The Impact of Black Women on Race and Sex in America* (New York: Bantam, 1984), and Bettina Aptheker, *Woman's Legacy: Essays on Race, Sex, and Class in American History* (Amherst: U of Massachusetts P, 1982).

6. Detailed discussion of the club movement can be found in Giddings, *When and Where I Enter*, and in Karen Blair, *The Clubwoman as Feminist: True Womanhood Redefined, 1868–1914* (New York: Holmes & Meier, 1980).

7. A word on terminology and focus. When generalizations apply to all women, I use the term *women*. Otherwise I have tried throughout to use specific terminology: *women of color, white women, African American women,* and so forth. In terms of focus, there were at the turn of the century in the book publishing literary world too few Native American and Asian American women writers to comprise groups of authors. Therefore, the generalizations in my introduction usually apply specifically to African American or to white women or to those two groups together. In every case, however, the women I have in mind are specified. I do offer more detailed information about Asian American women at the turn of the century in Chapter 7, where I focus on Sui Sin Far, a woman of mixed English and Chinese parentage who embraced her Chinese ancestry and as a writer identified herself as Chinese American. Also I provide some information about the situation of Native American women in my discussion of Humishuma in Chapter 8. Finally, although the first short fiction in English by a Latina writer, María Cristina Mena, was published early in the twentieth century (as I discuss in Chapter 9), to the best of my knowledge there were no Latinas writing novels in English or collections of fiction in English in the United States during the years I am considering.

8. Barbara Welter, *Dimity Convictions* (Athens: Ohio UP, 1976).

9. Carroll Smith-Rosenberg, *Disorderly Conduct: Visions of Gender in Victorian America* (New York: Oxford UP, 1985), p. 176.

10. Ibid.

11. Giddings, *When and Where I Enter*, p. 137.

12. Ibid., p. 108.

13. Ibid., pp. 108–9.

14. Gerda Lerner, ed., *Black Women in White America: A Documentary History* (New York: Random House, 1972), pp. 442–43.

15. Giddings, *When and Where I Enter*, p. 54.

16. Nina Baym, *Woman's Fiction: A Guide to Novels by and about Women in America, 1820–1870* (Ithaca: Cornell U, 1978), p. 32.

17. See Louise Michele Newman, *Men's Ideas/Women's Realities: Popular Science, 1870–1915* (New York: Pergamon Press, 1985), or Rosalind Rosenberg, *Beyond Separate Spheres: Intellectual Roots of Modern Feminism* (New Haven: Yale UP, 1982).

18. The result of this tension personally, as I examine in Chapter 8 in particular and as critics such as Sharon O'Brien and Josephine Donovan have already argued in detail about individual figures, was a fundamental conflict between gender and art for many serious women writers at the turn of the century. See O'Brien, *Willa Cather: The Emerging Voice* (New York: Oxford UP, 1987), and Donovan, *After the Fall: The Demeter-Persephone Myth in Wharton, Cather, and Glasgow* (University Park: Penn State UP, 1989).

19. It may be that, although Humishuma is widely referred to as the first Native American woman novelist, she was preceded by Sarah Callahan. See Rayna Green, Introduction, *That's What She Said: Contemporary Poetry and Fiction by Native American Women* (Bloomington: Indiana UP, 1984), p. 3. Also, I use the name Humishuma, following Green's example, although it is most common to see the author referred to as Mourning Dove.

20. F. Stanly Godbold, Jr., *Ellen Glasgow and the Woman Within* (Baton Rouge: Louisiana State UP, 1972), p. 29.

21. See, for example, Grant M. Overton, *The Women Who Make Our Novels* (New York: Moffat, Yard & Co., 1918).

22. Helen Gray Cone, "Woman in Literature," in *Woman's Work in America*, ed. Annie Nathan Meyer (New York: Henry Holt & Co., 1891), pp. 107, 108.

23. Ibid., p. 122. For a valuable contemporary caution against constructing essential differences, see Nina Baym, "Rewriting the Scribbling Women," *Legacy* 2 (Fall 1985), 3–12.

24. Myra Jehlen, "Archimedes and the Paradox of Feminist Criticism," *Signs* 6 (Summer 1981), 584, 585.

25. Audre Lorde, *Sister Outsider* (Trumanburg, NY: The Crossing Press, 1984), p. 110.

26. Peggy Kamuf, "Replacing Feminist Criticism," *Diacritics* 12 (Summer 1982), 44, 45.

27. Robert E. Spiller et al., *Literary History of the United States* (New York: Macmillan, 1974), vol. 1, p. 1216.

28. For the Ellmann discussion, see *Thinking about Women* (New York: Harcourt, Brace and World, 1968). As I have worked on this book, large, new literary historical projects have been underway, one, for example, to come out from Cambridge University Press, another already issued from Columbia University Press, *The Columbia Literary History of the United States* (1988). How fundamentally new they will be or are remains an open question. See, for instance, Lawrence Buell's remark that his entry on the American Renaissance for the Columbia volume is, to his surprise, not very new ("Literary History Without Sexism? Feminist Studies and Canonical Reconception," *American Literature* 59 [1987], 102–3). For an excellent challenge to the Columbia and Cambridge projects early in their creation, when they were still being conceived and therefore could benefit from it, see Annette Kolodny, "The Integrity of Memory: Creating a New Literary History of the United States," *American Literature* 57 (1985), 291–307.

29. Spiller, *Literary History*, p. 1212.

30. An outdated book in this category that is nevertheless of particular interest because of its extreme and overt hostility to the politics of the authors it groups is Josephine Lurie Jessup's *The Faith of Our Feminists: A Study in the Novels of Edith Wharton, Ellen Glasgow, Willa Cather* (New York: R. R. Smith, 1950).

31. Lauter, "Race and Gender," pp. 435–63.

32. Ibid., p. 444.

33. Ibid.

34. James R. McGovern, "David Graham Phillips and the Virility Impulse of the Progressives," *New England Quarterly* 38–39 (1965–66), 335–36.

35. Cone, "Woman in Literature," p. 115.

36. F. L. Pattee, *The New American Literature, 1890–1930* (New York: Cooper Square, 1930), p. 268.

37. Cone, "Woman in Literature," pp. 126–27.

38. Judith Fetterley makes this point about earlier writers; see Introduction, *Provisions: A Reader from Nineteenth-Century Women* (Bloomington: Indiana UP, 1985).

39. Kamuf, "Replacing Feminist Criticism," p. 47.

40. Kolodny, "The Integrity of Memory," p. 301.

Chapter 2

1. Anna Julia Cooper, *A Voice From the South* (Xenia, OH: Aldine Printing House, 1892), p. i. This book is available in at least two reprints, one published in New York by the Negro Universities Press, 1969; and the other appearing with an introduction by Mary Helen Washington in The Schomburg Library of Nineteenth-Century Black Women Writers, gen. ed. Henry Louis Gates, Jr. (New York: Oxford UP, 1988).

2. Bettina Aptheker, *Woman's Legacy: Essays on Race, Sex, and Class in American History* (Amherst: U of Massachusetts P, 1982), p. 2.

3. See Erlene Stetson, ed., *Black Sister: Poetry by Black American Women, 1746–1980* (Bloomington: Indiana UP, 1981), and Joan Sherman, *Invisible Poets: Afro-Americans of the Nineteenth Century* (Urbana: U of Illinois P, 1974).

4. For an excellent introduction to writing by black women in the nineteenth century, see the forty-volume set of reprints titled The Schomburg Library of Nineteenth-Century Black Women Writers, gen. ed. Henry Louis Gates, Jr. (New York: Oxford UP, 1988 and 1991).

5. At issue for some people is whether to define *Our Nig* as an autobiography or as a novel, although the question may be unanswerable until more information about Wilson surfaces, if it exists. For discussion of what is presently known about Wilson, see Henry Louis Gates, Jr., Introduction, *Our Nig* (New York: Random House, 1983).

6. For a very interesting comparison of Harper and Alice Walker, e.g., see Deborah E. McDowell, " 'The Changing Same': Generational Connections and Black Women Novelists," *New Literary History* 18 (1986–87), 281–302.

7. See the annotated list of novels by African American women at the turn of the century in Carole McAlpine Watson's *Prologue: The Novels of Black American Women, 1891–1965* (Westport, CT: Greenwood Press, 1985); the discussion of the period in Hazel V. Carby's *Reconstructing Womanhood: The Emergence of the Afro-American Woman Novelist* (New York: Oxford UP, 1987); and the introductions to the volumes of fiction in the The Schomburg Library of Nineteenth-Century Black Women Writers.

8. See Penelope L. Bullock, *The Afro-American Periodical Press, 1838–1909* (Baton Rouge: Louisiana State UP, 1981).

9. This fiction and more detailed discussion of it can be found in Elizabeth Ammons, ed., *Short Fiction by Black Women, 1900–1920*, in The Schomburg Library of Nineteenth-Century Black Women Writers (1991). Other African American magazines probably carried fiction by women as well. For instance, *Woman's World*, founded in 1900, almost certainly did, and the *Colored Woman's Magazine*, founded in 1907, probably did. However, no copies of any issues of these publications have been located. See Bullock, *Afro-American Periodical Press*, p. 169.

10. Rayford W. Logan, *The Negro in the United States: A Brief History* (Princeton, NJ: D. Van Nostrand Co., 1957), p. 39.

11. Aptheker, *Woman's Legacy*, p. 57.

12. See Thomas F. Gossett, *Uncle Tom's Cabin and American Culture* (Dallas: Southern Methodist UP, 1985). pp. 348ff.

13. Excellent discussion of the club movement, as well as of the racism of white women in white clubs, who time after time proved themselves to be undependable allies and, often, adversaries, can be found in Aptheker, *Woman's Legacy* and Paula Giddings, *When and Where I Enter: The Impact of Black Women on Race and Sex in America* (New York: Bantam, 1984).

14. As Giddings explains: "Women's rights were an empty promise if Afro-Americans were crushed under the heel of a racist power structure" (*When and Where I Enter*, p. 7).

15. Gerda Lerner, ed., *Black Women in White America: A Documentary History* (New York: Pantheon, 1972), p. 171.

16. Ibid., p. 245.

17. As Giddings explains:

In times of racial militancy, Black women threw their considerable energies into that struggle—even at the expense of their feminist yearnings. However, when militancy faltered, Black women stepped forward to demand the rights of their race from the broader society, and their rights as women from their men. The latter demand was not seen in the context of race *versus* sex, but as one where their rights had to be secured in order to assure Black progress. (*When and Where I Enter*, p. 7)

18. Jessie Redmon Fauset, *The Sleeper Wakes*, in *Crisis* 20 (Oct. 1920), 271. This fiction is reprinted in Ammons, *Short Fiction by Black Women, 1900–1920*.

19. Giddings, *When and Where I Enter*, p 6.

20. Ibid., p. 85.

21. For lynch figures, including the fact that for known lynch victims between 1882 and 1946 only 23 percent were even accused of rape, see Aptheker, *Woman's Legacy*, pp. 60–61.

22. Giddings, *When and Where I Enter*, p. 28. For extended discussion of the rape fantasy embedded in lynching, see Jacquelyn Dowd Hall, *Revolt Against Chivalry: Jessie Daniel Ames and the Women's Campaign Against Lynching* (New York: Columbia UP, 1979).

23. Quoted in Herbert G. Gutman, *The Black Family in Slavery and Freedom, 1750–1925* (New York: Pantheon, 1976), p. 536; cited in Giddings, *When and Where I Enter*, p. 31.

24. Aptheker, *Woman's Legacy*, p. 62.

25. Giddings, *When and Where I Enter*, p. 87.

26. Ibid.

27. Lerner, *Black Women in White America*, p. 470.

28. Ida B. Wells, *Southern Horrors: Lynch Law in All Its Phases* (New York: The New York Age Print, 1892), p. 4.

29. Quoted in Hall, *Revolt Against Chivalry*, p. 79.

30. Giddings, *When and Where I Enter*, p. 29; Dorothy Sterling, *Black Foremothers: Three Lives* (Old Westbury, NY: The Feminist Press, 1979), p. 82; and Carby, *Reconstructing Womanhood*, p. 109. For detailed discussion of black feminist thought at the end of the nineteenth century as a context that enabled fiction writers such as Harper and Pauline Hopkins, see Carby's superb chapter " 'In the Quiet, Undisputed Dignity of My Womanhood': Black Feminist Thought after Emancipation," in *Reconstructing Womanhood*, pp. 95–120.

31. Frances Ellen Watkins Harper, *Iola Leroy, or Shadows Uplifted* (1892; rpt. New York: Arno, 1969), p. 208. References in the text are marked *IL* and are to this edition. The book has also been reissued, with an introduction by Frances Smith Foster, in The Schomburg Library of Nineteenth-Century Black Women Writers (1988), and exists in a paperback edition, ed. Hazel V. Carby (Boston: Beacon Press, 1987).

32. See William Still, *The Underground Railroad* (Philadelphia: Porter and Coates, 1872; rpt. Arno, 1968), p. 772. For a more detailed introduction to Harper's career than I provide here, see my "Profile" of her in *Legacy* 2 (Fall 1985), 61–66.

33. Carby, *Reconstructing Womanhood*, p. 63.

34. Harper wrote poems memorializing some of Stowe's characters, "Eliza Harris" and "Eva's Farewell," and also, in certain very interesting ways, modeled *Iola Leroy* on Stowe's *Uncle Tom's Cabin*. The two poems can be found in *Poems on Miscellaneous Subjects* by Frances Ellen Watkins (Philadelphia: Marrihew and Thompson, 1857), pp. 9–11, 32, as well as in *Complete Poems of Frances E. W. Harper*, ed. Maryemma Graham, in The Schomburg Library of Nineteenth-Century Black Women Writers (1988). For detailed discussion of the connection between Stowe's and Harper's novels, see Elizabeth Ammons, "Stowe's Dream of the Mother-Savior: *Uncle Tom's Cabin* and American Women Writers before the 1920s," in *New Essays on Uncle Tom's Cabin*, ed. Eric J. Sundquist (Cambridge: Cambridge UP, 1986), pp. 155–95.

35. Helen Gray Cone, "Woman in Literature," in *Woman's Work in America*, ed. Annie Nathan Meyer (New York: Henry Holt, 1891), pp. 113, 116.

36. Audre Lorde, "Age, Race, Class, and Sex: Women Redefining Difference," in *Sister Outsider* (Trumanburg, NY: The Crossing Press, 1984), p. 421.

37. Giddings, *When and Where I Enter*, p. 136.

38. Sterling, *Black Foremothers*, p. 73.

39. McDowell, " 'The Changing Same,' " p. 284.

40. Among the early praise for Harper's novel was G. F. Richings's statement in *Evidences of Progress Among Colored People*: "I am confident if such books written by Colored writers could be read by the leading White people of our country, much good might be done in breaking down the awful prejudice which now exists" (Philadelphia: G. S. Ferguson Co., 1896), p. 415.

41. The historical reality was bluntly pointed out by Mary Church Terrell. In the prestigious *North American Review* in 1904, she reminded her primarily white audience that along with "the white men who shoot negroes to death and flay them alive" were "the white women who apply flaming torches to their oil-soaked bodies." Quoted in Lerner, *Black Women in White America*, p. 209.

Chapter 3

1. Josephine Silone-Yates, "Parental Obligation," *Colored American Magazine* 12 (Apr. 1907), 285.

2. Helen Gray Cone, "Woman in Literature," in *Woman's Work in America*, ed. Annie Nathan Meyer (New York: Henry Holt & Co., 1891), p. 113.

3. Quoted in Charlotte Perkins Gilman, *The Living of Charlotte Perkins Gilman: An Autobiography* (New York: Harper & Row, 1935: rpt. 1975), p. 119.

4. Ibid., p. 120.

5. Ibid., pp. 120–21.

6. Some recent discussions of "The Yellow Wallpaper" are Susan Gubar, "*She* in *Herland*," in *Coordinates: Placing Science Fiction and Fantasy*, ed. George Slusser (Carbondale: Southern Illinois UP, 1983), pp. 139–49; Annette Kolodny, "A Map for Rereading: Or, Gender and the Interpretation of Literary Texts," *New Literary History* 11 (Spring 1980), 451–67; Elaine Hedges, Afterword, *The Yellow Wallpaper* (Old Westbury, NY: The Feminist Press, 1973), pp. 37–67; and Conrad Shumaker, " 'Too Terribly Good to be Printed': Charlotte Gilman's 'The Yellow Wallpaper,' " *American Literature* 57 (Dec. 1985), 588–99. Also of interest is the idea that periods of cultural turmoil—and certainly the turn of the

century was one—have a liberating effect on women's speech; see Patricia S. Yaeger, " 'Because a Fire Was in My Head': Eudora Welty and the Dialogic Imagination,'' *PMLA* 99 (Oct. 1984), 955–73.

7. Ellen L. Bassuk, "The Rest Cure: Repetition or Resolution of Victorian Women's Conflicts?,'' in *The Female Body in Western Culture: Contemporary Perspectives,* ed. Susan Rubin Suleiman (Cambridge: Harvard UP, 1986), p. 141.

8. Ibid.

9. Ibid.

10. Charlotte Perkins Gilman, *The Yellow Wallpaper* (Boston: Small, Maynard, 1899; rpt. Old Westbury, NY: The Feminist Press, 1973), p. 9. References in the text are to this separately published edition of the story and are abbreviated *YW.*

11. For extensive development of Gilman's belief that the Victorian feminine ideal was a completely eroticized version of woman, see *Women and Economics* (Boston: Small, Maynard, 1898; rpt. New York: Harper & Row, 1966). There she argues, for example, that even women's hands and feet have been made into secondary sex characteristics and a woman is expected to dress "in garments whose main purpose is unmistakably to announce her sex; with a tendency to ornament which marks exuberance of sex-energy, with a body so modified to sex as to be grievously deprived of its natural activities" (pp. 45, 53).

12. Helene Cixous, "The Laugh of the Medusa," *New French Feminisms,* eds. Elaine Marks and Isabelle de Courtivron (New York: Schocken Books, 1981), p. 244.

13. Ibid., p. 256.

14. See Susan S. Lanser, "Feminist Criticism, 'The Yellow Wallpaper,' and the Politics of Color in America," *Feminist Studies* 15 (Fall 1989), 415–41.

15. Gilman, *The Living of Charlotte Perkins Gilman,* p. 121.

16. Gilman says: "I sent him a copy [of "The Yellow Wallpaper"] as soon as it came out, but got no response. However, many years later, I met some one who knew close friends of Dr. Mitchell's who said he had told them that he had changed his treatment of nervous prostration since reading 'The Yellow Wallpaper.' If that is a fact, I have not lived in vain" (ibid., p. 121). For an excellent discussion of Mitchell that focuses in particular on his own creative writing—the novels he published—see Eugenia Kaledin, "Dr. Manners: S. Weir Mitchell's Novelistic Prescription for an Upset Society," *Prospects* 11 (1986), 199–216.

17. One of the central arguments of *Women and Economics* is the implicitly racist one that women, and by this Gilman meant white, American-born women, should be liberated from Victorian restrictions, ranging from corsets to unemployment, in order to be stronger, healthier mothers of stronger, healthier (white) babies and thus future citizens.

18. Rosalind Rosenberg, *Beyond Separate Spheres: Intellectual Roots of Modern Feminism* (New Haven: Yale UP, 1982), p. xiv.

19. See Ruth Bleier, *Science and Gender: A Critique of Biology and Its Theories on Women* (New York: Pergamon, 1984), p. 171. Also of interest here is Carroll Smith-Rosenberg's observation in a discussion of antiabortion debate at the turn of the century that the threatening figure changed dramatically depending on who was doing the analysis. When bourgeois women analyzed the abortion issue, for example, it was men, not middle-class ambitious women, who posed the threat: "In their pages, images of marital rape, of unwanted pregnancies, of marriage as legalized prostitution replaced male images of unnatural aborting mothers and willful urbane ladies. . . . For the women . . . the husband who forced unwanted pregnancies upon his wife, and not the willful and fashionable matron, constituted the dangerous and disorderly figure." *Disorderly Conduct: Visions of Gender in Victorian America* (New York: Oxford UP, 1985), p. 243.

20. Grant Allen, "Woman's Place in Nature," *Forum* 7 (May 1889), 263; quoted in Louise Michele Newman, *Men's Ideas/Women's Realities: Popular Science, 1870–1915*

(New York: Pergamon Press, 1985), p. 54. Allen, an Englishman who declared himself "an enthusiast on the Woman Question," declared in another essay in 1889:

> For what is the ideal that most of these modern women agitators set before them? Is it not clearly the ideal of an unsexed woman? Are they not always talking to us as though it were not the fact that most women must be wives and mothers? Do they not treat any reference to that fact as something ungenerous, ungentlemanly, and almost brutal? Do they not talk about our "casting their sex in their teeth?"—as though any man ever resented the imputation of manliness. . . . Women ought equally to glory in their femininity. A woman ought to be ashamed to say she had no desire to become a wife and mother. (Quoted in Newman, p. 127)

21. For analysis of Darwin from this point of view, see Ruth Hubbard, "Have Only Men Evolved?," in *Biological Woman: The Convenient Myth* (Cambridge, MA: Schenkman Books, 1982), pp. 17–45.

22. Quoted in Rosenberg, *Beyond Separate Spheres,* p. 7.

23. Ibid., pp. 8–9.

24. See Newman, *Men's Ideas/Women's Realities,* p. 85.

25. Theodore Roosevelt, "Prefatory Letter," in *The Woman Who Toils: Being the Experiences of Two Ladies as Factory Girls* by Mrs. John Van Vorst and Marie Van Vorst (New York: Doubleday, Page & Co., 1903), p. viii. Although Roosevelt applied this statement to either the man or the woman who shunned parenthood, it is clear from the letter, as well as from the Van Vorst material which inspired it, that his concern was with women who shirked their biological duty.

26. Gilman, *The Living of Charlotte Perkins Gilman,* p. 119.

27. Ibid., p. 5

28. Ibid., p. 9.

29. Ibid., pp. 10–11.

Chapter 4

1. Willa Cather on *Death Comes for the Archbishop,* in *Willa Cather on Writing,* ed. Stephen Tennant (New York: Alfred A. Knopf, 1949), p. 12.

2. Josephine Donovan, "Nan Prince and the Golden Apples," *Colby Library Quarterly* 22 (March 1986), 21.

3. Sharon O'Brien, *Willa Cather: The Emerging Voice* (New York: Oxford UP, 1987), Ch. 15.

4. She regretted Stowe's practice of not revising her work, for example, which reflected her inability, in Jewett's opinion, to put her art before her domestic and maternal obligations. See Annie Fields, ed., *The Letters of Sarah Orne Jewett* (Boston: Houghton Mifflin, 1911), pp. 46–47.

5. I discuss Harper and Jewett's attachment to midnineteenth century maternal values, as well as the attachment of other women writers such as Harriet E. Wilson, Louisa May Alcott, Elizabeth Stuart Phelps, and Angelina Grimké, in "Stowe's Dream of the Mother-Savior: *Uncle Tom's Cabin* and American Women Writers before the 1920s," in *New Essays on Uncle Tom's Cabin,* ed. Eric J. Sundquist (Cambridge: Cambridge UP, 1986), pp. 155–95.

6. Th. Bentson [Marie Thérèse de Solms Blanc], "Family Life in America," *Forum* 21 (March 1896), 12, 19, 20.

7. Sarah Orne Jewett, *The Country of the Pointed Firs,* ed. Mary Ellen Chase (1896; rpt. New York: Norton, 1981), p. 1. My citations in the text are to this edition and are

abbreviated *CPF*. Also, for excellent extended discussion of the Persephone-Demeter myth in Jewett's work, see Sarah Way Sherman's biography, *Sarah Orne Jewett, an American Persephone* (Hanover, NH: UP of New England, 1989), and the chapter on Jewett in Josephine Donovan, *After the Fall: The Demeter-Persephone Myth in Wharton, Cather, and Glasgow* (University Park: Penn State UP, 1989).

8. Richard Cary, *Sarah Orne Jewett* (New York: Twayne Publishers, 1962), p. 83.

9. George R. Stewart, *American Place-Names* (New York: Oxford UP, 1970), p. 152.

10. I discuss Jewett and witches in detail in "Jewett's Witches," in *Critical Essays on Sarah Orne Jewett*, ed. Gwen Nagel (Boston: G. K. Hall, 1984), pp. 165–84.

11. For detailed discussion of how Jewett exploits the category of minor in "A White Heron," turning "minor" into a source of strength rather than weakness, see Louis A. Renza, *"A White Heron" and the Question of Minor Literature* (Madison: U of Wisconsin P, 1984).

12. Richard Cary, ed., *Sarah Orne Jewett Letters* (Waterville, ME: Colby College Press, 1967), p. 29.

13. "A White Heron" also shows her ability to manipulate conventional plot structure in interesting ways; see Elizabeth Ammons, "The Shape of Violence in Jewett's 'A White Heron,' " *Colby Library Quarterly* 22 (March 1986), 6–16.

14. Concerned specifically with the marriage plot, Boone says:

Implicit in this notion of the reader's pleasure in excitation, deferral, and release [is the fact that] the developmental trajectory of such narratives, it would appear, reflects the trajectory ascribed to the reader's own desires. Yet, as the sexual imagery pointed out above suggests, the reader hypothesized here is male; the pattern of desire being evoked follows a linear model of sexual excitation and final discharge most often associated, in both psychological and physiological terms, with men. If this is so, the erotic dynamic of the traditional love plot, however much it may play to female desire, nonetheless would seem to encode at the most elementary level of narrative a highly specific, male-oriented norm of sexuality fostering the illusion that all pleasure (of reading or of sex) is ejaculatory. (Joseph A. Boone, "Modernist Maneuverings in the Marriage Plot: Breaking Ideologies of Gender and Genre in James's *The Golden Bowl*," *PMLA* 101 [May 1986], 375–76)

15. For this etymology I am grateful to my colleague, Sylvan Barnet.

16. I have borrowed the contrasting images of web and ladder from Carol Gilligan, *In a Different Voice: Psychological Theory and Women's Development* (Cambridge, MA: Harvard UP, 1982), on whose theory of gender polarity I relied extensively in my initial working out of this part of my argument in "Going in Circles: The Female Geography of Jewett's *Country of the Pointed Firs*," *Studies in the Literary Imagination* 16 (1983), 83–92. While I still find the contrasting images of web and ladder helpful, I now find more useful as a description of the complex development of adult personality the analysis of Jessica Benjamin, to whom I turn at the end of this discussion of Jewett's book.

17. See Willa Cather, ed., *The Best Stories of Sarah Orne Jewett* (Boston, New York: Houghton Mifflin, 1925). For the thought that Cather was probably just following the lead of Jewett's publishers, who added stories to posthumous editions of the book (1910, 1919), see Francis Fike, "An Interpretation of *Pointed Firs*," in *Appreciation of Sarah Orne Jewett: Twenty-nine Interpretive Essays*, ed. Richard Cary (Waterville, ME: Colby College Press, 1973), p. 179, n. 2; rpt. from *New England Quarterly* 34 (Dec. 1961), 478–79. Happily, Jewett's original version of *The Country of the Pointed Firs* is now available in the 1981 Norton paperback edited by Mary Ellen Chase.

18. As sociologist Nancy Chodorow observes of the domestic activities of women in the modern west, they "have a nonbounded quality. They consist, as countless housewives can

attest and as women poets, novelists, and feminist theorists have described, of diffuse obligations.'' Therefore, in contrast to ''work in the labor force—'men's work'—[which] is likely to be contractual, to be more specifically delimited, and to contain a notion of defined progression and product,'' ''the work of maintenance and reproduction [in the home] is characterized by its repetitive and routine continuity, and does not involve specified sequence or progression.'' See Chodorow, *The Reproduction of Mothering: Psychoanalysis and the Sociology of Gender* (Berkeley: U of California P, 1978), p. 179.

19. Ibid., p. 178.

20. Carroll Smith-Rosenberg, ''The Female World of Love and Ritual: Relations between Women in Nineteenth-Century America,'' *Signs* 1 (Autumn 1975), 1–30; collected in Smith-Rosenberg, *Disorderly Conduct: Visions of Gender in Victorian America* (New York: Oxford UP, 1985), pp. 53–76.

21. See Smith-Rosenberg *Disorderly Conduct,* pp. 64–65.

22. Cather, Preface, in *Best Stories,* p. xviii.

23. Marjorie Pryse, ''Introduction to the Norton Edition,'' in *The Country of the Pointed Firs and Other Stories* by Sarah Orne Jewett, ed. Mary Ellen Chase (1896; rpt. New York: Norton, 1981), p. xv.

24. Christine Downing, *The Goddess: Mythological Images of the Feminine* (New York: Crossroad Publishing Co., 1981), p. 135.

25. Ibid., p. 143.

26. Fields, *Letters of Sarah Orne Jewett,* pp. 172–73.

27. Emrika Padus, *Woman's Enclyclopedia of Health and Natural Healing* (Emmaus, PA: Rodale Press, 1981), pp. 292, 299, 302.

28. Jessica Benjamin, ''The Oedipal Riddle: Authority, Autonomy, and the New Narcissism,'' in *The Problem of Authority in America,* eds. John P. Diggins and Mark E. Kann (Philadelphia: Temple UP, 1981), p. 215.

29. Ibid., p. 205.

Chapter 5

1. Ruby Ora Williams, ''An In-Depth Portrait of Alice Dunbar-Nelson,'' unpublished Ph.D. dissertation, University of California at Irvine, 1974, p. 97.

2. Gloria T. Hull, *Color, Sex, and Poetry: Three Women Writers of the Harlem Renaissance* (Bloomington: Indiana UP, 1987), p. 54.

3. The Howells quotation, as well as detailed discussion of Alice Dunbar's debate with her husband on accommodation to white expectations, can be found in Williams, ''In-Depth Portrait of Alice Dunbar-Nelson,'' pp. 53ff.

4. Ibid., p. 81.

5. Ibid.

6. James Weldon Johnson, Preface, *The Book of American Negro Poetry* (New York: Harcourt, 1931); quoted in Henry Louis Gates, Jr., *Figures in Black: Words, Signs, and the "Racial" Self* (New York: Oxford UP, 1987), p. 182.

7. Gates, *Figures in Black,* pp. 185–86.

8. Hull, *Color, Sex, and Poetry,* pp. 52, 90.

9. This story, as well as many other writings previously unavailable or difficult to locate, can be found in *The Works of Alice Dunbar-Nelson,* vols. 2 and 3, in The Schomburg Library of Nineteenth-Century Black Women Writers, gen. ed. Henry Louis Gates, Jr. (New York: Oxford UP, 1988). *The Goodness of St. Rocque and Other Stories* and *Violets and Other Tales* are reprinted in *The Works of Alice Dunbar-Nelson,* vol. 1. All three volumes include an excellent introduction by Gloria T. Hull, who edited them.

10. *The Works of Alice Dunbar-Nelson,* vol. 2, pp. 261–62.

11. See McDowell's introduction to *Quicksand and Passing* (New Brunswick: Rutgers UP, 1986).

12. Hull, *Color, Sex, and Poetry,* pp. 57–58.

13. Ibid., pp. 53, 57, 58, 64.

14. Alice Dunbar, *The Goodness of St. Rocque and Other Stories* (New York: Dodd, Mead & Co., 1899; rpt. Arno 1969), pp. 7–8. References in the text are to this edition and will be preceded by the abbreviation *GSR.*

15. Information about St. Roch (also spelled Rock and Rocco) can be found in any standard source; I used *Butler's Lives of the Saints,* eds. Herbert Thurston, S. J., and Donald Attwater (New York: P. J. Kenedy & Sons, 1956), vol. 3, p. 338.

16. For explicit identification of this symbolism, see Dunbar-Nelson's later story, "Cupid and the Phonograph," in *The Works of Alice Dunbar-Nelson,* vol. 3, p. 90.

17. Mary L. Shaffter, "Creole Women," *The Chautauquan,* 15 (June 1892), 346; rpt. in *The Awakening,* ed. Margaret Culley (1899; rpt. New York: Norton Critical Edition, 1976), p. 119. Note also the protest of the white author M. H. Herrin in *The Creole Aristocracy: A Study of the Creole of Southern Louisiana, His Origin, His Accomplishments, His Contributions to the American Way of Life* (New York: Exposition Press, 1952): "The word [Creole] is never to be used to identify persons with both white and Negro blood"—the appropriate term for such people being instead "Colored Creole," a label suggested by the white journalist Lafcadio Hearn as a "convenient term to distinguish the colored people who claim a partly Latin origin from the plainer 'American' colored folk who have neither French nor Spanish blood in their veins and to whom the Creole dialect is unintelligible" (p. 28).

18. Williams, "In-Depth Portrait of Alice Dunbar-Nelson," p. 98.

19. For examples, see *The Works of Alice Dunbar-Nelson,* vol. 2.

20. Williams, "In-Depth Portrait of Alice Dunbar-Nelson," p. 98.

21. Ibid.

22. Anzia Yezierska, *Red Ribbon on a White Horse* (New York: Charles Scribner's Sons, 1950; rpt. Persea, 1981), p. 162; emphasis added.

23. Hull, *Color, Sex, and Poetry,* p. 44.

24. Williams, "In-Depth Portrait of Alice Dunbar-Nelson," p. 84.

25. "The Stones of the Village" is in volume 3, and "Brass Ankles Speaks" in volume 2, *The Works of Alice Dunbar-Nelson.* For discussion of both, see Gloria T. Hull, "Shaping Contradictions: Alice Dunbar-Nelson and the Black Creole Experience," *The New Orleans Review* 15 (Spring 1988), 34–37.

26. What little is known at this point about Dunbar-Nelson's lesbianism can be found in Hull's biographical discussions of her in *Color, Sex and Poetry; The Works of Alice Dunbar-Nelson;* and *Give Us Each Day: The Diary of Alice Dunbar-Nelson* (New York: W. W. Norton, 1984).

27. The fact that she was bisexual rather than exclusively heterosexual or lesbian reinforces this idea; see Hull, *Give Us Each Day,* pp. 24–25.

28. Mary Russo, "Female Grotesques: Carnival and Theory," in *Feminist Studies, Critical Studies,* ed. Teresa de Lauretis (Bloomington: Indiana UP, 1986), p. 218.

29. For excellent discussion of Dunbar-Nelson's life and work in the 1920s, see Hull, Introduction and headnotes, *Give Us Each Day.*

30. Quoted in Per Seyersted, *Kate Chopin: A Critical Biography* (New York: Farrar, Straus and Giroux, 1980), pp. 58–59.

31. Allen F. Stein opens his discussion of Chopin with this statement as well. See *After the Vows Were Spoken: Marriage in American Literary Realism* (Columbus: Ohio State UP, 1984), p. 163.

32. Kate Chopin, *The Awakening*, ed. Margaret Culley (1899; rpt. New York: Norton Critical Edition, 1976), pp. 10, 12. References in the text are to this edition and will be preceded by the abbreviation *A*.

33. I take the term and the concept "wild zone" from Elaine Showalter's classic essay, "Feminist Criticism in the Wilderness," collected in *The New Feminist Criticism: Essays on Women, Literature, and Theory*, ed. Elaine Showalter (New York: Pantheon, 1985), pp. 243–70.

34. Discussion of the treatment of race in Chopin's work can be found in Seyersted, *Kate Chopin*, and in Anne Goodwyn Jones's excellent chapter on Chopin in *Tomorrow Is Another Day: The Woman Writer in the South, 1859–1936* (Baton Rouge: Louisiana State UP, 1981), pp. 135–84. Also important on *The Awakening* is the discussion of Chopin in Sandra M. Gilbert and Susan Gubar, *No Man's Land: Sexchanges* (New Haven: Yale UP, 1989), ch. 3.

35. Toni Morrison, "Unspeakable Things Unspoken: The Afro-American Presence in American Literature," *Michigan Quarterly Review* 28 (Winter 1989), 12.

36. Willa Cather, Review of *The Awakening* in the *Pittsburgh Leader* (July 8, 1899); quoted in Culley, ed., *The Awakening*, p. 153.

37. Morrison, "Unspeakable Things Unspoken," p. 11.

38. Emily Toth, "Timely and Timeless: The Treatment of Time in *The Awakening* and *Sister Carrie*," *Southern Studies* 16 (Fall 1977), 271.

39. Peggy Skaggs, "Three Tragic Figures in Kate Chopin's *The Awakening*," *Louisiana Studies* 13 (Winter 1974), 346.

40. Quoted in Jones, *Tomorrow Is Another Day*, p. 147.

41. Pauline E. Hopkins, *Contending Forces: A Romance Illustrative of Negro Life North and South* (Boston: The Colored Co-operative Publishing Co., 1900; rpt. Carbondale: Southern Illinois UP, 1978), pp. 14–15. References in the text are to this edition, which will be abbreviated as *CF*.

42. In her diary, Alice Dunbar-Nelson recalls being in West Medford in 1896–97. See Hull, *Give Us Each Day*, p. 50, and *Color, Sex, and Poetry*, p. 33.

43. Pauline E. Hopkins, "Famous Women of the Negro Race," *Colored American Magazine* 3 (Apr. 1902), 369.

44. "Pauline E. Hopkins," *Colored American Magazine* 2 (Jan. 1901), 219, 218.

45. Pauline E. Hopkins, *Of One Blood. Or, The Hidden Self*, in *The Magazine Novels of Pauline Hopkins*, with an introduction by Hazel V. Carby (New York: Oxford UP, 1988), p. 451. References in the text, abbreviated as *OB*, and are to this edition. *The Magazine Novels*, which also include *Hagar's Daughter, A Story of Southern Caste Prejudice* and *Winona, A Tale of Negro Life in the South and Southwest*, collect the novels that Hopkins serialized in the *Colored American Magazine* from 1901 to 1903 and appear in The Schomburg Library of Nineteenth Century Black Woman Writers.

46. Published biographical information on Hopkins is scarce. In addition to the introductions to *Contending Forces* and *The Magazine Novels of Pauline Hopkins* in The Schomburg Library of Nineteenth-Century Black Women Writers, see the brief sketch of her in the *Colored American Magazine* cited above (n. 44); the entry by Dorothy B. Porter and the sources cited by her in the *Dictionary of American Negro Biography*, eds. Rayford W. Logan and Michael R. Winston (New York: Norton, 1982), pp. 325–26; Ann Allen Shockley, "Pauline Elizabeth Hopkins: A Biographical Excursion into Obscurity," *Phylon* 33 (Spring 1972), 22–26; and Claudia Tate, "Pauline Hopkins: Our Literary Foremother," in *Conjuring: Black Women, Fiction, and Literary Tradition*, eds. Marjorie Pryse and Hortense J. Spillers (Bloomington: Indiana UP, 1985), pp. 53–66. For information about her association with the *Colored American Magazine*, see Penelope L. Bullock, *The Afro-American Periodical Press, 1838–1909* (Baton Rouge: Louisiana State UP, 1981), pp. 106–18.

47. Hazel V. Carby, *Reconstructing Womanhood: The Emergence of The Afro-American Woman Novelist* (New York: Oxford UP, 1987), p. 136.

48. Ibid., p. 132.

49. Carole McAlpine Watson, *Prologue: The Novels of Black American Women, 1891–1965* (Westport, CT: Greenwood Press, 1985), p. 144.

50. See Bullock, *Afro-American Periodical Press,* p. 107.

51. Margaret Walker, "On Being Female, Black, and Free," in *The Writer on Her Work: Contemporary Women Writers Reflect on Their Art and Situation,* ed. Janet Sternburg (New York: W. W. Norton, 1980), pp. 95–106.

52. See Abby Arthur Johnson and Ronald M. Johnson, "Away from Accommodation: Radical Editors and Protest Journalism, 1900–1910," *Journal of Negro History* 62 (Oct. 1977), 325–29.

53. See Bullock, *Afro-American Periodical Press,* pp. 106–8.

Chapter 6

1. Mary Austin, *The American Rhythm: Studies and Reexpressions of Amerindian Songs* (New York: Harcourt, Brace and Company, 1923), p. 40.

2. Gertrude Stein, "Stanzas in Meditation," Stanza V; quoted in Richard Bridgman, *Gertrude Stein in Pieces* (New York: Oxford UP, 1970), p. 216.

3. Mary Austin, *Earth Horizon* (Cambridge, MA: Houghton Mifflin, 1932), p. 289.

4. For Stein's much-discussed attraction to Cézanne, to which I will return later in the chapter, see, e.g., her own remarks long after the fact in *Lectures in America* (New York: Random House, 1935), pp. 76–77.

5. Mary Austin, *The Land of Little Rain* (Albuquerque: U of New Mexico P, 1974), p. 3. Quotations in the text are from this edition and are abbreviated *LLR.* Also available is a new reissue of the text with an excellent introduction by Marjorie Pryse called *Stories from the Country of Lost Borders,* which includes both *The Land of Little Rain* and *Lost Borders* (New Brunswick: Rutgers UP, 1987).

6. For excellent detailed discussion of Stein's relation to Cézanne, see Jayne L. Walker, *The Making of a Modernist: Gertrude Stein, from Three Lives to Tender Buttons* (Amherst: U of Massachusetts P, 1984).

7. Richard Kostelanetz, *The Yale Gertrude Stein* (New Haven: Yale UP, 1980), p. xvi.

8. Ibid., p. xxiv. For book-length analysis of Stein's "anti-patriarchal" experimental writing from a critical perspective grounded in large part in deconstructionist and French feminist theories, see Marianne DeKoven, *A Different Language: Gertrude Stein's Experimental Writing* (Madison: U of Wisconsin P, 1983).

9. Kostelanetz, *Yale Gertude Stein,* p. xxvi. Kostelanetz earlier remarks on the "abolition of linear causality in the portrayal of character and activity" in Stein's development as a writer (p. xviii).

10. Mary Austin, *A Woman of Genius* (New York: Doubleday, Page & Company, 1912), p. 5.

11. Austin, *Earth Horizon,* p. 365.

12. Lisa Ruddick, "Modernism and Sacrifice: The Writings of Gertrude Stein," unpublished paper delivered at The Bunting Institute (Cambridge, MA), pp. 17, 24.

13. Austin, *Earth Horizon,* p. 362. Excellent discussion of other writers' attraction to Native American culture and art at about the same time as Austin—D. H. Lawrence, Mabel Dodge Luhan, Willa Cather, Jean Toomer—can be found in Lois Palken Rudnick, *Mabel Dodge Luhan: New Woman, New Worlds* (Albuquerque: U of New Mexico P, 1984).

14. Austin, *Earth Horizon,* p. 365.

15. See ibid., pp. 292–93.

16. Ibid., pp. 257, 221. That the relationship may have looked quite different to Austin's mother, and certainly did to at least some townspeople in Carlinville, Illinois, where Mary Hunter Austin grew up, is discussed by Austin's biographer. T. M. Pearce, who often found community members sympathizing with the peculiar author's mother. Poverty, overwork, and the burden of a daughter who frequently made up stories rather than telling the "truth" were what many of Susie Graham Hunter's neighbors recalled when they remembered the famous author's mother. See Pearce, *The Beloved House* (Caldwell, ID: The Caxton Printers, 1940), pp. 35–36. Austin's relationship with her mother also receives detailed attention in Augusta Fink's study, *I-Mary: A Biography of Mary Austin* (Tucson: U of Arizona P, 1983), and briefer comment in Marjorie Pryse's introduction to *Stories of the Country of Lost Borders by Marty Austin.* For a book-length discussion of Austin's life and work, see Esther Lanigan Stineman, *Mary Austin: Song of a Maverick* (New Haven: Yale UP, 1989).

17. Gretchen Bataille and Kathleen Mullen Sands, *American Indian Women: Telling Their Lives* (Lincoln: U of Nebraska P, 1984), p. 8.

18. Austin, *The American Rhythm*, p. 11.

19. Joan Lidoff, *Fluid Boundaries,* unpublished ms., p. 67.

20. Austin, *The American Rhythm,* pp. 18–19, 55.

21. Marilou Awiakta, Review of Marla N. Powers's *Oglala Women: Myth, Ritual and Reality,* in *Papers from the Center for Research on Women: Memphis State University* (Fall 1987), p. 6.

22. Awiakta, "Baring the Atom's Mother Heart," in *Homewords: A Book of Tennessee Writers,* eds. Douglas Paschall and Alice Swanson (Knoxville: U of Tennessee P, 1986), p. 186.

23. Paula Gunn Allen, *The Sacred Hoop: Recovering the Feminine in American Indian Traditions* (Boston: Beacon, 1986), pp. 81, 79.

24. Ibid., p. 78.

25. Ruddick, "Modernism and Sacrifice," p. 24.

26. Quoted in Kostelanetz, *Yale Gertrude Stein,* p. xx.

27. Ruddick, "Modernism and Sacrifice," pp. 1–2. For Edmund Wilson's statement to much the same effect forty years ago, see Lillian Faderman, *Surpassing the Love of Men: Romantic Friendship and Love Between Women from the Renaissance to the Present* (New York: William Morrow, 1981), p. 399.

28. Gertrude Stein, *Tender Buttons,* in *Selected Writings of Gertrude Stein,* ed. Carl Van Vechten (New York: Random House, 1945), p. 487.

29. Ruddick, "Modernism and Sacrifice," p. 23.

30. Ibid., pp. 27, 28.

31. Stimpson's essay was a paper prepared for the Harvard Feminist Literary Theory Seminar (Oct. 6, 1987). Lorde's essay, "The Master's Tools Will Never Dismantle the Master's House," can be found in Lorde, *Sister Outsider* (Trumansburg, NY: Crossing Press, 1984).

32. Xaviere Gauthier, "Existe-t-il une ecriture de femme?," trans. Marilyn A. August, in *New French Feminisms: An Anthology,* eds. Elaine Marks and Isabelle de Courtivron (New York: Schocken, 1981), pp. 162–63.

33. Ibid., p. 162.

34. Austin, *Earth Horizon,* p. 366.

35. Grant Overton, *The Women Who Make Our Novels* (New York: Moffat, Yard, & Company, 1918), pp. 168–69.

36. In her autobiography, Austin gives this account of her political work:

I took to the defense of Indians because they were the most conspicuously defeated and offended against group at hand. I should have done as much even without what

I afterward discovered among them of illumination and reformation of my own way of thought. . . . I got out of the actual activities [of fighting the U.S. government] . . . a knowledge of the persisting strain of bruteness, of emotional savagery, of greed and hypocrisy which taints the best of our Western civilization; precisely what my contemporaries learned by seeing strikers beaten up by policemen; citizens deprived by violence of their ^constitutional liberties; the lowly and underprivileged stripped of their economic opportunities. As for the other things that came to me by way of my Indian acquaintances, they are the gifts of a special grace. (*Earth Horizon,* pp. 266–67)

37. Austin, *The American Rhythm,* pp. 40–41.

38. Good discussion of Austin's racism, including mention of her attitudes toward black Americans, can be found in Richard Drinnon, *Facing West: The Metaphysics of Indian-Hating and Empire-Building* (Minneapolis: U of Minnesota P, 1980), ch. 16.

39. Gertrude Stein, *Three Lives* (New York: Alfred A Knopf, 1909; 1936)), p. 85.

40. Ibid., p. 86. For more detailed analysis of Stein's treatment of blacks, see Milton A. Cohen, ''Black Brutes and Mulatto Saints: The Racial Hierarchy of Stein's 'Melanctha,' '' *Black American Literature Forum* 17–18 (1983–84), 119–21.

41. Gertrude Stein, *The Autobiography of Alice B. Toklas* (New York: Harcourt, Brace, 1933), p. 100.

42. Discussions of ''Melanctha'' routinely point out that Stein's familiarity with African American life consisted of a two-month stint (which she hated) in a city hospital in Baltimore when she was a medical student. See, e.g., Cohen, ''Black Brutes,'' pp. 119–21.

Chapter 7

1. Sui Sin Far, ''Leaves from the Mental Portfolio of an Eurasian,'' *Independent* 66 (Jan. 21, 1909), 132. References are hereafter cited in the text as ''Leaves.''

2. In addition to this autobiographical essay, I am drawing in this paragraph on two excellent articles by Amy Ling, ''Edith Eaton: Pioneer Chinamerican Writer and Feminist,'' *American Literary Realism* 16 (Autumn 1983), 287–98, and ''Writers With a Cause: Sui Sin Far and Han Suyin,'' *Women's Studies International Forum* 9 (1986), 411–419; and on one by S. E. Solberg, ''Sui Sin Far/Edith Eaton: First Chinese American Fictionist,'' *MELUS* 8 (Spring 1981), 27–39.

3. Sui Sin Far provides this more complete list in her acknowledgment at the beginning of *Mrs. Spring Fragrance*: the *Independent, Out West, Hampton's,* the *Century, Delineator, Ladies' Home Journal, Designer, New Idea, Short Stories, Traveler, Good Housekeeping, Housekeeper, Gentlewoman, New York Evening Post, Holland's, Little Folks, American Motherhood, New England, Youth's Companion, Montreal Witness, Children's, Overland, Sunset,* and *Westerner.*

4. Ling, ''Edith Eaton,'' p. 292.

5. For discussion of the legal and economic situation for Chinese Americans at the turn of the century, see Ruthanne Lum McCunn, *An Illustrated History of the Chinese in America* (San Francisco: Design Enterprises of San Francisco, 1979); Judy Yung, *Chinese Women of America* (Seattle: U of Washington P, 1986); Him Mark Lai, Genny Lim, and Judy Yung, *Island: Poetry and History of Chinese Immigrants on Angel Island, 1910–1940* (San Francisco: HOC DOI, 1980); and Ronald Takaki, *Strangers from a Different Shore: A History of Asian Americans* (Boston: Little Brown, 1989). The 5 percent statistic comes from a workshop led by Ronald Takaki, ''Asian Women in American History: Scholarship and Methodology,'' Tufts University, November 2, 1988.

6. Sui Sin Far, *Mrs. Spring Fragrance* (Chicago: A. C. McClurg & Co., 1912), p. 3. References in the text are to this edition and are abbreviated *MSF.*

7. Ling, "Edith Eaton," p. 293; and "Writers With a Cause," p. 415.

8. Willa Cather and Mary Austin, for two famous examples, wrote stories about Chinese in America. See Cather's "A Son of the Celestial" and "The Conversion of Sum Loo," or Austin's "The Conversion of Ah Lew Sing." The way in which these authors' publishing careers overlapped and intersected becomes especially clear in the literal juxtaposition of the work of Sui Sin Far and Mary Austin in the July 1899 issue of the *Overland Monthly* (vol. 34). Sui Sin Far's story "A Chinese Ishmael" ends on the same page (p. 49) on which Mary Austin's poem "Inyo" is printed.

9. I am indebted for this insight to my colleague at Tufts, Professor Shuk-Mei Ho.

10. I discuss several of these stories in more detail and in a different context in "The New Woman as Cultural Symbol and Social Reality: Six Women Writers' Perspectives," in *The Cultural Moment: 1915*, eds. Lois Rudnick and Adele Heller (New Brunswick: Rutgers UP, 1991).

11. Solberg, "Sui Sin Far," pp. 32, 33, 35. Particularly critical of Sui Sin Far as an artist is the remark, largely inaccurate, in the introduction to *AIIIEEEEE! An Anthology of Asian-American Writers*, eds. Jeffery Paul Chan, Frank Chin, Lawson Fusao Inada, and Shawn H. Wong (Washington, DC: Howard UP, 1974): "Working within the terms of the stereotype of the Chinese as laundryman, prostitute, smuggler, coolie, she presents 'John Chinaman' as little more than a comic caricature, giving him a sensibility that was her own" (rpt. in *Three American Literatures: Essays in Chicano, Native American, and Asian-American Literature for Teachers of American Literature*, ed. Houston A. Baker, Jr. [New York: Modern Language Association of America, 1982], p. 204). One of the arguments of this introduction is that Asian American literature has suffered from being emasculated, as evidenced by the number of women as opposed to men writers who have been published. This bias against women writers, standard enough in the 1960s but, curiously, not emended in the 1982 reissue, may help explain the authors' skewed statement about Sui Sin Far quoted above. On the other hand, many of their general statements about racism, language, and silencing are excellent (see, e.g., p. 217) and no doubt apply importantly to Sui Sin Far.

12. Sui Sin Far's opinion about pretending to be Japanese rather than Chinese may be contained in this strong statement by one of her characters in "A Chinese Ishmael," a story not collected in *Mrs. Spring Fragrance*: "This I do say: I am only a slave, but still a Chinese maiden. He is a man who, wishing to curry favor with the white people, wears American clothes, and when it suits his convenience passes for a Japanese." *Overland Monthly* 34 (July 1899), 44.

13. See Houston A. Baker, Jr., *Modernism and the Harlem Renaissance* (Chicago: U of Chicago P, 1987).

14. For an excellent introduction to her concept of "the narrative of community," see Sandra Zagarell, "Narrative of Community: The Identification of a Genre," *Signs* 13 (Spring 1988), 498–527.

15. Amy Ling, *Between Worlds: Women Writers of Chinese Ancestry* (New York: Pergamon, 1990), p. 27. For the comparison of Sui Sin Far and Sherwood Anderson mentioned below, see Ling, "Edith Eaton," p. 292.

16. Ibid., p. 291.

17. Ibid., p. 287.

18. See "Leaves," passim.

19. I am indebted to Yilan Liu for showing me the English words in the name Sui Sin Far. As Yilan Liu explains, because Anglicized spellings of Chinese sounds were not standardized at the time that Sui Sin Far wrote, she could have spelled her name any way she wished and thus avoided the words *sin* and *far*. For example, she could have written *sing* or *xin* or *xing* and *fah* or *fa*; she did not have to encode the Chinese sounds in western words that have clear meanings. (Another interesting spelling of her name that shows up in print,

though far more rarely, is Sui Seen Far.) By her own admission, Sui Sin Far did not know Chinese ("Leaves," p. 131), so it is possible that the western words in her Chinese-looking name were totally accidental and not of her design (this is especially true if the name was given to her in childhood rather than taken on by her as an adult). However, given the fact that she was a writer and that words were her business, it seems highly unlikely that the western possibilities of the Anglicized code "Sui Sin Far," even if accidental, escaped her. (On this subject of naming, a large unexamined topic in *Mrs. Spring Fragrance* is the significance of characters' names and the extent to which Sui Sin Far is or is not in control of their meanings and appropriateness.)

Chapter 8

1. Jewett wrote this to Cather in 1908 after reading her story, "On the Gull's Road," in *McClure's Magazine.* Quoted in Lillian Faderman, *Surpassing the Love of Men: Romantic Friendship and Love Between Women from the Renaissance to the Present* (New York: William Morrow, 1981), p. 202.

2. Mary Austin, *Lost Borders,* collected in *Stories from the Country of Lost Borders,* ed. Marjorie Pryse (New Brunswick: Rutgers UP, 1987), p. 258.

3. See Nina Baym, *Woman's Fiction: A Guide to Novels by and about Women, 1820–1870* (Ithaca: Cornell UP, 1978); Mary Kelley, *Private Woman, Public Stage: Literary Domesticity in Nineteenth-Century America* (New York: Oxford UP, 1984); and Jane Tompkins, *Sensational Designs: The Cultural Work of American Fiction, 1790–1860* (New York: Oxford UP, 1986).

4. See Sharon O'Brien, *Willa Cather: The Emerging Voice* (New York: Oxford UP, 1987).

5. Francis Whiting Halsey, ed. *Women Authors of Our Day in Their Homes: Personal Descriptions and Interviews* (New York: James Pott & Co., 1903), p. 251.

6. For Hopkins's serial on Lydia Maria Child, see the *Colored American Magazine* 6 (1903).

7. Per Seyersted, *Kate Chopin: A Critical Biography* (New York: Farrar, Straus and Girous, 1980), pp. 52, 89, 25, 65, 51.

8. E. Stanly Godbold, Jr., *Ellen Glasgow and the Woman Within* (Baton Rouge: Louisiana State UP, 1972), pp. 44, 43.

9. Quoted in Josephine Donovan, *New England Local Color Literature: A Women's Tradition* (New York: Frederick Ungar, 1983), p. 100.

10. Willa Cather, "Miss Jewett," in *Not Under Forty* (New York: Alfred A. Knopf, 1936), p. 89. Cather emphasizes that Jewett did not refer to herself or to her own writing as "great," thereby qualifying her aspirations as an artist. At the same time, she thought well enough of her own potential and work to take Flaubert, one of the few "great" writers in her view, as one of her mentors. In other words, though modest in her aspirations as an artist in one way, she was bold and confident in another.

11. Carolyn Wedin Sylvander, *Jessie Redmon Fauset, Black American Writer* (Troy, NY: Whitson Publishing Co., 1981), p. 107.

12. Dunbar-Nelson expressed these ambitions in letters to her future husband, Paul Laurence Dunbar, in the 1890s. See Ruby Ora Williams, "An In-Depth Portrait of Alice Dunbar-Nelson," unpublished Ph.D. dissertation, University of California at Irvine, 1974, p. 78.

13. Godbold, *Ellen Glasgow,* p. 47.

14. Quoted by Thadious Davis, "Nella Larsen and the Harlem Renaissance," public lecture, Harvard University, March 18, 1987.

15. Quoted in Seyersted, *Kate Chopin,* p. 59.

218 NOTES

16. Anzia Yezierska, *Red Ribbon on a White Horse* (New York: Charles Scribner's Sons, 1950; rpt. Persea, 1981), p. 87.

17. Edith Wharton, "George Eliot," *Bookman* (May 1902), 247–51; and Pauline Hopkins, *Of One Blood*, in *The Magazine Novels of Pauline Hopkins*, with an introduction by Hazel V. Canby, in the Schomburg Library of Nineteenth-Century Black Women Writers, gen. ed. Henry Louis Gates, Jr. (New York: Oxford UP, 1988), passim.

18. Cather, "Katherine Mansfield," in *Not Under Forty*, p. 147.

19. Mary Austin, *Earth Horizon* (Cambridge, MA: Hougton Mifflin, 1932), pp. 23, 105.

20. See Rosalind Rosenberg, *Beyond Separate Spheres: Intellectual Roots of Modern Feminism* (New Haven: Yale UP, 1982). In Chapter 3, I give a brief summary of Rosenberg's thesis.

21. Austin, *Earth Horizon*, p. 136.

22. For detailed discussion of the conflicts apparently felt by many popular nineteenth-century American women novelists, see Kelley, *Private Woman, Public Stage*.

23. Helen Gray Cone, "Woman in Literature," in *Woman's Work in America*, ed. Annie Nathan Meyer (New York: Henry Holt & Co., 1891), p. 115.

24. Ibid., p. 122–23.

25. These statements are quoted in O'Brien, *Willa Cather*, pp. 174 and 177, and can be found in their entirety in William M. Curtin, ed., *The World and the Parish: Willa Cather's Articles and Reviews, 1893–1902* (Lincoln: U of Nebraska P, 1970), vol. 1, pp. 275, 362.

26. O'Brien, *Willa Cather*, pp. 5–6.

27. O'Brien argues this thesis throughout her biography of Cather's early development.

28. See Annie Feilds, ed. *Letters of Sarah Orne Jewett* (Boston: Houghton Mifflin, 1911), p. 250.

29. I discuss *Alexander's Bridge* in detail in "The Engineer as Cultural Hero and Willa Cather's First Novel, *Alexander's Bridge*," *American Quarterly* 38 (1986), 746–60. Briefly, I argue in that essay that Cather's first novel, written in imitation of Henry James, was an attempt at a "masculine"novel and that the exercise, failing, freed her to write the books about strong women that would truly launch her career: *O Pioneers!*, *The Song of the Lark*, and *My Ántonia*.

30. Willa Cather, *The Song of the Lark* (Boston: Houghton Mifflin, 1915; rev. 1937) p. 368. References in the text are to this edition and are abbreviated *SOL*.

31. Cather's statement that the making of art parallels pregnancy is especially interesting in this context; see Blanche H. Gelfant, *Women Writing in America: Voices in Collage* (Hanover, NH: UP of New England, 1984), p. 240. Gelfant offers many perceptive observations about Cather in this book, as well as about Mary Austin.

32. Paula Gunn Allen, *The Sacred Hoop: Recovering the Feminine in American Indian Traditions* (Boston: Beacon Press, 1986), p. 149.

33. For an excellent discussion, see Judith Fetterley, "*My Ántonia*, Jim Burden and the Dilemma of the Lesbian Writer," in *Gender Studies: New Directions in Feminist Criticism*, ed. Judith Specter (Bowling Green, OH: Bowling Green State UP, 1986), pp. 44–59.

34. Quoted in Sarah Way Sherman, *Sarah Orne Jewett: An American Persephone* (Hanover, NH: UP of New England, 1987), p. 221.

35. Willa Cather, *My Ántonia* (Boston: Houghton Mifflin, 1918), p. iii.

36. Susan J. Rosowski, *The Voyage Perilous: Willa Cather's Romanticism* (Lincoln: U of Nebraska P, 1986), pp. 76–77; and Judith Fryer, *Felicitous Space: The Imaginative Structures of Edith Wharton and Willa Cather* (Chapel Hill: U of North Carolina P, 1986), p. 274.

37. Rosowski, *Voyage Perilous*, p. 77.

38. Cather's most famous theoretical announcement of this aesthetic of simplification can be found in "The Novel Démeublé," in *Willa Cather on Writing*, ed. Stephen Tennant (New York: Alfred A. Knopf, 1949).

39. See, e.g., Phyllis Rose, "Modernism: The Case of Willa Cather," in *Modernism Reconsidered*, ed. Robert Kiely, with assistance from John Hildebidle (Cambridge, MA: Harvard UP, 1983), pp. 123–45.

40. For the Morrison essay, see Toni Morrison, "Unspeakable Things Unspoken: The Afro-American Presence in American Literature," *Michigan Quarterly Review* 28 (Winter 1989), 1–34. For my discussion of *My Ántonia*, see my essay, "*My Ántonia* and African American Art," in *New Essays on My Ántonia*, ed. Sharon O'Brien (Cambridge: Cambridge UP, forthcoming).

41. In 1938 Willa Cather stated directly that she attempted "two experiments in form" in *The Professor's House*. The first was the insertion of "a *Nouvelle* into the *Roman*," a shorter narrative into the longer one. The second was the imitation of the Dutch painting technique of creating a crowded domestic scene in which, through a window, one can see the sea and ships: "In my book I tried to make Professor St. Peter's house rather overcrowded and stuffy with new things; American proprieties, clothes, furs, petty ambitions, quivering jealousies—until one got rather stifled. Then I wanted to open the square window and let in the fresh air that blew off the Blue Mesa, and the fine disregard of trivialities which was in Tom Outland's face and in his behaviour" (*Willa Cather on Writing*, pp. 30–32.).

42. Ibid., p. 12.

43. See in particular the closing paragraphs of Book VII, in *Death Comes for the Archibishop* (1927; rpt. Boston: Houghton Mifflin, 1938), pp. 271–73.

44. Blanche H. Gelfant, "The Forgotten Reaping-Hook: Sex in *My Ántonia*," *American Literature* 43 (1971), 60–82. This essay is collected in Gelfant, *Women Writing in America*, pp. 93–116; and in *Critical Essays on Willa Cather*, ed. John J. Murphy (Boston: G. K. Hall, 1984), pp. 147–64.

45. Cather, *My Ántonia*, p. 184. I use this simply as an example; the pages about Blind d'Arnault are full of such language and images.

46. See E. A. Mares, "Padre Martinez: Defender of the People," *New Mexico Magazine* (June 1985), 57–60; and T. M. Pearce, *The Beloved House* (Caldwell, ID: Caxton Printers, 1940), p. 176. Also relevant here is Cordelia Candelaria, "Song of the Dark: Cather's Unwitting Portrayals of Bigotry," unpublished paper, Spring 1989.

47. I discuss these issues, and the need to address them more directly in both teaching and writing about Willa Cather, in "Cather's Racism," Keynote Paper at "The Santa Fe Conference on Willa Cather: A Critical Reappraisal," August 1989.

48. O'Brien, *Willa Cather*, p. 44.

49. Ibid., p. 45.

50. Willa Cather, *Sapphira and the Slave Girl* (1940; rpt. New York: Random House, 1975), p. 70. References in the text are to this edition and are *SSG*.

51. For a different point of view, see James Woodress who says of *Sapphira* that it is "particularly distinguished for its credible black men and women, something new in Cather's fiction. . . . There is not a stereotype in the lot." *Willa Cather: A Literary Life* (Lincoln: U of Nebraska P, 1987), p. 488.

52. For a very interesting discussion of how the illustrations that Cather commissioned for *My Ántonia* contribute to her subtextual commentary on Jim Burden as narrator, see Jean Schwind, "The Benda Illustrations to *My Ántonia*: Cather's 'Silent' Supplement to Jim Burden's Narrative," *PMLA* 100 (1985), 51–67.

53. Hum-ishu-ma or "Mourning Dove," *Cogewea, The Half-Breed* (1927; rpt. Lincoln:

U of Nebraska P, 1981), p. 264. Quotations in the text are to this edition and are abbreviated as *CHB*.

54. Alanna Kathleen Brown, "Legacy Profile: Mourning Dove," *Legacy* 6 (1989), 51–56.

55. Ibid., p. 54. Discussion of *Cogewea* can also be found in Mary V. Dearborn, *Pocahontas's Daughters: Gender and Ethnicity in American Culture* (New York: Oxford UP, 1986), pp. 18ff.

56. Brown, "Legacy Profile," p. 54. Also quoted in the introduction by Dexter Fisher to the University of Nebraska edition of *Cogewea*.

57. Dexter Fisher encourages this interpretation in his thoughtful and thought-provoking introduction to *Cogewea*.

58. I take some of my remarks here from my earlier essay "Crossing the Color Line: White Feminist Criticism and Black Women Writers," paper presented to the Modern Language Association, 1986.

59. See Paula Giddings, *When and Where I Enter: The Impact of Black Women on Race and Sex in America* (New York: Bantam, 1984), p. 137.

60. See Jacqueline Jones, *Labor of Love, Labor of Sorrow: Black Women, Work, and the Family from Slavery to the Present* (New York: Basic Books, 1985).

Chapter 9

1. Carolyn Wedin Sylvander, *Jessie Redmon Fauset, Black American Writer* (Troy, NY: Whitson, 1981), p. 107.

2. A junior at Cornell at the time, Fauset wrote to Du Bois of *Souls*:

> Professor Du Bois I am going to thank you, as though it had been a personal favor, for your book "The Souls of the [*sic*] Black Folk." I am glad, glad you wrote it— we have needed someone to voice the intricacies of the blind maze of thought and action along which the modern, educated colored man or woman struggles. It hurt you to write that book, didn't it? The man of fine sensibilities has to suffer exquisitely, just simply because his feeling is so fine. (*The Correspondence of W. E. B. Du Bois,* ed. Herbert Aptheker [Amherst: U of Massachusetts P, 1973], vol. 1, p. 66)

3. Sylvander, *Jessie Redmon Fauset,* p. 78.

4. In response to Alain Locke's charge in the January 1934 issue of *Opportunity* that her style was mid-Victorian, for example, Jessie Fauset wrote to him, as Sylvander explains, "a scathing letter. . . . 'I have always disliked your attitude toward my work,' she begins, continuing with comments on the pedantry, stuffiness, and poverty of thought in his works, his inept writing, his prejudice as a critic in favor of whites, his malice and lack of discrimination. She challenges him to point out one page where 'mid-Victorian style prevails' " (Ibid., p. 76).

5. For example, the review of *There Is Confusion* in the *Literary Digest International Book Review* in 1924 states that Fauset "neither demands nor makes any sentimental concessions. She possesses the critical insight and resolute detachment of the novelist, and her picture of the society which her novel surveys is achieved with an art as impersonal as that of Mrs. Wharton. Her novel is neither propaganda nor apology but art." Quoted in Sylvander, *Jessie Redmon Fauset,* pp. 71–72.

6. Wharton has been attacked for being hostile to women in her fiction and for being male-identified as an author. Fauset has been criticized for being hidebound and Victorian— too ladylike—and not sufficiently "black." For examples of the former, see Janet Malcolm's review of a new edition of selected Wharton novels in the *New York Times Book Review*

(Nov. 16, 1986), or Josephine Donovan's chapter on Wharton in *After the Fall: The Demeter-Persephone Myth in Wharton, Cather, and Glasgow* (University Park: Penn State UP, 1989). Examples of the latter can be found in Alain Locke's quote in note 4 above; in two of the critics cited in Deborah E. McDowell's introduction to *Plum Bun* (London: Pandora Press, 1985)—David Littlejohn, *Black on White: A Critical Survey of Writing by American Negroes* (New York: Viking, 1966), pp. 50–51, and Robert Bone, *The Negro Novel in America* (1958; rpt. New Haven: Yale UP, 1972), pp. 65, 95–107—or in Barbara Christian, *Black Women Novelists: The Development of a Tradition, 1892–1976* (Westport, CT: Greenwood, 1980), pp. 41–47.

7. For discussion of black women's lives and occupational options at the turn of the century, see Paula Giddings, *When and Where I Enter: The Impact of Black Women on Race and Sex in America* (New York: Bantam, 1984), and Jacqueline Jones, *Labor of Love, Labor of Sorrow: Black Women, Work, and the Family from Slavery to the Present* (New York: Basic Books, 1985).

8. Deborah E. McDowell, "A Portrait in Pieces," unpublished paper, Tufts University, March 9, 1987.

9. Both Giddings, *When and Where I Enter,* and Jones, *Labor of Love,* offer good discussions of the lives of such women.

10. Edith Wharton, *The Touchstone* (New York: Charles Scribner's Sons, 1900), p. 4. References in the text are to this edition and are abbreviated *T.*

11. I discuss Ellen as an artist in some detail in "Cool Diana and the Blood-Red Muse: Edith Wharton on Innocence and Art," in *American Novelists Revisited: Essays in Feminist Criticism,* ed. Fritz Fleischmann (Boston: G. K. Hall, 1982), pp. 209–24. In this essay I comment on the absence of important successors to Edith Wharton in the 1920s (p. 222)—a completely erroneous statement in light of the careers of Fauset and Nella Larsen. The statement reflects my own ignorance and blindness at the time, and I call attention to it here both to correct the error and to emphasize how skewed and inaccurate literary history is when white scholars (myself in this case) fail to educate themselves about all, rather than just white, American authors.

12. Quoted in E. Stanly Godbold, Jr., *Ellen Glasgow and the Woman Within* (Baton Rouge: Louisiana State UP, 1972), p. 178.

13. Wharton's letters to Fullerton can be found in R. W. B. Lewis and Nancy Lewis, eds., *The Letters of Edith Wharton* (New York: Charles Scribner's Sons, 1988).

14. See Elizabeth Ammons, *Edith Wharton's Argument with America* (Athens: U of Georgia P, 1980). Other recent extended discussions of Wharton include: R. W. B. Lewis, *Edith Wharton: A Biography* (New York: Harper & Row, 1975); Cynthia Griffin Wolff, *A Feast of Words: The Triumph of Edith Wharton* (New York: Oxford UP, 1977); Judith Fryer, *Felicitous Space: The Imaginative Structures of Edith Wharton and Willa Cather* (Chapel Hill: U of North Carolina P, 1986); Sandra M. Gilbert and Susan Gubar, *No Man's Land 2: Sexchanges* (New Haven: Yale UP, 1989), ch. 4; Josephine Donovan, *After the Fall,* ch. 3; and Susan Goodman, *Edith Wharton's Women* (Durham, NH: UP of New England, 1990).

15. María Cristina Mena, "The Vine-Leaf," *Century Magazine* 89 (Dec. 1914), 291. There is very little written about Mena. Brief biographical information can be found in Matthew Hoehn, ed., *Catholic Authors* (Newark, NJ: St. Mary's Press, 1948), pp. 118–19. A short, dismissive, and largely misrepresentative discussion of her stories can be found in Raymond A. Paredes, "The Evolution of Chicano Literature," in *Three American Literatures: Essays in Chicano, Native American, and Asian-American Literature for Teachers of American Literature,* ed. Houston A. Baker, Jr. (New York: Modern Language Association of America, 1982), pp. 49–51.

16. Jessie Redmon Fauset, *There Is Confusion* (New York: Boni and Liveright, 1924), p. 68. References in the text are to this edition and are abbreviated *C.*

17. Quoted in Sylvander, *Jessie Redmon Fauset,* p. 73.

18. As Deborah E. McDowell remarks: "Given Joanna's mindset throughout the novel, Fauset's ending seems forced and inconsistent, not growing organically out of the novel, but rather, 'tacked on' to it. . . . Joanna's growth from stubbornly independent careerist to dependent, self-abnegating wife rings false." See "The Neglected Dimension of Jessie Redmon Fauset," in *Conjuring: Black Women, Fiction, and Literary Tradition,* eds. Marjorie Pryse and Hortense J. Spillers (Bloomington: Indiana UP, 1985), p. 98. McDowell goes on in this essay to offer the very plausible argument that Fauset's conservative conclusion reflects, at least in part, a necessary compromise with readers' expectations in order to get published.

19. Sylvander, *Jessie Redmon Fauset,* p. 212.

20. Edith Wharton, *Summer* (New York: Charles Scribner's Sons, 1918), p. 192; references in the text are to this edition and are abbreviated *S.* Wharton uses this image of Charity to open Chapter 27, the penultimate chapter in the book.

21. See Ammons, *Edith Wharton's Argument with America,* ch. 5.

22. For detailed discussion of this change in outlook, see ibid., ch. 6.

23. McDowell, Introduction, *Plum Bun,* pp. ix–xxiv.

24. See, e.g., a number of the stories in *Short Fiction by Black Women, 1900–1920,* ed. Elizabeth Ammons, in The Schomburg Library of Nineteenth-Century Black Women Writers, gen. ed. Henry Louis Gates, Jr. (New York: Oxford UP, 1991).

25. McDowell, Introduction, *Plum Bun,* p. xvii.

26. Ibid., p. xx.

27. Ibid., pp. xx, xxii.

28. As Sylvander points out in her very interesting discussion of the novel, *The Chinaberry Tree* is also heavily influenced by Fauset's knowledge of classical literature. See Sylvander, *Jessie Redmon Fauset,* p. 198.

29. Jessie Fauset, *Comedy: American Style* (1933; rpt. College Park, MD: McGrath Publishing, 1969), p. 8. References in the text are to this edition and abbreviated *CAS.*

30. Hugh Gloster, *Negro Voices in American Fiction* (1948; rpt. New York: Russell & Russell, 1965), p. 138. Quoted in Sylvander, *Jessie Redmon Fauset,* p. 212.

31. On Wharton, see my discussion of *The Reef* and of *Ethan Frome* in *Edith Wharton's Argument with America,* pp. 56–96; on Fauset, see McDowell, both her introduction to *Plum Bun* and her essay, "The Neglected Dimension . . . ," in *Conjuring.*

32. Charlotte Perkins Gilman, *The Man-Made World, or Our Androcentric Culture* (New York: Charlton Co., 1911), p. 70. Two excellent recent discussions of gender and the genre of the novel are Rachel Blau Du Plessis, *Writing Beyond the Ending: Narrative Strategies of Twentieth-Century Women Writers* (Bloomington: Indiana UP, 1985), and Joseph Allen Boone, *Tradition Countertradition: Love and the Form of Fiction* (Chicago: U of Chicago P, 1987).

33. Gilman, *Man-Made World,* pp. 72–78. For a superb discussion of the relationship between Gilman's theory of gender and her experimentation with form in *Herland* (1915), see Christopher P. Wilson, "Charlotte Perkins Gilman's Steady Burghers: The Terrain of *Herland,*" *Women's Studies* 12 (1986), 271–92.

34. M. M. Bakhtin, "Discourse in the Novel," in *The Dialogic Imagination: Four Essays,* trans. Caryl Emerson and Michael Holquist (Austin: U of Texas P, 1981), p. 367.

35. In a 1902 article on George Eliot, for example, Wharton scoffed at what she labeled the "prejudice" of declaring certain subjects, such as science, off limits for women and invoked the well-known image of misogynist "Dr. Johnson" to show just how antiquated such notions were: "Is it because these [Tennyson, Goethe, Milton] were men, while George Eliot was a woman, that she is reproved for venturing on ground they did not fear to tread?

Dr. Johnson is known to have pronounced portrait-painting 'indelicate in a female'; and indications are not wanting that the woman who ventures on scientific studies still does so at the risk of such an epithet.'' See Wharton, ''George Eliot,'' *Bookman* (May 1902), 248.

36. Lewis and Lewis, *The Letters of Edith Wharton,* p. 124.

37. Nina Baym states this position particularly forcefully in an essay on pedagogy, ''The Feminist Teacher of Literature: Feminist or Teacher,'' *PLL* 24 (1988), 255.

38. For a description of this event, see Lewis, *Edith Wharton: A Biography,* pp. 467–68.

39. Lewis and Lewis, *The Letters of Edith Wharton,* pp. 457, 481; also see the 1921 letter to Sinclair Lewis, p. 445.

40. Ibid., p. 480.

Chapter 10

1. Anzia Yezierska, ''What Makes a Writer,'' lecture at Purdue University, October 1965. Quoted in Louise Levitas Henriksen, with assistance from Jo Ann Boydston, *Anzia Yezierska: A Writer's Life* (New Brunswick: Rutgers UP, 1988), p. 195.

2. Henriksen, *Anzia Yezierska,* pp. 142–43.

3. Quoted in ibid., p. 149.

4. Ibid., p. 183.

5. Anzia Yezierska, ''My Own People,'' in *Hungry Hearts and Other Stories* (1920; rpt. New York: Persea, 1985), p. 225. Quotations in the text are to this edition, which is abbreviated as *HH*.

6. Henriksen, *Anzia Yezierska,* p. 79; see also p. 197.

7. On formal repetition in folklore, and particularly in the Russian folk tale, which is the cultural tradition out of which Yezierska came, see Vladimir Propp, *Morphology of the Folktale,* trans. Laurence Scott (Austin: U of Texas P, 1968), ch. 2.

8. Henriksen, *Anzia Yezierska,* p. 120. Quoted from Yezierska's book *Children of Loneliness* (New York: Funk and Wagnalls, 1923) and from an essay by Yezierska, ''My Ambitions at 21 and What Became of Them,'' *American Hebrew* (Aug. 25, 1922).

9. Ellen Glasgow, *A Certain Measure: An Interpretation of Prose Fiction* (New York: Harcourt, Brace and Co., 1943), p. 167.

10. Anne Firor Scott, *Making the Invisible Woman Visible* (Urbana: U of Illinois P, 1984), pp. 191–92; see also p. 224. As Scott explains of the ruling-class white South: ''Early in the nineteenth century the South had adopted a more rigid definition of the role of women than any other part of the country and had elevated that definition to the position of a myth'' (p. 223).

11. Excellent discussion of these women can be found in ibid., pp. 212–21.

12. Linda Wagner, *Ellen Glasgow: Beyond Convention* (Austin: U of Texas P, 1982), p. 22.

13. Ellen Glasgow, *Barren Ground* (1925; rpt. Charlottesville: U of Virginia P, 1938), p. 248. Quotations in the text are to this edition of the novel which is abbreviated *BG*.

14. Wagner, *Ellen Glasgow,* p. 97.

15. Ibid., p. 117. Wagner argues that Glasgow, given the period in which she lived, had to mask her identity as a woman: ''What should have been a strength became a liability, and even at her most assertive—at the end of her life—she had to title her autobiography *The Woman Within*. Glasgow the writer was—or should have been—somehow unsexed. Only under the mask, inside the writerly disguise, could a woman exist.''

16. Anne Goodwyn Jones, *Tomorrow Is Another Day: The Woman Writer in the South, 1859–1936* (Baton Rouge: Louisiana State UP, 1981), p. 203.

17. Ellen Glasgow in a letter to Douglas Southall Freeman on January 26, 1925, in *Letters of Ellen Glasgow,* ed. Blair Rouse (New York: Harcourt, Brace and Co., 1958), p. 74.

18. In *Letters,* pp. 107, 118.

19. Glasgow, *A Certain Measure,* pp. 152, 159, 191–92.

20. Ibid., pp. 194, 162–63.

21. See E. Stanly Godbold, Jr. *Ellen Glasgow and The Woman Within* (Baton Rouge: Louisiana State UP, 1972), p. 204.

22. The Table of Contents of *Virginia,* e.g., reads: Book One: The Dream; Book Two: The Reality; Book Three: The Adjustment.

23. Glasgow's deep interest in Darwin is particularly well documented in Julius Rowan Raper's book, *Without Shelter: The Early Career of Ellen Glasgow* (Baton Rouge: Louisiana State UP, 1971), which emphasizes the radical significance of Glasgow's attraction as a Southerner to Darwin. As Raper says: "What Darwin proposed implied the total annihilation of southern ideology, replacing its emphasis upon hierarchical order, stability, uniformity, and protection of the innocent, with an emphasis on change, diversity, and struggle" (p. 42). For Darwin's image of the tangled bank that I draw on in my discussion, see the last paragraph of *The Origin of Species* (1859; rpt. New York: NAL, 1958), p. 450. I wish to thank my colleagues in the Tufts American Studies Summer Faculty Workshop on Darwin, 1986, especially biology professors Saul Slapikoff and Nancy Milburn, for reintroducing me to Darwin's work.

24. Although the charge of misandry occurs repeatedly in the criticism of Glasgow (as it also does in Wharton criticism), probably the most overt articulation can be found in the early study, Josephine Lurie Jessup, *The Faith of Our Feminists: A Study in the Novels of Edith Wharton, Ellen Glasgow, and Willa Cather* (New York: R. R. Smith, 1950). Also of interest in this connection is Godbold's observation that Glasgow (here again there is a strong parallel with Wharton) frequently preferred the company of homosexual to heterosexual men; see Godbold, *Ellen Glasgow,* p. 142.

25. Glasgow, *A Certain Measure,* p. 167.

26. Adrienne Rich, "Education of a Novelist," in *The Fact of a Doorframe: Poems Selected and New, 1950–1984* (New York: W. W. Norton, 1984), pp. 314–17. For Glasgow's account of Lizzie Jones's and her joint fiction-making, which Glasgow herself presents as the major influence on her development as an artist, see *A Certain Measure,* pp. 192–94, and *The Woman Within* (New York: Harcourt, Brace & Co., 1954), pp. 18–25.

27. Rich, "Education," p. 317.

28. Glasgow, *A Certain Measure,* p. 177.

29. See C. Hugh Holman, *Windows on the World: Essays on American Social Fiction* (Knoxville: U of Tennessee P, 1979); Wagner, *Ellen Glasgow;* and Raper, *Without Shelter,* and ed., *Ellen Glasgow's Reasonable Doubts: A Collection of Her Writings* (Baton Rouge: Louisiana State UP, 1988). Two other important recent studies are Anne Goodwyn Jones, *Tomorrow Is Another Day,* ch. 6; and Josephine Donovan's chapter on Glasgow in *After the Fall: The Demeter-Persephone Myth in Wharton, Cather, and Glasgow* (University Park: Penn State UP, 1989).

30. Quoted in Godbold, *Ellen Glasgow,* p. 287.

31. Ibid., p. 204.

32. Ibid., p. 208.

33. Edith Summers Kelley, *Weeds* (1923; rpt. Old Westbury, NY: The Feminist Press, 1982), p. 15. Quotations in the text are to this edition and are abbreviated *W.*

34. See Bruccoli's afterword to *Weeds* (Carbondale: Southern Illinois UP, 1972) and to *The Devil's Hand* (New York: Popular Library, 1976, which is a reprint of the 1974 Southern

Illinois UP edition); and Goodman's afterword to *Weeds* (Old Westbury, NY: Feminist Press, 1982), as well as her essays, "Widening Perspectives, Narrowing Possibilities: The Trapped Woman in Edith Summers Kelley's *Weeds,*" in *Regionalism and the Female Imagination: A Collection of Essays,* ed. Emily Toth (New York: Human Sciences Press, 1985), pp. 93–106, and "Portraits of the *Artiste Manque* by Three Women Novelists," *Frontiers* 5 (1980), 57–59.

35. See Bruccoli, Afterword, *Weeds,* p. 341.

36. Quoted in Goodman, Afterword, *Weeds,* pp. 359, 360.

37. Bruccoli, Afterword, *The Devil's Hand,* pp. 293, 294.

38. For example, to what extent was Glasgow's suicide attempt in 1918 prompted by a love affair going bad, which is the usual interpretation offered, and to what extent might it have sprung as well from her construction of herself as an artist in the modern mold—suffering, alienated, etc.? In any case, suicide would not have contradicted her concept of artist, as it would have in other periods and other cultures.

Chapter 11

1. *Colored American Magazine* 6 (March 1903), 400.

2. Probably the best-known literary study of the American 1920s is still Frederick J. Hoffman, *The Twenties: American Writing in the Postwar Decade* (New York: Viking, 1965 [rev. ed.]).

3. A good overview of this political history can be found in Dorothy M. Brown, *Setting a Course: American Women in the 1920s* (Boston: G. K. Hall, 1987).

4. See Joseph A. Hill, *Women in Gainful Occupations 1870–1920: A Study of the Trend of Recent Changes in the Numbers, Occupational Distribution, and Family Relationship of Women Reported in the Census as Following a Gainful Occupation,* Census Monograph 9 (Washington, D.C.: United States Printing Office, 1929).

5. For excellent discussion of Dunbar-Nelson's career as a poet, see Gloria T. Hull, *Color, Sex, and Poetry: Three Women Writers of the Harlem Renaissance* (Bloomington: Indiana UP, 1987).

6. See, e.g., the way that Houston Baker connects the Harlem Renaissance to the turn-of-the-century literary strategies of Booker T. Washington and W. E. B. Du Bois, in *Modernism and the Harlem Renaissance* (Chicago: U of Chicago P, 1987); or think of Stein's and Wharton's expatriation to Paris well before the twenties. For excellent discussion of them as well as other women expatriates in Paris, see Shari Benstock, *Women of the Left Bank: Paris, 1900–1940* (Austin: U of Texas P, 1986).

7. For detailed discussion of Hurston's life, see Robert E. Hemenway, *Zora Neale Hurston: A Literary Biography* (Urbana: U of Illinois P, 1977).

8. The date usually given for Hurston's birth is 1901; however, Cheryl Wall has established that she was actually born in the early 1890s and lied about her age. See Robert E. Hemenway, Introduction, Zora Neale Hurston, *Dust Tracks on a Road: An Autobiography,* 2nd ed. (Urbana: U of Illinois P, 1984), pp. x–xi.

9. Hemenway, *Zora Neale Hurston,* pp. 68–70.

10. See Ibid., p. 115.

11. Zora Neale Hurston, *The Eatonville Anthology,* in *I Love Myself When I Am Laughing. . . . ,* ed. Mary Helen Washington (New York: The Feminist Press, 1979), p. 188.

12. Ibid., pp. 177–87.

13. Nella Larsen, *Quicksand and Passing,* ed. Deborah E. McDowell (1928 and 1929; rpt. New Brunswick: Rutgers UP, 1986), p. 1. Citations in the text to these two novels are to this edition and are abbreviated, respectively, *Q* and *P.*

Index